ARMENIA

arat

CASPIAN SE

PARTHIA

ASSYRIA

MEDIA

od

ur

raris

• Nuzi

POTAMIA

• Ecbatana

PERSIA

• Eshnunna

• Akkad

BABYLONIA

• Babylon

• Nippur

• Susa

• Isin

• Lagash

• Erech

• Larsa

PERSIAN GULF

Darton, Longman and Todd Ltd
1 Spencer Court
140–142 Wandsworth High Street
London SW18 4JJ

First published as *The Bible for Children* in 1996

This edition © 1999 Darton, Longman and Todd Ltd
Published under licence from Les Éditions du Cerf, Paris

2/1

ISBN 0–232–52332–0

New Jerusalem Bible text edited by Sandy Waldron
Notes translated by Joanne Monk
Text design by Sandie Boccacci

Phototypeset by Intype, London
Printed and bound in France

THE BIBLE
or
THE BOOK

W hy give this title to what is after all only one book among many? True, for thousands of years, it has been the world's most widely read and translated text. But its importance is not to be measured by its success; it is truer to say that its success follows from its importance.

The Bible contains the product of two thousand years of human experience; two thousand years during which people have faced a huge range of situations and asked all the fundamental questions we still ask today. Why life and death? Where do we come from and where are we going? What is God and what is the nature of Evil? Can we hope to find happiness in the future, and what exactly is "happiness"?

Thoughts: not presented as intellectual arguments, but in a very concrete form: witnesses from the past recount their experiences and the conclusions they have drawn from them. They tell us how, throughout history, they have discovered the call of a loving God who shows himself to anyone who is really prepared to look for him, and to give up the desire to have everything they want, as it were, on a plate.

Before they were written, many of the accounts in the Bible were learned by heart and passed on by word of mouth from generation to generation.

What the Bible is not

We can say immediately what the Bible is not, what we will not find in it.

It is not a scientific textbook. In contrast to modern research, it does not aim to tell everything known about the evolution of the world nor the nature of humankind as a species in scientific terms. The people who wrote the Bible saw the world in a way which is now unfamiliar to us. They used the ideas current in their own time to show God in action. It is for us to make the same discovery but using the scientific knowledge available today.

It does not contain only history, but many other types of literature. Of course the writers of the Bible reported historical events to us; and present-day archaeological research confirms many of their claims. In general their aim was to make us understand historical events, to explain how they saw them and what they learned from them. So they told things their way, emphasising things which seemed important to them and which were often invisible even to the best of reporters.

God taught his people gradually, step by step. For this reason, many of the stories in the Bible appear to us immoral. But it is often through mistakes and sins that we come to see most clearly the true nature of goodness and truth.

It is not even a collection of religious truths, though of course the authors do tell us about their faith in God, for example, that faith often goes in fits and starts. It takes a long time to understand the full meaning behind certain key ideas.

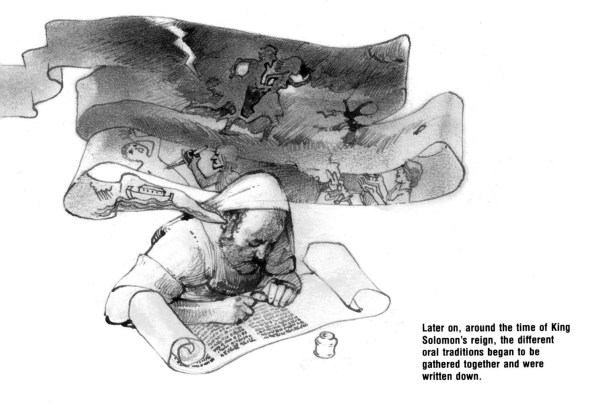

Later on, around the time of King Solomon's reign, the different oral traditions began to be gathered together and were written down.

What the Bible is

In a way, the Bible is a book of the past: those who wrote it are dead, and the events they were writing about could never happen again.

It is definitely a collection of statements by people having a passion for seeking God's Truth. In another sense, though, it is always up-to-date: what we read in it makes us think about our own lives and lets us discover God there.

When we realise what the Bible is giving us, we discover that its words (which can appear dead on the page) are really still alive. Its message does concern us and is addressed to us.

For believers, the Bible is the Word of God. It is as if we can hear a voice speaking to us through the texts, and calling us to set out on the marvellous spiritual adventure of the chosen people, which means the whole human race in search of Truth, and guided by God to find it.

The "Book" or many books?

The Bible, "The Book", is in fact a collection of many books. It is like a library: seventy-five pieces of writing altogether, written in the course of many centuries.

There are texts of all kinds in this little library: historical chronicles and legendary tales, short stories and poetry, proverbs and rules, letters . . .

It is important that we know which kind a book belongs to when we read it because we cannot read a short story or a history book, a sermon or an epic poem in exactly the same way. The introductions given with each book will help you not to misinterpret the meaning of the passages chosen.

For more than a thousand years, "Holy Scriptures", meaning the Bible, was copied and re-copied by hand by hundreds of scribes.

A basic division in the Christian Bible

The main part of the Bible consists of writings collected by the Jews around the year AD 100.

Jerusalem and its Temple had just been destroyed. If the recently-divided people were to hold on to their spiritual identity, then they needed to identify clearly the texts in which everyone could recognise themselves, those which would bear true witness to their faith. It was then that some of their leaders "canonised" (made official) what we now call the Scriptures.

The Christians, as spiritual heirs to the Jews, also used the Scriptures. They added other texts which had not been passed on (or "canonised") by the Jewish leaders since they were in Greek rather than Hebrew. They also added their own writings about Jesus and the early Church to the Scriptures.

They called the Jewish canon of texts the Old Testament, or the expression of the old Covenant formed between God and the people of Israel; and they called their own writings the New Testament: which means the expression of the new relationship God established with those who listened to the message of Jesus Christ.

The Old Testament, then, is common to both Jews and Christians. The New Testament is holy only to Christians, for whom there is no strict division between the Old and New Testaments. The words and actions of Jesus and his disciples shed light on a long story in which all of us can see ourselves.

Until the day when, in about 1440, Johann Gutenberg invented the printing-press. The Bible has never stopped being the world's bestseller since that time.

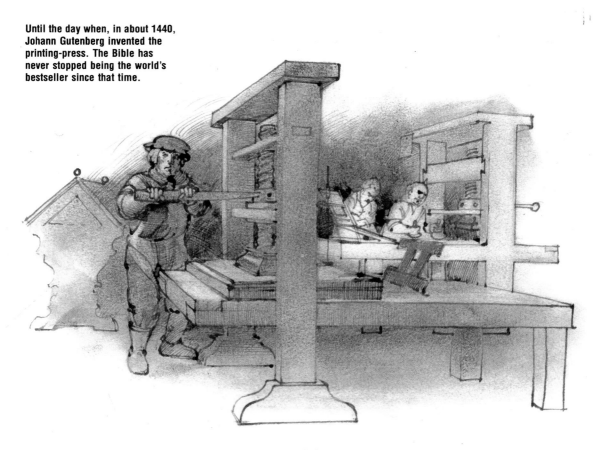

How to read the Bible

Nobody reads every book in a library, beginning with the first and ending with the last. We pick out whichever book we need at the time.

In the same way, we do not read the Bible by starting at the beginning and reading it in order to the end, even though that is perfectly possible.

The best way to read it is to use a good reading guide, or subject list, which helps us to find the texts which deal with the questions we are asking.

In the Bible presented here, we have included only the most important texts from the Old Testament. As for the New Testament, we have printed the whole of one of the Gospels, that by Mark, which is probably the earliest of the four and certainly the easiest to understand. We have included only certain extracts from the other Gospels, where they complement and differ from Mark's account.

We have been able to include only a small part of the so-called "apostolic" texts (the Epistles, the Acts of the Apostles and the book of Revelation).

In spite of these inevitable disadvantages, our selection is intended to make reading Scripture easier for younger readers, who may feel discouraged by the size of the whole text.

The notes which accompany the biblical texts are intended to make it easier to grasp the meaning of passages and to explain them by giving useful additional information. *The Illustrated Bible* can be used to the end of schooldays and beyond. It is also ideal for parents and children to read together.

THE OLD TESTAMENT

THE PENTATEUCH

HOW A PEOPLE
FOUND ITS IDENTITY

Human beings are always asking who and what they really are. They feel lost if they do not find answers to their questions. They lose their sense of direction when they doubt themselves.

This is true of individuals, but also of groups of people. A community can only hold together if there is a feeling of identity between its members, and a sense that they are different from other communities.

The Hebrews realised they were a people set apart even from early times. Having thought about the reasons for this uniqueness, they came to a deep certainty: they were called by God to play a unique role in the world's development, as forerunners leading the way towards a new humanity.

There was however a moment when they doubted both themselves and God; it was when their nation collapsed after the destruction of the kingdom of Israel, the exile and the return from captivity in Persia (in the sixth century BC). They wondered if their old traditions, the very customs that had made them so certain of their mission on earth, were really right after all.

It was then that a scribe, probably Ezra, tried to encourage his people again by taking the writings and oral traditions of the past and using them to explain the difficult times through which they were passing. This led him to write a new version of the history through which Israel had discovered its unique mission. That history was the Pentateuch (which means "five cases", which today comprise the first five books of the Bible).

The scribe showed through his use of the Pentateuch that the Lord had not abandoned his people. God was carrying out his plan to save the world by saving Israel. Believers could trust in him and face the future with confidence.

We can see, then, why the Jews called these five books the *Torah*. This word is sometimes translated as "the Law" but in fact it means much more than a simple list of rules (although one of the five books, Leviticus, and parts of the others do contain many rules). The Torah is the "way", a direction in life revealed as a gift from God coming to give wisdom to humankind.

These five fundamental books are: Genesis, Exodus, Leviticus, Numbers and Deuteronomy.

GENESIS

GENESIS, SUGGESTING A MEANING FOR HUMAN LIFE

T he book of Genesis enables us to see God's way of understanding our existence as human beings on this earth. It states that the human race was created by God and that life only makes sense when it is seen in terms of a relationship with the Creator. However, although created for happiness, humankind has always been tempted to reject the path leading to it, because it appears too difficult: people want security here and now and so lose the ability to meet with God and with others in true love. But God does not give up on his plans: he goes after guilty humanity and, slowly but surely, leads it back onto the path to true victory.

Genesis expresses this certainty in two very different ways:

1. The story of the origins of the human race

The first eleven chapters of the book do not report historical events, nor do they give a scientific description of the origins of the universe — they tell us about the place of the human being at the heart of the created universe.

By using stories and images, it shows us the important destiny of the human race: we are called to live in fellowship with God. Through the description of the earthly paradise, the author shows that the human being was essentially made for happiness, but is prone to sin, a fact which is illustrated by three stories. However, God did not abandon his work of Creation; this is the message of the pact with Noah, after the Flood.

2. The story of the patriarchs

God chose one of these sinful human beings and called on him to become the leader of a new people: his name was Abraham. Through his descendants, Isaac, then Jacob, he became the ancestor of the Israelites who were the nation with whom God formed a covenant. The story of a small group of wandering nomads emerges gradually as the beginning of an amazing human and spiritual adventure. The writers of the Bible recognised the image of their own people in the image of these people as they anxiously wandered in search of pastureland to safeguard their future: all of us are on that journey, in search of the land of plenty where there will be no more death to fear.

REFLECTIONS ON HUMANITY AND THE WORLD

Contrary to popular belief, the author of the first eleven chapters of Genesis is not trying to tell us how the universe, the earth and human beings were made. His aim is, rather, to answer questions about the meaning of life, of evil, and of God. In the face of belief in the astral gods of Mesopotamia, he stated that there is only one God, the Creator of all the visible world. To those who believed that the gods created human beings to be their slaves, to perform the unpleasant jobs for them, he stated that God created humankind out of love, and invited all people to enter into a loving relationship with him. He explained to those who thought humanity was condemned to suffering and death that the root of evil is in the heart: God can lead his creation on toward salvation and new life. The writer takes up a number of traditional and legendary stories in order to express all this, and organised them in such a way as to show the growth of Israel's faith over the centuries.

THE CREATION AND THE FALL

The first account of creation

This poem was composed, during the exile in Babylon in the sixth century BC and acts as an introduction to the Bible. The author accepts without question the view of the universe which was current at the time (see picture opposite). However, he disagreed with the Babylonian religion which worshipped the moon and the stars as gods: there is only one God who is Creator of the universe, and with human beings as the summit of his Creation.

1: 1—2: 4a

In the beginning God created heaven and earth. Now the earth was without form and void, there was darkness over the deep, with a wind from God sweeping over the waters.

God said, "Let there be light," and there was light. God saw that light was good, and God divided light from darkness. God called light "day", and darkness he called "night". Evening came and morning came: the first day.

God said, "Let there be a firmament through the middle of the waters to divide the waters in two." And so it was. God made the firmament, and it divided the waters under the firmament from those above it. God called the firmament "heaven". Evening came and morning came: the second day.

God said, "Let the waters under heaven come together into a single mass, and let dry land appear." And so it was. God called the dry land "earth" and the mass of waters "seas", and God saw that it was good.

God said, "Let vegetation grow on the earth: seed-bearing plants, and fruit trees producing fruit according to their own species." And so it was. (. . .) God saw that it was good. Evening came and morning came: the third day.

God said, "Let there be lights in the firmament of heaven to divide day from night, and let them mark festivals, days and years. Let them be lights in heaven to shine on the earth." And so it was. God made two great lights: the greater to rule over the day, the smaller to rule over the night, and the stars. God set them in the firmament of heaven to shine on the earth, to rule over the day and the night and to divide light from darkness. God saw that it was good. Evening came and morning came: the fourth day.

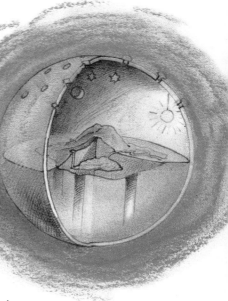

God said, "Let the waters be alive with living creatures, and let birds fly above the earth across the firmament of heaven." And so it was. God created great sea-monsters and all the creatures that glide and teem in the waters in their own species, and birds in their own species. God saw that it was good. God blessed them, saying, "Be fruitful, multiply, and fill the waters of the seas; and let the birds multiply on land." Evening came and morning came: the fifth day.

God said, "Let the earth produce every kind of living creature: cattle, creeping things and wild animals of all kinds." And so it was. (. . .) God saw that it was good.

God said, "Let us make man in our own image, in the likeness of ourselves, and let them be masters of the fish of the sea, the birds of heaven, the cattle, all the wild animals and all the creatures that creep along the ground." God created man in the image of himself, in the image of God he created him, male and female he created them.

God blessed them, saying to them, "Be fruitful, multiply, fill the earth and subdue it. Be masters of the fish of the sea, the birds of heaven and all the living creatures that move on earth." God also said, "Look, to you I give all the seed-bearing plants on the surface of the earth, and all the trees with seed-bearing fruit; this will be your food. And to all the wild animals, all the birds of heaven and all the creatures that creep along the ground, I give all the green leaves of the plants as their food." And so it was. God saw all he had made, and indeed it was very good. Evening came and morning came: the sixth day.

Thus heaven and earth were completed with all their array. On the seventh day God had completed the work he had been doing and he rested. God blessed the seventh day and made it holy, because on that day he rested having finished his creation.

This is the story of the creation of heaven and earth.

A very important statement: humanity was not complete until it included both "man and woman". The love that binds the sexes together is part of what makes them the "image of God".

God gave human beings the power to rule over all of nature. It was their job to organise the environment, not according to their own whim, but in line with the order established by God: that is the real "ecology".

God's day of rest on the seventh day was recalled in Exodus (20:11) to justify the idea of the Sabbath: so, people fit in with the natural rhythm of all Creation.

Paradise, and the test of free will

2: 4b–25

At the time when the Lord made earth and heaven there was as yet no wild bush on the earth nor had any wild plant yet sprung up, for the Lord God had not sent rain on the earth, nor was there any man to cultivate the soil. Instead, water flowed out of the ground and watered all the surface of the soil. The Lord God shaped man from the soil of the ground and blew the breath of life into his nostrils, and man became a living being.

The Lord God planted a garden in Eden, which is in the east, and there he put the man he had made. From the soil, the Lord caused to grow every kind of tree, pleasing to look at and good to eat, with the tree of life in the middle of the garden, and the tree of the knowledge of good and evil. A river flowed from Eden to water the garden, and from there it divided to make four streams. (. . .) The Lord God took the man and settled him in the garden of Eden to cultivate and take care of it. Then he gave the man this command, "You are free to eat of all the trees in the garden, except the tree of knowledge of good and evil; for, the day you eat of that, you will die."

The Lord God said, "It is not right that the man should be alone. I shall make him a helper." So from the soil the Lord God fashioned all the wild animals and all the birds of heaven. These he brought to the man to see what he would call them; each one was to bear the name the man would give it. The man gave names to all the cattle, all the birds of heaven and all the wild animals. But he did not find a helper suitable for him. Then, the Lord God made the man fall into a deep sleep. And, while he was asleep, he took one of his ribs and immediately closed the flesh up again. The Lord God fashioned the rib he had taken from the man into a woman, and brought her to the man. And the man said: "This one at last is bone of my bones and flesh of my flesh! She is to be called Woman, because she was taken from Man."

This is why a man leaves his father and mother and becomes attached to his wife, and they become one being.

Now, both of them were naked, the man and his wife, but they felt no shame before each other.

The author added a second, older, account of Creation to the first. It is much richer in images than the first and seems almost naïve: this one emphasises the fact that the human race was called to find fulfilment through love, in the presence of a God who was very close to them. Human beings had to accept their own limitations if that was to happen since they were not the providers of the law but merely stewards of someone else's estate. That is the meaning of the tree bearing forbidden fruit.

To name everything and know how to distinguish things one from another is what science does. But science can never satisfy the human being's deepest need, which is to communicate with a living partner. Once again, the author emphasises the fact that people find the meaning of their lives through love. Without love we are condemned to be alone forever. In the beginning, the attraction of the opposite sex was fundamentally pure: it enabled us to accept others as they were, naked and undisguised, and to be equally open themselves. Man in Hebrew is *Ish*, and woman is *Isha*, so the original text contained a play on words.

The Fall

3: 1–23

How do we explain the presence of evil in the world? The biblical author answered this question using a symbolic story: the real drama was sin, an evil which came from the very beginning of time and into which everyone falls before realising their involvement. The story of the Fall shows the tempting nature of the forbidden fruit and how people could drag one another into sin. The story also showed that sin was caused by humankind's refusal to accept their status as God's creatures. They wanted to set themselves up as "little Gods" and so behave as though they were unbeatable or immortal. They wanted it all and they wanted it now.

From this point onwards, man and woman lost their original harmony. Each hid from the other's gaze and from the eyes of God; other people always seem to be a threat to those acting like "little Gods". It is also typical of such people to refuse to recognise their own guilt or to accept responsibility for their own actions.

Christian tradition took up this old text and applied it to Mary whose son, Jesus, triumphed over the tempter at the moment of his death on the cross.

The author presented all the evil and back-to-front values in the world as the result of humankind's original sin. The order of creation had been destroyed.

Now, the snake was the most cunning of all the wild animals created by the Lord. It asked the woman, "Did God really say you were not to eat from any of the trees in the garden?" The woman answered the snake, "We may eat the fruit of the trees in the garden. But of the fruit of the tree in the middle of the garden God said, 'You must not eat it, nor touch it, under pain of death.' " Then the snake said to her, "No! You will not die! God knows in fact that the day you eat it your eyes will be opened and you will be like gods, knowing good from evil." The woman saw that the tree looked appetising and good to eat, and she was attracted by the wisdom that it could give. So she took some of its fruit and ate it. She also gave some to her husband who was with her, and he ate it. Then their eyes were opened and they realised that they were naked. So they sewed fig-leaves together to make themselves loin-cloths.

The man and his wife heard the sound of the Lord God walking in the garden in the cool of the day, and they hid from him among the trees. But the Lord God called to the man. "Where are you?" he asked. "I heard the sound of you in the garden," he replied. "I was afraid because I was naked, so I hid." "Who told you that you were naked?" God asked. "Have you been eating from the tree I forbade you to eat?" The man replied, "It was the woman you put with me; she gave me some fruit from the tree, and I ate it." Then the Lord God said to the woman, "Why did you do that?" The woman replied, "The snake tempted me and I ate."

Then the Lord God said to the snake, "Because you have done this, you are cursed among all wild and tame animals! You will creep on your belly and you will feed on the dust for as long as you live. I shall put hatred between you and the woman, and between your descendants and hers; it will bruise your head and you will strike its heel."

To the woman he said: "I shall give you intense pain in childbirth, you will give birth to your children in pain. Your desire will be for your husband, yet he will dominate you."

To the man he said, "You listened to the voice of your wife and ate the fruit I had forbidden you to eat. The soil is cursed because of you! You will have to work hard to get your food from it as long as you live. It will yield you brambles and thistles, as you eat the produce of the land. You will earn your food by the sweat of your brow, until you return to the ground from which you were taken. For you are dust and you shall return to dust." (. . .)

So the Lord God threw him out from the garden of Eden, to cultivate the soil from which he had been formed. He banished the man and in front of the garden of Eden he posted great winged creatures and the fiery flashing sword, to guard the way to the tree of life.

Cain and Abel

4: 1–16

The man had intercourse with his wife Eve. She became pregnant and gave birth to Cain. "I have had a son with the help of the Lord," she said. She gave birth to a second child, Abel, the brother of Cain. Now Abel became a shepherd and kept flocks, while Cain worked on the land. Time passed. Cain brought some of the produce he had grown as an offering to the Lord, while Abel brought the first-born lambs of his flock, fattened ready to be killed. The Lord was pleased with Abel and his offering. But he did not accept Cain and his offering. Cain was very angry and his face fell. The Lord asked Cain, "Why are you angry and why is your face so depressed? If you are doing right, surely you ought to hold your head high! But if you are not doing right, beware! Sin is crouching at the door like a wild animal ready to pounce. You can still master it." But Cain said to his brother Abel, "Let us go out"; and while they were in the open country, Cain attacked his brother Abel and killed him.

Humankind wanted affirmation of independence from judgement and God did not deny them this freedom. But they had to give up their desire for eternal life — a divine privilege which they could not achieve for themselves since life can only be given by Grace, and then at the end of a long search. The final chapter of the Bible, in Revelation, shows paradise regained, by Jesus' grace.

This story is like a second account of original sin. But this time, the sin was directed against another human being by Cain. He cultivated the land and was jealous of his brother Abel, who was a shepherd whose lot seemed better than his own. Cain killed his brother because he felt like a fool when compared with Abel.

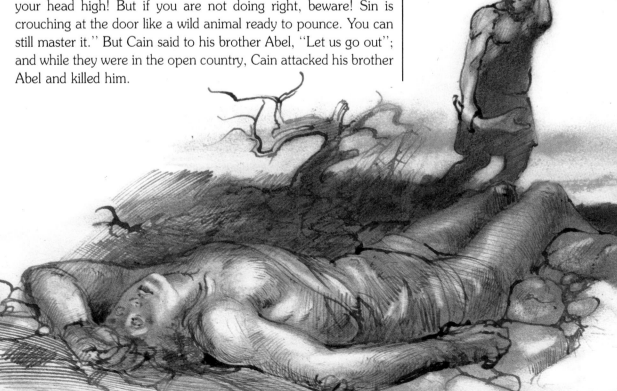

"Where is your brother?" The question is still relevant in our violent world.

But God, although he condemns evil, did not reject Cain completely, that dark face of humanity who turned towards the ground. Cain still had to leave his land, though, and travelled east towards the rising sun. One day his descendants, the Canaanites, were reunited with the people of Israel, the descendants of Abel, who found favour with God. Thus Cain himself was eventually included in the general salvation and was reconciled with his brother.

The Lord asked Cain, "Where is your brother Abel?" "I do not know," he replied. "Am I my brother's guardian?" The Lord asked, "What have you done? Listen! Your brother's blood is crying out to me from the ground. Now be cursed and banned from the ground that has opened up to receive your brother's blood shed by your hands. When you cultivate the ground it will no longer give you its produce. You will be a restless wanderer on the earth." Cain then said to the Lord, "My punishment is greater than I can bear. Look, today you are driving me from the face of the earth. I must hide from you, and be a restless wanderer on earth. Why, whoever comes across me will kill me!" "Very well, then," the Lord replied, "if anyone kills Cain, he will be avenged seven times." So the Lord put a distinctive mark on Cain, so that no one coming across him would kill him. Cain left the Lord's presence and settled in the land of Nod, east of Eden.

The following biblical account shows how humanity sank ever deeper into sin. Admittedly, we see the cultural development of the human race but the life of human society was ruined by the spirit of intolerance and pride. Was divine creation a failure?

The flood

6: 5–14, 17–19

The Lord saw that there was so much human wickedness on the earth and that human hearts planned nothing but evil schemes all day long. The Lord regretted having made human beings on earth and he was sad in his heart. And he said, "I shall rid the earth of the human beings whom I created, as well as the animals, the creeping things and the birds of heaven, for I regret having made them."

But Noah won the Lord's favour. God said to Noah, "I have decided to put an end to all life, for the earth is full of violence because of human beings. So I am now about to destroy them and the earth. Make yourself an ark out of resinous wood. (. . .) For my part I am going to send the flood, the waters, on earth, to destroy all living things; everything on earth is to die. But I shall make my covenant with you and you will go aboard the ark, yourself, your sons, your wife, and your sons' wives along with you. You must take aboard the ark a pair of all the living creatures, to save their lives with yours." (. . .)

Sin could not be allowed to continue to destroy the world! Was God's work an utter failure? Fortunately, Noah came along. The story of the Flood was based on an old near-Eastern tradition about an ancient catastrophe, and was intended to show how humankind would have been wiped out due to its own violence were it not for the intervention of a righteous man, someone able to stand in a healthy relationship to both God and his fellow human beings. This righteous man carried the rest of Creation along behind him and supported humankind through good times and bad. The ark became the symbol of the Church for Christians who were saved from the hell of sin by following Jesus, the new Noah.

Noah built the ark according to God's specifications. A tempest blew for forty days after Noah entered the ark, together with all the creatures chosen by God for rescue. The floods drowned everything and everyone not present in the ark. Noah released a raven after many months, and later a dove, to find out the state of the outside world. After the second trip:

This story brings together several earlier versions, not always consistent one with another. The author made them into one story, more or less successfully.

the dove came back to him and there in its beak was a freshly-picked olive leaf! So Noah realised that the waters were going down. After waiting seven more days, he released the dove, and this time it did not come back. (. . .) He lifted back the hatch of the ark and looked out. The ground was dry!

Now there was a real re-creation of the world. Noah offered a sacrifice which pleased the Lord, and God promised that he would never again destroy the world. He made a firm pact with Noah and his family.

There were many people who lived in fear of seeing "the sky fall on them". But the story of the covenant with Noah shows Israel's confidence that there was a certain order of the world, guaranteed by God. Despite its sinfulness the human race can go forward without irrational fears. The source of this freedom was the secure future God promised the earth.

9: 1, 9, 11–16

God blessed Noah and his sons and said to them, "Have children, multiply and fill the earth." (. . .)

"I am now making my covenant with you and your descendants after you, and with every living creature that was with you. (. . .) Never again will the waters of a flood destroy all living creatures, never again will a flood devastate the earth."

And God said, "This is the sign of the covenant which I am now making between myself and you and every living creature for all generations to come: I now put my bow in the sky and it will be the sign of the covenant between me and the earth. (. . .) When the bow is in the sky I shall see it and remember the eternal covenant I have made between God and every living creature."

Why are people divided? The author of Genesis explained it as the result of pride. Humankind's attempts to rival God ended only in chaos. The tower at first appeared as a sign of creative optimism, but in fact represented humanity's desire for power. The building was so ridiculously small that God could not even see it from a distance. He could not grant humankind's wish to take over the heavens, which could only be theirs if given freely by God. This is, in a way, a new form of the story of original sin but using the legend of the gigantic towers (Ziggourats) of the pagan city of Babylon (Babel).

The account of Pentecost, in the Acts of the Apostles, shows how the gift of tongues sent by the Holy Spirit had the opposite effect to this scattering at Babel.

The tower of Babel

11: 1–9

At this time, the whole world spoke the same language, and used the same words. As people moved eastwards they found a valley in the land of Shinar where they settled. They said to one another, "Come, let us make bricks and bake them in the fire." For stone they used bricks, and for mortar they used bitumen. "Come," they said, "let us build a city and a tower with its top reaching heaven. Then we will become famous and we will not get scattered all over the world."

Now the Lord came down to see the city and the tower that the people had built. "So they are making themselves a single people with a single language!" he said. "Now nothing will stop them finishing what they have set out to do. Come, let us go down and confuse their language, so that they can no longer understand one another." The Lord scattered them from there all over the world, and they stopped building the city. That is why it was called Babel, since in that place the Lord confused the language of the whole world, and from there he scattered them all over the world.

Chapter 11 of Genesis concludes with the introduction of the family of Terah, Abram's father. Terah left Ur, in Chaldaea, and climbed along the fertile crest to Haran. The author thus began to explain the origins and history of his people, showing how God intervened to change the world: humanity began to rise again after its initial fall.

II: THE STORY OF ABRAHAM

The call of Abram   12: 1–9

The Lord said to Abram, "Leave your country, your people and your father's house for a country which I shall show you. I shall make you a great nation, I shall bless you and make your name famous. You are to be a blessing!

I shall bless those who bless you,

I shall curse those who curse you,

because of you, all the families of the earth will be blessed."

So Abram left as the Lord had told him to. He was seventy-five years old when he left Haran. He took with him Sarai, his wife, Lot, his nephew, all the possessions they had acquired and the people who had joined their household in Haran. They set off for the land of Canaan, and arrived there.

Abram travelled through the country until he reached the holy place at Shechem, the Oak of Moreh. The Canaanites lived in the country at the time. The Lord appeared to Abram and said, "I shall give this country to your descendants." And there, Abram built an altar to the Lord who had appeared to him. From there he travelled on to the mountainous district east of Bethel, where he pitched his tent, with Bethel to the west and Ai to the east. There he built an altar to the Lord and called on his name. Then Abram made his way to the Negeb, setting up camp at various places during the journey.

As he reflected on the memory of the Israelites' ancestor who immigrated to the country, the writer described the beginning of an adventure that was both earthly and spiritual. Earthly, because Abram travelled the length and breadth of the land which was later to become the home of his descendants, and spiritual because Abram was responding to a call which he recognised as coming from God. He responded immediately, in faith, thus starting out on the journey which would lead the human race to its true goal: the Kingdom proclaimed by Jesus, where he will welcome all whose faith has made them "sons of Abraham".

Abram returned to Canaan after a short stay in Egypt. As a result of disputes between his shepherds and those who worked for his nephew Lot, the two groups separated leaving Lot the best pastures in the Jordan Valley. God then showed himself to Abram again:

13: 14–18

The Lord said to Abram, "Look all round from where you are, to north and south, to east and west. I shall give to you and your descendants all the land you can see for ever. I shall make your descendants as numerous as the dust on the ground. When people succeed in counting the specks of dust, then they will be able to count your descendants too! On your feet! Travel the length and breadth of the country, for I mean to give it to you."

So Abram moved his tent and went to settle at the Oak of Mamre, at Hebron, and there he built an altar to the Lord.

God rewarded Abram's generosity by opening out great prospects to him: the world and the future were his.

The stay in Canaan was difficult. An alliance of local kings was a threat to Lot and his family. But Abram rescued his nephew from prison. He met Melchizedek when he returned from this daring exploit. This stranger was both a king and a priest of Almighty God who offered bread and wine to Abram and gave him a blessing.

The covenant and divine promises

15: 1–6

Some time later, the word of the Lord came to Abram in a vision: "Do not be afraid, Abram! I am your shield and shall give you a very great reward."

Abram replied, "Lord God, what use are your gifts to me, since, as I go on my way, I have no child of my own? Since you have not given me any descendants, one of my servants will be my heir." Then the Lord said to him in reply, "No, that will not be so, your heir will come from your own body." Then taking him outside, he said, "Look up at the sky and, if you can, count the stars. Just so will your descendants be." Abram put his faith in the Lord and because of this the Lord considered him righteous.

Abram could not believe that it was really possible to have a son by Sarai, his wife, who was already an old woman. So he used a tactic that was perfectly legal at the time: he had a child by a slave-girl, Hagar. Ishmael was born but was not the promised son. After renewing his covenant with the man (who was now called Abraham) God confirmed that it was by Sarai (from now on called Sarah) that the patriarch would have his son.

The apparition at Mamre

18: 1–15

The Lord appeared to Abraham at the oak of Mamre while he was sitting by the entrance of the tent during the hottest part of the day. He looked up, and saw three men standing near him. As soon as he saw them he ran to greet them, bowing to the ground. "My lord," he said, "please, do not pass so near to my home without doing me the honour of stopping. Let me have someone

Another version of the divine promise. This story emphasises the warmth of Abraham's welcome.

It was God himself that Abraham welcomed when he offered hospitality to the three strangers: God reveals himself through human beings.

bring you some water, so that you can wash your feet and then have a rest under the tree. Let me fetch a little bread and you can get your strength back before going further, now that you have come so near to my home." They replied, "Do as you say."

Abraham hurried to the tent and said to Sarah, "Quick, take three measures of best flour and make loaves." Then, running to the herd, he took a fine and tender calf and gave it to a servant, who hurried to prepare it. Then taking curds, milk and the calf which had been prepared, he laid it all before them. They ate while he remained standing near them under the tree.

"Where is your wife Sarah?" they asked him. "She is in the tent," he replied. Then his guest said, "I shall come back to you next year, and your wife Sarah will have a son." Sarah was listening at the entrance of the tent behind him. Now Abraham and Sarah were old, very old, and Sarah had passed the age for having children. So she laughed to herself, thinking, "Now that I am past the age of childbearing, and my husband is an old man, am I to enjoy such pleasure again?" But the Lord asked Abraham, "Why did Sarah laugh and say, 'Am I really going to have a child now that I am old?' Nothing is impossible for the Lord. I shall come back to you at the same time next year and Sarah will have a son." Sarah said, "I did not laugh," lying because she was afraid. But he replied, "Oh yes, you did laugh."

Abraham walks with the Lord

18: 16–32

From there the men set out for Sodom. Abraham walked with them to speed them on their way. The Lord wondered, "Shall I hide from Abraham what I am going to do?" (. . .)

The River Jordan and the Dead Sea had failed and this was said to have been caused by a disaster in which two towns with a bad reputation had been destroyed. The author of the book of Genesis took up this story and included Abraham in it, extracting a valuable lesson. He emphasised first of all the close relationship between Abraham and the Lord.

Then the Lord said, "The outcry against Sodom and Gomorrah is so great and their sin is so serious, that I shall go down and see whether or not they have really done what they are being accused of. Then I shall know." (. . .)

Abraham approached the Lord and said, "Will you really destroy the innocent with the guilty? Suppose there are fifty innocent people in the city. Will you really destroy it? Will you not spare the place for the sake of the fifty innocent people who live there? You can't do that: put the innocent to death with the guilty, so that the innocent are treated in the same way as the guilty! Should the judge of the whole world not act justly?" The Lord replied, "If I find fifty innocent people in the city of Sodom, I shall spare the whole place because of them."

Abraham spoke up again, "It is very bold of me to speak to the Lord, I who am only dust and ashes: But suppose the fifty innocent were five short? Would you destroy the whole city because of five?" "No," he replied, "I shall not destroy it if I find forty-five there." Abraham persisted, "Suppose there are forty to be found there?" He replied, "If there are forty there, I shall not do it."

Abraham said, "Lord, don't be angry if I go on: Suppose there are only thirty to be found there?" "I shall not do it," he replied, "if I find thirty there." Abraham said, "It is bold of me to speak to you, Lord: Suppose there are only twenty there?" "I shall not destroy it," he replied, "for the sake of the twenty." Abraham said, "I trust my Lord will not be angry if I speak once more: perhaps there will only be ten." "I shall not destroy it," replied the Lord, "for the sake of the ten."

He showed the importance of prayer in the world. At a time when it was considered normal for a group of people to be collectively punished when someone had done wrong, he reversed the idea: God could pardon the guilty because of the innocent people in the group. The righteous had earned salvation for everyone, because God was merciful and took them into account.

The city did not contain ten good people so it was destroyed by a great disaster. Only Lot and his children were saved.

The divine promise came true after these events. Sarah had a son named Isaac. She then insisted on the departure of Ishmael, the son of Hagar the slave-girl. Abraham reluctantly sent the child away. According to the Bible, he became the ancestor of the Arabs. The continuity of Abraham's family now seemed assured. It was then that God put Abraham to a severe test.

The sacrifice of Isaac

22: 1–19

Some time later God put Abraham to the test. "Abraham, Abraham!" he called. "Here I am," he replied. God said, "Take your son Isaac, your only son, whom you love so much, and go to the land of Moriah. There you are to offer him as a sacrifice on one of the mountains which I shall point out to you."

Early next morning Abraham saddled his donkey and took with him two of his servants and his son Isaac. He chopped wood for the sacrifice and started out on his journey to the place which God had told him about. On the third day Abraham looked up and saw the place in the distance. Then he said to his servants, "Stay here with the donkey. The boy and I are going over there; we shall worship the Lord and then come back to you."

Abraham took the wood for the sacrifice and loaded it on Isaac. He carried the fire and the knife, and then the two of them set out

In ancient civilizations, the sacrifice of the eldest son was normal practice. They believed that this would gain them the favour of the gods, who were thought to be jealous of human beings. The author of Genesis took this idea only to overturn it: God did not want human sacrifices. He also used it to show that Abraham had complete faith in the divine promise, even when the Lord seemed to be contradicting himself by demanding the sacrifice of the son he himself gave Abraham. Abraham passed the test, and gave new hope to the people of Israel who, despite their belief that they were the "people of the

together. Isaac spoke to his father Abraham, "Father?" "Yes, my son," he replied. "Look," Isaac said, "here are the fire and the wood, but where is the lamb for the sacrifice?" Abraham replied, "My son, God himself will provide the lamb for the sacrifice." And the two of them went on together.

When they arrived at the place which God had told him about, Abraham built an altar, and arranged the wood. Then he tied his son up and put him on the altar on top of the wood. He stretched out his hand and took the knife to kill his son.

But the angel of the Lord called to him from heaven and said, "Abraham, Abraham!" "Here I am," he replied. The angel said, "Do not raise your hand against the boy. Do not harm him, for now I know you fear God. You have not refused me your own beloved son."

Looking up, Abraham saw a ram caught by its horns in a bush. He took it and offered it as a sacrifice in place of his son. Abraham called this place "The Lord provides", and even today people say: "On the mountain the Lord provides." (. . .)

Abraham went back to his servants, and together they set out for Beersheba, where he settled.

promise", were often threatened with being wiped out.

For Christians, Jesus is the lamb of God, offering himself freely as a sacrifice for sin.

As far as land was concerned, Abraham was never to own more than the corner of a field and the cave he bought for the burial of his wife Sarah. He himself was also buried in this cave. But the story which began with him continued: Isaac married Rebecca and she later found she was expecting twins.

There was rivalry between the two brothers, Jacob and Esau, even from the beginning. Jacob became a farmer and Esau became a hunter when they grew up. Being the first-born, Esau had the birthright, which meant that his father's heritage went to him. But Jacob used his cunning to get the inheritance from his brother.

Esau gives up his birthright

25: 29–34

Once, when Jacob was cooking a stew, Esau returned, exhausted, from the countryside. He said to his brother, "Let me have some of your soup, I'm exhausted." Jacob said, "First, give me your birthright in exchange." Esau replied, "I am about to die, what use is a birthright to me?" Then Jacob said, "First give me your word." Esau gave him his word and sold his birthright to Jacob. Then Jacob gave him some bread and lentil stew. Esau ate, drank, got up and went away. That was all he cared about his birthright.

> Jacob took advantage of his elder brother's tiredness and naïvety. It seems that he was unable to find his place in the world without tricking other people: the early days of God's chosen one show he had much to learn!

Isaac was about to die. According to custom, he wanted to give his first-born son, Esau, the blessing which would assure him of a happy future. Rebecca preferred Jacob and advised her son to trick his father: as Isaac had gone blind, Jacob could take his brother's place. While Esau was out hunting to prepare a last meal for his father, Jacob got ready. He put on gloves made of hide as his brother was very hairy, and then took Isaac his meal. Isaac did not recognise Esau's voice so he made sure it was really him by touching his son's hand. He was convinced by his hairy gloves that it really was Esau and so he gave Jacob his blessing. Jacob had to flee when faced with his brother's anger. He headed towards Mesopotamia from which his ancestors had come and where he still had relatives. He made an important discovery on the way.

Jacob's dream

28: 11–22

When Jacob reached a certain place, he stopped for the night, since the sun had set. He took a stone, made it his pillow and lay down to sleep. He had a dream: a ladder reached from the earth right up to heaven; and God's angels were going up and down on it. And there was the Lord, standing beside him, saying, "I am the Lord, the God of Abraham your father, and the God of Isaac. I shall give to you and your descendants the ground on which you are lying. Your descendants will be as numerous as the dust on the ground. Your family will spread out to the west and east, to the north and south, and all peoples on earth will be blessed by you and your descendants. I am with you; I shall keep you safe wherever you go, and bring you back to this country, for I shall never leave you until I have done what I have promised you." Then Jacob woke up and said, "Truly, the Lord is in this place and I did not know!" He was afraid and said, "How awe-inspiring this place is! This is none other than the house of God, and the gate of heaven!" Early next morning, he took the stone he had used for his pillow, and set it up as a pillar, pouring oil over it. He called the place Bethel. (Before that the town had been called Luz.)

    Jacob then made this vow, "If God remains with

> Jacob's dream was no doubt influenced by the memory of the Ziggourats, the towers of Babylon's sanctuaries, whose staircases were supposed to lead up to the heavens. The aim of the story is to show that the covenant established between God and Abraham was still valid. Jacob was the heir to the promise.

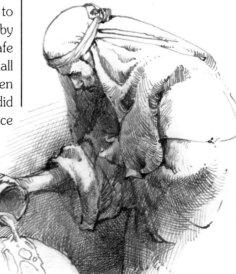

Jacob was still materialistic. He agreed to be faithful only on condition that God helped him. The time of his full conversion was yet to come.

me and keeps me safe on this journey, if he gives me food to eat and clothes to wear, and if I come home safe and well to my father's home, then the Lord shall be my God. This stone I have set up as a pillar will be a house of God, and I will give you a tenth of everything you give me."

At last Jacob reached the home of a distant relative called Laban. Wishing to marry his second daughter, Rachel, he was tricked by his father-in-law who made him first marry the eldest, Leah, before he would allow him to marry the daughter he preferred. Jacob became rich and powerful in his own right, and set off towards Canaan with his family and all his possessions. When he reached the river Jabbok, which marked the frontier, he met with a mysterious opponent.

This strange tale is probably based on old legends concerning a river god, but the author used it to present a very deep experience undergone by the people of Israel. Jacob's whole existence was shaken to the core at this turning-point in his life. The man who had always succeeded through trickery suddenly saw his selfish schemes collapse about his ears.

Jacob wrestles with God
32: 25–33

Later on, this strange fight would appear to him as a struggle with God himself. He tried to win by finding out his opponent's name (which was seen as a way of getting the better of him). It was only when he accepted the fact that he was a weak man that he won. He was a different person when he emerged, and marked forever by the experience (he had a limp). It was a new beginning — he was given a new name — and at last he could be reconciled to his brother.

Then someone wrestled with Jacob until daybreak. When this person saw that he could not get the better of Jacob, he struck him on the hip, and Jacob's hip was dislocated during the struggle. The stranger said, "Let me go, for day is breaking." But Jacob replied, "I will not let you go unless you bless me." The other said, "What is your name?" "Jacob," he replied. He said, "You will no longer be called Jacob, but Israel since you have shown your strength against God and men and no one has got the better of you." Then Jacob asked, "Please tell me your name." He replied, "Why do you ask my name?" Then he blessed Jacob.

Jacob named the place Peniel, "Because I have seen God face to face, and have survived." The sun rose as he left Peniel, limping because of his hip. (. . .)

Jacob looked up and saw Esau coming with four hundred men. He bowed to the ground seven times, as he went up to his brother. But Esau ran to meet him, took him in his arms, threw himself on his neck and wept as he kissed him.

Thus the people of Israel, struggling with God throughout their history, were called upon to live in brotherly love with all people.

Jacob had twelve sons from his double marriage. They became the ancestors of the twelve tribes of Israel. The second to last son, Joseph, was always fighting his brothers.

THE STORY OF JOSEPH SOLD BY HIS BROTHERS

Joseph was his father's favourite. In a dream, he saw himself lording it over his brothers (their sheaves bowed down to his). The brothers were filled with jealousy and took advantage of Joseph's joining them in the fields to sell him as a slave and to tell their father he was dead.

When he reached Egypt, Joseph at first became a household steward, but was then thrown into prison following the false accusations of his master's wife. He was taken from the prison and made Chief Officer to Pharaoh owing to his ability in interpreting dreams. He met his brothers again during a famine in Canaan when they came to Egypt in search of food. He had his father brought to him after many romantic adventures and the whole family settled in Egypt.

This lovely story emphasises the faithfulness of God, who never abandons those he loves.

EXODUS

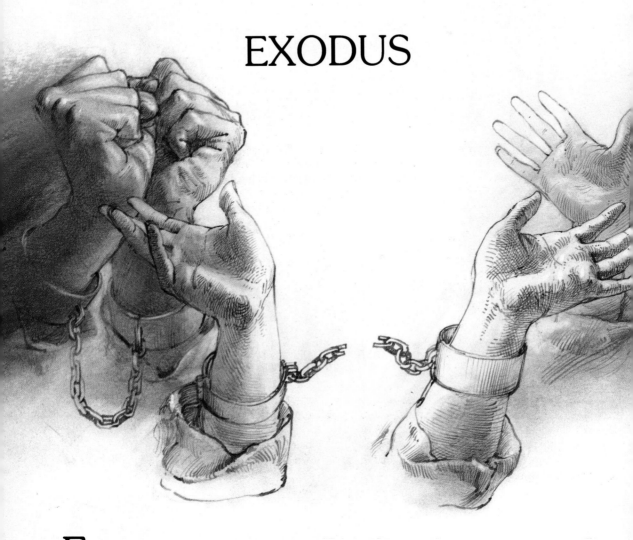

Freedom! For all those suffering under cruel tyrants, the word symbolises hope. But what follows is so often disappointing — those who rallied together for the fight disperse and new difficulties emerge. Should we despair, then? Should we not rather discover that one day's freedom often leads to others? And that this progress, from freedom to freedom, is in itself the sign of God in action at the heart of human life? That is the real meaning of the Exodus account.

God calls people to freedom

Life was hard for the descendants of the patriarchs who had fled to Egypt around the thirteenth century BC. They were reduced to slavery and also faced a real threat of being wiped out. The dominant religion at the time stated that the established order could not be changed. What hope was there for the future?

The true God, the God of their ancestors, intervened through Moses. Moses had appeared to be on the

side of their Egyptian masters but came back to support his brothers. It was then that he heard God calling him to set his people free. On the night of the Passover and in spite of Pharaoh's opposition, he led his people into the desert and towards the Promised Land and freedom. The people who left Egypt acquired a totally new idea of God at the time of the crossing of the Red Sea: their God was a God of freedom who came to save his people from their slavery and to form a covenant with them. The sign of that covenant was the Law, the charter of a humanity that was truly free. The people were still far from ready to accept that Law. True freedom involves an endless struggle against the forces pulling us backwards.

A story that is always in our thoughts

We rewrite the story as we think about the deep significance of the events which founded the Israelite people. With hindsight, the Hebrews were to see more clearly the fundamental events which made them who they were: they had really been called upon by God to establish a new humanity. The author emphasises their discovery of God's intervention by elaborating on events and reorganising them to make them easier to understand. Present-day scientific research however confirms that the main points of the account are historically accurate.

An Exodus which continues to this day

As the adventure which began with the Exodus continued, the need for freedom at a deeper level than that represented by the crossing of the Red Sea became clear. The Jews meditated on this and came to believe that this event in the distant past was a picture of a second Exodus, a second Passover, through which the divine plan to free humankind would be truly fulfilled.

This is how Christians see the work of Jesus. They see him as the new Moses, saving humanity from the slavery of sin, and bringing them into the true Promised Land: the Kingdom of God.

THE BEGINNING OF MOSES' STORY

The Hebrews lived happily in Egypt for a long time until one day a new Pharaoh emerged (perhaps Rameses II, who lived BC 1290–1224). He began to worry about the growth of the immigrant population. He reduced them to slavery and put them to work making bricks. He also ordered the massacre of all new-born baby boys.

One day, a woman managed to save her son

by putting him in a basket made of rushes and leaving it on the Nile. The child, Moses, was adopted by Pharaoh's daughter and educated at the royal court. Later, he realised the poverty his people lived in and he killed an Egyptian guard while defending one of them. He then had to flee into the desert of Midian where he soon married. That was when he had a surprise meeting with God.

The burning bush 3: 1–6

Moses was looking after the flock of his father-in-law Jethro, the priest of Midian. He led the animals to the far side of the desert and came to Horeb, the mountain of God. The angel of the Lord appeared to him in a flame of fire blazing from the middle of a bush. Moses looked; the bush was in flames, but it was not being burnt up. Moses said to himself, "I must go and find out why the bush is not being burnt up." When God saw him going across to look, he called to him from the middle of the bush: "Moses, Moses!" "Here I am," he replied. "Do not come any nearer," God said. "Take off your sandals, for the place where you are standing is holy ground. I am the God of your ancestors, the God of Abraham, the God of Isaac and the God of Jacob." Then Moses covered his face, because he was afraid to look at God.

The mission of Moses 3: 7–12

God said, "I have seen the suffering of my people in Egypt. I have heard them crying for help because of their slave-drivers. I have come down to rescue them from the power of the Egyptians and bring them out from there to a large, fertile country, to a country flowing with milk and honey (. . .). The Israelites' cry for help has reached me, and I have seen the cruel way in which the Egyptians are oppressing them. So now I am sending you to Pharaoh. Bring my people, the Israelites, out of Egypt."

Moses said, "Who am I to go to Pharaoh and bring the Israelites out of Egypt?" God said, "I shall be with you. This is the sign by which you will know that I was the one who sent you. After you have led the people out of Egypt, you will worship God on this mountain."

The divine name revealed 3: 13–15

Moses said to God, "Look, if I go to the Israelites and say to them, 'The God of your ancestors has sent me to you,' and they say to me, 'What is his name?' what am I to tell them?" God said to Moses, "I am who I am." And he said, "You will say to the Israelites, 'I am has sent me to you.' " God said to Moses again, "You are to tell the Israelites, 'Yahweh, the God of your ancestors, the God of Abraham, the God of Isaac and the God of Jacob, has sent me to you.' This is my name for all time, and this is what all generations are to call me."

Moses discovered in his hour of need that the God of his ancestors, apparently forgotten, was still there. He made himself known as the one who would set his people free. He appeared as the Almighty, but at the same time as very close to men and women. Moses was inspired by this image.

Moses was called to put God's plan into action. He felt overwhelmed when faced with such a calling, so God gave him a solemn promise, saying "I shall be with you".

In that ancient universe with, it seemed, so many gods, which one was speaking? Moses wanted to know, not least because, according to Jewish beliefs, to know a god's name was to have the power to call on him. But God answered him in a strange way: "I am who I am": in Hebrew "*Yahweh*". In effect this is God's name, but the Jews avoid using this name out of respect. That is why, in this Bible, we have translated it as *the Lord*.

Moses is given miraculous powers

4: 1–17

Moses replied to God, "But suppose they will not believe me or listen to me, but say to me, 'The Lord has not appeared to you'?" The Lord then said to him, "What is that in your hand?" "A staff," he replied. "Throw it on the ground," said the Lord. Moses threw it on the ground; the staff turned into a snake and Moses ran away from it. The Lord then said to Moses, "Reach out your hand and catch it by the tail." Moses reached out his hand, caught it, and in his hand it turned back into a staff. "This is so that they may believe that the Lord, the God of their ancestors, the God of Abraham, the God of Isaac and the God of Jacob, has appeared to you."

Next, the Lord said to him, "Put your hand inside your tunic." Moses did so, then drew it out again: his hand was like a leper's hand, white as snow. The Lord then said to him, "Put your hand back inside your tunic." Moses did so, and when he drew it out, it was healthy, just like the rest of his body. "If they do not believe you and are not convinced by the first sign, the second sign will convince them. But if they do not believe you, even with both signs, you are to take some water from the river and pour it on the ground. The water you have taken from the river will turn to blood on the dry land."

Moses said to the Lord, "Please, my Lord, I have never been good with words, I never have been and your speaking to me hasn't changed that. I am slow and hesitant." "Who gave a person a mouth?" the Lord said to him. "Who makes a person dumb or deaf, gives sight or makes blind? Is it not I, the Lord? Now go, I shall help you speak and tell you what to say."

Moses replied, "Please, my Lord, send anyone you decide to send!" At this, the Lord grew angry with Moses. He said to him, "There is your brother Aaron the Levite, is there not? I know that he is a good speaker. He is coming to meet you. When he sees you, he will be very happy. You will speak to him and tell him what to say. I shall help you speak, and him too, and tell you what to do. He will be your spokesman and speak to the people in your place. You will be like God telling him what to say. Take this staff in your hand. With it you will perform the signs."

The author emphasised that Moses was able to beat the Egyptian magicians at their own game, thanks to God.

Faced with predictable problems and with the power of Egypt, Moses felt helpless and wanted to refuse the task God was giving him. But God reminded him that he, the Lord, was the sole source of all power. He would act through his chosen one even if that one was weak. All he would give Moses was the help of his brother, Aaron.

So Moses returned to Egypt and asked Pharaoh to free the Hebrews. The Egyptian king wanted nothing to do with him and even ordered his men to be more severe with the slaves. Tension mounted, against both Pharaoh and Moses, because the Hebrews were furious with Moses for making the king angry.

Then Moses took drastic measures. He caused nine disasters to take place one after the other: a plague of frogs, one of locusts, one of hail, etc. Pharaoh pretended to back down after each one but quickly went back on his word and stubbornly refused to release the Hebrews. At last, Moses announced a tenth 'plague', more terrible than all the others: God would kill all the first-born children of Egypt. He told the Hebrews to get ready to leave as they celebrated the feast of the Passover.

The Passover

12: 1–14

In the land of Egypt the Lord said to Moses and Aaron, "This month must be the first month for you; it will be the first month of your year. Speak to the whole community of Israel and say, 'On the tenth day of this month each man must take an animal from the flock for his family: one animal for each household. If there are too few people in the household to eat the whole animal, they must join up with their nearest neighbours, depending on the number of people. When you choose the animal, take into account how much each person can eat. It must be an animal without any defects, a one-year-old male, either a sheep or a goat. Keep it till the fourteenth day of the month when the whole community of Israel will slaughter it at twilight. Some of the blood must then be taken and put on both the door-posts and the lintel of the houses where it is eaten. That night, the meat must be eaten, roasted with unleavened bread and bitter herbs. Do not eat any of it raw or boiled in water, but it must all be roasted including the head, feet and internal organs. You must not leave any of it until the morning: if any is left, you must burn it. This is how you must eat it: with a belt round your waist, your sandals on your feet and your staff in your hand. You must eat it quickly: it is a Passover in the Lord's honour. That night, I shall go through Egypt and kill all the first-born, both men and animals, and shall bring justice on all the gods of Egypt. The blood will be a sign marking the houses where you are. When I see it I shall pass over you, and you will escape the plague of destruction which I am bringing on Egypt. You and all future generations will remember this day, and keep it as a feast in the Lord's honour. This is a decree for all time.' "

The Hebrews adapted an old nomadic religious rite and gave it new meaning. In spring, they sprinkled the blood of an animal on the tent-post to gain protection for its inhabitants. From now on, the blood of the Paschal lamb would commemorate the protection provided by God to his people, on the night of the Egyptian terror, and the departure for the land of freedom.

The old rite was repeated again by Jesus with yet another meaning: Christ himself was the Paschal lamb and the shedding of his blood marked the beginning of true freedom for humankind.

Everything happened as the Lord had said. The Egyptians were devastated and wanted nothing more than to see the Hebrews go. Pharaoh gave in at last. The Hebrews left quickly and marched off into the Sinai peninsula.

God leads his people   13: 21–2

The Lord went in front of them, by day in a pillar of cloud to show them the way, and by night in a pillar of fire to give them light. This meant they could march both by day and by night. The pillar of cloud never left its place ahead of the people during the day, nor the pillar of fire during the night. (. . .)

The Egyptians pursue the Israelites   14: 5–14

When Pharaoh, the king of Egypt, was told that the people had fled, he and his officials changed their attitude towards them. They said, "How could we have allowed the people of Israel to leave our service?" So Pharaoh had his chariot made ready and set out with his troops. He took his six-hundred best chariots and each of them carried an officer. The Lord made Pharaoh stubborn, and he gave chase to the Israelites while they marched confidently away.

The author shows the people travelling in an impressive procession, all in order, and with God himself as their guide. The event became an epic adventure in the Israelites' memory, with God seen to act in an extraordinary way.

He caught up with them where they had set up camp beside the sea (. . .). As Pharaoh approached, the Israelites looked up and saw the Egyptians in pursuit of them! They were terrified and cried out to the Lord for help. They said to Moses, "Are there not enough graves in Egypt, that you had to lead us out to die in the desert? What was the point of bringing us out of Egypt? Did we not tell you as much? Leave us alone, we said, we would rather work for the Egyptians! We prefer to work for them than to die in the desert!" Moses said to the people, "Do not be afraid! Stand firm. You will see what the Lord will do to rescue you. The Egyptians you see today you will never see again. The Lord will do the fighting for you. All you need to do is to keep calm."

The Hebrews were in great danger and so they rebelled against Moses, who was their hero only the previous day. The people were not prepared to risk their lives to gain freedom. They still thought like slaves and were forever looking back with regret on their former security.

The miracle of the sea

14: 15–31

The Lord said to Moses, "Why cry out to me? Tell the Israelites to march on. Raise your staff and stretch out your hand over the sea and divide it, so that the Israelites can walk through the sea on dry ground. I shall make the Egyptians so stubborn that they will follow them, and I shall win glory for myself at the expense of Pharaoh and all his army, chariots and horsemen. The Egyptians will then know that I am the Lord when I cause my glory to be seen at their expense."

Then the angel of God, who went in front of the army of Israel, moved his position and followed behind them. The pillar of cloud also moved from their front and took position behind them, so that it came between the Egyptian camp and that of Israel. The cloud was dark, and the night passed without either side drawing any closer to the other. Then Moses stretched out his hand over the sea, and all night long the Lord drove the sea back with a strong easterly wind: he made the sea into dry land and divided the waters. The Israelites walked on dry ground right through the sea, with walls of water to the right and to the left of them. The Egyptians gave chase, and all Pharaoh's horses, chariots and horsemen went into the sea after them. In the morning, the Lord looked down from the pillar of fire and cloud and threw the Egyptian army into confusion. He made their chariot wheels stick in the mud so that it was very difficult for them to drive. The Egyptians began to say, "Let us get away from Israel, for the Lord is fighting on their side against us!" Then the Lord said to Moses, "Stretch out your hand over the sea and let the waters flow back onto the Egyptians and onto their chariots and horsemen." Moses stretched out his hand and, as day broke, the sea flowed back onto its bed. As they fled, the Egyptians ran straight into it, and the Lord overthrew them in the middle of the sea. The returning waters covered the chariots and horsemen of Pharaoh's entire army, which had followed the Israelites into the sea. Not one of them was left. The Israelites, however, had marched through the sea on dry ground, with walls of water to the right and to the left of them. That day, the Lord rescued Israel from the threat of the Egyptians, and Israel saw the Egyptians lying dead on the sea-shore. When Israel saw the great power that the Lord had used against the Egyptians, they put their faith in him and in his servant Moses.

Many consider that it is possible to explain the passage of the Red Sea as a natural phenomenon, but those who were actually there saw in it the intervention of God. The story is recounted time and again, enriched with colourful details which the author of the book of Exodus has included.

The miracle of the "crossing of the Sea of Reeds" was regarded from that time as God's greatest work. It was the experience which really marked the foundation of the people of Israel. Its echoes were to recur throughout their history.

The account puts together several traditions from different sources. The author did not want to sacrifice any of them.

Song of victory   15: 1–5, 9–10, 21

Then Moses and the Israelites sang this song in the Lord's honour:

"I shall sing to the Lord, for he has covered himself in glory, he has thrown horse and rider into the sea.

The Lord is my strength and my song, I owe my rescue to him.

He is my God, my father's God, and I shall praise and glorify him.

The Lord is a warrior; the Lord is his name. He has thrown Pharaoh's chariots and army into the sea. The pick of his officers have been drowned in the Sea of Reeds.

The ocean has closed over them; they have sunk to the bottom like a stone. (. . .)

The enemy said, 'I shall give chase and overtake, I shall share out the spoils of battle and gorge myself on them, I shall draw my sword, I will kill them.'

But you blew with your breath, and the sea closed over them; they sank like lead in the terrible waters.

Lord, who is like you among the gods? Awesome in glory, worker of miracles! (. . .)

Sing to the Lord, for he has covered himself in glory, he has thrown horses and riders into the sea."

Beyond the event itself — the destruction of Pharaoh's armies — Jews and Christians down the ages have referred to this song in order to praise God who works for the salvation of his people in all circumstances.

The manna
16: 2–5

The road to freedom was hard and the people were on the verge of rebelling. However the discovery of an unexpected provision of food appeared as a wonderful sign from God. When the author tells us how the manna for the Sabbath had to be collected the day before and stored, he reminds us that although a human being does need food for his body, "he does not live on bread alone". This text was quoted by Jesus during his temptation.

The whole community of Israelites began complaining about Moses and Aaron in the desert. They said to them, "Why did we not die at the Lord's hand in Egypt, where we used to sit round the pots of meat and could eat to our heart's content! As it is, you have led us into this desert to starve us all to death!"

The Lord said to Moses, "Look, I shall rain down bread for you from the heavens. Each day the people must go out and collect their ration for the day. I am going to test them in this way to see whether or not they will follow my law. On the sixth day, however, they are to bring in and prepare twice as much as usual."

Sure enough, in the morning, the Israelites found a strange dew of large whitish grains. Moses told them, "It is the bread the Lord has given you to eat". Some people gathered more of the food than they needed because they lacked faith, but found that it had gone rotten the next day (except on the eve of the Sabbath).

The water from the rock
17: 1–7

The author of the account emphasises how the people still did not trust God in spite of all that had happened. God rose to their challenge: he gave them the water they needed. The memory of the water flowing from the rock was kept alive in Israel; Jesus also referred to it when he described himself as the water of life which satisfied people so that they need never be thirsty again.

Massah means *test*. Meribah means *opposition* or *conflict*.

The whole community of Israelites left the desert of Sin, travelling by stages as the Lord instructed them. They pitched camp at Rephidim where there was no water for them to drink. The people complained to Moses: "Give us water to drink." Moses replied, "Why are you grumbling? Why do you put the Lord to the test?" But the people were desperately thirsty and complained to Moses, "Why did you bring us out of Egypt, only to make us, our children and our animals, die of thirst?" Moses cried out to the Lord for help: "How am I to deal with these people? Any moment now they will stone me!" The Lord said to Moses, "Go on ahead of the people with some of the elders of Israel. Take the staff with which you struck the River with you, and go. I shall be waiting for you there on the rock. Strike the rock, and water will come out for the people to drink." Moses did this in the presence of the elders of Israel. He gave the place the names *Massah* and *Meribah* because the Israelites complained and put the Lord to the test, saying: "Is the Lord with us, or not?"

They travelled on with all their difficulties. They had to fight the Amalekites, an enemy bedouin tribe. The Israelites won in response to Moses' prayers. The group also had internal difficulties: Moses was unable to meet everyone's needs. On the advice of his father-in-law, who had come to meet him on the way, he began to organise the group by choosing helpers to help people settle their disputes.

At last they came to the foot of Mount Sinai.

God shows himself
to his people
19: 16–24

At daybreak two days later, there were peals of thunder and flashes of lightning, dense cloud over the mountain and a very loud trumpet blast. In the camp, all the people trembled. Then Moses led them out of the camp to meet God. They stood at the bottom of the mountain. Mount Sinai was totally covered with smoke, because the Lord had come down on it in the form of fire. The smoke rose into the air as it does from a furnace and the whole mountain shook violently. The sound of the trumpet grew louder and louder. Moses spoke, and God answered him in the thunder. The Lord came down onto the top of Mount Sinai, and called Moses to come to him there. Moses went up. The Lord then said to Moses, "Go down and warn the people not to cross over the boundary to look at the Lord, or many of them will die. Even the priests, who may come close to the Lord, must sanctify themselves, or the Lord may become very angry with them." Moses said to the Lord, "The people cannot come up Mount Sinai; you yourself warned us to mark out the limits of the mountain and declare it holy." The Lord replied, "Go down! Then come back bringing Aaron with you. But do not allow the priests and people to step over the boundary to come up to the Lord, or he may break out in anger against them." (. . .)

All the previous events recounted in the Bible lead up to this central moment. God had saved his people unconditionally but the people had to take another step: they had to stop being like children, led by the hand, and freely accept God's call to join with him by a contract of alliance. The account of this alliance, or covenant, is the basis of the social and religious life of Israel.

The Law began with a reminder of their rescue from Egypt. A people freed from slavery should not be like other people who are slaves to their instincts and desires. In particular, they should not make gods in their own image, that is to say, gods who conform to their own desires. They must also stop being guided by their own desires. The Ten Commandments committed them to the way of life commanded by God himself.

But the attitude with which the people would obey this Law remained to be seen. Jesus revealed its full significance by presenting it as the expression of love. But many people will always see it as a list of rules, taking their freedom away, rather than as the way to eternal life.

The Ten Commandments

20: 1–21

Then God spoke and said: "I am the Lord your God who brought you out of Egypt, where you lived as slaves.

"You shall have no other gods before me.

"You shall not make yourself a carved image or any likeness of anything in heaven or on earth or in the waters under the earth.

"You shall not bow down to these gods or worship them. For I, the Lord your God, am a jealous God. Among those who hate me, I bring punishment for a parent's fault on the children, the grandchildren, and the great-grandchildren. But I show faithful love towards thousands of those who love me and keep my commandments.

"You shall not use the name of the Lord your God in any wrong way, for the Lord will not leave unpunished anyone who uses his name wrongly.

"Remember the Sabbath day and keep it holy. For six days you shall labour and do all your work, but the seventh day is a Sabbath, set aside for the Lord your God. You shall do no work that day, neither you nor your son nor your daughter nor your servants, nor your animals nor the stranger living with you. For in six days the Lord made the heavens, the earth and the sea and all that these contain, but on the seventh day he rested. This is why the Lord has blessed the Sabbath day and made it holy.

"Honour your father and your mother so that you may live a long life in the land that the Lord your God is giving you.

"You shall not kill.

"You shall not commit adultery.

"You shall not steal.

"You shall not give false evidence against your neighbour.

"You shall not set your heart on your neighbour's house.

"You shall not set your heart on your neighbour's wife, or servant, or ox, or donkey, or any of your neighbour's possessions."

Seeing the peals of thunder, the flashes of lightning, the trumpet blasts and the smoke covering the mountain, the people were all terrified and kept their distance. They said to Moses, "Speak to us yourself, and we will obey; but do not let God speak to us, or we shall die." Moses said to them, "Do not be afraid; God has come to test you, so that your fear of him may keep you from sinning." The people kept their distance while Moses approached the dark cloud where God was.

The Covenant is sealed

24: 1–11

God said to Moses, "Come up to the Lord, you and Aaron, Nadab and Abihu, and seventy of the elders of Israel, and bow down some distance away. Moses alone will approach the Lord; the others will not approach, nor will the people come up with him."

Moses told the people all the Lord's words and all his laws. They answered with one voice, "We will carry out all the words the Lord has spoken!" Moses put all the Lord's words into writing, and early next morning he built an altar at the foot of the mountain, with twelve standing-stones for the twelve tribes of Israel. Then he sent some young Israelites to offer sacrifices. Moses took half the blood from the bullocks and put it into basins, and he sprinkled the rest of the blood on the altar. Then, he took the Book of the Covenant and he read it to the people, who said, "We shall do everything that the Lord has said." Moses then took the blood and sprinkled it over the people saying, "This is the blood of the covenant which the Lord has made with you with all these conditions."

Moses, Aaron, Nadab, Abihu and seventy elders of Israel then went up the mountain, and they saw the God of Israel. Beneath his feet there was what looked like a sapphire pavement, as pure as the heavens themselves. God did not harm the elders of Israel. They actually gazed on God, and they then ate and drank.

The alliance (or covenant) agreed between God and his people was a solemn pact. The people agreed to observe the Law and God promised to help his people. The rite of sprinkling blood expressed the sacred nature of this two-way promise and the relationship with God. It reappears in a new form in Christianity: Jesus introduced a new kind of relationship with God by shedding his own blood through love: the new alliance (or "new Covenant") is a call on us all to discover the father-child relationship between the human race and its Father God.

Most texts in the Bible insist that God could not be seen. We have a different tradition here, but even in this case where God is seen, he remains a mysterious presence.

Moses on the mountain

24: 12–18

The Lord said to Moses, "Come up to me on the mountain. Stay there, and I will give you the stone tablets — the law and the commandment — which I have written to teach them how to live." Moses got ready, with Joshua his assistant, and they went up the mountain of God. (. . .)

Cloud covered the mountain. The glory of the Lord rested on Mount Sinai and the cloud covered it for six days. On the seventh day the Lord called to Moses from the cloud. To the watching Israelites, the glory of the Lord looked like a fire burning on the mountain top. Moses went right into the cloud and went on up

Moses would always be Israel's great law-giver, but the manner in which the story is told made it perfectly clear that the Law came above all from God.

One day, on another mountain and in another cloud, the apostles of Jesus were to have a vision of the founder of their people coming to bear witness to the fact that Jesus Christ had come to fulfil "the Law and the prophets".

the mountain. He
stayed there for forty days and
forty nights.

The golden calf

32: 1–6

When the people saw that Moses seemed to be staying on the mountain a long time, they gathered round Aaron and said to him, "Get to work, make us a god to go ahead of us, for we do not know what has happened to Moses, who brought us here from Egypt." Aaron replied, "Take off the gold rings in the ears of your wives and your sons and daughters, and bring them to me." The people took off the gold rings from their ears and brought them to Aaron. He took the gold, melted it down in a mould and made a statue of a calf. The people shouted, "Israel, here is your God who brought you here from Egypt!" Seeing this, Aaron built an altar before the statue and announced, "Tomorrow will be a feast in the Lord's honour."

Early the next morning they offered sacrifices. The people then sat down to eat and drink, before getting up to amuse themselves.

In pagan fertility rites it was common for God to be represented by the image of a bull, a symbol of wealth and power. So the people made themselves an image of a bull. It was a terrible sin against the Law they had just agreed to obey but it was too difficult to hold on to a God who could not be seen, that is, a God they had no hold over! They wanted to possess and own him.

The account remained in the memory of the Israelites as the symbol of the sin they constantly slid into; they were always setting up false images of God in one form or another.

In his anger at this sin, the Lord told Moses that he was going to destroy the people. But he promised Moses that he would make him the leader of a great nation.

The prayer of Moses
32: 11–14

Moses tried to pacify the Lord his God. He said, "Lord, why should your anger rage at your people, whom you have brought out of Egypt by your great power and might? The Egyptians will come and say, 'He intended to do them harm when he brought them out, to let them die in the mountains and wipe them off the face of the earth.' Give up your anger; relent and do not bring this disaster on your people. Remember your servants Abraham, Isaac and Jacob, to whom you swore by your very self when you made this promise: 'I shall make your descendants as numerous as the stars of heaven, and I shall give them the whole of the country of which I have spoken, and it will be theirs for ever.' " The Lord then relented over the disaster which he had intended to bring upon his people.

Moses refused to abandon his own people even when he had the chance to save himself by doing so. Moses appeared as a man torn between God and the people he represented. He was often caught in this way.

A gilded bronze calf, discovered in Byblos.

Moses was furious when he returned to the camp. He broke the stone tablets of the Law in his rage and had the guilty parties punished severely. Considering that what had just happened was a real breaking of the Covenant, he announced it would be necessary to renew it completely. Moses had set up a tent some distance from the camp, the one called the "Tent of Meeting", and he prayed to God in it.

Moses prays again   33: 12–23

Moses said to the Lord, "Listen, you said to me, 'Make the people move on,' but you have not told me whom you are going to send with me. You have said, however, 'I know you by name and you enjoy my favour.' If indeed you are pleased with me, show me your plans, so that I can understand you and can continue to please you. Remember too that this nation is your people." The Lord then said, "I myself shall go with you and I shall give you rest." Moses replied, "If you do not come yourself, do not make us move on from here. For how can it be known that I and my people enjoy your favour, if you do not come with us? But if you do come with us, we shall be different from all the other peoples on the earth." The Lord then said to Moses, "I shall do what you have asked, because you enjoy my favour and because I know you by name."

Moses then said, "Please show me your glory." The Lord said, "I shall make all my goodness pass before you, and I shall speak the name Lord to you. I am gracious to those I wish to be gracious to and I take pity on those I wish to take pity on. But you cannot see my face, for no human being can see me and live." Then the Lord said, "Here is a place near me. You will stand on the rock,

The admirable prayer of a man who "knows God by his name" and who is "known to him by his name" (the sign of deep intimacy): Moses dared to ask God to go with them himself, without an intermediary, for the entire journey. The God of Israel would be "God with us" or, in Hebrew, "Emmanuel".

Exodus tells us that Moses saw God face to face (chapter 11). The apostle Philip asked Jesus: "Lord, show us the Father: that is all we ask". But God cannot be seen until we have been made completely holy, through death.

Until then, he will show himself only through his works and through his messengers, of whom the greatest is his Son, Jesus.

and when my glory passes by, I shall put you in a cleft of the rock and shield you with my hand until I have gone past. Then I shall take my hand away and you will see my back. But my face, you cannot see!''

The Lord renewed the broken Covenant while on the mountain. He showed himself to be the God who was "slow to anger, abounding in grace and faithfulness".

Moses comes down from the mountain 34: 29–35

Moses was radiant. Anyone who comes so close to God is transformed visibly by the experience. Later, Jesus was described as "transfigured".

When Moses came down from Mount Sinai, he was carrying the two tablets of stone with the words of the covenant written on them. He did not know that his face was radiant because he had been talking to the Lord. When Aaron and all the Israelites saw him, his face was so radiant that they were afraid to go near him. But Moses called to them, and Aaron and all the leaders of the community went to him and he talked to them. Then all the Israelites came closer, and he passed on to them all the orders that the Lord had given to him on Mount Sinai. When he had finished speaking to them, he put a veil over his face. Whenever Moses went into the Lord's presence to speak with him, he took the veil off until he came out. And when he came out, he would tell the Israelites what orders he had been given, and the Israelites would see that Moses' face was radiant. Then Moses would put the veil back over his face until he went in to speak to the Lord again.

The book of Exodus ends with the description of the building of the sanctuary, built following the plans given by God himself: it was to be the place of his presence.

LEVITICUS

Any organised group of people starts by giving themselves laws and rules of how to behave. Although this may appear to limit the freedom of the individual, if we look closely, we see that it does make things easier: because everyone knows exactly what he or she can expect from other people. They understand the meaning of their actions and their attitudes.

The Israelites called the first five books of the Bible the Law, or Torah, because they were the books establishing the basic rules for living which were to be followed when starting out on the road towards true freedom. The Israelites regarded the Torah as a gift from God, a gift of grace, because it enabled those following its teachings to become human in the truest sense.

This Torah, or Law, contained very specific orders, or commandments: the Decalogue (cf. Exod. 20: 2–17). We are no longer dealing with general instructions about life, but with rules which clearly define the moral behaviour of the new person, freed from slavery.

Leviticus is made up of a list of decrees applied to everyday life. It went into detail, for it was a complete code, particularly useful to the Levites, who were responsible for making sure the religious practices were followed.

It is important to know how to behave both towards God and other people. The two go together.

Leviticus lays particular emphasis on the worship in the Temple and consequently has lost much of its interest for us today: its rules about sacrifices and definitions of ritual cleanliness no longer concern us.

It is important, however, to see that our religious lives cannot be separated from our attitude towards other people. It is also important to see how, underlying all the detailed commands, there is an essential message: we are called to be as perfect as God himself is.

These are the rules which particularly concerned the poor, the weak, the disabled, the stranger and justice in general. The reason for these commandments is continually and forcefully repeated: "I am the Lord who brought you out of the land of Egypt". So the Israelites had to be as generous and open towards others as God himself was, "for I, the Lord, your God, am holy".

Jesus' teaching is already here. He quoted this text in Matt. 5: 43–8 and 22–9.

Moral and religious regulations

19: 1–18, 33–7

The Lord said to Moses: "Speak to the whole community of Israelites and say:

'Be holy, for I, the Lord, am holy.

'Each of you will respect your father and mother, and you will keep my Sabbaths, for I am the Lord your God.

'Do not turn to worship idols and do not make metal gods for yourselves. I am the Lord your God.

'If you offer a communion sacrifice to the Lord, offer it in the way that pleases him. (. . .)

'When you bring in the harvest of your land, do not reap to the very edges of the field, and do not gather the gleanings of the harvest; do not strip your vineyard bare, and do not pick up the fallen grapes. You will leave them for the poor and the stranger. I am the Lord your God.

'You will not steal, nor try to defraud or cheat your fellow-citizen. You will not swear by my name in an effort to deceive someone and bring dishonour to the name of your God. I am the Lord. You will not exploit your neighbour or rob him. You will not keep back your worker's wage until the next morning. You will not curse the dumb or put an obstacle in the way of the blind, but you will fear your God. I am the Lord.

'You will not be unjust when you administer justice. You will neither favour the poor nor be in awe of the great, but will administer justice fairly. You will not slander your own family, nor will you put your neighbour's life at risk. I am the Lord. You will not hate your brother in your heart. Reprove your neighbour firmly, so that you do not share in his guilt. You will not take revenge on, nor bear a grudge against, the members of your people. You will love your neighbour as yourself. I am the Lord. (. . .)

'If foreigners live in your country, you will not take advantage of them. You will treat them as though they were your fellow-countrymen and love them as yourself, for you yourselves were once foreigners in Egypt. I am the Lord your God.

'You will not be dishonest in administering justice as regards measures of length, weight or capacity. You will have accurate scales and accurate weights and measures. I am the Lord your God who brought you out of Egypt. Keep all my laws and all my customs and put them into practice. I am the Lord.' ''

NUMBERS

T he book of Exodus described the Israelites' journey through the wilderness to Sinai, and the covenant God made with his people. The book of Numbers continues the epic up to the entry into Canaan, forty years later. Although the author of the book wanted to recall the events of the past, he also showed how the sins committed by the people were already typical of the sins that Israel continued to fall into throughout its history, and which led eventually to their catastrophe and exile. Their basic sin was always a lack of trust in God: instead of going forward boldly, they never stopped looking back. They felt homesick for Egypt, the land of their slavery, because they still dreamt of security and were discouraged by the difficulty of the road to freedom.

On leaving Sinai, the people seemed at last to have jelled as a group since the description of the "order of march" for the tribes is written in the form of a list of all the families (this is where the title of the book comes from). To judge by the oral traditions passed on by priests over the centuries, the Israelites moved forward in the manner of a liturgical procession, guided by the cloud and the pillar of fire. But, very soon, they began to have difficulties. They grew tired of the manna, and began to complain against Moses. He was very unhappy with this.

The prayer of Moses

11: 10–15

Moses heard the people weeping, each family at the door of its tent. The Lord was extremely angry and Moses too was very displeased. He said to the Lord: "Why do you treat me, your servant, so badly? Have you then no pity on me that you give me the responsibility for all these people? Was it then I who conceived

Moses, who had always until now defended his people, could take no more. God was asking too much of him — his mission seemed impossible.

them or was I their father? You say to me, 'Carry them in your arms, as a nurse carries a baby, and take them to the country which I promised to give to their fathers.' Where am I to find meat to give all these people? They pester me with their tears and say, 'Give us meat to eat.' I cannot carry all these people on my own. It is too much for me. If this is really what you expect of me, please kill me here and now! If only I could win your favour for I can no longer bear my unhappiness!''

The Lord replies   11: 16–17

The Lord said to Moses, "Call together seventy of the elders of Israel. Bring them to the Tent of Meeting, and let them stand with you. I shall come down and talk to you. I shall take some of the spirit which is on you and put it on them. Then they will help you to carry the burden of the people, and you will no longer be on your own." (. . .)

God recognised that responsibility for the people could not rest entirely on one man. So he promised to raise up helpers for Moses to share his vision.

The gift of the Spirit   11: 24–30

Moses called together seventy of the elders, and stationed them around the Tent. The Lord came down in the cloud. He spoke to Moses, then he took some of the spirit that was on him and put it on the seventy elders. When the spirit came on them they prophesied, but only once.

Two men had stayed back in the camp: one was called Eldad and the other Medad. Their names had been included with the others but they had not gone to the Tent. The spirit came down on them and they began to prophesy in the camp. A young man ran to tell Moses this, "Look, Eldad and Medad are prophesying in the camp." Joshua son of Nun, who had served Moses since he was a boy, spoke up, "My lord Moses, stop them!" Moses replied, "Are you jealous on my account? If only all the Lord's people could be prophets and could receive his spirit." Moses then went back to the camp with the elders of Israel.

God sent his Spirit upon the leaders of the people to enable them to take up their responsibilities. But the Spirit burst through the limits they tried to define for it. In fact, Moses did not resent this as a threat to his authority because he wished that one day all Israel would be filled with the Spirit: on that day, the people really would be as one, going forward together rather than as a straggling group.

Moses' authority was questioned, even by his sister Miriam and his brother Aaron. But he was a very humble leader! God had to intervene and punish those who were grumbling. Everything seemed to settle down, and they arrived at the southern frontier of the land of Canaan. Moses sent out spies to scout out the territory they were seeking. The exploring team returned bringing magnificent fruits that made everyone want to conquer such a rich country. But they described the inhabitants as terrifying giants. Two of the scouts suggested that they go on boldly, but the others spread frightening rumours: "It is a land which devours those who live in it".

The rebellion of Israel

14: 1–9

The whole community cried out in distress, and the people wept all night. All the Israelites complained against Moses and Aaron. They said to them, "Why did we not die in Egypt? Or why, even, did we not die in the desert! Why has the Lord brought us to this country, for us to die by the sword, and for our wives and children to be captured by the enemy? Would it not be better for us to go back to Egypt?" And they said to one another, "Let us appoint a leader and go back to Egypt."

At this, Moses and Aaron threw themselves on their faces in front of the whole community of Israelites. Then two of the men who had explored the country, Joshua son of Nun and Caleb son of Jephunneh, tore their clothes and said to the people: "The country we went to explore is a good country, an excellent country. If the Lord is pleased with us, he will lead us into it and give it to us. It is a country flowing with milk and honey. But do not rebel against the Lord or be afraid of the people there, for we shall gobble them up. Their protecting shade has deserted them, while we have the Lord on our side. Do not be afraid of them."

> The people feared for the future. They wanted to turn back towards what they saw as security. Their lack of faith was the greatest of all sins.

The Lord's anger and Moses' prayer

14: 10–19

The whole community was talking of stoning them, when the glory of the Lord appeared to all the Israelites, inside the Tent of Meeting. The Lord said to Moses: "How much longer will these people treat me with contempt? How much longer will they refuse to trust me, in spite of all the signs I have given them? I am going to strike them down with a plague and wipe them out. But I shall make a new nation of you, greater and mightier than they are."

Moses said to the Lord:

"But the Egyptians now know about your power — the power with which you brought these people out of their country. They speak of it everywhere. They have learnt that you, Lord, are with this people, and that you, Lord, show yourself to them face to face; that your cloud stands over them; that you go before them in a pillar of cloud by day and a pillar of fire by night. If you kill this people now, with a single blow, then the nations who have

> A dramatic confrontation between Moses and the Lord. Once again, Moses refused to abandon his people. He obtained forgiveness by pointing out the need to save God's reputation.

heard about you will say, 'The Lord was not able to bring this people into the country he had promised them, and so he has murdered them in the desert.' No, my Lord! Show them rather your power. You have said, 'The Lord is slow to anger and rich in faithful love, he forgives faults and sins and yet he lets nothing go unpunished, making the children to the third and fourth generation pay for their parents' sin.' In your most faithful love, please forgive this people's guilt, as you have done from Egypt until now."

Pardon and punishment

14: 20–33

The people were forgiven but punished severely, with the exception of those who had shown faith in the Lord's strength.

The Lord said, "I forgive them as you ask. But just as truly as I live, and as the glory of the Lord fills the whole world, not one of these people who have seen my glory and the signs that I worked in Egypt and in the desert, who have put me to the test ten times already and not obeyed my voice, not one shall see the country which I promised to give their ancestors. Not one of those who have treated me with contempt will see it. (. . .) Only Caleb, Joshua and your children, who you said would be captured, will enter the land you rejected. But, as for you, your dead bodies will fall in this desert and your children will be nomads here for forty years, as punishment for your faithlessness, until the last one of you lies dead in the desert." (. . .)

The community changed its tune at these words. In spite of warnings from Moses, Joshua and Caleb, they fought the Amalekites and the Canaanites, but were defeated.

So the people began their journey through the desert. They sinned time and again, particularly when Moses had to make water spring from the rock again to quench the thirst of those who complained. But the author tells us that at this point Moses himself had a moment of doubt, for which he was punished by the announcement that he would never enter the Promised Land.

Moses also had to deal with the rebellion of Korah, Dathan and Abiram but God supported his chosen one, and his brother Aaron.

The long march continued. There were many obstacles. They could not return to the proper path until they were forgiven their backsliding. The Israelites arrived at last at the frontier of the land of Moab, which barred their way to Canaan to the east of the Dead Sea.

Asked for a safe-conduct, the king of Moab pleaded with a prophet, Balaam, to curse the advancing people and thus condemn them to defeat. But the account tells us in a very amusing way that Balaam was unable to intervene because his ass, who was more intelligent than he was, argued with him. God was with Israel, and the prophet was forced in spite of himself to give them a blessing promising a glorious future in store for the chosen race. In spite of their sins, the Israelites won victory after victory, conquering the whole area east of the Jordan. They were now on the very doorstep of the Promised Land. A new stage in history was about to begin.

DEUTERONOMY

Around the eighth century BC, long after the events recorded in Exodus and Numbers, some of the Israelites saw with sorrow that their kings and fellow countrymen were abandoning the religion of their ancestors. They began to think about the past, about the teachings of Moses and God's promises. Witnessing the catastrophes befalling their country, they said, "Moses warned us that if we betrayed the covenant then God would abandon us". So they began to compile a new version of the journey to the Promised Land, in order to shed light on what was happening in the present. They gave their account in the form of "Moses' Will". Moses was supposed to have addressed the people one last time just before his death, and suggested that they learn from their experiences in the wilderness and warning them to beware of temptation.

The product of this exercise was Deuteronomy, or the "Second Law". It gives us deep religious insights by presenting God as a God of love, who invited the chosen people to join themselves to him for love.

We have here a few of the "lessons" learnt from past events, relevant to the contemporaries of the writer. They were all attributed to Moses as a conclusion to the account of events in the wilderness.

True wisdom

4: 1–9

"And now, Israel, listen to the laws and customs which I am
teaching you today, so that, by keeping them, you may live to take
possession of the country which the Lord, God of your ancestors,
is giving you. You must add nothing to what I command you, and
take nothing from it, but keep the commandments of the Lord
your God just as I give them to you. (. . .) Keep them, put them
into practice, and the people of other nations will admire your
wisdom and understanding. Once they know what all these laws
are, they will exclaim, 'No other people is as wise and understanding as this great nation!' And indeed, what great nation is there
that has its gods as near to them as the Lord our God is to us
whenever we call to him? And what great nation has laws and
customs which are as fair as this Law which I am laying down for
you today?

"But take care. Do not forget the things which you have seen,
or let them slip out of your heart for as long as you live. Rather,
teach them to your children and to your grandchildren."

Loving the Lord is the heart of the Law

5: 32—6: 25

"Do not stray away either to the right or to the left.
Follow the way that the Lord has marked out for you.
Then you will live, you will know happiness and long life
in the country which you are going to possess.

"These, then, are the commandments, the laws and the customs
which the Lord your God has instructed me to teach you so that
you can put them into practice in the country which you are on
your way to receive as your inheritance. If you respect the wishes
of the Lord your God all the days of your lives and keep all his
laws and commandments, which I am teaching you today, you will
have a long life, you, your child and your grandchild. Listen then,
Israel, be careful to keep and put into practice what will make you
happy and will make you a large nation, as the Lord, God of your
ancestors, has promised you, in giving you a country flowing with
milk and honey.

"Listen, Israel: the Lord our God is the one, the only Lord. You
must love the Lord your God with all your heart, with all your soul,
with all your strength. Let the words I am giving you today stay in
your heart. Repeat them to your children when you are sitting at

home, when you are walking down the street, when you are lying down and when you are standing up. Fasten them on your hand as a sign and on your forehead as a headband. Write them on the doorposts of your house and on your gates. (. . .)

"In times to come, when your child asks you, 'What do these instructions, laws and customs mean which the Lord our God has laid down for you?' you are to say: 'Once we were Pharoah's slaves in Egypt, and the Lord brought us out of Egypt by his great power. Before our eyes, he worked great and terrible signs and wonders against Egypt, against Pharaoh and his household. And he brought us out of there, to lead us into the country which he had promised our ancestors he would give us. And the Lord has commanded us to put into practice all these laws and to honour him so as to be happy for ever and to live, as we do to this day. For us, right living will mean this: to keep and put into practice all these commandments in obedience to the Lord our God, as he has commanded us.' "

when asked to give a summary of the Law (cf. Matt. 23: 35–40).

God chose his people freely
7: 7–14

"If the Lord set his heart on you and chose you, it was not because you were more in number than any other people on the earth, for indeed you were the smallest nation. But it was because of his love for you and because he meant to keep the promise he made to your ancestors. That is why he rescued you from the country where you were slaves and, with his mighty power, snatched you out of Pharaoh's hands. From this you can see that the Lord your God is the true God, the faithful God. He is true to his covenant and his faithful love for a thousand generations of those who love him and keep his commandments, but he punishes those who hate him. (. . .) So you must keep the commandments, laws and customs which I am giving you today and you must put them into practice.

The chosen people could not claim to have any rights to God's favour. The Lord had chosen them freely and loved them, and Israel could rely on his faithfulness if they remained faithful to the law of the covenant — and then they would find happiness.

"If you listen to these laws and put them into practice, the Lord your God will keep his covenant and show you the love which he promised to your ancestors. He will love you and bless you and make your numbers grow. He will bless your children and the produce of your land, your corn, your new wine, your oil, the young of your sheep and cattle, in the land which he promised your ancestors he would give you. You will receive more blessings than all the other peoples of the earth."

The ordeal in the desert   8: 2–6

"Remember the long road by which the Lord your God led you for forty years in the desert, to make you humble, to test you and know what was in your heart — whether you would keep his commandments or not. He made you humble, he made you feel what it was like to be hungry. He fed you with manna which neither you nor your ancestors had ever known, to make you understand that man does not live on bread alone but on every word that comes from the mouth of the Lord. Your clothes did not wear out and your feet were not swollen, all those forty years.

"Learn from this that the Lord your God was training you as a father trains his child. Keep the commandments of the Lord your God; follow his ways and fear him."

The Promised Land and its temptations   8: 7–18

"But the Lord your God is bringing you into a fine country, a land of streams and springs (. . .), of wheat and barley, of vines, of figs, of pomegranates, a land of olives, of oil, of honey, a land where bread will not be rationed, where you will lack nothing, a land where you will find iron and copper. You will eat and have all you want and you will bless the Lord your God for the good land he has given you.

"Be careful not to forget the Lord your God, by neglecting his commandments, customs and laws which I am giving you today. When you have eaten all you want, when you have built fine houses to live in, when you have seen your flocks and herds grow, your silver and gold increase, do not let your heart become proud. (. . .) Beware of thinking to yourself, 'My own strength and ability have enabled me to succeed.' Remember the Lord your God; he was the one who gave you the strength to act like this, and in so doing, was keeping the covenant which he made with your ancestors."

The two ways

30: 15–20

"Look, today I am offering you life and happiness, or death and disaster. If you obey the commandments of the Lord your God, which I am giving you today, if you love the Lord your God and follow his ways, if you keep his commandments, his laws and his customs, you will live and become a large nation, and the Lord your God will bless you in the country which you are about to enter and make your own. But if your heart turns away from him, if you refuse to listen to him, if you let yourself be drawn away to worship other gods and serve them, I tell you today, you will most certainly die; you will not live for long in the country which you are crossing the Jordan to enter and make your own. Today, I call heaven and earth to be my witnesses: I am offering you life or death, blessing or curse. Choose life, then, so that you and your descendants may live, in the love of the Lord your God, obeying his voice and being faithful to him; for in this your life consists, and on this depends the length of time that you stay in the country which the Lord promised to give to your ancestors Abraham, Isaac and Jacob."

"This Law which I am laying down for you today is not beyond your strength or beyond your reach . . . No, the word is very near to you, it is in your mouth and in your heart for you to put into practice", the text declares. To be free means that we must choose the path we want to take. Our death and final destiny depend upon our choice. God hopes that destiny will be life.

After this reminder to the people of the Law of the covenant, and after repeating some of the commandments, Moses blessed the twelve tribes of Israel. Having laid his hands on Joshua, his successor, he climbed up Mount Nebo which overlooked the land of Canaan and died there. "Moses was a hundred and twenty years old when he died, his eyes undimmed, his vigour unimpaired . . . since then, there has never been such a prophet in Israel as Moses, the man the Lord knew face to face".

THE BOOK
OF JOSHUA

We all tend to look back nostalgically to the good old days when the present seems hard and the future bleak. This follows because life in former times seemed full of promise and we felt strong and encouraged — indeed, capable of overcoming any obstacle. If only those days could come again!

These were the feelings of the Jews exiled in Babylon following the collapse of the kingdom of Judah in BC 587. The Jews remembered how God had given them a land but they had ruined everything by their sin. There seemed to be no hope, and they could only weep.

The writer of this book says that nothing is impossible for God if we truly believe in him. The writer gives a new account of the old memories of the conquest of Canaan. The result is the book of Joshua and is presented in the form of a triumphal epic. The author portrayed the entry into the Promised Land as a real triumph. It was like a military display, or rather a procession, for it was not the strength of their armies that conquered the land but the Lord himself, and with the ark of the covenant marching at the head of the troops. Only those among the native peoples who joined the chosen nation survived since all others were swept away and massacred.

So, the Jews should not lose hope. The return to the Promised Land seemed impossible but God would one day show his strength again. The people would return to their own land when that time arrived — if only they would believe in him!

The author did not hesitate in his account to present God as cruel in calling for the destruction of his enemies. God was guiding a people who were fighting desperately for survival. It was to be a long time before they understood that the real Promised Land that God wants to lead humankind into is the Kingdom of heaven, and heaven is meant for all human beings. The words of the prophets, the message of the gospel and the death of Christ, were intended to enable believers to see beyond any cruel image they still had of the Lord, and discover that in fact he is a loving Father.

Jesus was the one to introduce this new vision of God and open up a new way of life. But this new Joshua (in Hebrew, Jesus and Joshua are the same name) would show that the might of God is not a warlike force but is the power of love. A love that opens up the future.

The conquest of the promised land

God called Joshua to take on the leadership of the Hebrews following Moses' death. He renewed his promise to let his people enter Canaan but reminded him of his condition of obeying the Law.

Joshua sent spies to a fortress town guarding the eastern entrance to the land. This was Jericho. The spies' source of help there was unexpected: a prostitute named Rahab had realised that God was on the Hebrews' side. She took the spies into her house and hid them. She managed to smuggle them from the city over the wall after the closing of the gates. The spies returned to their camp full of confidence: "The Lord has delivered the whole country into our hands, and its inhabitants all tremble already at the thought of us", they announced.

So Joshua organised the crossing of the Jordan. It was to be a procession. The ark of the covenant would lead the way, and the people would follow at a respectful distance after their ritual purification.

Crossing the Jordan   3: 15–17, 4: 13–18

As soon as those carrying the ark reached the Jordan and the feet of the priests carrying the ark touched the waters, the waters coming down from upstream stopped flowing and formed a mass a great distance away, completely cut off from the waters flowing down to the Salt Sea. For the Jordan overflows its banks during the whole time of harvest. The people crossed opposite Jericho. The priests carrying the ark of the covenant of the Lord stood still on dry ground in the middle of the River Jordan, while all Israel crossed on dry ground. (. . .)

Some forty thousand armed warriors, they crossed in the Lord's

We have here the last written version of an old epic account. It was probably compiled by priests who saw the conquest as a result of the perfect celebration of a liturgical rite.

The crossing of the Jordan is similar in many ways to the crossing of the Sea of Reeds. The fall of Jericho and the victory at Ai were definitely not accomplished by the might of the Israelite armies but by the Lord's intervention. These amazing episodes illustrate God's power.

presence, ready for battle, towards the plain of Jericho. That day, the Lord made Joshua great in the eyes of all Israel, who respected him as they had respected Moses, as long as he lived.

The Lord said to Joshua, "Order the priests carrying the ark to come up out of the Jordan." (. . .) When they came out, no sooner had the soles of their feet touched solid ground, than the waters of the Jordan returned to the river-bed and flowed on, flooding its banks as before.

Jericho stood in the way. It was a fortress that the small Hebrew forces could not hope to take. But who can resist God? Joshua organised another procession:

Capture of Jericho 6: 6–25

**This account was written at the time of the Babylonian exile and aims to comfort those in exile. Did they think it was impossible to return to their land? Hadn't God shown that nothing was impossible for him?
Didn't he miraculously cause the walls of the enemy fortress to collapse when Israel's forces were weak? What had happened previously could always happen again.**

Joshua called the priests and said to them, "Take the ark of the covenant, and let seven priests carry seven ram's-horn trumpets ahead of the ark of the Lord." To the people he then said, "Forward! March round the city, and let the advance guard march ahead of the ark of the Lord!" Everything was done as he had ordered. Seven priests, carrying seven ram's-horn trumpets in the presence of the Lord, moved forward blowing their trumpets. The ark of the covenant followed. The advance guard marched ahead of the priests, who blew their trumpets, the rear-guard followed the ark. The men marched, the trumpets sounded.

Joshua had given the people the following orders, "Do not shout out, do not let your voice be heard. Do not say a single word until I say, 'Raise the war cry.' That is when you must raise the war cry."

He made the ark go once round the city, then they went back to camp, where they spent the night. (. . .) The second day they marched once round the city and went back to camp. They did this each day for six days. On the seventh day, they got up at dawn and, in the same way, marched round the city seven times. The seventh time, the priests blew their trumpets and Joshua said to the people, "Raise the war cry, for the Lord has given you the city!" (. . .)

The people raised the war cry, the trumpets sounded. When the people heard the sound of the trumpet, they gave a mighty shout and the wall collapsed then and there. At once they stormed the city and captured it. They killed all they found: men and women, young and old, including the oxen, the sheep and the donkeys. (. . .) But Joshua spared the lives of Rahab the prostitute, her father's family and all who belonged to her. She is still living in Israel even today, because she hid the messengers whom Joshua sent to spy on Jericho.

> Woe to those who dared to oppose the people of God but happy are those who realised whose side God was on! There was no doubt in the minds of a people who were concerned above all to assert their identity: there are both "goodies" and "baddies". God could not possibly spare the baddies and so they were destroyed mercilessly.

Defeat at Ai and the final taking of the city

They now advanced on Ai which was the next fortress. The conquest appeared easy but the Hebrews were surprised when the inhabitants attacked them and beat them. They were thrown into confusion: could God have abandoned his people?

God's response to Joshua's complaints was to accuse the people of disobeying his orders. Part of the spoils had secretly been kept after Jericho had fallen, and had not been burned as the Lord had commanded. This could not be allowed.

Joshua found out who the guilty man was and had him executed along with his entire family.

Then God was no longer angry and the people could attack the city again. They employed a strategy suggested by the Lord by pretending to flee before the counter-attack, much as they had been forced to do the previous day. They then ambushed the troops coming from behind the city. The enemy were split into two groups and were scattered. The city was taken. Joshua ensured that everyone was indeed massacred and all the spoils destroyed. God's orders were not to be taken lightly!

The treaty with the Gibeonites

All the people in the land were seized with fear when they heard the news that the two towns had fallen. The inhabitants of the city of Gibeon decided on a strategy to save themselves from destruction. They sent messengers who pretended to have come from very far away. These men arrived looking exhausted, with no provisions and with their clothes worn out: in fact, they had only travelled a very short distance. The Hebrews were convinced that the Gibeonites had really come from beyond the territories they wished to conquer and agreed willingly to form a covenant with them. They were tricked before they realised what was happening, but it was too late. They had sworn to the messengers that they would not attack their territory. Here we have an intelligent group of people who understood that it was best to be on the

Hebrews' side! The new allies very soon had occasion to see how right they were to take sides in this way. Five neighbouring kings decided to punish the Gibeonites for being allied to the invaders. They came to besiege Gibeon. Joshua's help was sought to rescue the city. God intervened during the battle by making huge hailstones fall on the fleeing men, killing them. Joshua requested God to stop the sun in its tracks to enable the people to win a total victory before nightfall. The five enemy kings took refuge in a cave but were made prisoner and hanged. It was a total victory. Now the whole of the southern territories were in the hands of the Hebrews and their allies.

The conquest of the North and the division of the land

The kings of the North then formed an alliance against the Hebrews. They had troops as countless as the sands of the sea, with numerous horses and chariots. But God had said to Joshua, "Have no fear of these men, for by this time tomorrow Israel shall see them all cut to pieces; you shall hamstring their horses and burn their chariots". The victory was indeed total. The Israelites then ransacked the country, took their towns and possessions and killed all the inhabitants.

The conquered regions could now be shared out. What joy! They had acquired a magnificent land to which they now had an indisputable right — all thanks to God!

Each tribe received its own territory. Some of them were able to go home because they had already settled in the lands east of the Jordan and had agreed to help their sister-tribes to conquer the lands west of the river.

Everything seemed to have turned out well. God had kept his promise and the people had found peace in their land.

Joshua was now very old. He gathered all the people together before he died and gave them his last instructions.

Joshua's last speech

23: 3–16

The spiritual will of Joshua is another version of the one in Deuteronomy attributed to Moses. The author comments on its sadness; he was writing later during the years of exile and wondered why the people did not listen to Joshua's warnings.

"You have witnessed all that the Lord your God has done to all these nations for your sake. The Lord your God himself has fought for you. (. . .)

"Be very firm about keeping and doing everything written in the Book of the Law of Moses, not swerving from that either to the right or to the left. Never mix with the peoples who are still left living beside you. Do not speak the names of their gods, do not serve them and do not bow down to them. On the contrary, you must remain loyal to the Lord your God as you have been till now. (. . .) No one so far has been able to resist you. One of your men was able to chase a thousand of them, since the Lord your God was himself fighting for you, as he had promised you. Be very careful to love the Lord your God, for your life depends on it.

"But should you in any way fail to live up to this, if you make friends with the nations still living alongside you, (. . .) then know that the Lord your God will most certainly stop giving you the lands of these nations. They will become a trap for you, a pit for you to fall into, until you vanish from this fine country given to you by the Lord your God.

"Remember that all the promises made to you by the Lord your God have been fulfilled. But just as he has kept every promise, so he will keep every threat he has made. If you break the covenant which the Lord your God has made with you, if you go and serve other gods, then the Lord will become very angry with you and you will quickly disappear from the fine country which he has given you."

Joshua invited the people to renew the covenant of Sinai; this was after reminiscing about the patriarchs.

The great assembly at Shechem

24: 15–28

"If serving the Lord seems a bad thing to you, today you must make up your minds whom you do mean to serve, whether the gods whom your ancestors served beyond the River, or the gods of the Amorites in whose country you are now living. As regards my family and me, we shall serve the Lord."

The people replied, "Far be it from us to desert the Lord and to serve other gods! The Lord our God was the one who brought us and our ancestors here from Egypt. He kept us safe all along the way we travelled and among all the peoples through whom we passed. We too shall serve the Lord, for he is our God."

Joshua then said to the people, "You will not be able to serve the Lord, since he is a holy God, a jealous God who will not tolerate either your faults or your sins. If you desert him and serve the foreigners' gods, he will destroy you." The people replied to Joshua, "No! The Lord is the one we mean to serve." That day Joshua made a covenant for the people at Shechem. He gave them laws and rules to follow. Joshua wrote these words in the Book of the Law of God. He then took a large stone and set it up, under the oak tree in the Lord's sanctuary. Joshua then said to all the people, "Look, this stone will be a witness to us, since it has heard all the words that the Lord has spoken to us: it will be a witness against you, in case you should deny your God." Joshua then sent the people away, everyone to his own land.

After this, Joshua died. He was a hundred and ten years old.

The assembly at Shechem probably took place around BC 1200. It was an important event in the history of Israel. Apparently it was then that certain tribes, who had not been through the Exodus, decided also to follow the traditions of those who had come out of the wilderness. For the older generation it meant renewing old promises but for the younger ones it was a new beginning. It was a time of unity for the Hebrews as a people.

The event is presented in the form of a celebration and we can still find traces of it in Christian worship today: for example, on the night of the Passover, when baptismal promises are renewed, Christians are invited to confirm their original choice between the two possible ways of life, either following the Devil, or following the true God who leads us into life.

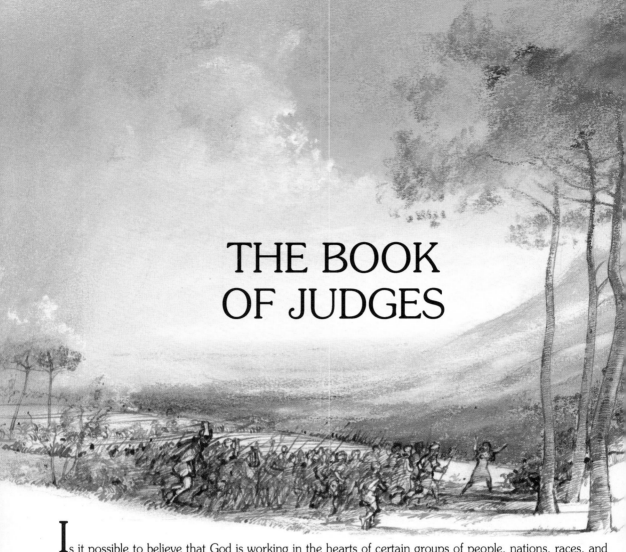

THE BOOK
OF JUDGES

Is it possible to believe that God is working in the hearts of certain groups of people, nations, races, and societies even when the observer can see nothing but chaos, brutality and even savagery?

The book of Judges answers this question. It shows that there were signs that God was at work amidst the obvious lawlessness which was a feature of the early days of the Hebrews in Palestine. God slowly educated the people who were still governed by their animal instincts. He raised leaders over them ("the Judges") and gradually made the people aware that it was not sufficient to occupy a land in order to live there in peace: unity was also essential.

The situation of the Hebrews in Palestine around BC 1200 was different from that described in the book of Joshua. Each tribe made its way to its own territory following the conquest, and their unity under Joshua was soon no more than a distant memory. Such division caused weakness and they were continually being attacked by groups of marauding bedouins.

But then, leaders began to appear spontaneously who regrouped them and spurred them into action, scattering armies and fighting off the enemy. It was a call to order and a promise for those people who had been tempted quickly to forget their identity and to drift into the customs of the land, by adopting foreign gods and foreign customs: God remembers his people and delivers them, when they return to him.

Some of these leaders may appear rather primitive to us and in fact some were downright brutal. But the account of their exploits, even when exaggerated by popular legend, was sufficient to restore courage and confidence to those Hebrews who still remembered the covenant and who wondered if the Lord had forgotten his people. The "Judges" were real comic-strip heroes and reminded them that God did not forget his own, the "goodies" persecuted by their "wicked" enemies.

The present book of Judges probably dates from the end of the exile. It was at that time that a writer put the old tales into their final form. Previously they had been handed down through the generations. He wanted to show how Israel had needed a long time of testing in order to find its true identity.

Judgement on an era 2: 10ff.

When the generation that knew Joshua had gone, another generation followed it which neither knew the Lord nor what he had done for the sake of Israel.

The Israelites then did what is evil in the Lord's eyes and served the Baals. They turned away from the Lord, God of their ancestors, who had brought them out of Egypt, and they followed other gods. Then the Lord grew angry with Israel. He handed them over to raiders who plundered them; he delivered them to the enemies surrounding them, and they could no longer resist them. They were in very deep distress.

The Lord then appointed them judges, who rescued them from the hands of the raiders. (. . .) The Lord was with the judge and he rescued them from their enemies as long as the judge lived, since he was moved by their groans. But once the judge was dead, the Israelites began to behave in even worse ways than their ancestors had done. The Lord then became extremely angry with Israel, and he said, "Since this people has broken the covenant which I made with their ancestors, since they have not listened to my voice, in future I shall not drive out of their land any one of those nations which Joshua left when he died." He intended to use them to put Israel to the test.

Here, the final editor of the book of Judges indicated the "lesson" in the stories he told. The Israelites were victorious over their enemies as soon as they stopped betraying the covenant and started being the "goodies" again.

The story of Deborah

The Israelites in the north of the country were being crushed by a powerful Canaanite leader called Jabin. A lady of very high status named Deborah invited Barak to take command of the troops recruited from the two tribes but the general would only agree to continue the campaign if Deborah herself came along. God thus used a woman as his intermediary in saving his people. The enemy army was seized by panic at the foot of Mount Tabor. The leader of Jabin's armies was Sisera and he fled on foot. He died at the hand of a woman in whose tent he tried to hide.

Deborah then composed a song to celebrate the wonders of the Lord.

"And the land enjoyed rest for forty years."

The story of Gideon

Israel betrayed the covenant once again and the Lord handed them over to the Midianites, a marauding tribe from the desert who destroyed the Israelites' crops. The Israelites repented of their sins. It was then that God showed himself to a simple peasant called Gideon. Gideon was a man of great humility so at first he refused the divine mission because he felt unable to perform it. He was convinced eventually that it was indeed the Lord's will and he started a revolt, initially by throwing down statues of the pagan gods. His actions shook the people of God. He set out to attack the Midianite camp with those men who had joined the fight.

God then gave them the peculiar order to reduce the size of the army! This was because Israel could otherwise have claimed all the credit for the victory by thinking that they had won by their own efforts and not because of God's help. So Gideon sent twenty-two thousand men home and kept only ten thousand. God still said there were too many men. Gideon eventually fought with only three thousand warriors who had previously passed a sort of test.

The men were divided into three groups. They advanced while carrying horns and torches hidden in empty jars. They sounded the horns, broke the jars and held up their torches at a given signal during the night. The Midianites were terrified and fled. Their leaders were captured and beheaded.

The Israelites offered to make Gideon their king as a result of this victory, but he humbly refused, saying, "It is not I who shall rule over you, nor my son; the Lord shall rule over you."

Abimelech's kingship

There was a character who did try to make himself king but the prophet Jotham attacked his plans by telling a parable:

Jotham's idea was rich with meaning: the most important thing is service. This was the basis of the criticism which was later to be levelled at the descendants of David. Jesus echoed it also when he said that anyone who wanted to be great must be a servant. Jesus only admitted to being a king when asked directly by Pontius Pilate immediately before being nailed to the cross.

Many kings are no more than conceited tyrants, real "thorn bushes" to their subjects.

9: 8–15

One day the trees went out to choose a king to rule them. They said to the olive tree, "Be our king!" The olive tree replied, "Must I give up my oil which gives honour to gods and men, to stand and sway over the trees?"

Then the trees said to the fig tree, "You come and be our king!" The fig tree replied, "Must I give up my sweetness and my excellent fruit, to go and sway over the trees?"

Then the trees said to the vine, "You come and be our king!" The vine replied, "Must I give up my wine which makes gods and men rejoice, to go and sway over the trees?"

Then the trees all said to the thorn bush, "You come and be our king!" And the thorn bush replied to the trees, "If you are choosing me to be your king in good faith, come and shelter in my shade."

Abimelech succeeded in forcing his way into power but the final result was a disastrous civil war. Abimelech even went as far as destroying Shechem in order to put down the rebellion but was killed in the battle. Those who had helped him to power lost their lives, which was a just punishment for forgetting that only God is king in Israel.

THE ADVENTURES OF SAMSON IN THE LAND OF THE PHILISTINES

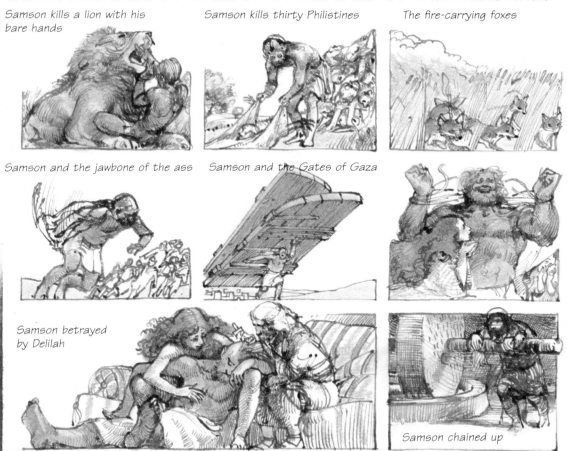

Samson kills a lion with his bare hands

Samson kills thirty Philistines

The fire-carrying foxes

Samson and the jawbone of the ass

Samson and the Gates of Gaza

Samson betrayed by Delilah

Samson chained up

More or less all the stories concerning the nation's glory are legendary. The legend which the Israelites liked to remember best is the colourful story of Samson.

Samson's revenge

The oppressors of the Israelites in the south of the country were the Philistines. They were a people who had come by sea and settled on the coast.

God freed his people at that time by raising up a powerful hero called Samson. It was said in Israel that he had been born in an amazing way from a woman who was incapable of having a child. The Lord made known to her his will that the child she was to bear was to be dedicated to him.

Samson fell in love with Delilah when he grew up. She was a Philistine girl and so caused a great scandal in his family. They saw his marriage as betraying the people of God. His father and mother failed to understand that God would use the marriage to start a war between Samson and the Philistines.

Samson made the Philistines furious by posing them riddles they could not solve. Delilah one day used her tears to influence Samson, and obtained the solution to a riddle on which he had laid a heavy bet, and then slipped the answer to her fellow countrymen. Now, Samson's strength was extraordinary. He was furious when he realised he had been betrayed by his wife, so he went out and killed thirty Philistines and used their money to pay his debts. The war was started!

The Israelites joyfully told tales in their evenings of how Samson had once caught three hundred foxes and tied them tail to tail in pairs, with a torch between each pair of tails. The creatures had caused a huge fire when released among the enemies' crops. The Philistines got their own back by murdering Samson's father-in-law.

One day Samson entered the Philistine city of Gaza. The inhabitants hoped to take him prisoner by locking the gates, but he tore them down and carried them on his shoulders to the top of a far-away hill.

Samson was finally betrayed by Delilah. This time came when, in his weakness, he gave in to her pleas and told her that the secret of his great strength was his hair which had never been cut because it was the sign of his dedication to God. Delilah seized some scissors one night and cut off her husband's hair while he slept. Samson was lost. The Philistines took him prisoner and put out his eyes.

They gathered together one day to worship their god, Dagon. Samson was brought into the temple, to be mocked:

Samson's death was that of a hero since he gave his life as he used his God-given strength one last time for his people.

16: 26–30

Samson then said to the boy who was leading him by the hand, "Lead me where I can touch the pillars supporting the building, so that I can lean against them." Now the building was crowded with men and women. (. . .) Samson called on the Lord and cried out, "Lord, I beg you! Remember me; give me strength once more, O God, and let me take revenge on the Philistines at one blow for my lost eyes." And Samson took hold of the two central pillars supporting the building, and braced himself against them. He shouted, "Let me die with the Philistines!" He then heaved with all his might, and the building fell on the chiefs and on all the people there. Those whom he killed at his death were more in number than those whom he killed during his life.

The Hebrews' situation became more and more critical despite these great deeds. The tribes were divided and fought against one another in an endless cycle of blood feuds. How could they hope to survive in such conditions? The author was a strong supporter of the monarchy and commented, "In those days there was no king in Israel, and every man did as he pleased." Would God come eventually to save his people from their distress?

THE BOOK OF RUTH

A LESSON IN UNIVERSALISM

It is common to see groups, families or nations isolating themselves from others because they want to keep their race pure. They are so full of their own dignity. This terrible temptation occurs when the élite forgets that its true destiny is the service of others.

It was arrogance which caused the Jews to isolate themselves when they returned from exile. In fact, they forced anyone who had married a foreigner to divorce his wife. This practice was doubtless condoned within the Law of Moses, but that had been written at a time when the people were unsure of themselves and needed to preserve their identity. The situation was now rather different, so how could they continue to seek "purity" just as they were beginning to appreciate they were called to be a blessing to the world? Wasn't it now their duty to welcome foreigners, if they recognised that God wanted to use Israel to speak to the whole human race?

This is the lesson that the author of the book of Ruth wanted to put across. He reminded people of the tradition saying that King David (of whom they were so proud) was descended from a foreigner, a Moabitess. The book was written around the fifth century BC and follows the book of Judges in the Bible since the events in the story took place at that time.

Elimelech lived in Bethlehem. He had gone to a foreign country with his wife Naomi and their two sons. Each son married a native woman, Orpah and Ruth, but both men died childless.

Naomi was now widowed. She decided to return to Bethlehem while her daughter-in-law, Orpah, decided to stay in the Moabite country. Her other daughter-in-law, Ruth, was determined to accompany her mother-in-law and said, "wherever you go, I will go; wherever you live, I will live. Your people shall be my people,

and your God, my God," and thus showed her wish to belong to the chosen race. The two women came to live near the land owned by a relative of Elimelech called Boaz. They lived poorly by gleaning among the ears of corn left from the rich owner's harvest. Boaz generously arranged for the harvesters to let Ruth glean among the sheaves.

The laws of that time stated that if a man died childless then his closest relative had to marry the widow and thus continue the dead man's family line. Discovering the relationship which linked him to Ruth's dead husband:

The origins of the family into which Jesus was later to be born were already marked out by divine intervention. The anti-racist message of the story is accompanied by a spiritual lesson: it is through the poor and the weak that God, the Redeemer, delivers his people.

4: 13–17

Boaz took Ruth and she became his wife. The Lord blessed her, and she became pregnant and had a son. The women said to Naomi, "Blessed be the Lord who has not left you without anyone to redeem you. May his name be praised in Israel! The child will be a comfort to you and a support in your old age." (. . .) And they called the child Obed. This was the father of Jesse, the father of David.

THE BOOKS
OF SAMUEL

Any nation or community of people feels the need of a leader when there is no law and order. Only a strong power can unite the groups within the society and give it back a sense of community.

The choice of a leader itself poses problems. To begin with, it is rare for the choice to be unanimous and, moreover, it is very easy for power to be used wrongly. The achievement of unity is short-lived and always fragile. It is common to see new crises occurring later which lead to the decline or even the total collapse of the group united in this way.

That was what happened to the Hebrews around BC 1030. The tribes of Israel were divided and fought amongst themselves. They felt the need to become united in order to stand up to the Philistines who were becoming a threat to them. The Philistines had probably come from Crete and had settled on the coast. They had set up camp among the hills and so were particularly threatening to the Hebrews.

But the decision to appoint a king in Israel was not free of problems. The religious "judge" who held together the tribes which lived around the sanctuary at Shiloh where the ark of the covenant was kept was Samuel. Samuel reminded the tribes that God alone was king. Any man who tried to take that role away from God was in danger of becoming a dictator himself by setting himself up as God. Pharaoh had done that in the past. The Israelites were giving up the basic freedom to which the Lord had called them by wanting to choose a king for themselves.

Samuel did however anoint a king — and at God's command. The first king chosen was a Northerner called Saul. It was soon apparent that he was a disappointment. He also interfered with Samuel's power when the prophet's health was poor. His reign ended in catastrophe.

The second man to be chosen was David from the southern tribe of Judah. David was a clever man with a deep faith. He also unified the country. He conquered Jerusalem and made it his capital, and the city also became the new centre of religious worship. His reign left a prestigious memory to which the Israelites looked back continually during the difficult times that followed, in particular it was hoped that an heir would come to restore the kingdom to all its glory. This was called the messianic hope.

The faults predicted by Samuel were already evident within the royal house, however, and David used his powerful position to commit a terrible sin. He did repent later but the rot had now set in making the kingdom's decline inevitable. This decline soon revealed that even what appeared to be the stablest of political powers could not ensure "life in its fullness" for which the people had longed since the days of their ancestor Abraham.

Jesus was the true "son of David". It was only with his coming that the people were to realise that the real Kingdom could not be built by humankind since it could only be a gift from God. This God is the God of love coming to transform the hearts of men and women by removing their selfishness, their thirst for power and their desire for security at any price.

There are two books of Samuel which have been separated artificially. They were compiled at the time of the exile and came from old sources, especially the royal archives which were written shortly after the events had actually occurred. They use colourful stories to present us with some deep thoughts on the way power can be used both for good and for evil.

FIRST BOOK OF SAMUEL

SAMUEL

The tribes of Israel were politically divided in those days but gathered together at a place of worship called Shiloh where the ark of the covenant was kept. It was kept there to demonstrate the religious unity of the people.

Eli was the priest in charge of the sanctuary. He saw a woman crying there one day and, thinking she was drunk, wanted to ask her to leave. The woman was Hannah and she told him of her troubles: she had no child and was begging the Lord to give her one. Eli was filled with compassion and told her that the Lord would answer her prayer. Hannah did indeed give birth to a son whom she named Samuel. She dedicated her son to the Lord and composed a beautiful song of gratitude to God, which was later to inspire the Virgin Mary's *Magnificat*.

The people of God seemed to be in decline at that time. Even at Shiloh, the sons of Eli were taking advantage of their father's power in order to accept bribes from the worshippers. God then intervened.

God calls Samuel   3: 1–20

The boy Samuel was serving the Lord in the presence of Eli. (. . .)
One day, Eli was lying down in his room. His eyes were beginning
to become weak and he could no longer see. Samuel was lying in
the sanctuary, where the ark of God was kept. The Lord called,
"Samuel! Samuel!" He answered, "Here I am," and, running to
Eli, he said, "Here I am, as you called me." Eli said, "I did not
call. Go back and lie down." He did so. And again the Lord called,
"Samuel! Samuel!" He got up and went back to Eli and said,
"Here I am, as you called me." He replied, "I did not call, my son;
go back and lie down." As yet, Samuel did not know the Lord and
the word of the Lord had not yet been revealed to him. Again the
Lord called, the third time. He got up and went to Eli and said,
"Here I am, as you called me." Eli then understood that the Lord
was calling the child, and he said to Samuel, "Go and lie down,
and if someone calls to you again say, 'Speak, Lord, for your
servant is listening.' " So Samuel went and lay down.

   The Lord then came and stood by, calling as he had done before,
"Samuel! Samuel!" Samuel answered, "Speak, Lord, for your
servant is listening."

Samuel's birth required divine
intervention but he still had to
accept his call from God for
himself. The author of the book
gives a lively and descriptive
account of his call. He was to be
a prophet. Samuel responded
immediately to God's voice as
soon as he realised who was
speaking.

The Lord told Samuel that Eli's descendants were condemned, for his sons had not been faithful to the
responsibility they have been given.

Samuel grew up. The Lord was with him. All Israel knew that God
had made Samuel his prophet. The Lord continued to make himself
known at Shiloh, revealing himself to Samuel there.

The ark captured by the Philistines

The troubles continued. The Hebrews were defeated by the Philistines. They decided to return to the attack
so they carried the ark of the covenant in front of them. It was hoped this action would guarantee the
Lord's presence and thus make victory certain. In fact they were defeated and the ark fell into the hands
of the enemy. Eli's two sons were both killed in the fight and Eli himself died when he heard the news of
the disaster.

   The ark brought trouble to the Philistines. They had carried it victoriously to their temple but the statue
of their (pagan) god Dagon fell and was shattered before the ark. Then the inhabitants of the region fell
victim to a plague of tumours. It was crucial to send away the ark of this foreign God who brought nothing
but death and destruction. The Philistines decided to return it to Israel together with a large guilt-offering.
It was loaded onto a cart. The cows pulling the cart were more intelligent than their masters for they knew
of their own accord the right route back. The Israelites welcomed the ark's return with joy. The ark was a
holy object; it was the symbol of the presence of God and was to be treated with awe; several of the
Israelites were struck down because they came too close to it.

   Samuel understood the meaning of what had happened. He brought order back into the religious life of
the people which resulted in the immediate and final defeat of the Philistines.

SAMUEL AND SAUL

The people ask for a king 8: 4–19

This text reflects the anti-royalist attitude of the Israelites following David's reign. They felt justified later when, at the time of the exile, they looked back upon the new monarchy as a disaster. The problem that arose here concerns the meaning of *power*. Jesus taught that true power was in fact service. He refused to call himself king until the very moment when he was sentenced to death.

The elders of Israel gathered together, went back to Samuel at Ramah, and said, "Look, you are old, and your sons are not following your example. So give us a king to judge us, like the other nations." Samuel was displeased, so he prayed to the Lord. But the Lord said to Samuel, "Do as the people ask because it is not you they have rejected but me. They do not wish me to reign over them any more. (. . .) Only, you must give them a solemn warning, and must tell them what the king who is going to reign over them will do."

Samuel then told the people who were asking him for a king everything that the Lord had said. He said, "This is what the king who is going to reign over you will do. He will take your sons and make them serve in his chariotry and cavalry, and they will run in front of his chariot. (. . .) He will take your daughters as perfumers, cooks and bakers. He will take the best of your fields, your vineyards and your olive trees and give them to his officials. (. . .) He will take a tenth of all your flocks. When that day comes, you will cry aloud because of the king you have chosen for yourselves, but on that day the Lord will not answer you."

The people refused to listen to Samuel. They said, "No! We are determined to have a king, so that we can be like the other nations."

Why did they insist on being "like the other nations" when they were the "people of God"?

Samuel's choice fell upon Saul. He was a handsome man in the prime of life. The prophet consecrated Saul with the oil which made him the "anointed" (or messiah) of the Lord. Samuel thought Saul must be God's chosen one. Saul suddenly seemed to be a changed man and came under the power of the Holy Spirit. This was thought to prove that he was qualified to take on the leadership of the Hebrew armies.

So Samuel gathered the people together and confirmed his choice in the presence of the tribes.

In Israel, however, a different version of Saul's election as king was remembered. Saul was said to have been seized by divine fury on a day when the neighbouring Ammonites were threatening to attack the region; he was said to have called together warriors from all the tribes and to have totally demolished the enemy. It was then that he was proclaimed king.

Samuel considered his own role as leader to be at an end. He retired soon after the king was enthroned. He wanted to put the people on their guard against going astray in the future and told them to remember the Lord's goodness and never think that their success came through a king: success depended only on their obedience to the Law of the covenant.

Saul governed the new kingdom with the help of his son Jonathan. He created a standing army and led a revolt against their Philistine oppressors. The Philistine armies were undoubtedly better equipped but God was with his people and they had a decisive victory.

There was trouble in the new kingdom, particularly when some strict religious rules were broken again and again. Jonathan himself was in a difficult position at one stage when, on the eve of a battle, he did not keep the ritual fast which was supposed to guarantee God's presence with the troops. The victory was indeed theirs but was it not still necessary to put to death the person who had nearly caused the Lord to abandon them? Saul decided to spare his son when all the people spoke up on his behalf. They were no longer in the days of Jephthah.

A much more serious problem was the breaking of sacred laws by Saul himself. After a victorious battle against the Amalekites, for example, he kept some of the herds taken from the enemy, yet the old commandment of the "anathema" (which means the total destruction of the enemy's belongings) was still in force. Samuel intervened and angrily rebuked the king for his transgression. He told Saul, "Since you have rejected the word of the Lord, he has rejected you as king." Saul asked in vain for pardon. Saul was haunted by Samuel's curse from that moment and felt abandoned by God. He sank gradually into an obsession with being persecuted which was to lead him to catastrophe.

SAUL AND DAVID

It was then that a new hero appeared. David was a shepherd boy from Judah who was soon to take the place of Saul.

It was Samuel himself who chose David according to one early version of the consecration. The man of God was said to have travelled to Bethlehem at the Lord's command and gone to the home of Jesse who introduced Samuel to his seven sons in order of age. They were all good-looking men but God had warned Samuel, "Take no notice of his appearance or his height . . . God does not see as human beings see; they look at appearances but the Lord looks at the heart." Samuel rejected all those he saw. So an eighth son was brought to him, the youngest, who looked after the flocks. Samuel recognised this son as God's chosen one and secretly anointed him to be king.

Another version tells that David had been introduced to the royal court because, as poet and player of the zither, he alone was capable of calming the king's fits of madness which were becoming the mark of his psychotic illness.

David then distinguished himself by an amazing exploit. The war against the Philistines had broken out once more. There was a giant called Goliath among the enemy ranks who was apparently unbeatable and was spreading terror. Saul had promised the hand of his daughter to any man who would kill this terrible enemy. David was furious when he heard Goliath getting away with challenging the Israelite army. David was sustained by his faith in God, although weak and unarmed, but he was still determined to confront the giant. The Lord who had enabled him to protect his sheep from the claws of lions and wolves would give him the strength to face the Philistine! David refused any of the weapons offered because they weighed him down too much, so he marched toward his opponent armed only with a sling. Goliath insulted David and was filled with scorn at the sight of such a youth daring to challenge him. But David replied:

17: 45–7

"You come to me armed with sword, spear and scimitar, but I come to you in the name of the Lord of hosts, God of the armies of Israel, whom you have challenged. Today, the Lord will hand you over to me. I shall cut off your head. Today, I shall give your corpse and the corpses of the Philistine army to the birds of the air and the wild beasts, so that the whole world may know that there is a God in Israel. Everyone will know that the Lord does not use swords or spears to win victory, for the Lord is lord of the battle and he will hand you over into our power."

The text shows how, through David, an apparently defenceless people discovered that their true strength lay in their faith. Everything is possible for God: this certainty was borne out of the Exodus and confirmed by the memory of David. It was to sustain the people of Israel throughout their history.

David struck the Philistine between the eyes with a pebble from his sling. Goliath fell to the ground and David cut off the giant's head with his own sword. Panic seized the Philistine camp and the Israelites won a decisive victory.

David was welcomed warmly by Saul. He immediately began an inseparable friendship with the king's son, Jonathan.

The king was soon jealous when he heard the people cheering David more than himself. Twice, while the young hero was singing to him, Saul tried to pin him to the wall with his spear but missed each time. This frightened the king even more since it indicated the Lord was protecting the young man.

Saul had promised his daughter to the killer of Goliath but decided to raise the asking price. David had to kill a hundred Philistines before he could become the king's son-in-law. David went into battle and brought back the proof that he had killed two hundred. This only increased the king's jealousy. Eventually he had to agree to the marriage of David and his second daughter, Michal. David's faithful friend, Jonathan, intervened and managed to dissuade his father temporarily from the idea of getting rid of this "dangerous rival".

OPEN HOSTILITIES BETWEEN SAUL AND DAVID

Saul grew more and more afraid of David's growing popularity and was obsessed by the fear of losing his throne. He tried openly to have his rival assassinated but David was saved by his wife.

David's greatest good fortune was his deep friendship with Jonathan. The king's son did everything in his power to defend David from Saul. Jonathan helped David to escape because he realised the great risk his friend was running by remaining at the court.

David then led the life of a guerilla soldier and benefited from the help of the population of the southern tribes. He even enlisted himself in the service of the Philistines but carefully avoided helping them whenever they were fighting his own people.

Saul had done everything in his power to arrest the man he most feared and had even massacred those who helped him. David's life became ever more difficult for he had simultaneously to avoid the king's traps and being taken hostage by the Philistines. He continued to think of these latter as the real enemies of his people.

The text tells how David twice found himself in the ideal situation to get rid of his adversary but he refused to harm Saul, for he continued to regard the king as the "Lord's anointed". David could easily have taken him by surprise and killed him. Saul repented each time he learned of David's integrity but, very quickly, he was again overcome by madness and fear. Saul was convinced that David was going to seize the throne from his family. In his madness, he did a most peculiar thing: the man who had strictly banished all magic makers from his kingdom went to consult a witch. He asked her to conjure up for him the soul of Samuel who had died shortly before. But this only added to his despair for Samuel's spirit confirmed that God had turned away from him and that the kingdom would soon be snatched from his hand and given to David.

Saul went to war against the Philistines at Mount Gilboa shortly after this and was wounded fatally. He pleaded in vain with his armour-bearer to kill him but eventually fell upon his own sword. His three sons were killed at the same time. Thus his unhappy reign ended in a national catastrophe. The institution of the monarchy was undermined.

THE SECOND BOOK OF SAMUEL

David, King of Judah

David returned from a raid on the Amalekites to find a message announcing the defeat of Israel and the death of Saul. The messenger claimed to have killed Saul himself. This might have been a ploy to gain the favour of his future king but David had the man executed because he had dared to raise his sword against a king. The murder of a king was the worst of all crimes to David because, right to the end, he had continued to respect his opponent as the rightful ruler. David wept bitterly for those who had fallen at Gilboa and composed a funeral hymn in their honour. He particularly expressed his grief at losing so dear a friend as Jonathan to whom he had sworn eternal loyalty.

David now returned to his own land without fear. The southern tribes made him their king at Hebron which is the capital city of Judah. The new king cleverly congratulated the people of the North who had faithfully seen to Saul's burial. The northern tribes then elected one of Saul's surviving sons as their king and war broke out between the two rival groups in Israel, each led by a son of Saul. It turned to the advantage of Joab, the leader of David's armies.

David composed a lament following his conquest to celebrate the greatness of his former enemy. He thus ensured the acceptance of the northern tribes who were moved by the sight of a Judaean respecting their own heroes.

Only one of Saul's sons now lived. He was therefore the only remaining obstacle to David's total victory. He was later killed by two traitors. The assassins were filled with pride and took the boy's head to the new king, thinking David would reward them. David was loyal to the end though and had the two men executed.

Only one of Saul's descendants now remained and he was a cripple. David showed great kindness to him for his dead friend Jonathan's sake. David gave him a place of honour at his court although he could have had him killed in fear that the northern tribes would use him as a figurehead.

David, King of Judah and of Israel

David was now the undisputed king of all the tribes of Israel.

David had just taken Jerusalem from the Jebusites so he moved the capital there. This was in order to avoid humiliating the northern tribes if he had set up his capital in Hebron, which belonged to the tribe of Judah. This transfer of power was a great moment for the new "City of David" which was to become the centre of the nation's life: it was the symbol of a monarchy which seemed to fulfil God's promise to Abraham that the land would be given to his descendants.

David could now deal with the real enemy.

He defeated the Philistines. He even destroyed their idols which was an obvious sign that David had help from God. The Philistines were never again a serious threat to the people of God.

The ark in Jerusalem

David realised that his power needed a religious basis and decided to have the ark of the covenant transported to his new capital. The ark was a symbol of the exodus but had been neglected somewhat since its return to the Israelites by the Philistines.

The bringing of the ark to the city was the occasion of a magnificent feast. Jerusalem now became the Holy City. The king himself led the procession and danced while singing hymns he had composed himself to honour the occasion. One of his wives was shocked to see her husband, the king, displaying himself in a way she considered degrading but David replied that nothing was too demeaning if it enabled him to sing the Lord's praises: the Lord had given him the crown and victory over all his enemies.

The ark was placed inside a tent. David was later filled with remorse and summoned Nathan, the prophet who served him as a counsellor. He asked Nathan whether he should build a proper Temple to the God of Israel; after all, David had built himself a beautiful palace!

Nathan gave a strange reply after giving the matter some thought and having consulted God:

This text is essential if we are to understand what follows in Israel's history. From that moment on, even in their darkest hours, the people lived in the hope that one day God would restore the kingdom of David by sending a new "anointed one", or "Messiah", to lead God's people to victory.

Nathan carefully explained God's refusal to let himself be confined to a temple as the pagan gods were. He was a God who travelled along with his people.

Solomon later built the Temple that David had to give up plans for, and Nathan's prophecy contains a clause to justify this. But the main idea was that human beings cannot build a house to contain God since it is God who makes his home among human beings. The Christians later interpreted this phrase by explaining that the Temple in which God lives is Jesus, and through him, the community of believers.

7: 5–18

The Lord says this: "Are you to build me a temple for me to live in? I have never lived in a house from the day when I brought the Israelites out of Egypt until today. I have kept travelling with a tent for shelter. In all my travels with the Israelites, did I say to any of the judges of Israel: 'Why do you not build me a temple from cedar-wood?' (. . .) I took you from the pasture, from following the sheep, to be leader of my people Israel. I have been with you wherever you went. I have got rid of all your enemies for you. I am going to make you as famous as the most famous people on earth. I am going to provide a place for my people Israel; I shall plant them there, and they will never be disturbed again; nor will they be oppressed by the wicked, as they were in the past. The Lord tells you that he will make you the first of a royal line of kings. And when your days are over and you fall asleep with your ancestors, I shall appoint your heir, and I shall make his royal throne secure for ever. I shall be a father to him and he a son to me. (. . .) I will never take my faithful love away from him as I took it away from Saul. Your royal line and your sovereignty will always stand firm before me and your throne will be secure for ever."

Nathan told David everything that the Lord had revealed to him. Then King David went in, sat down in the Lord's presence, and gave thanks.

David's sin

David's reign began well and got better. The Lord really was with him. The king successfully defended the country from threatening tribes in the north-east of the land, particularly the Ammonites and the Arameans. David had been obedient to God's Law until then, but now he committed a terrible sin for which the

THE TERRIBLE SIN OF KING DAVID

punishment should have been death. From his balcony one day he saw a very beautiful woman. He later discovered that she was Bathsheba, the wife of a foreign general in his service named Uriah the Hittite, who was currently on campaign against the Ammonites. David was obsessed and had Bathsheba kidnapped. He learned some time later that she was expecting his child. He realised the difficulty of his situation and ordered Uriah to return from the campaign; David hoped that Uriah would sleep with his wife while on

leave and that it would thus be possible to claim that the child was Uriah's. The general refused to spend even one night under his own roof out of respect for his comrades who were still out fighting. David decided in the end that he had to get rid of Uriah. He had the Hittite sent back to the army and gave orders for him to be given the most dangerous job. Uriah was killed and David could now add the wife of the man he had murdered to his harem. It was a terrible crime: simultaneously committing adultery and murder. It was even worse because the sin was committed by the king, God's representative on earth, who thereby had the power of life and death over his subjects.

David's sin fulfilled Samuel's predictions at the time the monarchy was created. God's chosen one has allowed himself to be corrupted by power and the new political system has revealed its weakness. Its failure was more and more evident from that time forward and it finally led Israel to disaster. David did repent humbly but the same cannot be said of all his successors. So we have to ask ourselves: what political system would enable them to live in peace and justice?

12: 1–15

The Lord sent the prophet Nathan to David. He went to the king and said: "In the same town there were two men, one rich, the other poor. The rich man had many flocks and herds; the poor man only had one ewe lamb, which he had bought. He cared for it and it grew up with him and his children, eating his bread, drinking from his cup, sleeping in his arms; it was like a daughter to him. A traveller came to stay with the rich man. He would not take anything from his own flock or herd to provide for the traveller. Instead, he stole the poor man's lamb and prepared that for his guest."

David became extremely angry with the man. "As the Lord lives," he said to Nathan, "the man who did this deserves to die." (. . .)

Nathan then said to David, "You are the man! The Lord, God of Israel, says this, 'I anointed you king of Israel, I saved you from Saul's hands. (. . .)

'Why did you show contempt for the Lord, by doing what displeases him? Because of this, members of your family in every generation will be killed by the sword, since you showed contempt for me and took the wife of Uriah the Hittite, to make her your wife.'" (. . .)

David said to Nathan, "I have sinned against the Lord." Nathan then said to David, "The Lord, for his part, forgives your sin; you are not to die. But, since you have angered the Lord by doing this, the child born to you will die." And Nathan went home.

Bathsheba's child died in fact, but she had another son — Solomon, who continued the line of David from which the future Messiah was born. He would be the descendant of the great King David, and thereby linked to guilty humanity. He would come to take their sins away.

The story of Absalom

Nathan predicted a crisis which came very quickly. There was great rivalry between David's numerous offspring from his different wives. One of them, Absalom, was particularly cunning. He began by arranging for one of his half-brothers to be assassinated.

He obtained the king's pardon despite David having sworn to punish the culprit. Absalom was an influential and attractive man and used his skills in speaking to gain the goodwill of the people and get them on his side. He then organised an outright revolt.

David suddenly noticed the danger of the situation and fled from the Holy City. He was surrounded by loyal followers who refused to abandon him. He did not, however, take the ark of the covenant with him although he was advised to do so; he realised how sinful he was and was therefore unwilling to appear to force God's hand in his favour — he wanted the Lord himself to decide.

He was humiliated and fled. The old grudges still harboured by the former supporters of Saul now re-emerged but the king did not punish those who insulted him as he rode along because he accepted their opposition as a punishment for his sin.

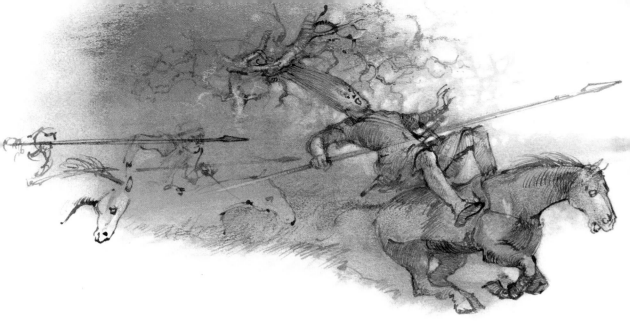

Absalom appeared to have won and arrogantly settled in the royal palace. He even took over his father's harem.

David was able to regroup his forces beyond the Jordan. A battle began between the respective armies of father and son. God showed his hand and Absalom was beaten and forced to flee. David had not lost any love for his son and gave orders that he should not be killed.

Absalom's hair was caught fast in the branches of a tree as he fled on horseback from the battle. He was left hanging while his horse ran off. Joab caught up with him and thrust three lances into his heart. It was the final victory.

David, however, never ceased hoping that his son would return. For him it was a day of mourning. He refused to hide his grief until told that it was dangerous to mourn openly for a mere traitor.

David could now return to Jerusalem amid the acclamation of the people whose opinion had now turned back in his favour. His friends urged him to take revenge on those who had insulted him when he was a fugitive. But the king generously refused. He did not want any more hatred or division among his people. But he knew how to distinguish between those who were truly loyal to him and those who rallied to him only out of self-interest.

In fact, the kingdom was riddled with deep divisions despite its appearance of unity. The end of David's reign was darkened by these divisions.

The great king remained profoundly faithful to the Lord in spite of all his faults. He composed a final song of praise at the end of his life which was like so many of the psalms he had written since his youth:

22: 2ff.

The Lord is my rock and my fortress, my God is my deliverer.

I take refuge in him, my rock, my stronghold, my place of refuge.

My Saviour, you have saved me from violence;

I call to the Lord, who is worthy of praise, and I am saved from my enemies.

The waves of death surrounded me. (. . .) I called to the Lord in my distress, I cried to my God for help.

My cry came to his ears! (. . .)

He pulled me out of the deep waters, and rescued me from my mighty enemy. (. . .)

For this I will praise you, Lord, and sing praise to your name.

It is not certain that all the psalms attributed to David are really his but we do know that the king was a great religious poet. He was also the creator of a whole tradition of songs which were taken up throughout the ages, and sometimes enriched with new ideas.

THE BOOKS
OF THE KINGS

**ILLUSION
AND
DISILLUSION**

Whenever a catastrophe causes a group to begin to fall apart, be it a nation or a family, the good old days are remembered with nostalgia. How could anyone have made all the mistakes which, looking back, so obviously led to disaster?

The Jewish believers were feeling just like that, exiled in Babylon after the fall of the kingdom. Everything had begun so well! The failures observed at the end of David's reign had quickly been forgotten under Solomon. Everything started to fall apart when he died: the North and the South were divided and the two kingdoms, brothers and yet enemies, began to fight one another. It was traumatic for the faithful who continued to believe in the divine destiny of their people in being called to lead humanity in God's way. The northern kingdom of Israel gradually slipped further and further away from God despite warnings from the prophets: Elijah, Elisha, Amos, Hosea kept reminding them of the covenant. The kingdom was rotten to the core and fell to the Assyrians in BC 721.

The southern kingdom of Judah survived longer. The people there were more faithful to the religion of their ancestors. Some kings of Judah were influenced by the prophets and undertook religious and moral reforms which slowed the kingdom's decline. Although some kings were good (like Hezekiah and Josiah), many of the others had a disastrous political and moral stance. Godlessness, arrogance and injustice destroyed the chosen people from the inside, and Jerusalem no longer had the strength to fight off the Chaldaean invaders.

The authors of the books of Kings contemplated this painful past. They used the archives to rewrite the story in the light of the covenant established by Moses; they were anxious to teach the future generations which illusions and sins should be avoided; they stressed God's faithfulness; and they held on to the hope that one day Israel would be reunified and would rise again with a new David as Messiah. He would come at last to establish the kingdom of joy as an example to all humanity. The lessons of the past should be used to prepare a better future.

FIRST BOOK OF KINGS

DAVID'S SUCCESSION

David was now a sick old man and plots concerning his successor were multiplying around him. Each of his wives in the royal harem hoped to see her own son on the throne. Nathan the prophet had no doubt that God's chosen one was Solomon, son of Bathsheba; she helped Nathan to frustrate the schemes of Adonijah who was so sure of being king that he was already feasting with his friends to celebrate his triumph. Nathan consulted with David and hurriedly arranged to have his own candidate anointed as king. Adonijah was terrified and was sure that he was about to be put to death and could do nothing but surrender. Solomon generously allowed his rival to live.

David finally died. His will was a call to be faithful to the covenant. This was the end of a brilliant forty-year reign that was above all deeply marked by faith in the Lord. The memory of David's reign would never die for the people of Israel.

There were then some old scores to be settled. Solomon eventually had Adonijah put to death for his ambitiousness was dangerous, as was that of his followers. Joab, David's former general, had also become a threat. Shimei, the man who had cursed David during Absalom's revolt, was also punished. Solomon's throne was now secure.

THE REIGN OF SOLOMON THE MAGNIFICENT

The wisdom of Solomon

The new reign had a bright beginning. Solomon was not only a great man but a wise one. It was said that, having gone to Gibeon, he had seen God in a dream. The Lord had promised to grant him his greatest wish and in response the king had asked for wisdom rather than wealth or power.

This was soon demonstrated by the way he handled even the thorniest problems in his capacity as judge. Everyone had heard of his most famous judgement: two prostitutes had lived in the same house and had each given birth to a son. One night, however, one of the children died and his mother took the child still living and claimed it as her own. When the two mothers came to plead their case before the king, he ordered that the living child be cut in two, and one half of it given to each woman. The false mother agreed to the arrangement while the real mother begged him to give the child to the other woman rather than kill it. The king returned the child to the rightful mother having thus discovered the truth.

Solomon also created a model administration which was so efficient that the kingdom prospered.

The fame of the new ruler grew: neighbouring kings heard about his wisdom and knowledge and brought him gifts to honour him.

Solomon the builder

Solomon then decided to build the Temple his father had dreamed of. He organised a gigantic building project on the hill overlooking Zion (where his own palace stood). Nothing was too good for this sanctuary which was to demonstrate the glory of the God of Israel to everyone. The best craftsmen were brought in from neighbouring countries to construct a building which was to outdo anything else existing at that time.

The day of the dedication arrived and God at last had a home at the heart of his land. The ark of the covenant was solemnly carried into the Holy of Holies which was the holiest part of the new sanctuary. Then a bright cloud filled the Temple. This cloud was the same as the one which had guided the people as they wandered in the wilderness. God was making his presence known.

Solomon gave a great speech showing how the whole of the past had led up to that moment. The new Temple was a visible confirmation of the covenant formed at Sinai. Then the king raised his hands to the heavens and prayed this prayer:

God had refused to live in a house built by human hands during David's reign! Solomon thought he was both doing his religious duty and giving praise to God by building the Temple. But the rest of the story shows that the new building also brought difficult issues to light.

8: 22–9

"Lord, God of Israel, there is no god like you either in heaven above or here on earth. You remain loyal to your covenant and faithful in love to your servants as long as they walk wholeheartedly in your way. You have kept the promise you made to your servant, my father David, as you promised him you would. Today you have carried it out by your power. And now, Lord, God of Israel, keep the promise which you made to your servant David when you said,

KING SOLOMON IN ALL HIS GLORY!

The wisdom of Solomon

The riches of Solomon

The Temple of Jerusalem built by Solomon near his palace

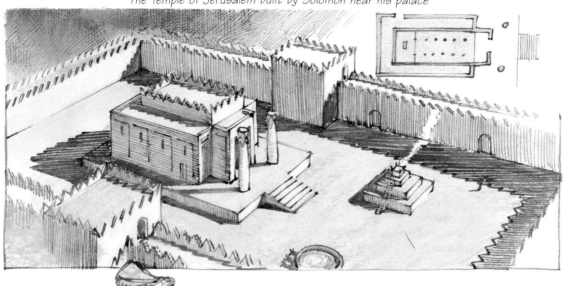

Solomon and the Queen of Sheba

It became too easy to believe that Israel was secure while God was in the Temple. The Temple became a sign of God's presence at the heart of his people for those who truly believed; but it was like a lucky charm for others, and would be destroyed one day. So a fundamental question must be asked: where and how do we meet God?

'There will always be one of your descendants sitting before me on the throne of Israel, provided that your sons are careful how they behave and walk before me as you yourself have done.' So now, God of Israel, let the words come true which you spoke to your servant, my father David. Yet will God really live with human beings on earth? Why, the heavens, the highest of the heavens, cannot contain you. How much less this temple which I have built! Even so, listen favourably to the prayer and request of your servant, Lord my God. Listen to the cry and to the prayer which your servant makes to you today: day and night may your eyes watch over this temple, over this place of which you have said, 'My name will be there.' Listen to the prayer which your servant offers in this place.''

Solomon begged the Lord to pardon Israel if it ever slipped back into sin. He also prayed for all the foreigners who would come to pray in the Temple after discovering the greatness of the Lord's name. The celebrations ended with a blessing on the crowd and with countless sacrificial offerings.

Solomon's power was now evident. God was with him! Wealth poured in from all sides and the kingdom became an economic power. Even the famous Queen of Sheba visited in great pomp to see the ruler whose glory was boasted of everywhere.

The dark side of the reign

Unfortunately, Solomon's reign also had negative aspects: for example, he was very like the cruel Pharaohs in some ways — and God had saved his people from them! The people of the land were forced to do military service while those foreigners allowed to settle had to become slaves. Furthermore Solomon kept a large harem as was common for any great ruler anxious to show off his power. He had taken wives from amongst the princesses of neighbouring lands for political reasons but had allowed them to introduce their pagan cults into the kingdom. It was a serious sin and broke the rules of the covenant. Further afield, certain enemies had not laid down their arms although they were under control.

Even worse: the hatred between the North and the South of the country still continued, and at the root of the division was the past fighting between the houses of Saul and David. The northern tribes were wealthy and hated being politically inferior to Judah. It was said how a high-court official called Jeroboam had met with a prophet who had divided his cloak into twelve pieces and given ten of them to him, thus foretelling the time in the not too distant future when the tribes of Israel would divide. Solomon saw the danger and tried to get rid of this man who was too clever, and therefore dangerous, but Jeroboam fled to Egypt.

Solomon died after reigning for forty years. What was to become of the kingdom?

THE POLITICAL AND RELIGIOUS SPLIT

The assembly at Shechem

12: 1–19

Rehoboam then went to Shechem, for it was to Shechem that all Israel had come to proclaim him king. Jeroboam and the whole assembly of Israel came. And they said to Rehoboam, "Your father made us carry a cruel yoke. If you will lighten your father's cruel slavery, that heavy yoke which he forced upon us, we are willing to serve you." He said to them, "Go away for three days and then come back to me." And the people went away. (. . .)

On the third day Jeroboam and all the people came to Rehoboam. (. . .) And the king gave the people a harsh answer. (. . .) He said, "My father made your yoke heavy. I shall make it heavier still! My father controlled you with a whip, but I shall use a spiked lash!" (. . .) When all Israel saw that the king refused to listen to them, they answered:

"What is our share in David? We have no inheritance in the son of Jesse! Away to your tents, Israel! Now, David, look after your own House!"

So Israel went home again.

The thoughtlessness of David's heir caused a political split. It was a dramatic turning-point in the history of God's people and unity was destroyed. They could only dream from then on and hope that eventually the descendant promised to David by Nathan would come to re-establish it: this was the "anointed of God".

Even worse than the political division was the religious split that went with it. Jeroboam became king of Israel but he did not want to allow his subjects to come to Jerusalem. So he had an altar set up at a former shrine that had been neglected since the Temple was built. There at Bethel he appointed priests who did not come from the family of Levi and, worse still, had two golden calves made as images of God. Despite fierce protests from a man of God and God himself using miraculous signs to show his anger against this outrageous behaviour, Jeroboam continued with his plans. Those who had remained faithful to the true covenant began to regard those of the northern kingdom as traitors and as heretics.

The decline had begun. Rehoboam's reign in Judah was disastrous but fortunately his successor was Asa who could remedy the situation. In Israel, though, ruler after ruler was overthrown; the monarchy lost its rightful base and fell into the hands of the most powerful contender. Omri reigned between BC 885 and 874 and established his capital in Samaria. His son was Ahab who was to be even worse than all his predecessors combined. He married a pagan princess from Sidon called Jezebel and officially introduced the cult of Baal into the kingdom. This cult was increasingly taking the place of faith in the God of the covenant.

ELIJAH

The great drought

It was not long before God's punishment fell upon the kingdom of Israel. Elijah was a prophet raised up by the Lord. He foretold that there would be a drought — and then famine!

But Elijah himself was a source of blessing to those who welcomed him. Thus he multiplied the bread and oil at the home of the poor widow. But he did much more:

The widow's son raised to life   17: 17–24

Luke was careful to tell the tale of the widow's son being brought back to life at Nain because he was anxious to show that Jesus had come to fulfil the work begun by Elijah (7: 11ff.).

The son of the woman who owned the house became sick and his illness was so serious that in the end he died. Then the woman said to Elijah, "What quarrel have you got with me, man of God? Have you come here to bring my sins home to me and to kill my son?" "Give me your son," he said. He took the boy, carried him to the room upstairs where he was staying and laid him on his bed. He cried out to the Lord, "Lord my God, do you really mean to bring such sorrow to the widow who is looking after me by making her son die?" He stretched himself on the child three times and cried out to the Lord, "Lord my God, I beg you, may the soul of this child come into him again!" The Lord heard Elijah's prayer and the child's soul came back into his body and he revived. Elijah took the child, (. . .) gave him to his mother, and said, "Look, your son is alive." And the woman replied, "Now I know you are a man of God and the word of the Lord in your mouth is truth itself."

The king, urged on by Jezebel, had meanwhile massacred almost all the priests still faithful to the covenant. Elijah challenged the king: why not gather together all the priests of the two rival cults and let God show which was the true faith?

The day of the contest arrived. The action took place in the middle of a great gathering on Mount Carmel. Elijah told the priests of Baal to prepare their sacrifice while he prepared his own. God himself would set fire to the offering he chose to accept and in this way would show which side he was on.

The priests of Baal ranted and raved and even gashed themselves but it was no use. "Call louder," Elijah jeered at them, "perhaps your god is preoccupied or is busy, or he has gone on a journey; perhaps he is asleep and will wake up." But nothing happened.

Then Elijah called on the Lord in his turn. "Lord, God of Abraham, Isaac and Israel, let them know today that you are God in Israel, that I have done all these things at your command. Answer me, Lord, answer me, so that this people may know that you, Lord, are God and are winning back their hearts." The fire of God fell upon the sacrifice at that very moment and the offering was burnt up at once despite Elijah having first drenched the altar with water.

God's judgement was so clear that Elijah had the priests of Baal seized and then he killed them. God immediately showed his mercy to those people who had rid themselves of the pagan priests; rain then fell. The times of plenty had returned.

Elijah at Horeb

Queen Jezebel was determined to take revenge on the prophet so Elijah was forced to flee for his life.

He wanted to return to Horeb, or Sinai which was the mountain where God had revealed himself to Moses and his people. The crossing of the desert was a terrible testing time for Elijah and more than once he was tempted to give in to despair. But he was strengthened by the "angel of God" and reached the end of his journey.

19: 9–15

He went into a cave and spent the night there. Then the word of the Lord came to him: "What are you doing here, Elijah?" He replied, "I am full of jealous zeal for the Lord Almighty, because the Israelites have abandoned your covenant, have torn down your altars and put your prophets to death with the sword. I am the only one left, and now they want to kill me." Then he was told, "Go out and stand on the mountain before the Lord." For at that moment the Lord was going by. A mighty hurricane split the mountains and shattered the rocks before the Lord. But the Lord was not in the hurricane. And after the hurricane, there was an earthquake. But the Lord was not in the earthquake. And after the earthquake, there was fire. But the Lord was not in the fire. And after the fire, there was the sound of a gentle murmur. And when Elijah heard this, he covered his face with his cloak and went and stood at the entrance of the cave. Then a voice came to him: "What are you doing here, Elijah?" He replied, "I am full of jealous zeal for the Lord Almighty." (. . .)
Then the Lord said, "Go back by the same way to the desert of Damascus."

This text is one of the most beautiful accounts of "theophany", which means God revealing himself to a human being. Elijah was always remembered as a hero by the chosen people because he was faithful to the covenant: he was a real "second Moses". At the time of a later "theophany" when Jesus was transfigured on the mountain, Christians told how the two representatives of the first covenant came to bear witness that Jesus had come to fulfil God's plan for the human race.

Elijah courageously returned to his people to continue the struggle he had begun. He called Elisha to help him and become his successor. He went again before the king but Ahab was involved in continuous wars against his Aramean neighbours and remained deaf and blind to the prophet's God-given warnings.

Naboth's vineyard

Then Ahab committed a real crime which put the whole covenant-based social structure of Israel at risk. He decided to extend his personal garden by purchasing for himself a vineyard owned by his neighbour Naboth. This man did not want to part with it because all land in Israel belonged to God: people consequently had no right to sell land since the Lord had entrusted it to their families.

This was intolerable to Jezebel who, as a pagan princess, was accustomed to thinking of the king as having all the rights. So, she encouraged her husband to hatch a plot accusing Naboth of treason against the king. Witnesses who were prepared to lie were easily found and Naboth was stoned to death having been convicted of rising up against the king.

Elijah acted as God's witness and protested vigorously against this breaking of the law. He delivered God's sentence: Ahab's descendants would be wiped off the face of the earth.

Another Aramean war and the death of Ahab

There was a short period of peace and then Ahab decided to reconquer a city which the Arameans had taken from him previously. The success of the operation was predicted by the official court prophets (who were really courtiers). Only Micah, God's true prophet, had the courage to tell him he would fail. Micah was immediately thrown into prison, yet the expedition was disastrous. The enemy concentrated all their forces against the king and he was shot by an arrow and died during the retreat. Dogs licked up his blood as Elijah had foretold. Thus the God of Israel triumphed at last over the godless king.

SECOND BOOK OF KINGS

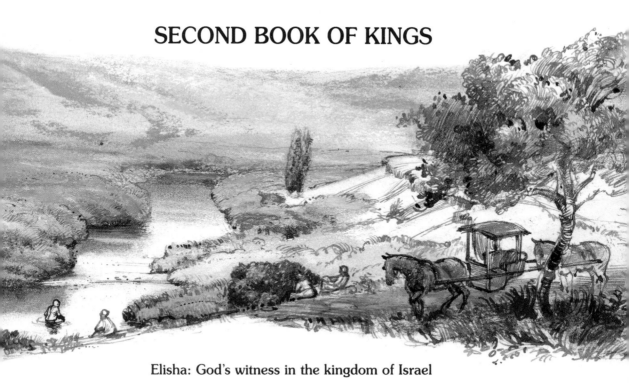

Elisha: God's witness in the kingdom of Israel

Tradition tells that Elijah did not die but was taken up into heaven. He was suddenly carried off in a chariot of fire when out with his disciple Elisha. From that day on, Israel expected the great man of God to return: rumour suggested that he would come back to prepare the way for the long-awaited Messiah.

Elisha collected Elijah's cloak from where it had fallen when the prophet was carried away to heaven. In this way Elisha showed that he was taking up his master's rôle. Others quickly realised that the spirit that had rested on his predecessor now rested on him.

A real golden legend spread about the new prophet. He was a source of blessing to all who respected him but he was a source of trouble to those who mocked him.

The popular imagination was particularly captured by one of his miracles: that of Naaman. This man was a general in the Aramean army who had heard rumours about Elisha. He asked the king of Israel to intervene and help him find a cure for his leprosy. The king did not believe in Elisha's power and thought that the Arameans were trying to invent an excuse for attacking him. The king was very frightened.

Naaman is healed   5: 8–15

Elisha sent word to the king, "Let him come to me, and he will find there is a prophet in Israel." So Naaman came with his team of horses and chariot and drew up at the door of Elisha's house. And Elisha sent him a messenger to say, "Go and bathe seven times in the Jordan, and your skin will become clean again." But Naaman was indignant and went off, saying, "Here was I, thinking he would be sure to come out to me, and stand there, and call on the name of the Lord his God, and wave his hand over the spot and heal the part that was diseased. Surely, Abana and Parpar,

Even a foreign general was allowed to share in Elisha's blessing. In order to do so he only had to trust the prophet and go down into the healing waters. Jesus later reminded the inhabitants of Nazareth of this episode when justifying the fact that he had also healed foreign believers (cf. Luke 4: 27).

the rivers of Damascus, are better than any water in Israel? Could I not bathe in them and become clean?'' And he turned round and went off in a fit of anger. But his servants approached him and said, ''Father, if the prophet had asked you to do something difficult, would you not have done it? Doesn't it make even more sense, then, when he says to you, 'Bathe, and you will become clean'?'' So he went down and bathed himself seven times in the Jordan, as Elisha had told him to do. And his skin became clean again like the skin of a little child. Returning to Elisha with his whole escort, he went in, presented himself to him and said, ''Now I know there is no other God anywhere on earth than the God of Israel.''

Elisha's interventions were also important on a national scale since they led to victory or defeat. His great deeds, however, only made the godlessness and unbelief of Ahab's successors even more evident. They persecuted him rather than listen to the prophet's words.

The story of Jehu

Elisha condemned Ahab's guilty line and called on the name of the Lord. He sent one of his followers to anoint a general of the army called Jehu as king. Jehu then personally executed Ahab's descendant, Jehoram, and had his body thrown into the field where the blood of Naboth had once been shed. The queen mother was Jezebel and was guilty of many crimes. Jehu gave orders for her to be thrown down from a window, and thus the punishment foretold by Elijah was carried out as dogs ate part of her corpse.

Jehu then ordered the massacre of the seventy sons of Ahab. He then had all the priests of Baal put to death and was used to carry out God's punishment. Jehu eventually became no more faithful to God than his predecessors had been, and hastened the kingdom's decline rather than stopping it.

Athaliah: a wicked queen

The terrible events in Israel had immediate repercussions in the southern kingdom.

The king of Judah from 848 to 841 was Jehoram. He married Athaliah, one of the daughters of Ahab (then the king of Israel). The kingdom was consequently involved with the political and religious dealings of its ungodly neighbour. Their son was Ahaziah who had become king in 841. He made an alliance with the king of Israel and they were both assassinated by Jehu when they were together one day. Athaliah heard about the death of her son and the massacre of the princes of her family and decided to take revenge by murdering the entire royal family to end the line of David. Fortunately, one of the children was saved from the massacre by his aunt. Jehoash was raised secretly in the Temple. A group of faithful believers organised an uprising by presenting the heir to the throne to the crowds. This was in BC 845. Athaliah was alerted by the noise. She was seized and put to death after coming to see what was happening. The mob then destroyed the temple of Baal.

In fact, the reign of Jehoash was no happier than that of his fathers: he chose to commit serious abuses of power against the religious authorities. Jehoash was finally assassinated by his own men in 796 but at least he had made sure that the line of David would continue. This was an important issue for a nation convinced that God's promise of a better world would be fulfilled through a descendant of the great king. Elisha died around this time.

THE RELIGIOUS DECLINE OF THE TWO KINGDOMS AND THE FALL OF SAMARIA

The histories of Judah and Israel were full of crises from that time onwards. The two kingdoms had an uneasy relationship, occasionally being allies but were enemies at other times. Israel tended to dominate. This fact was explained by the author of the book of Kings who said that God, in his divine patience, "had not yet decided to sweep the name of Israel from the face of the earth". The reign of Jeroboam II was particularly brilliant but the prophets Amos and Hosea spoke out strongly against the religious, moral and social decline of the kingdom during his period on the throne. The people felt that they could ignore the warnings presented to them by God's representatives. The future was alarming anyway because Assyria was becoming ever more powerful and dangerous.

Some of the kings of Judah did try to remedy the spiritual crisis but were unsuccessful. Religious life collapsed when Ahaz came to power (736–716). This king refused to trust in the God of the covenant despite Isaiah's interventions. Ahaz later called for help from Assyria (which was in fact his worst enemy) after having gone to war at the same time against both Israel and the Arameans, who wanted to drag him into an anti-Assyrian coalition. He adopted the Assyrian religions and customs because of this. The drama was getting hotter in the North.

17: 5–8

The king of Assyria invaded the whole country and laid siege to Samaria for three years. In the ninth year of Hoshea, the king of Assyria captured Samaria and took the Israelites back to Assyria as prisoners. He settled them in Halah on the Habor, a river of Gozan, and in the cities of the Medes.

This happened because the Israelites had sinned against the Lord

Unity was at an end from that time. Only the prophets kept alive any hope that one day the Lord would restore unity as he came to save all his people.

their God who had brought them out of Egypt, out of the grip of Pharaoh king of Egypt. They worshipped other gods. They followed the evil practices of the nations whose lands the Lord had given to them.

THE LAST DAYS OF THE KINGDOM OF JUDAH

Hezekiah, the prophet Isaiah and Assyria

The fall of the other kingdom's capital was a terrible blow for Judah despite the hatred existing between Jerusalem and Samaria. It frightened them. This explains the sense of national crisis during the reign of Hezekiah, son of Ahaz (716–687). Hezekiah was different from his father and trusted the prophet Isaiah and tried to stop the religious decline. The biblical author used this trust to explain Jerusalem's unexpected resistance toward Assyria.

Ahaz's former ally was now an enemy. Sennacherib was the new king of Nineveh and had destroyed the alliance existing between the minor Syrian kings. He intended to confront his main rival of Egypt. He destroyed Judah on his way there and Hezekiah had to surrender with subsequent payment of tribute.

Then the Assyrians attacked the capital of Judah. The frightened people fled as refugees toward Jerusalem. A messenger from the attackers came under the walls of the city and gave them an ultimatum. He advised the people to surrender and not to listen to their king's calls for resistance. He dared to say:

The aim of the speech was to make them give up and played on a common religious belief at the time: each country had its own special god who protected it and so wars were conflicts between rival gods of their respective peoples. Victory was given to the people whose god was the greater. The prophets may have proclaimed that the God of the Covenant was stronger than the other gods but the idea of a single God, Creator of the universe and common to all peoples, was still unacceptable. The fall of Jerusalem 120 years later made people doubt the Lord's power and caused a serious crisis of faith.

18: 29—19: 6

"Listen to the word of the great king, the king of Assyria: 'Do not let Hezekiah deceive you. He will not be able to save you from my hands. Do not trust him when he says: The Lord is sure to save us; this city will not fall into the king of Assyria's hands. (. . .) Make peace with me, surrender to me, and each of you will be free to eat the fruit of his own vine and of his own fig tree and to drink the water of his own storage-well until I come and take you away to a country like your own. (. . .) Has any god of any nation been able to save his country from the hands of the king of Assyria? (. . .) Did the gods save Samaria from my hands? Of all the local gods, which ones have saved their countries from my hands? Do you then think that the Lord will be able to save Jerusalem from my hands?' "

King Hezekiah tore his clothes, put on sackcloth and went to the Temple of the Lord. He sent messengers to the prophet Isaiah (. . .) who said to them, "Say to your master, 'The Lord says this: Do not be afraid of the words which you have heard or the blasphemies which the king of Assyria's servants have spoken against me.' "

Sennacherib was determined to defeat Jerusalem forever. He issued a new ultimatum to which Isaiah replied:

19: 21–34

"She despises you, she scorns you, the virgin daughter of Zion; she tosses her head at you, the daughter of Jerusalem! Whom have you insulted, whom have you blasphemed? Against whom have you raised your voice and lifted your eyes? Against the Holy One of Israel! Through your messengers you have insulted the Lord. (. . .) Because you have raved against me, and your arrogance has reached my ears, I shall put a hook through your nostrils and a muzzle on your lips. I shall make you return by the road by which you came. (. . .) Those of the House of Judah who still survive will produce new roots below the ground and fruit above it; for a remnant will come from Jerusalem, and survivors from Mount Zion. The Lord God Almighty's jealous love will bring this about.

"This, then, is what the Lord says about the king of Assyria: 'He will not enter this city, he will not shoot arrows at it. (. . .) I shall protect this city and save it for my sake and my servant David's sake.' "

The situation was suddenly reversed. The Bible says, "the angel of the Lord struck". Probably the Assyrian army was struck down by a plague epidemic, and was forced to withdraw. Sennacherib was assassinated shortly afterwards and so Jerusalem was saved. Salvation was apparently connected to the king's love for God and the king was faithful to the covenant. He had always looked to the Lord with confidence in contrast with so many of his predecessors. God had heard his prayers and had healed him of a grave illness the very same day.

A new religious crisis and an attempt at reform under King Josiah

Isaiah was unfortunately dismissed from the king's council following the death of Hezekiah. The moral and religious crisis returned — the conversion had been superficial and people went back to pagan cults. Under King Manasseh (687–642), the prophets could only protest in vain and foretell doom in the name of God. The king was now under the control of of Assyria and allowed the faithful to be persecuted. The situation continued to get worse under the reign of his successor, Amon (642–640).

However, a sudden upturn gave hope to the faithful.

King Josiah (640–609) was a believer whose political and religious rôle-model was David. A manuscript had just been discovered in the Temple. No doubt it had been placed there by Israelite believers as they took refuge in Judah following the fall of Samaria. Josiah took its contents very seriously; it was probably an early version of Deuteronomy. The prophets emphasised the seriousness of the threats announced against the chosen people should they betray the divine Law.

The solemn reading of the Law
23: 1–3

We are seeing a rediscovery of traditions. These traditions were enriched by the thoughts of people from the North: the compilers took advantage of the events of Deuteronomy being presented in the form of Moses' Will to add the lessons learnt from the people's fall.

The king then had all the elders of Judah and of Jerusalem summoned to him. He went up to the Temple of the Lord with all the inhabitants of Jerusalem, priests, prophets and all the people, high and low. In their hearing he read out the entire contents of the Book of the Covenant discovered in the Temple of the Lord. The king then, standing on the platform, made a covenant with the Lord, to follow the Lord, to keep his commandments, decrees and laws with all his heart and soul, and to carry out the terms of the covenant as written in this book. All the people promised to keep the covenant.

The faith and morals had been worn away by pagan cults which had now been eliminated. The weakening of the Assyrians made it possible to extend the reforms to cover certain areas in the former kingdom of Israel. This reconstruction of a sort of national unity was a hopeful sign, indeed, the Passover was celebrated solemnly in Jerusalem during the eighteenth year of King Josiah's reign. Didn't the return of the Covenant guarantee salvation?

Josiah was unfortunately killed while trying to oppose the Egyptian Pharaoh, who had come to the defence of Assyria (itself under threat from the Chaldaeans' rising political power). Israel's hopes collapsed.

The ruin of Jerusalem

There was no stopping the decline under Josiah's successors, Jehoahaz, Jehoiakim, Jehoiachin: it was one bad king after another. The prophet Jeremiah spoke out continually against the incompetence and weakness of these kings who were no more than puppets. Jerusalem was conquered in BC 598 by Nebuchadnezzar, king of Babylon. He took part of the population prisoner (among them Ezekiel, the priest-prophet) and placed a puppet king on the throne. This king, Zedekiah, was involved in a rebellion against his governors so the Chaldaeans besieged Jerusalem once more. The city was taken and destroyed. Zedekiah's sons were killed in front of their father before finally his eyes were put out. The Temple was destroyed, the majority of the population were taken to Babylon as prisoners. A bleak period of exile thus began.

The dream had collapsed. The people had thought that having a king would bring them happiness but it had brought only catastrophe. Were the people of God destroyed forever? It was all over in human terms and the divine promise appeared to be an illusion — even Jehoiachin had been taken into exile and he was the last of David's descendants. The only remaining hope was that the king was still alive. Perhaps it was still possible to believe in Nathan's prophecy that one day a descendant of the great king would come and make the dream come true.

THE BOOK OF CHRONICLES

A COMMUNITY
REDISCOVERS ITS LINKS WITH THE PAST

The account of the history of a nation varies according to the author's point of view and the problems he wants to address.

It was the year BC 350. The Jewish community felt isolated in the midst of the huge empires then dominating the Middle East (the Persians and then the Greeks). The splendour of David's kingdom was no more than a distant memory by now, so the Jews clung to the Temple and its religious practices — it was the only thing keeping their hopes for the future alive. Surely the Temple was where God would begin when he created his new world order?

The narrator of this history is known to us only as the Chronicler. He decided at that time to rewrite the history already recorded in the book of Kings. He emphasised different aspects of these same events because he wanted to show how the entire history of the world centred around the reality of the religious practices at Jerusalem; this aspect was essential to him and explains the endless genealogies which start from the supposed origins of humanity and move on progressively to David and Solomon. These two characters were very important to the narrator since they are at the origin of the Temple and its worship.

The Evangelist Matthew followed the example of the Chronicler by starting his account with a family tree. This was to emphasise that his "Good News" was rooted in the history of the Jewish people.

1: 1–25

Adam, Seth, Enosh, Kenan, Mahalalel, Jared, Enoch, Methuselah, Lamech, Noah, Shem, Ham and Japheth.

Sons of Japheth: Gomer, Magog, the Medes. (. . .)

2: 12–15

Boaz was the father of Obed, Obed was the father of Jesse. Jesse was the father of Eliab, his first-born, Abinadab second, (. . .) David seventh.

The account which follows is a real literary monument to the great king who, it appears, spent most of his life preparing the plans for the Temple his son was to build. Solomon's main ambition seems to have been the completion of this great project. The author is at pains to justify the worship practices of his own day by showing how each began at the time of the two great kings. His account omits to mention their sins which might have damaged their memory. On the other hand, he emphasises how enormous were the sins of the kingdom of Israel which, through the split, broke with both the rightful royal line and the sacrificial religious practices of the capital. This betrayal caused all the troubles suffered by those wicked people.

It has to be said that the track record for the kingdom of Judah was no better since it had also ended in catastrophe. The explanation was again simple: Judah had ignored the examples set by David and Solomon. But all praise to those who had remained faithful to their traditions, as was particularly the case with Hezekiah. The author writes at length about this king's reforms and proudly describes the details of the Temple's purification and the ceremonies which followed:

Worship begins again

29: 29–36

When the sacrifice was finished, the king and all those present with him fell to their knees and worshipped. Then King Hezekiah and the officials told the Levites to sing praise to the Lord in the words of David and Asaph the prophet. Joyfully they sang their praises, then knelt in worship.

Hezekiah spoke again, "Now that you have consecrated yourselves to the Lord, come forward and bring thanksgiving sacrifices to the Temple of the Lord." Then the congregation brought thanksgiving sacrifices and those who were generous brought burnt offerings. The number of offerings brought by the congregation was seventy bulls, a hundred rams and two hundred lambs, all as offerings to the Lord. The consecrated gifts amounted to six hundred bulls and three thousand sheep. The priests were too few, however, and were unable to kill all the offerings and get them ready, so their brothers, the Levites, helped them until the work was finished and the priests had sanctified themselves. The Levites had been more conscientious about sanctifying themselves than the priests had. (. . .) And so worship was restored in the Lord's Temple. Hezekiah and all the people rejoiced over what God had provided for the people, since everything had happened so suddenly.

The lessons drawn from this sort of account are clear: the people should understand the true source of real success and return to the religious customs of their ancestors. That way God could be seen in all his glory at the heart of his chosen nation.

The book of Chronicles mirrors the books of Kings but through its variations it allows us to understand the thinking of a group of people turning towards their past. Chronicles is followed by the books of Ezra and Nehemiah which are more original works. The writer's main concern is still to show how the holy traditions were restored after the exile by the rebuilding of the Temple and the reintroduction of the religious practices.

The people returned after a period of punishment and testing to the holy institutions they should never have neglected anyway.

THE BOOKS OF EZRA AND NEHEMIAH

It isn't easy to revitalise a community, a family or a nation and reunify its members if a storm has almost caused its collapse.

That was the problem the Jews had to solve following their release from exile in Babylon.

King Cyrus of Persia freed the Jewish captives in BC 538 and allowed them to go home. They dreamed of an ideal future when they returned to their homeland and were full of enthusiasm. Harsh reality soon changed them, though, and they were faced with rebuilding their lives in a ruined and sometimes barren land — even worse, the land was occupied by foreigners who were unwilling to give it up. The Jews had no resources and conflicting interests caused divisions among themselves. They had to fight against the Samaritans who were a mixed race of descendants of former Israelites and members of the foreign colonies introduced by the Assyrians. These people claimed they were faithful to the religious practices of the God of Israel and even asked to be allowed to take part in the rebuilding of the Temple. The returning exiles drove away this "impure race" and consequently had to face the hatred of the Samaritans. Additional problems concerning the organisation of power forced them to collaborate with the Persian occupiers.

The Chronicler had already written works honouring the memory of David and Solomon who had founded the Temple with its religious practices. He then wrote two more books to show how they had overcome the further difficulties and how they had finally managed to continue the old sacred traditions despite the time spent away during the exile. The Chronicler was writing around BC 350. The Jews had probably not been able to establish complete political independence at that time owing to Alexander's conquest of the country but they did have the bare essentials: they had the Law which governed the life of the nation and they had the Temple (which they rebuilt).

The Chronicler introduces two men who were greatly used by God: Ezra and Nehemiah who were a priest and a layman respectively. The author seems unconcerned about establishing an exact sequence of events, so he showed Ezra re-establishing the authority of the Holy Scriptures (although Ezra is thought to be the author of the final book of the Pentateuch). He also showed Nehemiah using his position at the Persian court to make it possible to rebuild the Holy City.

The two men really did more than simply rebuild the past. Judaism was born under their influence and was deeply marked by their time in exile. Its vision of God had been transformed. The hopes for the Jewish nation were now spiritual ones and God's victory would be obtained through obedience to his Law.

The reforms did, however, have a darker side: the Jewish leaders emphasised how special and different the Jews were. This idea arose from their anxiety to give a sense of identity back to the Jewish people, but it tended to make the Jews isolate themselves to maintain the ritualism of their lifestyle; the renewal of God's people went hand in hand with a temptation to cut themselves off. The Apostles, in common with Jesus, encountered this problem time and again. In fact, it has been a problem over the centuries and throughout the history of the Church.

THE BOOK OF EZRA

THE RETURN FROM EXILE AND THE REBUILDING OF THE TEMPLE

Having conquered Babylon, Cyrus was inspired by God to allow the exiled Jews to go back home. About fifty thousand people started on the journey home. He also returned to them the treasures which had been stolen from the Temple.

The first task the Jews performed on their arrival in Jerusalem was to rebuild the altar, as decreed by the Law of Moses. They sang hymns of God's grace before the assembled crowds, and wept with emotion.

They faced huge problems. The Samaritans wanted to help rebuild the Temple. Jeshua and Zerubbabel, the leaders of the people, refused to let them help and so the Samaritans set about trying to prevent the reconstruction of Jerusalem. Their aim was achieved by plotting with the Persians in a plan based on their mutual fear of seeing Israel regain its former power.

The prophets were calling for the Temple to be rebuilt while international debates occurred concerning the status of the Jewish community. Meanwhile Darius was the new Persian king. He found the decree issued by his predecessor, Cyrus, in the royal archives. This document gave permission for the sanctuary to be rebuilt.

Eventually in BC 515 — more than twenty years after their homecoming — the Jews solemnly celebrated the Passover: it was a memorable date and marked the re-establishment of the Jewish nation.

THE ORGANISATION OF THE COMMUNITY BY EZRA AND NEHEMIAH

Ezra arrived in Jerusalem at about this time. He was a priest whose life was dedicated to the study of God's Law in order to make Israel follow his rules and customs.

Ezra had the support of the new king of Persia, Artaxerxes, and was able to reorganise the system of justice. The Mosaic Law became the law of the land.

Reinstating the Law was a hard and painful process. Ezra arrived in Jerusalem after a difficult journey and was appalled to see how many Jews now had foreign wives. This practice went against Moses' stated command. Ezra then remembered how Solomon's foreign wives had led him into idolatry so, in a heart-rending prayer, he begged the people to make amends for their sin by divorcing these women.

Ezra's prayer of repentance provoked a real rise in nationalism: God's people had to re-establish their original purity. The strict application of the Law caused a backlash of racism, and was opposed in certain quarters (cf. book of Ruth).

9: 6–15

"My God, I am ashamed, I blush to lift my face to you, my God. For our sins have increased, until they are higher than our heads, and our guilt has risen as high as heaven. From the days of our ancestors until now we have been deeply guilty. Because of our sins, we, our kings and our priests, have been handed over to the kings of other countries; to the sword, to captivity, to pillage, and to shame. And now, for a brief moment, the Lord our God has been gracious to us. He has allowed some of us to escape and given us a home in his holy place. In this way our God has raised our spirits and revived us a little, despite our slavery. For we are slaves. But God has not forgotten us in our slavery. He has shown his faithful love to us even under the kings of Persia and revived us to rebuild the Temple of our God, restore its ruins and provide us with a refuge in Judah and in Jerusalem. But now, our God, what can we say? For we have abandoned your commandments, which you gave us through your servants, the prophets, who instructed us: 'The country which you are about to possess has been polluted by the people of the country and their disgusting practices, which have filled it with their filth from end to end. You are not to give your daughters in marriage to their sons, or let their daughters marry your sons. Do not concern yourselves about peace or good relations with them, and in this way you will grow strong. You will eat the best food of the land and leave it as an inheritance to your sons for ever.' (. . .)

"After all (. . .) are we to break your commandments again and join our hands in marriage with people with these disgusting practices? Would you not be so angry with us that you would destroy us? (. . .) We come before you in our guilt; because of it we cannot stand in your presence."

The crowds were overwhelmed by their emotion and decided immediately to send their foreign wives away. The chosen people thus regained their original racial purity. (There were only four people who dared to oppose this drastic measure.)

THE BOOK OF NEHEMIAH

Nehemiah was a high-ranking Jew living in the Persian capital of Susa. He heard of the difficulties experienced by his fellow countrymen and women in Jerusalem and wondered how he could accept the situation if he really believed in the mission of God's chosen people.

He decided to use his own influence to come to the people's aid and so asked the king for help. He obtained full powers enabling him to restart the rebuilding of the Holy City. He got hold of the necessary documents and went to Jerusalem to inspect the city.

The decision to rebuild the walls of Jerusalem

2: 11–20

And so I reached Jerusalem. After I had been there three days, I got up during the night with a few other men — I had not told anyone what my God had inspired me to do for Jerusalem — taking no animal with me other than my own mount. Under cover of dark I went out through the Valley Gate towards the Dragon's Fountain as far as the Dung Gate, and examined the wall of Jerusalem where it was broken down and its gates burnt out. (. . .) I went up the Valley in the dark, examining the wall. I then went in again through the Valley Gate. (. . .)

I then said to those involved, "You see what a sorry state we are in: Jerusalem is in ruins and its gates have been burnt down. Come on, we must rebuild the walls of Jerusalem and put an end to our humiliating position." And I told them how the kind hand of my God had been over me. (. . .) And they put their hands to the good work.

When Sanballat the Horonite, Tobiah the official of Ammon, and Geshem the Arab heard about this, they laughed at us and

The rebuilding of the city walls seemed impossible but it was surely possible with God's help? The city walls symbolised the Lord's protection for his people. They were rebuilt.

jeered. They said, "What is this you are doing? Are you going to revolt against the king?" But I gave them this answer, "The God of heaven will help us to succeed and we, his servants, mean to start building. As for you, you have no share or right or memorial in Jerusalem."

The workers always kept weapons within reach to defend themselves since the local populations were worried and tried to stop their progress.

Another problem arose: the poor performed all the work while the rich profited from their labour. Nehemiah negotiated with them to overcome the differences and insisted that people recognise his efforts to be impartial.

The great day came when the new buildings were dedicated to God. The sacred texts were read out solemnly during the ceremony planned by Ezra, the scribe who had re-introduced the Law. The celebrations lasted for seven days. It was a new beginning for the people of God.

A few days later came the celebration of *Yom Kippur*, the "day of repentance" which is still a part of the Jewish year. They remembered both the past and the sins Israel had committed, humbly asking for God's pardon.

"Standing, each man in his right position, they read from the book of the Law of the Lord, their God, for one quarter of the day; for another quarter they confessed their sins and worshipped the Lord, their God."

9: 7–33

"You are the Lord God, who chose Abram, brought him out of Ur in Chaldaea and changed his name to Abraham. Finding his heart was faithful to you, you made a covenant with him, to give him the country of the Canaanites, the Hittites, the Amorites. (. . .) You saw the distress of our ancestors in Egypt, you heard their cry by the Sea of Reeds. You displayed signs and wonders against Pharaoh. (. . .) You opened up the sea in front of them: they walked through it on dry ground. (. . .) You made your holy Sabbath known to them; you gave them commandments, statutes and laws, through your servant Moses. For their hunger you gave them bread from heaven, for their thirst you brought them water out of a rock. (. . .) But they became disobedient and rebelled against you and rejected your law behind their backs; they killed your prophets who had warned them in order to bring them back to you, and they committed terrible sins against you. So you put them at the mercy of their enemies who oppressed them. (. . .) But, because of your great compassion, you did not destroy them completely, for you are a gracious, compassionate God. Now God, our great, mighty and awe-inspiring God, who keeps your covenant and your faithful love, take into account all that we (. . .) have had to live through. You have been righteous in all that has happened to us, for you acted faithfully, while we did wrong."

The Israelites sought forgiveness for their sins (especially the sin of having taken foreign wives, who were pagans). They recalled God's past goodness to them, which now seemed like a pledge that he would continue to be faithful and to love them. The Jewish people often looked to the past in order to find courage when times were hard. The Bible contains many examples of this during their history, for example in the Psalms.

The Jewish community seemed to have found the ideal way of life once they had eliminated all foreigners from their community. Their faith grew with the rebuilding of Jerusalem. Nehemiah briefly left them to fulfil his duties to the Persian king. He found yet more disobedience to the Law on his subsequent return to Jerusalem. He had to enforce the Sabbath rest vigorously and forbid marriages to foreigners. Nehemiah was conscious that he was doing God's will by intervening firmly. Holiness is a continuous struggle: certainly, we can never fight hard enough against sin!

THE BOOK OF TOBIT

IS IT POSSIBLE
FOR A RIGHTEOUS PERSON
TO SUFFER
ALL HIS LIFE?

"What have I done that God should punish me like this?" is a question we often ask when we are unhappy. We can understand it when a bad person is being punished, but what about the sufferings of good people? The answer seemed obvious to the authors of the Bible when they began to ask this question. Good people should find their reward in this world: this conclusion was extremely important as the people of that era had no idea of an after-life. Suffering showed that people had offended God, even if by accident. The offence could have been caused, for example, by actions which did not fit in with the religious practices, or just by belonging to a group that had sinned. From the moment we begin to think of sin as a personal moral fault, it is no longer possible to hold on to this simplistic idea.

The book of Tobit was written after the exile. It tried to re-examine the question, concluding that good people will only suffer for a little while, as if they were taking part in a short-lived endurance test. God will always restore things to their proper order. All they need to do is keep hoping and trusting in God while they wait. The book of Job later showed that this way of seeing things is inadequate. But the Jews had to wait a long time before the answer to the essential question was to become known — as revealed through the death and resurrection of Jesus.

Tobit is not a historical book but is a story with a message, a short novel set within the context of captivity in Assyria. Tobit was the father of Tobias. He led the difficult life shared by all the Israelites deported to Nineveh, the land of their pagan oppressors. Already, he was one of only a few people who were still faithful to the Law in that foreign land. He showed his zeal for God by giving gifts to the poor and, of greatest importance, he buried his fellow Jews according to the rites dictated by the Law despite such practices being banned by the Chaldaeans. So it is understandable why he became the target of

persecution. But how could the writer explain the curious accident which blinded him at a time when he was doing his duty? Even his wife (who was irritated by the care he took to follow God's laws) asked him brutally, "What about your own gifts to the poor? What about your own good works? Everyone knows what return you have had from them."

A virtuous young Israelite called Sarah lived three hundred kilometres away. Unfortunately she had been married seven times and each time a terrible demon caused her husband to die on the very evening of the wedding. Each husband had died in this way. It was a real dishonour for her.

Tobit one day sent his son to visit Sarah's family to collect some money lent previously. Tobias was bombarded with advice before he left, being told to respect the Law in every way, to give to the poor, to be fair to people, and not to marry a foreign woman. Tobias sought for a good guide to show him to his intended destination of Media. In fact, the fellow traveller who offered to go with him was none other than the archangel Raphael who was Tobias' "guardian angel". Raphael had assumed a human form which allowed him to help.

This fellow traveller turned out to be an extraordinary person. He knew everything including the remedy to all ills and was a safeguard against all dangers. Thus one day when the two travellers had caught a huge fish, Raphael retained the entrails because of their medicinal properties. During the journey, he encouraged Tobias to marry Sarah but the young man said he was afraid of her reputation. Raphael replied that she had been destined to be his wife since the beginning of time, and that Tobias was called to be her saviour thanks to his own remedies. Tobias decided as soon as he arrived at Sarah's home that he would marry her, despite the warnings of her father Raguel. On the wedding night:

This short passage illustrates both the symbolic character of the story and certain aspects of Jewish piety. Even sex can be holy and should be placed in God's keeping. That is why, even today, some liturgical texts used in the Christian marriage ceremony make reference to Sarah.

8: 1–5

When they had finished eating and drinking and it seemed time to go to bed, the young man was taken from the dining room to the bedroom. Tobias remembered Raphael's advice; he went to his bag, took the fish's heart and liver out of it and put some on the burning incense. The stink of the fish distressed the demon, who fled through the air to Egypt. Raphael chased him there, chained him up and strangled him. (. . .) Tobias got up from the bed, and said to Sarah, "Get up, my sister! You and I must pray and ask our Lord for his grace and his protection." She got up, and they began praying for protection: "You are blessed, O God of our fathers; and your name is blessed for ever and ever. (. . .) And so now it is not for my own selfish pleasure that I take my sister, but with a sincere heart. Be kind enough to have pity on both her and on me and bring us to old age together."

Raguel already had the young man's tomb prepared because he was so convinced that Tobias would die. He was filled with joy next morning when he found that Tobias was alive and well. They held a lavish feast to celebrate.

Tobias left with his young wife after two weeks because he thought his parents would be getting worried. He was still accompanied by their guide. Raphael intervened after the joy of the reunion by anointing the blind man's eyes with ointment made from the entrails of the fish they had caught during the journey. Tobit was healed and gave praises to God, "Blessed be God! Blessed be his great name! Blessed be all his holy angels! . . . For he had afflicted me and now has had pity on me, and I see my son Tobias!"

The mysterious companion then revealed his true identity, for the greater glory of God. He explained the way the heavenly court worked: angels there were responsible for presenting the prayers of good people to God.

Raphael disappeared having said this and everyone there began to sing God's praises.

The vision of the book's author is expressed by a series of acts of grace. Tobit would one day save all his people just as he had been healed.

13: 1–16

Blessed be God who lives for ever. (. . .)
For he both punishes and pardons;
he sends people down to the underworld and rescues them from utter Destruction. (. . .)
Declare his praise before the nations, children of Israel!
For if he has scattered you among them, there too he has shown you his greatness. (. . .) Though he punishes you for your sins, he will take pity on you all;
he will bring you back from every nation. (. . .)
My soul praises the Lord, because Jerusalem will be rebuilt.

Everything turned out for the best. Tobit could die in peace. Tobias was now the wealthy heir to Raguel. He lived to be a hundred and seventeen years old and saw the cursed city of Nineveh fall.

JUDITH

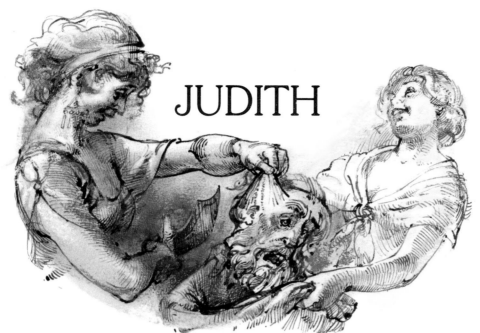

A "WEAK WOMAN" SAVES HER PEOPLE

It is such a pleasure to read stories where a weak person, the representative of God, triumphs over a strong representative of Evil. The Bible contains many such stories. Such victories in Scripture are always presented as a sign of God helping the oppressed over their oppressors.

The book of Judith follows this example. This little "historical novel" was probably written around the end of the second century BC. Its aim was to raise the morale of a weakened people who had just escaped the terrible persecution described in the book of Maccabees.

The heroine is Judith whose name means "the Jewess". God used her to bring about his victory although she was considered weak and in any case incapable of dealing with any problem as serious as war.

Christians see her legendary figure as pointing the way to another woman who had no skill in war but who played an essential part in freeing human beings from the rule of Evil: Mary. Hymns in honour of Judith, the Jewess, are also applied to the mother of Jesus.

Nebuchadnezzar was king of Nineveh. He decided to conquer the land and add it to his own empire; he had already done this to the Medes. The subsequent massacre and looting accompanying his victory showed the full power of evil. The king then turned against those, including Israel and Judah, who had refused to help him in his campaign. A formidable army was assembled under the leadership of Holofernes. No one could hold out against the invaders and those not submitting soon lost their lives. There was great anguish in Judah. The people took measures to defend themselves, the main one being prayer. Holofernes was a totally godless man, but his advisers explained to him how unusual the people of Israel were and how dangerous it could be to attack them.

The army laid siege to the fortress of Bethulia. The town soon ran out of water, thus causing panic: they would have to surrender. Uzziah, the governor of the town, managed to persuade an angry crowd of townspeople to hold out for another five days. If no help came in that time then he would agree with the wishes of the majority. Intervention then came from Judith, a widow well-known for her goodness. She rebuked those who were discouraged and protested against the idea of giving God a time-limit within which to act. Uzziah praised her highly for her religious speech but politely reminded her she ought just to pray for rain. Nothing more could be expected of a mere woman.

Judith did pray but not for rain: she asked God to support her in the action she had decided to take.

She left the town dressed in her best clothes and went to the first Assyrian post. She pretended that she was convinced that Holofernes' army was going to win and had decided to help him to take the city without any loss of life. She demanded to be taken to the general.

Holofernes was resting on his magnificent bed. Judith's beauty amazed and attracted him. How wonderful to have such a woman literally throwing herself into his arms! What a wonderful prospect it was of conquering a city full of such beautiful women! Judith flattered the general. She also explained to him that her people's God had abandoned them because they had sinned. That was why she had decided to change camps. But the general should nevertheless give the orders necessary to allow her to go each morning to the ravine to pray.

Holofernes held a magnificent banquet in honour of the woman he meant to seduce. He retired with her into his tent that evening but was completely drunk.

Judith kills Holofernes   13: 4–10

Judith's prayer shows clearly that God alone was the source of her strength. That God acts through the weak of this world had been demonstrated when David defeated Goliath.

Standing beside the bed, Judith murmured to herself: "Lord God, to whom all strength belongs, make my hands successful in what they are about to do for the greater glory of Jerusalem." (. . .) With that she went up to the bedpost by Holofernes' head and took down his sword; coming closer to the bed she grabbed him by the hair and said, "Make me strong today, Lord God of Israel!" With all her strength she gave two blows to his neck and cut off his head. She then rolled his body off the bed and pulled down the canopy from the bedposts. A little while later she went out and gave the head of Holofernes to her maid who put it in her food bag. The two then left the camp together, as they always did when they went to pray.

Judith then re-entered the besieged town and showed the head of their enemy to everyone. The people were amazed and filled with joy. Uzziah cried:

13: 18–20

For Christians, Mary is the new Judith who crushes the head of the serpent, the devil (cf. Gen. 3:15). The Christian liturgy uses the hymns from this book to praise her.

May you be blessed, my daughter, by God Most High, more than all the other women on the earth! Blessed be the Lord God, who guided you to cut off the head of the leader of our enemies!
Never will the trust which you have shown pass from human hearts; but they will remember the power of God for evermore.
God grant you may be always held in honour and rewarded with blessings, since you did not think about your own life when our nation was brought to its knees, but you averted our ruin, walking in the right path before our God.

The defenders then leapt to the attack. The Assyrians fled when robbed of their leader. The victory was total.

15: 9–10

You are the glory of Jerusalem!
You are the great pride of Israel!
You are the highest honour of our race! (. . .)
May you be blessed by the Lord Almighty
in all the days to come!

The end of Judith's life was that of the perfect widow. Nobody dared attack the Israelites again as long as she lived. She died at a very old age and a mourning period of seven days was decreed in her honour.

ESTHER

WILL GOD COME TO AVENGE
HIS PEOPLE?

Revenge! The cry continues to re-echo throughout the history of individuals and of groups of people.
It is understandable, when we know how distressing it must be for those whose families have been massacred
and who have been forced to live in extreme poverty.

The cry also re-echoes throughout the Bible as in the book of Esther here. This short story aims to show
that the people of God (who were forever threatened with being wiped out) used God's help to triumph
finally over those who sought their ruin. It also explains the origin of the Jewish festival of Purim, a sort of
joyous carnival celebrating the covenant of God with his people and poking fun at their enemies.

When considering the attitude we ought to take towards our enemies, the call for revenge is not the final
word in biblical revelation: Jesus pardoned those who had destroyed him even when on the cross. The
heart must be purified to a huge extent before we can reach such a loving attitude!

It is worth considering the problem posed by the book of Esther, which clearly reflects the tragic position
in which the Jews have found themselves throughout their history. It asks, "Will the lowly people God
came to save ever be able to break the vicious circle of vengeance?"

Ahasuerus was the king of Persia who reigned in Susa. Mordecai was a Jew under his authority who showed himself to be totally committed to the monarch's service. In particular, he had helped discover a plot against the king's life. He had an enemy at court, though, who was bent on his ruin: Haman.

Mordecai had a dream one day:

1: 1d–1k

The original book of Esther may have been a completely secular story. Later additions (which we know only from Greek versions) gave it a religious meaning: it showed how all the events had been foretold already by God to his faithful servant. God is the master of the story, which is presented using "apocalyptic" images (or images of the end-times).

There were cries and noise, thunder and earthquakes, and chaos over the whole earth. Then two great dragons came forward, each ready for the battle, and let out a great roar. At the sound of them every nation got ready to wage war against the nation of the just. A day of darkness and gloom, of suffering and distress, oppression and great upheaval on earth! The entire just nation was terrified at the thought of the evils awaiting it and prepared to die, crying out to God. Then from its cry, as from a little spring, there grew a great river, a flood of water. Light came as the sun rose, and the humble were raised up and destroyed the mighty.

The great king organised a magnificent banquet which ended badly. His queen, Vashti, refused to show herself before the people and the court officials; she was a very beautiful woman. Ahasuerus was irritated by this behaviour which humiliated him in front of everyone. His honour was in jeopardy so he decided to divorce her.

Which of the young girls in the royal harem was beautiful enough to be chosen as the first wife and queen? The competition was fierce: the chosen girl was Mordecai's niece, Esther.

Meanwhile, Haman had sworn to ruin Mordecai and all the Jews. His plot involved getting Ahasuerus to agree to an organised massacre to be held on the "day of destiny" (Purim). The royal decree permitting the massacre was sent out to all the provincial governors.

The Jews were in despair. It was providential that Esther was queen, but her intervention was a delicate matter since the king would not easily accept her interference in his affairs. The queen decided to take a terrible risk by trying to see the king without his having called for her.

The Jewish community then gave themselves to prayer and three days of fasting. Perhaps God would intervene. Mordecai's prayers were intense: he spoke of his confidence in a God capable of turning any situation on its head. Esther also prayed:

4: 17

A humble woman cried out to God from the depths of despair. Only he could enable his people to triumph in this desperate situation. Let him show himself again!

Remember, Lord; make yourself known at this time of danger. As for me, give me courage, King of gods and Master over all powers! Put persuasive words into my mouth when I face the lion; put hatred for our enemy into his heart, so that he may meet his end, and all those like him! As for ourselves, save us by your hand, and come to my help, for I am alone and have no one but you, Lord.

The dreadful moment came. Esther dared to come uninvited before Ahasuerus. He welcomed her and she was saved. She then invited him to eat with her along with his minister, Haman. Haman was triumphant at this proof of his success and did not know that Esther was Jewish by birth. Only the ruin of Mordecai

was lacking to make him completely happy. Ahasuerus was reminded of the plot that had been foiled thanks to Mordecai; this occurred while he was rereading the royal archives. How could he show his gratitude to such a faithful subject? When consulted, Haman thought that the king was talking about him, and suggested a triumphal procession and then found himself given the job of organising and directing the event. He was furious!

The day of the banquet arrived. The king promised to grant the queen a wish. Esther exposed the plots against her people and asked the king to have mercy on them. Haman realised that he was lost and threw himself at the queen's feet. The king was furious and ordered that Haman should be hanged.

A royal decree was issued to give justice to the Jews. Furthermore, the fates of the participants in the drama were reversed. The people joyfully massacred those who had been keen to see the ruin of the chosen race only the day before. Ahasuerus gave glory to God who is the source of all justice. The Jews praised Mordecai who declared:

10: 3a–f

"All this is God's doing. I remember the dream I had about these matters and nothing has failed to come true: the little spring that became a river, the light that shone, the sun, the flood of water. Esther is the river — she who married the king and became queen. The two dragons are Haman and myself. The nations are those that banded together to wipe out the name of Jew. The single nation is my nation, Israel, those who cried out to God and were saved."

> Mordecai's declaration underlines the lesson we should learn from this book: the Lord of Israel is all powerful. He never abandons his people, even in situations which appear hopeless.

MACCABEES,

OR
THE BOOK OF THE MARTYRS
OF ISRAEL

W hen terrible trials almost cause the destruction of a race of people, it is common for them to erect a monument to the glory of those whose resistance enabled them to survive. Thus they hope that remembering the heroes of the past will help them to hang on in the difficult times ahead.

That is the meaning of the book of Maccabees. It relates the exploits of those who successfully opposed their Greek oppressors during the persecution which began in the second century BC. The oppressors were Antiochus Epiphanes and his successors (all of whom were heirs of Alexander the Great).

The foreign princes had decided to bring unity to their territories (of which Judah was a part) by forcing them to accept the Greek religion and its accompanying world-view (this is called Hellenism). The Greeks found collaborators in Jerusalem who were traitors to their own traditions. But they were soon facing resistance from a group led by Judas Maccabaeus and his brothers. This resistance succeeded. Judah regained some measure of independence before falling under Roman rule. Two accounts report the events which took place between BC 167 and 134.

The first book of the Maccabees was written in about BC 100 and shows how the heavens (i.e. God) fought alongside the Maccabees as defenders of the Law. The persecution was a test which separated the faithful from the godless collaborators. The struggle led by the resistance was considered to be the continuation of the ancient battles recounted in the books of Judges and Kings.

The second book of the Maccabees summarises the work of Jason of Cyrene, a learned Jew who lived in the Greek world. The account has an element of the fantastic since God intervenes constantly in the battles. The author preaches a sermon while describing the events, reminding the reader that God punishes those who persecute his people. The sufferings of the righteous mean that the holy martyrs will be resurrected eventually and will enter into the glory of God.

Jason of Cyrene did show certain reservations about the descendants of the Maccabees. The members of the early resistance themselves became tyrants as they ruled over their people after they had taken power and freed Judah. Jesus was to clash against their power which the party of the Sadducees kept alive.

Christ also found himself in conflict with the Pharisees who were the heirs of those ordinary people who had created a movement of spiritual resistance to the Greek persecution.

The book of the martyrs of Israel gives on the one hand a true model of holiness but on the other, it reminds us that heroism can lose its way. Proud complacency can take its place, allowing us to forget that the Kingdom of peace and justice cannot come without the gift of God's mercy. Human beings cannot create peace and justice by their own efforts, that is, by using military means or moral pressure.

FIRST BOOK OF THE MACCABEES

Alexander the Great's generals shared out the empire at the time of his death in BC 323. Antiochus was reigning over Syria and Judaea in 167. He was a descendant of the Seleucids and was known as "Epiphanes", "manifestation of God". This arrogant man wanted to make his subjects accept the Greek religion and customs. He looted the Temple in Jerusalem with the support of collaborators there and made sacrifices to idols in the holy building.

Beginning of Greek persecution
1: 44–53, 62–6

Being faithful to the Law was interpreted as political rebellion and could lead to martyrdom. This even applied in the smallest details of daily life.

The king also sent edicts by messenger to Jerusalem and the towns of Judah, instructing them to adopt customs foreign to the country, banning burnt offerings, sacrifices and libations from the sanctuary, profaning Sabbaths and feasts, defiling the sanctuary and everything holy, building altars, shrines and temples for idols, sacrificing pigs and unclean beasts, leaving their sons uncircumcised, and prostituting themselves to all kinds of impurity and abomination, so that they should forget the Law and revoke all observance of it. Anyone not obeying the king's command was to be put to death. (. . .) Many of the people rallied to them and so committed evil in the country (. . .). Yet there were many in Israel who stood firm and found the courage to refuse unclean food. They chose death rather than allow themselves to be contaminated by such food or to profane the holy covenant, and they were executed. It was a time of dreadful retribution against Israel.

A Jewish priest called Mattathias started a holy war. His five sons were the Maccabaeus brothers. One of them, Judas, led a guerilla war from BC 166–160 following Mattathias' death. The Greco-Syrian army was beaten although superior in numbers in a similar way to the defeat of Goliath. The Jews sang the Hallel, a hymn of praise to their victorious God.

The enemy troops were beaten again despite having reinforcements. The rebels took Jerusalem and purified the desecrated Temple. This action was commemorated in later days by a Dedication feast. They were even able to reconquer parts of Galilee and areas around the Jordan.

The last days of Antiochus Epiphanes   6: 8–13

When the king heard this news he was amazed and deeply shaken; he threw himself on his bed and fell sick with grief, since things had not turned out for him as he had planned. And there he remained for many days, subject to deep and recurrent fits of melancholy, until he realised that he was dying. Then, summoning all his friends, he said to them, "I am not able to sleep, and my heart is overcome with anxiety. I have been wondering how I could have sunk into such deep distress, into the flood which now overwhelms me — I who was so generous and well-loved in my heyday. But now I recall how wrongly I acted in Jerusalem when I seized all the vessels of silver and gold there and ordered the massacre of the inhabitants of Judah for no reason at all. This, I am convinced, is why I am dying of melancholy in a foreign land."

Antiochus' "confession" is not a proven historical fact. His death in a foreign land did, however, cause his enemies to give glory to the God who had fought on the side of his people. The author of the book therefore shows the king repenting of his sins and giving glory to the Lord.

Antiochus' successor was Antiochus V. He chose for his generals to return to Judaea with an apparently unbeatable army which contained fighting elephants. The Jews fought courageously. One of them, Eleazar, went so far as to slip under the elephant he believed was carrying the king and died underneath the animal as he killed it. The Syrian army was victorious but the Greeks were divided. Antiochus V was finally forced to guarantee religious peace in the land he occupied.

A coup d'état carried Demetrius I to power. This was in BC 161. He chose a new high priest in Jerusalem but those who trusted this descendant of Aaron were quickly disillusioned. Judas Maccabaeus then restarted the resistance movement and the holy war began again.

The Syrian expeditionary force led by Nicanor was destroyed. The religious practices united the rival Jewish factions. Anyway, he was an enemy of the Temple. This army was defeated and Nicanor died following divine intervention. The unbelievers were punished!

Then Judas Maccabaeus made an alliance with the Romans. In fact, the Romans were careful not to intervene immediately and Judas was defeated eventually. He was mourned by everyone and died as a hero.

Jonathan, leader of the Jews and high priest

The Greeks seemed to have won but the intolerance of the Jewish collaborators caused a new rebellion to erupt. This time it was led by Jonathan, a brother of Judas.

The high priest at the time was Alcimus. He was a collaborator who had the nerve to destroy the wall of the Temple separating the court open to the gentiles from the one reserved for Jews. Alcimus was punished for his outrage against the holy place first by paralysis and then by death.

The collaborators failed in their attempt to get rid of Jonathan. The Syrian general, Bacchides, was beaten also. He made a pact with Jonathan and then left the country. Jonathan had won. He got rid of the unbelievers and rebuilt the Temple wall. He also had himself appointed high priest which caused new divisions since some people considered that he had seized this power wrongly. This new leader, however, knew how to divide and rule: he renewed the alliance with Rome and then made a treaty with the Spartans. He managed to restore the frontiers of David's former kingdom after obtaining powerful support from the Syrian authorities. He was trapped eventually by Tryphon, a Syrian general, and taken prisoner.

Simon the high priest and leader of the Jews

Simon, the eldest of the Maccabees, now took over. He was filled with religious ideals and gave fresh courage to the devastated Judaeans. Tryphon could not outwit Simon although he had managed to get the better of his brother. He had Jonathan put to death in his anger.

Demetrius II, who had been deposed by the rebel general Tryphon, was then restored to power. He decided to support Simon and so Israel was truly independent again for the first time since the exile. This was in BC 142. The Jews even regained access to the sea by use of a modern army. They seized the last enemy stronghold (the fortress protecting Jerusalem) in 141. Simon had another built, which later became Antonia.

The period of peace and prosperity that followed made people think that the promises made by the prophets were being fulfilled:

14: 8–15

This idyllic picture is inspired by the prophecies about the reign of the Lord, especially those of Micah.

The people farmed their land in peace; the land gave its produce, the trees of the plain their fruit. The elders sat at ease in the squares, all their talk was of their prosperity; the young men wore splendid armour. (. . .) Each man sat under his own vine and his own fig tree, and there was no one to make them afraid. No enemy was left in the land to fight them . . .

Simon encouraged the members of his people in difficult circumstances, and kept every wicked and godless man in check. He observed the Law, and gave new splendour to the Temple, enriching it with many sacred vessels.

The Jews were still dependent on the external friendships of Rome and Sparta. The new Syrian king was Antiochus VII. He had retaken the power that had temporarily been seized from his father. He was a friend of the Jews who had supported him and so he gave them the right to mint coins. He eventually took offence at Jewish independence so Simon proudly replied that he was only taking his inheritance which had belonged to his fathers by right. Antiochus tried to reconquer the country in 138 but failed.

Simon was assassinated by an ambitious son-in-law and his son, John, assumed the power over the country. The dynasty was assured of power for better or for worse. They were to keep it until the day when the Romans took advantage of their progressive decline as a ruling family.

SECOND BOOK OF THE MACCABEES

T he author of the second book went back to the days before the reign of Antiochus Epiphanes and continues the work of a certain Jason of Cyrene. Already Seleucus IV, king of Syria (187–175), had tried to pillage the Temple in Jerusalem by taking advantage of the divisions among the Jews. Seleucus' general, Heliodorus, was acting in the king's name when he tried to seize what had become a bank to support widows and orphans. The inhabitants of the city began to pray while in a state of anxiety. Heliodorus met a horseman in golden armour as he entered the Temple. The horseman was accompanied by two young men of great beauty who proceeded to beat the arrogant general. The high priest obtained the pagan's healing from God because he feared that Heliodorus would interpret this obviously divine intervention as a Jewish plot. Heliodorus was converted and announced to his king that:

3: 39

"He who has his dwelling in heaven watches over the place and defends it. He strikes down and destroys those who come to harm it."

Persecution under Antiochus

The collaborators had won. The new king, Antiochus Epiphanes, was acclaimed in the Holy City. It was scandalous! The position of high priest was sold to the highest bidder from that time onwards, and the result was religious in-fighting. Menelaus was the high priest at that time and ruled like a tyrant. The unfaithful Jews began to fight amongst themselves. Antiochus IV took advantage of the situation and looted the Temple (for the Lord was angry because of the sins of the inhabitants of the city). The persecution continued openly from that time. Faithfulness to the Law was punished severely. How can we explain all this?

6: 12–17

Now, I urge anyone who may read this book not to be dismayed at these disasters. They must believe that persecution is intended not to destroy our race but to discipline it. Indeed, when evil-doers are not left for long to their own devices but incur swift retribution, it is a sign of great benevolence. In the case of other nations, the

This declaration was inserted into the account to show that the author wanted to write a moral and religious work. God fights for his own people, but they must live as he wants them to if they are to succeed.

Master waits patiently for them to reach the full measure of their sins before he punishes them. But with us he has decided to deal differently, rather than have to punish us later, when our sins come to full measure. And so he never entirely withdraws his mercy from us; he may discipline us by some disaster, but he does not desert his own people. Let this be said simply by way of reminder.

The people of God had their heroes. It was suggested to Eleazar, a respected old man and a doctor of the Law, that he could avoid being executed if he just pretended to eat the forbidden meats. He replied:

6: 24–6

"Pretence", he said, "does not befit our time of life; many young people would suppose that Eleazar at the age of ninety had conformed to the foreigners' way of life and, because I had played this part for the sake of a brief spell of life, might themselves be led astray on my account . . . Even though for the moment I avoid execution by man, I can never, living or dead, escape the grasp of the Almighty."

The old man went to his martyrdom on his own two feet, as an example to Jews who were tempted to forget the Law. No less heroic was the action of a mother who saw six of her sons put to death. The king hoped that she would encourage the seventh to give in but she replied:

7: 27–40

Another story which praised the courage of the believers. The memory of these martyrs was to help the faithful survivors to hang on throughout the persecution. Earthly happiness was no longer the sole aim in life: the faithful ones now knew that their loyalty would earn them an eternal reward.

"My son, have pity on me; I carried you nine months in my womb and nursed you for three years, fed you and reared you to the age you are now. I implore you, my child, look at the earth and sky and everything in them. Consider how God made them out of what did not exist, and that human beings come into being in the same way. Do not fear this executioner, but prove yourself worthy of your brothers. Accept death, so that I may receive you back with them in the day of mercy."

She had hardly finished, when the young man said, "What are you all waiting for? I will not comply with the king's orders; I obey the orders of the Law given to our ancestors through Moses. As for you, who are the cause of all these evils against the Hebrews, you will certainly not escape the hands of God. We are suffering for our own sins. If, to punish and discipline us, our living Lord is briefly angry with us, he will be reconciled with us in due course. But you, unholy wretch and wickedest of villains, . . . will not escape the judgement of God the almighty, the all-seeing. Our brothers, having endured brief pain, for the sake of everlasting life have died for the covenant of God . . . I too, like my brothers, surrender my body and life for the laws of my ancestors, begging God quickly to take pity on our nation, and by trials and misfortunes to bring you to confess that he alone is God, so that with my brothers and myself there may be an end to the anger of the Almighty, rightly let loose on our whole nation."

The king fell into a rage and treated this one more cruelly than the others. (. . .) And so the last brother met his end undefiled and with perfect trust in the Lord. The mother was the last to die, after her sons.

The victory of Judaism

The author then took up the account of the Maccabaean revolt, which had already been given in the first book. He was so full of zeal when he reported the death of Antiochus Epiphanes that he even claimed Antiochus wrote to the Jews begging them to accept his son as their king!

The narrator emphasised that the victories are always due to God's help. He said this when describing the campaigns led by Judas Maccabaeus against Lysias, the general of Antiochus Eupator who had succeeded Antiochus Epiphanes. Lysias himself understood this lesson and gave the Jews the right to live according to their Law. Everyone trembled before "He who sees all". The true God triumphed.

But what a disappointment! The Jews lost many men during a campaign against Idumea, and God seemed to be "fighting" very half-heartedly. The explanation was simple: some of the soldiers had not obeyed the Law. They were punished and sacrifices of intercession were offered on their behalf.

12: 43–6

Judas' fine and noble action was prompted by his belief in the resurrection. For if he had not expected the fallen soldiers to rise again, it would have been useless and foolish to pray for the dead. Whereas if he had in view the splendid reward reserved for those whose death is holy, the thought was holy and devout. Hence, he had this expiatory sacrifice offered for the dead, so that they might be released from their sin.

The author of the book (or perhaps an editor writing later) explains the belief in resurrection here. Only resurrection can explain the practice of offering up sacrifices to allow the sins of dead men to be pardoned. This practice was to be inherited by Christianity.

The peace did not last although it remained clear that God was still with his people. Antiochus V caused Menelaus, the traitor, to be executed. The king's army was defeated at Modein despite his use of elephants. Eventually an outbreak of troubles in Antioch prevented Antiochus from continuing the struggle and so Judas was victorious.

The struggle against Nicanor

The writer then related how Nicanor tried to beat down the people he so hated (this man was a general to Demetrius and had seized Antiochus' throne). The writer added a number of details to the account of these events given in the first book of Maccabees to illustrate the merciless struggle between the godless pagans and those who were faithful to the Law. The heavenly powers were increasingly involved with the fighting on earth. Then the decisive battle arose. The Jews called on the God who had once destroyed the Assyrians as they besieged Jerusalem. The Jews' victory was total. Nicanor was killed, beheaded and his head displayed on the walls of Jerusalem.

"That was how it happened," concluded the narrator, "that was how the Jews regained their independence."

JOB

Why do suffering and death exist? Why does God allow evil if he is good?

Men and women have been seeking answers to these questions since the dawn of time. But even the cleverest explanations, which try to justify God, are rather weak.

It was the same in Israel. People started by thinking that suffering was a collective punishment when any member of the group committed a sin. Ezekiel proclaimed that it was impossible to accuse God of being so unjust; this was during the exile. He then said that every person was responsible for their own actions and was rewarded or punished according to their individual merits or sins.

This new idea clashed with brutal reality in the absence of any belief in an eternal life and in justice beyond death: then, as now, wicked people sometimes had happy lives while good people often suffered.

The book of Job is a long poem demonstrating the uselessness of all the explanations people had thought up. Job was a good man who experienced every possible evil. His friends tried to persuade him that what had happened was fair and that he must be a very guilty man. Job protested at this saying it was not true. His despair reached the point where he wondered whether God himself was unjust. He wanted to see God, to "have it out with him". When God spoke at last it was not to give the expected explanation but to ask Job what right he had to call his God to account. Job's friends had shown their ignorance, and Job himself should accept that he was just one of God's creatures and stop complaining! The only possible attitude toward suffering is trust in God. The end of the book shows how God generously rewarded Job's trust.

We will find evil shocking. Jesus himself was crucified despite his innocence and yet gave no explanation for it. He only demonstrated that it was possible to conquer evil through love and that this victory was the source of true life. The debate in the book of Job was introduced in a vivid account written in the style of oriental tales. Job was a man of total integrity. His material success, his fortune and his numerous children were a sign that he was favoured by God. The Lord was also very proud of his servant and quoted him as an example to his council. But Satan was a member of that council and questioned Job's integrity. "It is easy for him to be good because everything he does is successful. Let God put him to the test!"

God was annoyed and accepted the challenge. Job lost first his goods, then his children and finally his health, all one after the other. He refused to curse God although abandoned as on a dung-heap. In fact he was going through an intense inner struggle. He expressed his torment one day when his friends came to see him to sympathise with him.

3: 1–7

Job broke the silence and cursed the day of his birth:
If only the day on which I was born could be wiped out, and the
night when they gave the news that a boy was going to be born.
May that day be darkness (. . .), may no light shine on it. (. . .)
And may that night be sterile, without any cries of joy!

3: 11–16

Why was I not still-born,
or why did I not die as I left the womb?
Why were there knees to receive me,
breasts for me to suck?
Now I should be lying in peace,
in a deep and restful sleep (. . .),
or, like a child which dies before birth, I should not have existed,
like little ones that never see the light. (. . .)

3: 20–3

Why give light to a man of grief?
Why give life to those whose hearts are bitter,
who long for a death that never comes,
and hunt for it more than for buried treasure? (. . .)
Why give light to one who does not see his way,
whom God shuts in all alone?

Job cried out of despair to ask why he should continue living if life consisted of nothing but suffering? The nothingness and oblivion of death (as it was then perceived) were preferable by far.

The oldest of Job's friends suggested his own explanation: evil comes only to the guilty. Job was a good man, of course, but was he really so good in God's view? Job should repent and God would then take him back into his favour.

4: 1–9

Eliphaz of Teman spoke next. He said:
You have taught many others,
giving strength to feeble hands;
your words supported any who were unsure
and strengthened every knee that stumbled.
And now your turn has come, and you lose patience,
as soon as it touches you, you are overwhelmed!
Think back: has an innocent man ever lost his life?
Where then have the honest been wiped out?
I speak from experience: those who plough with evil actions
and sow disaster, reap just that.
Under the breath of God, they die (. . .).

God was obviously allowing Job to suffer. Why was God pursuing him in this way? God treated him as though he was important rather than as if he were just a passing breath of wind, so why did God deny him peace? Perhaps Job had sinned, but it was so insignificant — why was God so bothered about it?

6: 1–3

Job spoke next. He said:
If only my misery could be weighed,
and all my troubles be put together on the scales!
But they would be heavier than the sands of the seas (. . .).

6: 8–10

Will no one hear my prayer?
If only God himself would answer my request!
If only God would crush me!
If only he would let his hand do away with me!
Then I would at least have the comfort of knowing
that I never rebelled against the words of the Holy One.

7: 16–21

Leave me then, for my days are only a breath.
What are human beings that you should take them so seriously,
subjecting them to your scrutiny,
that morning after morning you should examine them
and at every moment test them?
Won't you even take your eyes off me
long enough for me to swallow my saliva?
Suppose I have sinned, what have I done to you,
you tireless watcher of humanity?
Why do you choose me as your target?
Why should I be a burden to you?
Can you not tolerate my sin, not overlook my fault?

For soon I shall be lying in the dust,
you will look for me and I shall be no more.

Job's friends were shocked by his words. His suffering implied that he must have done something terrible, because God was just. Job would have to acknowledge it and stop blaspheming by seeming to doubt God's perfection.

9: 1–3
Job spoke next. He said:
Indeed, I know it is as you say:
how could anyone claim to be just before God?
Anyone trying to argue matters with him,
could not give him one answer in a thousand.

Job protested that God's behaviour was inexplicable. It was impossible to ask him for reasons because he was stronger than he was, and Job would only feel crushed if he acted against him.

9: 15–16
Even if I am righteous, what point is there in answering him?
I can only plead for mercy with my judge!
Even if he saw fit to answer my cry for help,
I cannot believe he would listen to what I said (. . .).

9: 19–22
Shall I try force? Look how strong he is!
Or go to court? But who will summon him?
If I prove myself righteous, his mouth may condemn me;
even if I am innocent, he may declare me guilty.
But am I innocent? I am no longer sure.
Therefore I dare to say: he destroys innocent and guilty alike. (. . .)

10: 15
Woe to me, if I am guilty.
Even if I am innocent, I dare not lift my head.
I am so overwhelmed with shame and overcome with sorrow.

13: 4–7
As for you, you are only imposters, all worthless as doctors!
Will no one teach you to be quiet?
That is the only wisdom that becomes you! (. . .)
Do you mean to defend God by using false words
and dishonest argument?

13: 13–16
Be quiet! Kindly let me do the talking,
no matter what happens to me. (. . .)

Job's friends should stop saying stupid things by giving "explanations" which explained precisely nothing.

Let him kill me if wants to, I have no other hope
than to justify my conduct in his eyes,
And this is what will save me,
for a wicked man would not dare to appear before him. (. . .)

13: 18, 22–5

I shall proceed as in a court of law,
knowing that I am innocent. (. . .)
I shall speak and you will answer.
How many faults and crimes have I committed?
Tell me what I did wrong, what my sin was!
Why do you hide your face
and look on me as your enemy?
Do you want to frighten a leaf blown about by the wind
or chase a dry straw?

14: 1–3

A human being, born of woman,
has a short life but full of trouble.
Like a flower, such a one blossoms and withers,
passing as quickly as a shadow.
And this is the creature on whom you fix your gaze,
and bring to judgement before you!

14: 13–16

Will no one hide me in Sheol,
and shelter me there till your anger is past,
fixing a certain day for calling me to mind?
Can the dead come back to life?
Day after day of my service, I should be waiting
for my relief to come.
Then you would call, and I should answer,
you would want to see once more what you have made . . .
Then you would stop spying on my sin (. . .).

Job's friends were more and more shocked and accused him of having blasphemous ideas:

15: 4–6

You suppress the fear of God,
you make it seem useless to speak to God.
Your very fault prompts you to speak like this,
and that is why you talk in this cunning way.
Your own mouth condemns you (. . .).

Job showed the strength of his faith by continuing to protest. God should be careful that his fits of anger did not crush such fragile creatures. God should at least shelter Job temporarily to prevent his complete destruction. God could then show himself to be less severe after his anger had gone.

Sheol was the name the Hebrews gave to the country of the dead.

19: 1–3

Job spoke next. He said:

How much longer are you going to torment me
and crush me with your speeches?
You have insulted me ten times already:
are you not ashamed of ill-treating me?

19: 22–7

Must you persecute me just as God does,
and give my body no peace?
How I wish that my words could be recorded,
inscribed on some monument
with an iron chisel and engraving tool,
and cut into the rock for ever!
I know that my Defender lives
and that he will rise up at last, on the dust of the earth.
After my awakening, he will set me close to him,
and from my flesh I shall look on God.
The One I then see will be on my side:
my eyes will not be gazing on a stranger.

Job no longer knew where to turn for justice but he had a sort of hope despite everything. He saw that, beyond death, justice could be done by a "defender".

21: 6–7, 17

I myself am appalled at the very thought,
and my flesh creeps.
Why do the wicked still live on?
Why do they become even more powerful as they grow older?
(. . .)
Do we often see the light of the wicked put out,
or see him meet with disaster?
Does God in anger ever destroy his possessions? (. . .)

But Job's hope seemed to be contradicted by the facts. Experience showed that the wicked often seemed to succeed at everything they did and yet had no suffering.

21: 30–4

On the day of disaster, the wicked is spared,
on the day of anger, he is kept safe.
And who is there then to reproach him for his deeds
and to pay him back for the things he has done?
He is carried away to the cemetery,
and a watch is kept at his tomb.
The earth from the ravine lies easy on him,
and the whole population walk behind.
So what sense is there in your empty words of comfort?
Your answers are the result of lies!

23: 8–9, 13–16

Where is God? The eternal cry of humanity crushed by misfortune.

If I go to the east, he is not there;
or to the west, I still cannot see him.
If I seek him in the north, he is not to be found,
invisible as ever, if I turn to the south. (. . .)

But once he has made up his mind, who can change it?
He carries out whatever he plans.
There is no doubt that he will carry out my sentence,
like so many other decrees that he has made.
That is why I am full of fear before him.
The more I think, the more afraid I become.
God has made me lose my courage.

31: 35
Will no one give me a hearing?
I have said my last word; now let God reply!

God then showed himself to Job in the heart of the storm. Referring to all of his creation he makes a long speech:

38: 2–5

God "put Job in his place". His real sin was presuming to tell his Creator, who was much greater than him in every way, how to behave.

Who is this man who conceals my purposes
with his ignorant words?
Brace yourself like a fighter;
I am going to ask the questions, and you are to inform me!
Where were you when I laid the earth's foundations?
Tell me, since you are so well-informed!
Who decided its dimensions, do you know?
Or who stretched the measuring line across it? (. . .)

38: 12–13
Have you ever in your life given orders to the morning
or sent the dawn to its post,
to grasp the earth by its edges
and shake the wicked out of it? (. . .)

38: 16–17
Have you been right down to the sources of the sea
and walked about at the bottom of the Abyss?
Have you been shown the gates of Death,
have you seen the door-keepers of the Shadow dark as death?

No doubt Job's friends did say stupid things in their attempts to justify God but Job himself now humbly agreed to acknowledge his own ignorance, instead of trying to tell God how he should behave.

42: 1–6

This was the answer Job gave to the Lord:
I know that you are all-powerful:
every plan you make, you are able to perform.
I was the man who misrepresented your intentions
with my ignorant words.
You have told me about great works that I cannot understand,
about marvels which are beyond me, of which I know nothing . . .
Before, I knew you only from what others told me
but now, I have seen you with my own eyes.
I take back what I have said,
and repent in dust and ashes.

Job saw how arrogant he had been when he remembered all that God had done. He had tried to take issue with God. He admitted to God that he did not understand him. So he repented of his arrogant behaviour and decided to trust.

Job's response showed that he had eventually learned true wisdom which involved acknowledging his insignificance before God. The Lord could then reward him by returning everything Job had lost and doubling it. Job was then free to live a long and happy life.

THE PSALMS

**STATEMENTS
OF THE LOVE OF
GOD'S PEOPLE
FOR THEIR LORD**

Psalm **1** How blessed is anyone who rejects the advice
of the wicked
and does not stand in the path that sinners take,
nor sit in the company of cynics,
but who delights in the law of the Lord
and murmurs his law day and night.
Such a one is like a tree planted near streams;

Research using documents can sometimes enable us to find out about the history of a community or a family.

It cannot help us to imagine how the members of that group experienced their own history, though, unless it contains statements by the people themselves. Letters in which people express their impressions and feelings are particularly useful.

That is what we find in the book of Psalms. These prayers show us the very soul of Israel as the people talked to their God about their problems, their beliefs, and events which affected the lives of individuals and groups.

The people of God have always composed hymns to the glory of their Lord: the song of Miriam after the crossing of the Sea of Reeds (Exod. 15); the song of Deborah after the victory over the Canaanites (Judg. 5: 2–31); the song of Hannah when told she was going to have a son (1 Sam. 2: 1–9). Also, David was a poet-king and author of a great many songs which were collected together systematically soon after his death. The psalter we possess today contains several collections of poems which have been put together over the years.

The ancient songs can be expressed in fresh ways when adapting to new circumstances but then they lose their immediate link with the events causing their composition: their significance becomes more general. The beauty of the psalms is that they speak about human situations which are typical and so are always up-to-date. We still use them in our prayers today within the official Church liturgy.

They are easy to use because they are all so different. They all express great religious feeling such as wonder and praise for divine Creation, and for God's help throughout history; there are prayers for times of trouble; some ask forgiveness of sins committed while others offer thanksgiving for the Lord's goodness; some psalms are songs of joy in honour of the king God has given us, or in honour of the Holy City of Jerusalem; some express the hope of salvation and yet others the hope of the Messiah; there is the rather anxious wait for the "Day of the Lord"; and a loving meditation on the divine Law.

A prayer originally focusing on the interests of a specific group will become gradually more and more relevant until it forms part of God's great design for all humanity. These texts allow us to see how a spiritual life for God's people develops.

Jesus was following this same pattern when one day he taught his disciples the "Our Father". This prayer called them to open their minds and hearts to the vision of the Kingdom and to live in trust and love. The Psalms were the first prayers to express the spiritual meaning which Christ later condensed into a few words. He also led us towards the understanding to which they guide us.

it bears fruit in season
and its leaves never wither.
Every project succeeds.
How different the wicked, how different!
They are just like chaff blown around by the wind.
On the day of judgement they will not stand,
like sinners in a gathering of the righteous.
For the Lord watches over the path of the righteous,
but the path of the wicked is doomed.

There are two possible attitudes to God and we must choose between them: the believer decides to take that road which is the way of the Law leading to salvation.

Psalm 6

A continuation of Jeremiah's lament: a believer calls for help from the midst of difficulties and persecution. God seems sometimes to have forgotten him but he continues to trust in him.

Lord, do not rebuke me in your anger,
in your fury, do not come to punish me.
Have pity on me, Lord, for I am fading away.
Heal me, Lord, my bones are shaken,
my spirit is shaken to its very depths.
But, Lord, how long must I wait for you?
Lord, relent and save my life,
rescue me because of your faithful love.
For in death no one can remember you:
who could sing your praises in Sheol?
I am worn out with groaning.
Every night I drench my pillow, I soak my bed with tears
and my eyes are worn out with grief.
My enemies are full of arrogance!
Keep away from me, you evil-doers!
For the Lord has heard the sound of my weeping.
The Lord has heard my pleas for help.
He will accept my prayer.
Let all my enemies retreat, confused, shaken,
and suddenly overcome with shame.

Psalm 8

A hymn to the God of Creation. People can only praise his name when they remember the way in which the Lord called them to manage Nature and thus to share in his splendour.

O Lord our Lord,
how majestic is your name throughout the world!
Your praise reaches higher than the heavens.
When they declare your praise, the mouths of children and tiny babies
stand like a fortress, in the face of your enemies;
to crush the enemy and the rebel.
I look up at your heavens, shaped by your fingers,
at the moon and stars which you set in place,
what are human beings that you spare a thought for them,
or the child of Adam that you care for him?
Yet you have made him a little less than a god.
You have crowned him with glory and beauty,
you made him ruler over the works of your hands,
and put all things under his feet:
sheep and cattle, all of them,
and even the wild beasts,
birds in the sky, fish in the sea,
which make their way across the ocean.

O Lord, our Lord,
how majestic is your name throughout the world!

15

O Lord, who can find a home in your tent,
who can live on your holy mountain?
Whoever lives a blameless life,
who acts justly,
who speaks the truth from the heart,
without letting his tongue run away from him;
he who does not wrong a friend,
and does not make others have a low opinion
of his neighbour,
he who condemns those who disobey God,
but honours those who fear the Lord.
He who stands by his word at any cost,
who asks no interest on loans,
who would never take a bribe to harm the innocent.
No one who lives like this can ever be shaken.

It is only possible to meet with God if we live according to justice and truth. It is impossible to approach the Lord if we do not agree to live in his way. To "fear" God means to respect him.

16

Protect me, O God, my refuge is in you.
I said to the Lord, "You are my Lord,
my happiness is in none of the spirits of the earth." (. . .)

The Lord is my birthright, my cup;
you alone guarantee my destiny.
The measuring-line marks out a delightful place for me,
my birthright is all I could wish for.

I bless the Lord who is my counsellor,
even at night my heart instructs me.
I keep the Lord always before me,
for with him at my right hand, nothing can shake me.

So my heart rejoices, my soul delights,
my body too will rest secure,
for you will not abandon me to the depths of death,
you will not let your friend finish up in a pit.
You will teach me the path of life,
in your presence joy that knows no end,
at your right hand delight for ever.

The psalmist expresses the choice which enabled him to live in complete trust. He was not afraid of death any more, for he was sure that God was calling him to abundant life.

This text expresses a belief in resurrection and comes at the end of a long reflection on the meaning of life.

This long and painful lament comes from an innocent person who is being persecuted, but concludes with a declaration of trust. Righteous people contribute to the coming of God's reign through the sufferings they have accepted. Jesus identified himself with this servant. He cried out the first verse of this psalm at the moment of his death. Analysis of the Evangelists' texts shows how the entire Passion illustrates this psalm.

Psalm **22**

My God, my God, why have you forsaken me?
The words of my groaning do nothing to save me.
My God, I call by day but you do not answer,
at night, but I find no rest.
Yet you are the Holy One, and you make your home in the praises of Israel.
Our ancestors put their trust in you and you set them free.
They called to you for help and you rescued them.
They trusted in you and you did not disappoint them.
But I am a worm, less than human,
scorned by all mankind, ridiculed by the people.
All who see me jeer at me;
they sneer and shake their heads,
"He put his trust in the Lord, let the Lord set him free!
Let him deliver him, as he took such delight in him."

It was you who brought me out of my mother's womb
and soothed me on my mother's breast.
I have relied on you from my birth;
ever since I was born I have belonged to you.
Do not stay away from me, for trouble is upon me,
and I have no one to help me!

Many bulls are surrounding me, wild bulls are closing in on me.
Ravenous and roaring lions open their jaws at me.

My strength is trickling away, my bones are all disjointed;
my heart has turned to wax. (. . .)
My mouth is dry as earthenware,
my tongue sticks to the roof of my mouth.
You lay me down in the dust of death.
A pack of dogs surrounds me.
A gang of villains is closing in on me,
ready to hack off my hands and my feet.
I can count every one of my bones.
People stare at me and gloat.
They divide my garments among them
and cast lots for my clothing.
Lord, do not stay away from me!
You are my strength, come quickly to my help.
Rescue my soul from the sword,

the one life I have from the grasp of the dog!
Save me from the lion's mouth,
my poor life from the wild bulls' horns!
I shall sing of your name to my brothers.
I will praise you in the assembly of God's people:
"You who fear the Lord, praise him!
All the race of Jacob, honour him!
Fear him, all the race of Israel!"
For he has not despised
nor disregarded the poverty of the poor;
he has not turned his face away from them,
but has listened to their cry for help.
It is you I praise among the crowds of God's people.
I will carry out my vows before all who fear him.

The poor will eat and be filled.
Those who seek the Lord will praise him,
"May your heart live for ever."
The whole wide world will remember
and return to the Lord.
All the families, all the nations will bow down before him.
For kingly power belongs to the Lord, ruler of the nations.
All who prosper on earth will bow before him.
All who go down to the dust will revere him.
And those who are dead, their descendants will serve him,
they will proclaim his name to generations still to come;
and they will tell of his saving justice to a people yet unborn!
For he has brought justice!

Psalm **23** The Lord is my shepherd, I lack nothing.
He lets me lie down in grassy meadows.
He leads me by quiet streams, to restore my spirit.
He guides me in paths of saving justice because
of his name's sake.
Even were I to walk in a ravine as dark as death
I should fear no danger, for you are at my side.
Your staff and your crook are there to soothe me.
You prepare a table for me under the eyes of my enemies;
you anoint my head with oil; my cup brims over.
Kindness and faithful love pursue me every day of my life.
I make my home in the house of the Lord for all time to come.

The Lord is the shepherd of his people! This image means a great deal to a people of shepherds and is also present in the writings of the prophets. It was used by Jesus who was the "Good Shepherd".

Psalm **27**

The Lord is my light and my salvation.
Whom should I fear?
The Lord is the fortress of my life. Whom should I dread?
When the wicked advance against me to eat me up,
they, my opponents, my enemies,
are the ones who stumble and fall.
Though an army pitch camp against me, my heart will not fear.
Though war break out against me, my trust will never be shaken.
One thing I ask of the Lord, one thing I seek:
to dwell in the Lord's house all the days of my life;
to enjoy the sweetness of the Lord, to seek out his temple.
For he hides me away under his roof on the day of evil,
he hides me in the secret places of his tent,
he sets me high on a rock.
Now I can hold my head up high when I face
the enemies who surround me;
I will come into his tent to bring my offering,
my sacrifice of praise. (. . .)

The believer is filled with a feeling of security, even when confronted with battles to be fought, since he has complete confidence in the Lord.

Psalm **51**

Have mercy on me, O God, in your faithful love,
in your tenderness wipe away my sins.
Wash me clean from my guilt, purify me from my sin.
For I am well aware of what I have done wrong.
My sin is constantly in my mind.
Against you, you alone, I have sinned,
I have done what you see to be wrong.
So that your saving justice may be seen
when you pass sentence,
and your victory may be evident
when you give your judgement,
remember, I was guilty from the moment I was born,
a sinner from the moment I was conceived.
But you delight in a sincere heart,
and in secret you teach me wisdom.
Purify me with hyssop till I am clean,
wash me till I am whiter than snow.
Let me hear the sound of joy and gladness,
and the bones you have crushed will dance.
Turn your face away from my sins, and wipe away all my guilt.

The psalmist is aware of his sin and calls humbly for God's forgiveness. The Lord leads him back to life and enables him to offer a purified heart which is the only "sacrifice" really able to please God.

God, create in me a clean heart.
Give me once again a right spirit.
Do not push me far away from your presence,
do not take your holy spirit away from me.
Give me back the joy of your salvation,
let your generosity flood through me.
I shall teach the wicked your paths, and sinners will return to you.
Set me free from the guilt of murder, God, God of my salvation,
and my tongue will shout aloud of your saving justice.
Lord, open my lips, and my mouth will speak out your praise.
For you take no pleasure in sacrifice;
you do not desire burnt offerings.
The sacrifice that pleases you is a broken spirit;
you never reject a broken, contrite heart. (. . .)

God is the source of all life, so
the believer who discovered
God's splendour expresses his
heartfelt desire to come nearer
to him.

Im **63** God, you are my God, I search for you;
my heart thirsts for you, my body longs for you,
as in a dry and thirsty land where there is no water.
I have gazed on you in the sanctuary,
seeing your power and your glory.
For your faithful love is better than life itself;
my lips will praise you.
Thus I will bless you all my life,
I will lift up my hands in your name.
All my longings will be fulfilled as at a banquet,
a song of joy on my lips and praise in my mouth.
On my bed when I think of you,
I meditate on you in the watches of the night.
For you have always been my help;
safe in the shadow of your wings I rejoice.
My heart clings to you,
your right hand supports me. (. . .)

Psalm **88** Lord, God of my salvation,
when I cry out to you in the night,
may my prayer reach your presence. Hear my cry for help.
For I am filled with misery, my life is on the brink of Sheol.
People already think of me as dead. I am done for.
I am left alone among the dead, like a corpse lying in a grave,
whom you remember no more, cut off from your protection.
You have plunged me to the bottom of the grave,
into the darkness, into the depths.
Your anger pours over me, like waves crashing against me.
You have driven my friends away from me,
you made me repulsive to them.
I am imprisoned, with no escape.
My eyes are worn out with suffering.
I call out to you, Lord, all day long,
I stretch out my hands to you. (. . .)
I cry out to you, Lord,
every morning my prayer comes before you.
Why, Lord, do you push me away?
Why do you turn your face away from me? (. . .)

The believer feels as though God has abandoned him when overwhelmed by trials and tribulations. If only he would stop hiding himself and return!

Psalm **103** Bless the Lord, O my soul,
from the depths of my being, bless his holy name.
Bless the Lord, my soul.
Never forget all his acts of kindness.
He forgives all your sins, and cures all your diseases.
He redeems your life from the pit,
and crowns you with faithful love and tenderness;
he makes you content with good things all your life,
and renews your youth like an eagle's.
The Lord acts with righteousness,
with justice to all who are oppressed.
He revealed his ways to Moses,
his great deeds to the children of Israel.
The Lord is tenderness and pity,
slow to anger and rich in faithful love;
his anger does not last for ever,
nor does his displeasure remain for all time.
He does not treat us as our sins deserve.
He does not pay us back for what we have done wrong.
As high as the heaven above the earth,

so strong is his faithful love for those who fear him.
As far as the east is from the west,
so far does he put our faults from us.
As tenderly as a father treats his children,
so the Lord treats those who fear him.
He knows what we are made of,
he remembers that we are dust.
As for a human person — his days are like grass,
he blooms like the wild flowers.
As soon as the wind blows he is gone,
never to be seen there again.
But the Lord's faithful love for those who fear him
is from eternity and lasts for ever;
and his saving justice carries on for their children's children;
as long as they keep his covenant, and carefully obey his will.
The Lord has fixed his throne in heaven,
his kingly power rules over all.
Bless the Lord, all his angels,
mighty warriors who fulfil his commands,
attentive to the sound of his words.
Bless the Lord, all his armies, servants who fulfil his wishes.
Bless the Lord, all his works, in every place where he rules.
Bless the Lord, my soul.

104
Bless the Lord, O my soul.
Lord, my God, how great you are!
Clothed in majesty and splendour, wearing the light as a robe!
You stretch out the heavens like a tent,
and you build your palace even higher than that!
You make the clouds your chariot,
you glide on the wings of the wind.
You appoint the winds as your messengers,
and flames of fire as your servants.
You fixed the earth on its foundations,
for ever and ever it shall not be shaken.
You covered it with the oceans like a garment,
and the waters covered the mountains.
At your reproof the waters fled,
at the voice of your thunder they rushed away,
flowing over mountains, down valleys,
to the place you had fixed for them.

Praise be to God whose love shows itself in so many ways. In particular, praise him for the way he forgives people despite his intimate knowledge of their weakness.

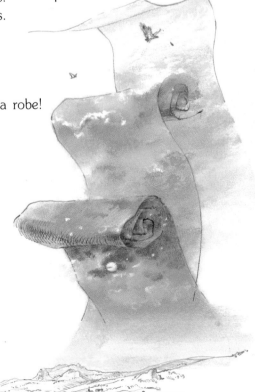

This psalm was inspired by the famous hymn of the Pharaoh Akenaton to the one true God. It exalts God through the splendours of his Creation, which are described lyrically. God is the source of life — of all forms of life, and the psalmist takes pleasure in mentioning them all.

You made a limit they were not to cross,
they were not to return and cover the earth.
In the valleys you opened up springs,
running down between the mountains,
supplying water for all the wild animals.
The wild asses quench their thirst.
On their banks the birds of the air make their nests,
they sing among the leaves.
From the heavens above you water the mountains,
satisfying the earth with the fruit of your works.
For cattle you make the grass grow,
and for people the plants they need:
to produce food from the earth,
and wine to cheer people's hearts,
oil to make their faces glow,
food to make them strong in heart.
The trees of the Lord have as much water as they need,
the cedars of Lebanon which he sowed.
There the birds build their nests,
on the highest branches the stork makes its home.
For the wild goats there are the mountains,
in the crags the rabbits find refuge.
He made the moon to mark the seasons,
the sun knows when to set.
You bring on darkness, and night falls,
when all the forest beasts roam around;
young lions roar for their prey, asking God for their food.
The sun rises and away they steal, back to their lairs to lie down.
Then man goes out to work, to labour till evening falls.
How many are your works, Lord.
You made them all so wisely!
The earth is full of your creatures.
Then there is the sea, with its vast expanses
teeming with countless creatures, creatures both large and small.
There ships pass to and fro,
and the seadragon whom you made to make you laugh.
They all depend upon you, to feed them when they need it.
You provide the food they gather.
You open your hand and they take their fill.
Turn away your face and they panic;
take back their breath and they die and become dust again.

Send out your breath and life begins;
you renew the face of the earth. Glory to the Lord for ever!
May the Lord find joy in his creatures!
At his glance the earth trembles,
at his touch the mountains pour out smoke.
I shall sing to the Lord all my life,
make music for my God as long as I live.
May he be pleased with my song, for the Lord gives me joy.
May sinners disappear from the earth,
and the wicked exist no more! Bless the Lord, my soul.

n **119** 1–3
How blessed are those whose way is blameless,
who walk in the Law of the Lord!
Blessed are those who follow his commands,
who seek him with all their hearts,
and, doing no evil, who walk in his ways.
9–10
How can a young man keep himself on the right path?
By keeping your words.
With all my heart I seek you,
do not let me stray from your commandments. (. . .)
25
I grovel in the dust;
true to your word, pick me up again.
29
Keep me far from the way of lies,
grant me the grace of your Law.

Only a small portion of this very long psalm has been printed here. The psalm has been called a summary of divine love or, in other words, a condensed account of what God's love means. The believer considered the paths of his life and remembered how God led his people by the gift of the Torah, the Law leading to life. He then appreciated the good life obtained by obeying that Law.

34–5

Give me understanding and I will keep your Law,
and follow it with all my heart.
Guide me in the way of your commandments,
for that is my delight.

169–176

May my cry come up to you, O Lord.
Give me understanding by your word.
May my prayer come up to you, rescue me as you have promised.
May my lips proclaim your praise, for you teach me your will.
May my tongue speak of your promise,
for all your commandments are righteous.
May your hand be there to help me,
since I have chosen to follow your commands.
I long for your salvation, Lord, your Law is my delight.
May I live only to praise you, may your judgements be my help.
I am wandering like a lost sheep. Come and look for your servant.

Psalm **124**

The psalm starts with a threat to the whole nation; then the psalmist emphasises that Israel would have been lost without the Lord. But God freed the bird caught in the trap. Praise to his name!

If the Lord had not been on our side
— let Israel repeat it —
if the Lord had not been on our side
when our enemies attacked us,
they would have swallowed us alive in the heat of their anger.
Then water was washing us away.
A torrent was running right over us;
running right over us then were raging waters.
Blessed be the Lord who snatched us from their teeth!
We escaped like a bird from the fowlers' net.
The net was broken and we escaped.
Our help is in the name of the Lord, who made heaven and earth.

Psalm **126**

The return from exile was a new exodus and announced the day when the Lord would gather together all his people. At present they were scattered all over the earth: "then the seed that fell to earth will bear fruit", as Jesus said.

When the Lord brought the captives back to Zion, we lived in a dream;
then our mouths were filled with laughter, and our lips with song.
Then the nations kept saying,
"What great deeds the Lord has done for them!"
Yes, the Lord did great deeds for us, and we were overjoyed.
Lord, bring our people back from captivity
like torrents gushing out in the desert!
Those who sow in tears sing as they reap.
He went off, went off weeping, carrying the seed.
He comes back, comes back singing, bringing in his sheaves.

130 From the depths I call to you, Lord.
Lord, hear my cry.
Listen attentively to the sound of my prayer!
If you kept a record of our sins,
Lord, who could stand in front of you?
But with you is forgiveness, that we may learn to fear you.
I rely, my whole being relies, Lord, on your promise.
My whole being hopes in the Lord,
more than watchmen for daybreak;
more than watchmen for daybreak let Israel hope in the Lord.
For with the Lord is faithful love: he redeems with a generous heart. He will redeem Israel from all its sins.

136 Alleluia! Give thanks to the Lord for he is good,
for his faithful love lasts for ever.
Give thanks to the God of gods, for his faithful love lasts for ever.
Give thanks to the Lord of lords, for his faithful love lasts for ever.
He alone works wonders, for his faithful love lasts for ever.
In wisdom he made the heavens, for his faithful love lasts for ever.
He set the earth firm on the waters, for his faithful love lasts
for ever.
He made the great lights, for his faithful love lasts for ever.
The sun to rule the day, for his faithful love lasts for ever.
Moon and stars to rule the night, for his faithful love
lasts for ever.
Moon and stars to rule the night, for his faithful love lasts
for ever.
He killed the first-born sons of Egypt, for his faithful love
lasts for ever.
He brought Israel out from among them, for his faithful love
lasts for ever.
With mighty hand and outstretched arm, for his faithful love
lasts for ever.
He divided the Sea of Reeds in two, for his faithful love
lasts for ever.
He let Israel pass through the middle, for his faithful love
lasts for ever.
And drowned Pharaoh and all his army, for his faithful love
lasts for ever.
He led his people through the desert, for his faithful love
lasts for ever.
He killed mighty Kings, for his faithful love lasts for ever.

The Jews call this psalm the "Great Hallel" (action of Grace). It celebrates God's work of Creation, but also the story of the people of God: every opportunity to sing of the love of the Lord is a good one.

Slaughtered famous kings, for his faithful love lasts for ever.
Sihon king of the Amorites, for his faithful love lasts for ever.
And Og king of Bashan, for his faithful love lasts for ever.
He gave them their land as a birthright, for his faithful love lasts for ever.
A birthright to his servant Israel, for his faithful love lasts for ever.
He kept us in mind when we were humbled, for his faithful love lasts for ever.
And rescued us from our enemies, for his faithful love lasts for ever.
He provides food for all living creatures, for his faithful love lasts for ever.
Give thanks to the God of heaven, for his faithful love lasts for ever.

Psalm **137** By the rivers of Babylon we sat and wept
when we remembered Zion.
On the poplars there we had hung up our harps.
For there our gaolers asked us to sing them a song,
our captors to make them happy.
"Sing us one of the songs of Zion," they said.
How could we sing one of the Lord's songs in a foreign land?
If I forget you, Jerusalem, may my right hand wither!

The Jews sang about how homesick they were for their own land after being taken prisoner to

May my tongue stick to the roof of my mouth if I do not keep you in mind,
if I do not count Jerusalem the greatest of my joys. (. . .)

148

Alleluia! Praise the Lord from the heavens, praise him in the heights.

Praise him, all you his angels, praise him, all you his heavenly armies!
Praise him, sun and moon, praise him, all shining stars, praise him, highest heavens, praise him, waters above the heavens.
Let them praise the name of the Lord
for they were made at his command.
They were fixed in place for ever by a law that will never change.
Praise the Lord from the earth, sea-monsters and all the ocean depths,
fire and hail, snow and mist, stormy winds that obey his word,
mountains and every hill, orchards and every cedar,
wild animals and all cattle, reptiles and birds that fly,
kings of the earth and all nations, princes and all judges on earth,
young men and girls, old people and children together.
Let them praise the name of the Lord, for his name alone
is greater than all others.
His glory is above earth and heaven.
For he gives strength to his people,
so that all his faithful people praise him —
the children of Israel, the people close to him.

150

Alleluia!

Praise God in his holy place,
praise him in the heavenly firmament of his power,
praise him for his mighty deeds,
praise him for all his greatness.
Praise him with fanfare of trumpet,
praise him with harp and lyre,
praise him with tambourines and dancing,
praise him with strings and pipes,
praise him with the clamour of cymbals,
praise him with triumphant cymbals.
Let everything that breathes praise the Lord.
Alleluia!

Babylon. They thus expressed the feelings of all who know that "true life is beyond this world".

Men and women are called to sing God's praises in the same way as all of creation which, by its beauty and diversity, celebrates the splendour of the Lord.

All creation is called to praise God — like a huge orchestra.

THE PROVERBS

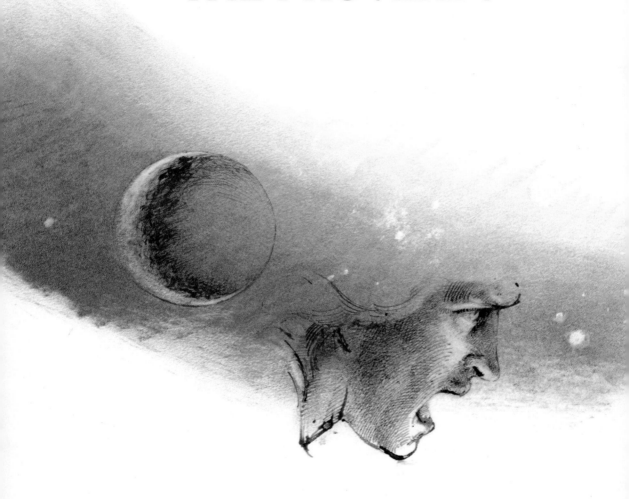

T he Jewish believers reminisced about experiences of God from their own history each time they considered how they ought to behave. The basis of their moral code was the Law of Sinai.

They did not hesitate to utilise the lessons of everyday life too, both from their own experiences, and those gleaned by adopting wise sayings from other peoples.

The wise person was someone who thought about divine revelation and had travelled, thereby building up a sum of practical experience. The results of these meditations were then recorded in the form of pithy phrases.

The book of Proverbs is a compilation of such phrases from nine collections deriving from different sources. Some of them possibly came from King Solomon and others can be traced to origins in Egyptian texts or works from neighbouring countries.

Wisdom is presented as a person who calls people to enter school and learn what leads to a successful life. It is assumed that virtue must lead to happiness and that vice will lead to death. This rather simplistic view is questioned in the book of Job, which shows such ideas to be only partially true in real life. The Jewish sages themselves said that reflections based on human experience alone are insufficient to answer the ultimate mysteries of life.

Recommendations of Wisdom

1: 7–16
The fear of the Lord is the beginning of knowledge;
fools despise wisdom and discipline.

Listen, my child, to your father's instruction,
do not ignore your mother's teaching (. . .).
If sinners try to make you do something wrong,
do not go along with them. If they say,"Come with us:
we'll lie in wait and murder our victim (. . .).
We shall find treasures of every sort,
we shall fill our houses with stolen goods." (. . .)
My child, do not follow the way they are going,
keep your steps out of their path
for their feet hurry to do evil, they are quick to shed blood.

1: 20–33
Wisdom cries out in the streets,
she raises her voice in the public squares;
she calls out at the street corners (. . .).
"You idiots, how much longer will you love your
foolishness? (. . .)
Pay attention to my warning. (. . .)
Since I have called and you have not listened (. . .),
since you have ignored all my advice,
I, for my part, shall laugh at your distress,
when terror comes upon you, like a storm,
when ordeal and anguish are forced upon you.
Then they will call me, but I shall not answer,
they will search for me and will not find me.
They have hated knowledge,
they have not chosen the fear of the Lord,
they have taken no notice of my advice. (. . .)
So they will have to eat the fruits of their own ways of life.

The Jews' "fear" of the Lord had nothing to do with being frightened but was a deep respect for God and his Law. It was shown by what we would call "religion" — a cultural moral practice.

Wisdom calls on everybody in their everyday life and is not reserved merely for a select few. Many people are unfortunate and fail to hear her but will regret it.

For the mistakes fools make kill them,
their complacency leads to their ruin.
But whoever listens to me finds security;
he will live in peace, without fear of harm."

2: 1–6, 9
My child, if you take my words to heart,
if you set store by my commandments,
tuning your ear to wisdom,
tuning your heart to understanding,
yes, if you plead for insight,
if you cry out for understanding (. . .),
then you will understand what the fear of the Lord is,
and discover the knowledge of God.
For it is the Lord who gives wisdom,
from his mouth come knowledge and understanding. (. . .)
Then you will understand what is right and just and fair,
the pathways to happiness.

Those who listen to wisdom learn to respect the Lord. They are on the path to happiness.

3: 1–7
My child, do not forget my teaching,
keep my principles in your heart,
since they will increase the length of your life,
and give you years of happiness and well-being.
Never let love and faithfulness leave you!
Tie them round your neck,
write them on the tablet of your heart.
In this way you will find favour and success
in the sight of God and of people.
Trust in the Lord with all your heart,
do not rely on your own way of thinking.
Acknowledge him in everything you do,
and he will see that your paths are smooth.
Never think of yourself as wise:
fear the Lord and turn your back on evil.

The first condition for gaining wisdom is to resist our arrogant confidence in our own powers of reasoning and to open up to God.

Wisdom as Creator
8: 22–31
The Lord created me, first of all,
before the oldest of his works.
From everlasting, I was firmly established,

from the beginning, before the earth came into being.
Before even the deep places existed, I was born,
before even the springs with their overflowing waters.
Before the mountains were settled in their place,
before the hills, I came into the world.
Before God had made the earth, the countryside,
and the first elements of the world,
when he set the heavens in place, I was there. (. . .)
I was beside the master craftsman,
giving him joy day after day.
I always played in his presence,
I played all over his earth,
delighted to be among men and women.

Invitation to Wisdom's banquet
9: 1–6

Wisdom has built herself a house,
she has carved out her seven pillars;
she has killed her beasts, poured out her wine,
she has laid her table.
She has sent out her maidservants
and shouted out from the highest places above the city,
"Who is simple? Let him come this way."
To the fool she says, "Come and eat my bread,
drink the wine which I have poured out for you!
Leave your foolish ways behind and you will live.
Follow the pathway of Knowledge."

Wisdom is presented as a person
and appears as a reality used by
God when he created the world.
Wisdom is part of creation but
her greatest joy is to show herself
among human beings. John used
similar expressions at the
beginning of his Gospel although
he talked about the "Word of
God" when speaking of Jesus'
coming into the world.

Wisdom invites us to her feast, in
a house with seven pillars, the
symbol of perfect stability.
  Jesus later sent out a similar
invitation for all people to come
to God's feast (Matt. 22: 1; Luke
14: 16). His suggestion of food
was his own body and blood.

The rest of the book contains a number of short maxims which are full of wisdom, irony, and humour. Each draws from an observation of everyday life and is therefore a reflection of the time when it was written while also continuing to be relevant to human nature throughout history.

Some good advice

11: 12
Anyone who looks down on a neighbour lacks good sense;
an intelligent person remains silent.

11: 22
A golden ring in the snout of a pig
is a lovely woman who lacks good judgement.

13: 4
A lazy person hungers but has no food;
hard workers get their fill.

13: 24
Anyone who fails to use the stick hates his child;
a person who corrects a child loves him.

14: 21
Anyone who looks down on the needy is at fault.
Anyone who takes pity on the poor is blessed.

15: 17
It is better to eat a plate of vegetables where there is love
than a fattened ox where there is hatred.

16: 18
Pride goes before destruction,
a conceited spirit before a fall.

16: 32
Better a patient person than a hero,
someone with self-control than one who conquers a city.

17: 22
A glad heart is
excellent medicine,
a depressed spirit
makes the bones
waste away.

23: 31–5
Do not gaze at wine, how red it is,
how it sparkles in the cup!
How smoothly it slips down the throat!
In the end it bites like a snake,
it stings like an adder!
Your eyes will see peculiar things,
you will talk nonsense from your heart.
You will be like someone sleeping in the middle of the ocean,
like someone asleep at the mast-head.
"Struck me, have they? But I'm not hurt.
Beaten me? I don't feel anything.
When shall I wake up?..
I'll ask for more of it!"

The perfect wife
31: 10
The truly capable woman — who can find her?
She is far beyond the price of pearls. (. . .)

14–15
She is like those merchant ships,
bringing her food from far away.
She gets up while it is still dark
giving her household their food (. . .).

18
She knows that her business affairs are going well.
Her lamp does not go out at night.

27–8
She puts her hand to the spinning-wheel,
her fingers grasp the spindle.
She holds out her hands to the poor,
she opens her arms to the needy.
Snow may come, she has no fears for her household,
with all her servants warmly dressed.
She keeps good watch on the way her household behaves,
she does not eat the bread of idleness.
Her children stand up and call her blessed,
her husband, too, sings her praises.

The book of Proverbs is not altogether sympathetic towards women. But the image presented here — certainly difficult to envisage! — nevertheless shows a very high estimation of the role they are able to play. This text has sometimes been regarded as a description of Wisdom personified.

QOHELETH

OR
ECCLESIASTES

Our hopes on the path of life often suddenly turn into doubt. We feel a kind of tiredness concerning our whole existence and are suddenly disillusioned. Are all our efforts in vain?

Ecclesiastes is the book of the Bible which most clearly reflects this mood among God's people. All actions, politics, love, pleasure are no more useful than chasing the wind. All that matters is to have a quiet and simple life without too much fuss. Of course, we have God but he is so far away that the whole world seems pointless. Our illusions are torn away by the Qoheleth (which means the man of the assembly, the preacher or delegate, or Ecclesiastes in Greek). The preacher speaks out against the lies we are tempted to tell ourselves in order to avoid painful feelings.

But he leads us to think more deeply than we would normally. He forces us to prepare ourselves despite our own little plans by showing us the dead end we have reached. Preparation for what? For the gospel, say Christians, since Jesus came to shatter the earthly limits of human experience.

The author of this philosophical work attributed it to King Solomon although the work was written much later since it dates from the last centuries BC. According to the author, the king possessed all the advantages of fortune and glory but eventually realised that everything was vanity.

Prologue
1: 2–11

How can we avoid a sense of hopelessness immediately we start thinking about life? Events go round and round in an endless cycle of repetition, and we fool ourselves if we think our own efforts can change the world.

Sheer futility, Qoheleth says. Sheer futility: everything is futile! What profit does a man get for all the work he puts in under the sun? A generation goes, a generation comes, yet the sun sets; it hurries back to its point of departure and there it rises again. The wind goes to the south, then turns to the north; it turns and turns again; then the wind goes back to its circling. Into the sea go all the rivers, but the sea is never filled. Yet the rivers still go on to their goal. All things are wearisome. No one can say that eyes have not had enough of seeing, ears their fill of hearing.

What was, will be again;
what has been done, will be done again;
there is nothing new under the sun!

If anyone says, "Look, here's something new!" it existed already in centuries past. We do not remember what has happened in the past, and so it will be for the centuries to come — our successors will not remember.

Life of Solomon

1: 2–18

I, Qoheleth, have been the king over Israel in Jerusalem. Wisely I have applied myself to investigation and exploration of everything that happens under heaven. What a tiresome task God has given humanity to keep us busy! I have seen everything that is done under the sun: how futile it all is, only chasing after the wind!

What is twisted cannot be straightened,

what is not there cannot be counted.

I thought to myself: I have gained more wisdom than anyone before me in Jerusalem. I myself have mastered every kind of wisdom and science. I have applied myself to understanding philosophy and science, stupidity and foolishness, and I now realise that all this too is chasing after the wind.

Much wisdom, much grief;

the more knowledge, the more sorrow.

2: 1–11, 17–20

I thought to myself, "Very well, I will try pleasure and see what enjoyment has to offer." And this was futile too. This laughter, I reflected, is a madness, this pleasure no use at all.

I decided to give myself over to drinking wine, while at the same time still continuing to look for wisdom; to take up foolishness, to discover the best way for people to spend their days under the sun. I worked on a grand scale. I built myself palaces, I planted vineyards. I got hold of slaves and servants; I had herds and flocks too (. . .). I stored up silver and gold, the treasures of kings and provinces (. . .). So I grew great, greater than anyone in Jerusalem before me. I did not deny myself anything I wanted, I did not deprive myself of any pleasure. Then I thought about all I had achieved and all the effort I had put into achieving it. What futility it all was, what chasing after the wind! (. . .)

The author put his reflections in the mouth of the great king. He was wise and rich and had all the material goods imaginable. But he was deeply disillusioned by the time his life ended. What remained of all that splendour now?

I have come to hate life, for what is done under the sun disgusts me; since all is futility and chasing after the wind. I have come to hate all that I have worked for under the sun and now hand over to my successor: who knows whether he will be wise or a fool? I have come to despair of all the effort I have put in under the sun.

Life flows towards death
3: 1–11, 19–20

There is a season for everything,
a time for every occupation under heaven:
A time for giving birth, and a time for dying;
a time for planting, and a time for pulling up
what has been planted;
a time for killing, and a time for healing;
a time for knocking down, and a time for building;
a time for tears, and a time for laughter;
a time for mourning, and a time for dancing, (. . .)
a time for keeping, and a time for throwing away;
a time for tearing, and a time for sewing;
a time for keeping silent, and a time for speaking;
a time for loving, and a time for hating;
a time for war, and a time for peace.

What do people gain from the efforts they make? I consider the task that God gives to humanity: all that he does is appropriate for its time. Although he has given us an awareness of the passage of time, we can grasp neither the beginning nor the end of what God does. (. . .)

For the fate of human and the fate of animal is the same. As the one dies, so the other dies; both have the very same breath. Human is in no way better off than animal — since all is futile.

Everything goes to the same place; everything comes from the dust, everything returns to the dust.

The vanity of riches
5: 9–10; 6: 2–3

No one who loves money ever has enough, no one who loves luxury has any income; this, too, is futile!

Where goods abound, parasites abound: what advantage does the owner have, apart from the joy of looking at it? Suppose someone has received from God riches, property and honours. He

For the wise man who wrote this book, the workaholic is the most foolish of people. All his efforts will end in death, just like an animal. How pointless this all is! Work cannot give us the meaning of life. The secret of life must be in God alone.

has nothing at all left to wish for. But God does not give him the chance to enjoy them, and some stranger enjoys them. This is futile, and cruel suffering too.

Or take someone who has had a hundred children and lived for many years. However, he has never enjoyed the good things of life and has not even got a tomb! A stillborn child is happier than he.

Old age

11: 7—12: 8

How sweet light is, and how delightful it is to see the sun!
However many years you live, enjoy them all,
but remember, there will be many days of darkness!
In the end all is futile.
Young man, enjoy yourself while you are young;
make the most of the days of your youth;
follow the prompting of your heart and the desires of your eyes;
but remember, God will call you to answer for everything.
Rid your heart of indignation, keep your body free from suffering.
But youth and the age of black hair are both futile.
Remember your Creator while you are still young,
before the bad days come,
before the years come which, you will say, give you no pleasure;
before the sun and the light, the moon and stars grow faint,
before the clouds return after the rain (. . .).
The time when the first cry of a bird wakes you up,
when all the singing has stopped;
when going uphill is an ordeal
and you are frightened at every step you take. (. . .)
Already you are on the way to your everlasting home
and the mourners are gathering in the street.
Before the silver thread snaps,
or the golden bowl is cracked,
or the pitcher shattered at the fountain,
or the pulley broken at the well-head:
before the dust returns to the earth
from which it came,
and the spirit returns to God who gave it.
Sheer futility, Qoheleth says, everything is futile!

Nothing remains of riches but disillusion.

Old age will come one day. Young people should remember how fleeting are the joys of youth. They will grow up and that will be the end of it.

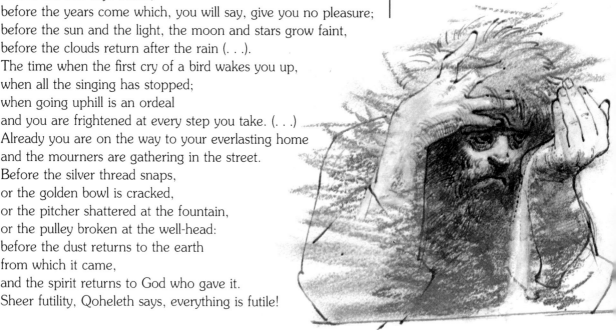

THE SONG OF SONGS

Can the love between a man and a woman have anything to do with religion? Surely human passions divert attention away from God?

No doubt erotic attraction can be degraded but the Bible states that love comes from God and makes us available to God. That was the fundamental message of the prophets when they compared the relationship between God and his people to that between a lover and his beloved.

It also explains why the Holy Scriptures include some poems that appear at first sight to concern earthly love alone. Two lovers describe their passion. They meet, lose one another, seek each other, find one another again and unite.

These songs were probably written to celebrate weddings but here they are used to describe the spiritual adventure of a soul exposing itself completely to the love of God. Great mystical writers repeatedly used the songs as inspiration when they wanted to sing of their profound relationship with God.

2: 8–11

Beloved: I hear my love.
See how he comes
leaping on the mountains,
bounding over the hills.
My love is like a gazelle,
like a young stag. (. . .)

My love lifts up his voice,
he says to me,
"Come then, my beloved,
my lovely one, come.
For see, winter is past,
the rains are over and gone."

These poems' main source of inspiration is nature. The poems concern a young man and a girl singing freely of their mutual love.

In this poem the girl is dreaming of her lover. He knocks on the door but she hesitates before she opens it. It is then too late and he is gone so that she must run after him to find him.

The author of Revelation cites Jesus as saying, "I am standing at the door, knocking" when he was reproaching a Christian community for their lack of enthusiasm (Rev. 3: 20). This shows what happens when people respond slowly to the Lord's call to love him.

4: 1,9

Lover: How beautiful you are, my beloved,
how beautiful you are!
Your eyes are doves, behind your veil (. . .).

You steal my heart,
my sister, my promised bride,
you steal my heart
with a single one of your glances,
with a single link of your necklace.

5: 2—6: 3

Beloved: I sleep, but my heart is awake.
I hear my love knocking.
"Open to me, my sister, my beloved,
my dove, my perfect one,
for my head is wet with dew,
my hair with the drops of night."

— "I have taken off my tunic.
Am I to put it on again?
I have washed my feet.
Am I to dirty them again?"

My love pushed his hand
through the hole in the door;
my whole being trembled. (. . .)
I opened to my love,
but he had turned and gone.
My soul failed at his flight,
I looked but could not find him,
I called, but he did not answer. (. . .)

Promise me, daughters of Jerusalem,
if you should find my love, what are you to tell him?
— That I am sick with love!

Chorus: Where did your lover go,
O loveliest of women?
Which way did your lover turn
so that we can help you search for him?

Beloved: My love went down to his garden,
to the beds of spices,
to pasture his flock on the grass
and gather lilies.
I belong to my love, and my love to me.
He pastures his flock among the lilies.

Epilogue

8: 6–8
Set me like a seal on your heart,
like a seal on your arm.
For love is strong as Death,
passion as relentless as Sheol.
The flash of it is like a flash of fire,
a flame of the Lord himself.
Floods of water cannot quench love,
no torrents can drown it.
Were a man to offer all his family wealth
to buy love,
he would gain nothing but contempt.

The song ends with a hymn to the love that is stronger than death. Nothing can stop it. It comes from God and can never be bought or earned.

THE BOOK
OF WISDOM

Young people are full of enthusiasm in the springtime of life but also tend to make "snap" judgements. We are happy indeed if we can still feel wonder and joy at the end of our experiences but have also learnt not to judge too quickly. We are truly wise if we have learnt to be young at heart.

This applies to the author of the book of Wisdom which was written in Greek during the first century BC. The Jewish author sang about the wonders of divine revelation which forged the identity of the chosen people. He was also able to draw on Greek influences which were considered to be absolutely incompatible with the true faith only a hundred years previously. He was amazed when he saw how God could touch the lives of even those who had been rejected with anger and scorn.

So he showed how the success of righteous people able to resist persecution and temptation is real success since they will have eternal life. He presented wisdom as a mysterious reality with a hidden meaning in the world that was able to reveal itself to all who sought it wholeheartedly. He finally recalled the old story of the Exodus and the conquest of the Promised Land; he did this to explain how God called patiently on all men and women to discover his presence at the heart of the world.

This book marked the exposure of Judaism to the surrounding cultural influences. It was right on the doorstep of the New Testament. John says in the introduction to his Gospel that Jesus is the Word of God, the true Wisdom. Jesus is coming to reach out to the whole universe and draw in all those who welcome him into the immense current of the Holy Spirit.

Life for the godless and the fate of the innocent

2: 1–20

Life is short for non-believers and so they live it to the full before it runs out. There are no limits allowed for there is no such thing as sin or punishment. Such people can only hate the righteous, since their way of life

And this is the false argument the godless use,

"Our life is short and dreary, there is no remedy for death, no one is known to have come back from the pit.

"We came into being by chance and afterwards it will seem as if we had never existed. (. . .)

"For our days are like the passing of a shadow,
when we die, we cannot return (. . .).
"Come then, let us enjoy the good things of today,
let us use created things with the passion of youth:
let us have our fill of the dearest wines and perfumes,
and on no account miss the flowers of spring (. . .).
Let us oppress the righteous man who is poor,
let us not spare the widow (. . .).
Let our might be our guide as to what is right,
since weakness only shows how useless it is.
Let us set traps for the righteous man, since he annoys us
and opposes our way of life (. . .).
We see him as a reproof to our way of thinking,
the very sight of him makes us feel depressed,
for his kind of life is not like other people's (. . .).
He proclaims that the final destiny of the righteous
is to be blessed,
and boasts of having God as his father.
Let us see if what he says is true (. . .).
Let us use cruelty and torture to test him,
and in this way explore this gentleness of his
and put his patience to the test,
since God will rescue him — or so he claims."

This is the way they reason, but they are misled,
since their malice makes them blind.
They do not know the hidden things of God.
They do not hope for the reward of holiness,
they do not believe in a reward for blameless souls.
For God created human beings to live forever,
he made them as an image of his own nature.
Death came into the world only through the Devil's envy,
as those who belong to him find to their cost.

3: 1–6
But the souls of the righteous are in the hands of God,
and no torment can touch them.
To the ignorant, they appeared to die,
their departure seemed to be disaster,
their leaving us seemed to wipe them out;
but they are at peace.

appears to reproach them. And
so, they become persecutors.

But non-believers do not realise
that God made human beings to
live for ever. The difficult life of
the righteous is a failure in their
eyes but in fact the virtuous
triumph through their trials and
tribulations.

If, as it seemed to us, they suffered punishment,
eternal life made them rich with hope.
God was putting them to the test
and has proved them worthy to be with him;
he has tested them like gold in a furnace,
and accepted them as a perfect offering.

A song of praise to wisdom

7: 22—8: 4

Introducing himself as King Solomon, the author considered the Wisdom which was evident throughout the whole world to be a reflection of the God who rules the universe. It is what makes human beings turn to God.

Wisdom is a spirit intelligent, holy, unique, diverse, subtle, moving, clear-sighted, spotless, lucid, invulnerable, kind, perceptive, irresistible, generous, friendly to human beings, steadfast, dependable, calm, almighty, all-surveying, penetrating all intelligent, pure and most subtle spirits. (. . .)

She is a breath of the power of God, pure outworking of the glory of the Almighty.

Nothing impure can find its way into her.

For she is a reflection of the eternal light, an untarnished mirror of God's active power, and an image of his goodness. (. . .)

Strongly she reaches from one end of the world to the other and she governs the whole world for its good.

I have loved and searched for wisdom from my youth;
I decided to have her as my bride,
I fell in love with her beauty.

She makes her birth even more noble by sharing God's life,
for the Master of All has always loved her.

Prayer for Wisdom

9: 1–4

Solomon asked God for wisdom when he came to the throne. This prayer could be the prayer of all believers. The author of the book attributed it to Solomon.

"God of our ancestors, Lord of mercy,
who made the universe by your word,
and in your wisdom have fitted human beings
to rule the creatures that you have made,
to govern the world in holiness and saving justice
and to dispense fair judgement with all honesty,
give me the one who shares your throne: Wisdom,
and do not reject me as one of your children."

ECCLESIASTICUS

OR

THE WRITINGS OF BEN SIRA

F aith is a response to God's call. But faith is empty if it fails to make itself clearly seen in our attitudes towards daily life. We must think carefully about what God expects of us in any given circumstance.

That was what Jesus Ben Sira did (his name means "son of Sira", sometimes called Siracide). This middle-class man was educated in the Israelite tradition but was also familiar with Greek culture. He wanted to teach his contemporaries the "wisdom" necessary to enable them to live a happy and balanced life. He was not ashamed of being a traditionalist and often thought about the lessons of the past, to which he added his own perceptive observations about the things he saw around him. His ideal in life was the "fear of God" (which today we would call a religion practised in everyday life as well as at church). This fear was shown through solid human qualities such as care and consideration for others and an awareness of self. Such a way of life would lead to happiness and peace since God rewards those who are faithful to him even in this world. Ben Sira did not mention a possible life after death because death, to him, was a law of nature that humankind could have avoided if sin had not existed. Creation was ultimately the best it could be. The writer's world-view was that of a man who had reached a certain inner peace at the end of his life. Perhaps this explains why his optimism seems rather glib at times.

He was strongly attached to his people and proud of their past. He looked forward to the day when Israel would return to its former unity and all the Jews of the "diaspora" (which means "dispersal" throughout the world) would return to their homeland. His book concludes with what we might call a "gallery of ancestors": he proudly remembered all the heroes of the Israelite faith, from Abraham through to Simon, the great high priest who had died recently.

The book was written towards the end of the second century BC and was translated into Greek about fifty years later by the author's grandson in Alexandria. The book consists mainly of short pithy phrases in a way which is reminiscent of the Proverbs.

Some advice about friends and enemies

9: 10

Do not desert an old friend; the new one will not match up to him.
New friend, new wine; when it grows old, you drink it with pleasure.

This is a good example of the small morsels of advice given by the author.

12: 8–12

In good times you cannot always tell a true friend,
but in hard times you cannot mistake an enemy.
When someone is doing well that person's enemies are sad,
when someone is doing badly, even a friend will keep at a distance.

This rather timid wisdom can be compared with one of the biblical proverbs which says, "Do not rejoice if your enemy falls; let not your heart exult if he stumbles." This proverb already foreshadows Jesus' instruction to "love your enemies" and has often been repeated within the tradition of the rabbis.

Do not ever trust an enemy;
just as bronze becomes tarnished, so does the spite of an enemy.
Even if he behaves humbly and comes bowing and scraping,
be wary and on your guard against him.
Behave towards him as if you were polishing a mirror,
you will find that his tarnish cannot last.
Do not stand him beside you
in case he pushes you out and takes your place.

Silence and speech

20: 4–7
Someone who tries to impose justice by force is like a eunuch trying to take a girl's virginity.
There is the person who keeps quiet and is considered wise, another incurs hatred for talking too much.
There is the person who keeps quiet, not knowing how to answer, another keeps quiet, knowing when to speak.
The wise will keep quiet till the right moment, but a talkative fool will always get it wrong.

The lazy person and the fool

22: 1–2
A lazy person is like a stone covered in filth,
everyone whistles at his disgrace.
A lazy person is like a lump of dung,
anyone picking it up shakes it off his hand.

22: 9–11
Teaching a fool is like gluing bits of pottery
together — you are trying to wake someone who loves to sleep. You might
as well talk to someone

sound asleep; when
you have finished the fool will say, "What's up?"
Shed tears for the dead, who has left the light behind; shed tears for the fool, who has left his wits behind. Shed quieter tears for the dead who is at rest, for the fool life is worse than death.

Some of Israel's great figures

44: 19–20

Abraham, the great ancestor of many nations, no one could equal his glory. He obeyed the Law of the Most High, and made a covenant with him.

45: 1–2

From the line of Jacob he produced a generous man who found favour in the eyes of all men and women. He was beloved by God and people, and the memory of this man, Moses, is blessed. He made him the equal of the holy ones in glory and made him strong, so that his enemies were terrified.

48: 1, 9–11

Then the prophet Elijah appeared like a fire, his word burning like a torch. (. . .) It was he who was taken up in the whirlwind of fire, in a chariot with fiery horses; by speaking out prophecies warning of doom he was appointed to appease God's anger before his rage breaks out, to turn the hearts of fathers towards their children, and to restore the tribes of Jacob. Blessed, those who will see you, and those who have fallen asleep in love; for we too shall certainly have life.

Elijah was traditionally said to have been carried up to heaven without having to go through death. Elijah would then return to announce the arrival of the Day of the Lord. Jesus explained that he had returned already in the person of John the Baptist.

THE PROPHETS

We sometimes say that certain people are "prophets" because they are especially far-sighted, able to analyse events and draw conclusions from them regarding the future. Such men and women played a large part in the lives of God's people. Not all of them were particularly intelligent or even well-educated: above all they were God's witnesses.

All the prophets were witnesses to the covenant and were inspired suddenly by a force which made them warn their fellow countrymen and women, put them on their guard, to make them see the consequences of their actions. This force was a gift from God, who chose to reveal himself to them through his Holy Spirit.

There were sometimes official prophets at the royal court who acted as religious counsellors to the king. David, for example, often consulted Nathan. Too often these prophets were tempted to say only what pleased those who were in power. The real prophets denounced these men as false prophets because they were only interested in flattering the king although they claimed to be inspired by God.

The real prophets invariably made people uneasy. They did not hesitate to rise against those in power when they thought the kings were betraying the covenant, by creating a political system that was no longer inspired by faith. They also spoke against abuses of power which allowed injustice. The logical consequence of this was that the prophets were misunderstood, slandered, persecuted and sometimes executed.

These prophets looked towards the future and believed in the divine promise. They announced that the day would come when the Lord would intervene to bring eternal peace and happiness to his people and, through the Jews, to all humanity. He had promised this to Abraham, Isaac and to Jacob.

It was the prophets who introduced the idea of a future Messiah, a new "Anointed One" (or Christ), who would eventually establish the rule of right and justice and allow order to return to the world. The prophets had glimpsed what the Messiah was to be, and what he would do.

Some of these prophets have left almost nothing but their names to posterity.

Some left no writing of their own, although the Bible tells us what they did. Others wrote proper works which we now refer to as the Books of Prophecy. The face of God revealed to us in these works is amazingly modern. Moreover, in the waiting for the future Messiah, Christians are able to see the image of Jesus Christ, who came to "fulfil" the Scriptures by realising God's plans for the world.

The Bible classifies the prophets according to the length of the works they left: the four "major" prophets are: Isaiah, Jeremiah, Ezekiel and Daniel (who is not considered to be a "prophet" by the Jews). The twelve "minor prophets" are: Hosea, Joel, Amos, Obadiah, Jonah, Micah, Nahum, Habakkuk, Zephaniah, Haggai, Zechariah and Malachi.

THE BOOK OF ISAIAH

Isaiah was a great nobleman at the court of Judah. He had a vision from God while in the Temple at Jerusalem around BC 740, and from then on he spoke in God's name. He questioned the king's political actions, which were unjust, immoral and unworthy of God's chosen people.

Assyria was becoming a threat in those days. The kingdom of Israel was allied to Syria, and wanted to force the kingdom of Judah to support their alliance against the Assyrian capital of Nineveh. Isaiah spoke out against these plots and reminded the people that the only guarantee of salvation lay in the allies' faithfulness to God. He was very critical of King Ahaz who had earlier sacrificed his son to pagan idols in the belief that this would earn him their protection. He announced to the King the birth of a new heir who would carry on the line of David. Beyond this child he glimpsed the coming of another descendant of the great king who was a marvellous being who would fulfil the divine promise and re-establish peace throughout the world.

Isaiah became counsellor to King Hezekiah, the reformer, in 719. The king was encouraged by Isaiah to defend himself against Assyria which had just destroyed the kingdom of Israel. In fact Jerusalem did successfully fight off the invaders in 701.

The old prophet disappeared from the public scene after the death of Hezekiah. He had tried to inspire his fellow countrymen by reminding them of their special relationship with God. But he had only postponed the country's decline. At least he knew the joy of glimpsing a glorious future beyond the inevitable catastrophe: a future which would be ushered in by the coming of the long-awaited Messiah.

The first few chapters of Isaiah speak out against the kingdom's decadence. The prophet unmasked the religious hypocrisy, the lawlessness within the society, and the pride of the rich and powerful. He summed up his descriptions with a parable:

THE PROPHET ISAIAH (ISA. 1–40)

The song of the vineyard

5: 1–24

Let me sing to my beloved the song of my friend for his vineyard.

My beloved had a vineyard on a fertile hillside. He dug it, cleared it of stones, and planted it with red grapes.
In the middle he built a tower, he made a wine press there too.
He expected fine grapes to grow; all it produced was wild grapes.

And now, citizens of Jerusalem and people of Judah,
I ask you to judge between me and my vineyard.
What more could I have done for my vineyard
that I have not done? Why did it produce wild grapes,
instead of the fine ones I expected?

Very well, I shall tell you what I am going to do to my vineyard!
I shall take away its hedge, for it to be grazed on,
I shall knock down its wall, for it to be trampled on.
I shall let it become a wasteland, unpruned, undug, overgrown by brambles and thorn-bushes.
I shall stop the clouds raining on it.

Now, the vineyard of the Lord of the universe is the House of Israel, and the plant he cherished is the people of Judah.
He expected fair judgement, but found injustice.
He hoped for justice, but found instead cries of distress.

Woe to those who add house to house and join field to field until there is nowhere left for anyone else and they are the sole inhabitants of the country. (. . .)
Woe to those who get up early to run after strong drink, and stay up late at night drunk with wine. (. . .)
Woe to those who call what is bad, good, and what is good, bad, who make the darkness become light and the light become darkness (. . .).

Isaiah summed up the situation he saw before him using a striking image. From his vineyard, meaning his people, God expected good fruit in return for his gifts but he reaped only injustice. So the vines had to be torn up by the roots.

Jesus used this parable again to speak out against the bad vine-growers and to announce that he had come to plant a new vine (cf. Mark 12: 1–9; Matt. 21: 33–43; John 15: 1–10).

Woe to those who let the guilty go free for a bribe and deny justice to the righteous. Yes, just as flames burn up the stubble, (. . .) their root will decay and their shoot will be carried off as if it were dust. For they have rejected the law of the Lord of the universe, they have despised the word of the Holy One of Israel.

The call of Isaiah

6: 1–13

In the year of King Uzziah's death I saw the Lord seated on a great, high throne; his train filled the sanctuary. Above him stood seraphs, each one with six wings. (. . .). They were shouting these words to each other: "Holy, holy, holy is the Lord of the universe. His glory fills the whole earth."

The door-posts shook at the sound of their shouting, and the Temple was full of smoke. Then I said: "Woe is me! I am lost, for I am a man with unclean lips and I live among a people with unclean lips, and my eyes have seen the King, the Lord of the universe."

Then one of the seraphs flew to me, holding in its hand a burning-hot coal which it had taken from the altar with a pair of tongs. It touched my mouth with it and said: "Look, this has touched your lips, your guilt has been taken away and your sin forgiven." I then heard the voice of the Lord saying: "Whom shall I send? Who will go for us?" And I said, "Here I am, send me." He said: "Go, and speak to this people. But I know that they will only harden their hearts." (. . .) I said, "Until when, Lord?" He replied, "Until towns are in ruins and deserted, until the land is devastated and the Lord has driven the people away and the country is totally abandoned. The people who are left will be like an oak, cut back to a stump. But this stump is a holy seed."

The coming of Immanuel

7: 10–16

The Lord sent this message to Ahaz: "Ask the Lord your God for a sign, either in the depths of the oceans or in the highest heavens."

But Ahaz replied, "I will not ask. I will not put the Lord to the test."

Isaiah then said:

Isaiah had his divine vision in the Temple at Jerusalem, close to the altar upon which there was a perpetually-burning flame. He saw the invisible God surrounded by winged creatures, similar to those found in the pagan temples of Mesopotamia.

Isaiah became aware of his own unworthiness when faced with this vision of God, but he believed that the Lord could purify him and make him capable of speaking in his name.

He had no illusions about the result of his mission: catastrophe was inevitable. But he held on to his confidence in the future: a remnant of the people would remain firm and faithful like a tree whose trunk stood up to the storm: new shoots would grow again.

King Ahaz was terrified by the threats of the kings who had united against him. He even sacrificed his son to the pagan gods to assure himself of their favour. The only help he refused to seek was that of the Lord. But God gave him a sign to show him that he remained faithful to his covenant: another son, with a revealing name: "God-with-us". Through this child, Isaiah began to see a happier future: would he be the dreamed-of Messiah? The Christians applied this text to Jesus, the true Immanuel, the son of the Virgin.

"Listen now,
House of David! Is it
not enough for you that
you try human patience,
that you try my God's
patience too? The Lord will give
you a sign in any case. It is this:
a young woman is with child and will
give birth to a son. She will call him
Immanuel. (. . .) Before the child knows how to
refuse the bad and choose the good, the lands whose two
kings are frightening you will be deserted."

Rescue has come

8: 23—9: 6

For is not everything dark as night for a country in distress?

In the past the country of Zebulun and the country of Naphtali were humbled, but in the future the country bordering the sea, beyond the Jordan and Galilee, will become great.

The people that walked in darkness have seen a great light; on the inhabitants of a country under a dark shadow light has shone. You give life to the nation, you make its joy increase. They rejoice before you as people rejoice at harvest time, as they sing for joy when they are dividing the spoils of battle. For you have broken the yoke that weighs your people down, the iron bar across their shoulders, the rod in the hands of those who oppress them, as you did in days gone by. The boots which pounded over the ground and the clothes stained with blood, will be thrown into the fire and burnt.

For a son has been born for us, a son has been given to us. The right to rule has been laid on his shoulders; and this is the name

The kingdom of Israel had just been raided by the invaders and the people had been deported, in chains. It was a bleak time. Isaiah dared to foretell that one day the light would return and all of the chosen people would regain the peace and prosperity they had lost: that would be when the wonderful child would come to restore the kingdom of David in righteousness and justice. Through love, God would send his Messiah.

As we saw in the Song of Songs, God loves his people to the point of possessiveness.

Isaiah told the people more about the Messiah, about whom Nathan had already prophesied to David. The descendant of the great king (who was himself the grandson of Jesse) would not only bring glory to his people, but would bring about a complete re-creation of the world: order and justice would reign. All creation would be at peace, for the human race would know God.

he has been given, "Wonderful Counsellor, Mighty God, Eternal Father, Prince of Peace" to extend his reign in a peace that will never end, over the throne of David and over his kingdom to make it secure and strong, with fair judgement and right actions. From this time onwards and for ever, the jealous love of the Lord of the universe will do this.

The descendant of David

11: 1–9

A shoot will spring up from the root of Jesse, a new shoot will grow from his roots. On him will rest the spirit of the Lord, the spirit of wisdom and insight, the spirit of counsel and power, the spirit of knowledge and fear of the Lord: his inspiration will lie in fearing the Lord. He will not judge by appearances, nor give his verdict on the basis of what others say. He will judge the weak with justice and give a fair sentence to the poorest in the land. He will strike the country with the rod of his mouth and with the breath from his lips he will bring death to the wicked. He will wear the belt of justice and he will be clothed in faithfulness. The wolf will live with the lamb, the panther will lie down with the kid. The calf, the lion and well-fed cattle will walk together, and a little boy will lead them. The cow and the bear will graze side by side, their young will lie down together. The lion will eat hay like the ox. The small child will play over the den of the adder; the baby will put his hand into the viper's lair. No hurt, no harm will be done

anywhere on my holy mountain, for the country will be full of the knowledge of the Lord as the waters cover the sea.

Foreign nations turn to God

19: 19–25

On that day there will be an altar dedicated to the Lord in the centre of Egypt and, close to the frontier, a pillar in his honour. This will be a sign bearing witness to the presence of the Lord of the universe in the land. When the Egyptians cry to the Lord for help because they fear those who oppress them, he will send them a Saviour to rescue them. The Lord will make himself known to them and they will know the Lord. They will offer their sacrifices and their offerings, they will make vows to the Lord and will carry them out. And if the Lord strikes the people of Egypt, he will heal them. They will turn to the Lord who will hear their prayers and heal them. On that day there will be a highway from Egypt to Assyria. Assyria will have access to Egypt and Egypt have access to Assyria. Egypt will serve alongside Assyria.

Although Isaiah threatened Israel with punishment, he was no softer towards the neighbouring lands. He criticised Babylon, Assyria and Egypt particularly strongly. The threat was never the last word, though, even when directed towards these countries: one day, the enemies themselves would be converted. That would be the beginning of peace and reconciliation under the eyes of the Lord, who would at last be acknowledged by everyone.

On that day Israel will make a third nation alongside Egypt and Assyria, and together they will be a blessing at the centre of the world, and the Lord of the universe will bless them in the words, "Blessed be my people Egypt, Assyria my creation, and Israel my heritage."

The divine banquet

25: 6–9

On this mountain, the Lord of the universe is preparing a banquet of rich food and fine wines for all the peoples of the earth. On this mountain, he has destroyed the veil of mourning which all the peoples wore, the dark curtain drawn over all the nations. He has destroyed death for ever. The Lord has wiped away the tears from every cheek. Throughout the earth he has saved his people from their shame. This is what the Lord has promised. On that day, it will be said, "Look, this is our God. We put our hope in him that he should save us. This is the Lord! We put our hope in him. Let us sing and rejoice since he has saved us."

A curse against Jerusalem

29: 3–12

I shall make my camp all round you, I shall surround you in a siege and mount siege-works against you. You will be brought low, your voice will come from the earth, your words will rise like a murmur from the dust. (. . .) The horde of your enemies will be like fine dust, the horde of the warriors like flying chaff. And suddenly, in an instant, you will be visited by the Lord of hosts with thunder, earthquake, mighty din, hurricane, tempest, and flames of burning fire. (. . .) It will be like the dream of a hungry man: he eats, then wakes up with an empty stomach; or like the dream of a thirsty man: he drinks, then wakes up exhausted with a parched throat. (. . .) Be shocked and stunned, go blind, unable to see, drunk but not on wine, staggering but not through drink. (. . .)

For every vision has become like the words of a sealed book to you. You give it to someone able to read and say, "Read that." He replies, "I cannot, because it is sealed." You then give the book to someone who cannot read, and say, "Read that." He replies, "I cannot read."

Isaiah never lost hope even in the darkest hours. He announced the joy that the Lord would one day bring to the land. The day the Lord intervened would be a day of great celebration.

The God who loves his people is also the one who punishes them severely. The prophetic texts do sing of the promise of salvation but this can only come after they have been purified. Isaiah predicted the siege of Jerusalem. The people would be completely lost and unable to understand the meaning of what was happening to them.

THE BOOK OF THE CONSOLATION OF ISRAEL
(Isa. 40–55)

The book of Isaiah as we know it is in fact a compilation. The second portion of the book was compiled much later than the first — close to the time when the exile was at an end. It has been joined on to the texts written by Isaiah himself since it develops the prophet's vision of hope.

The Judaeans had been deported into Babylon, the capital of Chaldaea. They went through a deep religious crisis. Could they still believe in the Lord when they were actually witnessing the magnificent feasts given in honour of the conquerors' own gods?

"God is not as you imagine him to be", the new prophet told them. He is the only Lord of the universe and not the God of only one people. The Chaldaean god who seemed to have beaten him was nothing but an idol. The true God created the moon and the stars. He was also the master of history.

The East was in turmoil. Cyrus, the king of the Persians, had a reputation for his liberal views. He was threatening the decadent Chaldaea. Could freedom be in sight? That was when a cry of joy went up in the name of the Lord. "Console my people!" Tomorrow Jerusalem would rise again and become the centre of the new world order. God was going to act through his chosen servant Cyrus.

But the perspective suddenly broadened: the one who would truly renew the world would not be a warrior. It would have to be a real servant of God, able to change people from the *inside*, an "anointed one" of God, the Messiah. The prophet tried to describe him in terms which were sometimes difficult to understand for people in his own day, for they contradicted the image of the victorious "avenger" the Jews liked to imagine. Who would this person be? The question was to be asked with more and more urgency. It opened the door to hope.

The promise of rescue 40: 1–11

"Console my people, console them," says your God. "Speak to the heart of Jerusalem and tell her that her period of slavery has come to an end, that her guilt has been atoned for, that she has received double punishment from the Lord for all her sins."

A voice cries, "Prepare a way for the Lord in the desert. Make a straight road across the desert places for our God. Let every

Babylon could fall at any moment. This was a sign to the prophet that God had forgiven his people at last. Like thieves, they had been forced to give back twice as much as they had taken. The exile was going to end and they were about to return to their homeland. There would be another exodus.

Once, the sea had opened up before the chosen people. Now, the road was to be made level for them. The Word of God was going to act: it was all-powerful. The Lord would guide his people as a shepherd guides his sheep.

valley be filled in, every mountain and hill be made level, every cliff become a plateau, every escarpment a plain. Then the glory of the Lord will be revealed and everyone will see it together: for this is the word of the Lord."

A voice said, "Shout out!" and I said, "What shall I shout?" — "All people are like grass and their beauty is like the wild flower's. The grass withers, the flower fades when the breath of the Lord blows on them: the grass withers, the flower fades, but the word of our God remains for ever!"

Go up on a high mountain, messenger of Zion. Shout as loud as you can, messenger of Jerusalem! Do not be afraid, shout to the towns of Judah, "Here is your God."
Here is the Lord coming with power,
he will make his authority known.
He carries his reward with him,
and his prize goes ahead of him.
He is like a shepherd feeding his flock,
gathering lambs in his arms,
holding them against his chest
and leading the mother ewes to a place where they can rest.

The greatness of God
40: 12–31

Until the time of the exile, Israel had been strong in "their God" and had never thought about the problem of other peoples' gods, although they did accept that other peoples had their own gods to protect them. The defeat of Israel therefore seemed to confirm that Marduk, the Babylonian moon-god, was stronger than the Lord.

Who was it measured the water of the sea in
the hollow of his hand?
Who calculated the size of the heavens to the nearest inch?
Estimated the dust of the earth to the nearest bushel,
weighed the mountains in scales, and the hills in a balance?
Who directed the spirit of the Lord?
What counsellor could ever have instructed him? (. . .)
See, the nations are like a drop of water in a bucket,
they count as a grain of dust on the scales.

Islands weigh no more than fine powder. (. . .) All the nations are as nothing before him, to him they are insignificant and empty.
To whom can you compare God?
What image can you make of him?

The craftsman casts an idol in metal, a goldsmith overlays it with gold and casts silver chains for it.
Someone who is too poor to afford to buy a sacrifice chooses a piece of wood that will not rot; he then finds a skilled craftsman to carve out an idol that will last.
Did you not know, had you not heard?
Were you not told from the beginning?
Have you not understood how the earth was created?
God sits on his throne above the circle of the earth,
the inhabitants of which are like grasshoppers,
he stretches out the heavens like a cloth,
he spreads them out like a tent to live in.
He reduces princes to nothing (. . .).
"To whom can you compare me, or who is my equal?" says the Holy One.
Who created these stars?
The Lord leads out their army in order, summoning each of them by name.
His power and strength are so great,
that not one of them fails to answer.
Israel, how can you keep on saying:
"The Lord pays no attention to me,
he does not care about my rights?"
Did you not know? Had you not heard?
The Lord is the everlasting God,
he created the remotest parts of the earth.
He does not grow tired or weary, his understanding is beyond our grasp.
He gives strength to the weary,
he strengthens the powerless.
Youths grow tired and weary,
the young stumble and fall,
but those who hope in the Lord will regain their strength.
They will be like eagles with outspread wings,
though they run they will not grow weary,
though they walk they will never become tired.

The prophet reacted strongly against the idea: there was only one God, who was the Creator of the entire universe. He alone was the ruler of all people everywhere. Let nobody think that the Lord would forget his own people or be indifferent to their fate! He alone was the source of all their strength.

41: 8–11, 14
But you, Israel, my servant,
Jacob whom I have chosen,
descendant of Abraham my friend,
whom I have taken to myself from the remotest parts of the earth
and called from countries far away,
to whom I have said, "You are my servant!
I have chosen you. I have not rejected you."
Do not be afraid, for I am with you.
Do not be alarmed, for I am your God. (. . .)
Those who picked quarrels with you will be reduced to nothing
and will (. . .) die.
Do not be afraid, Jacob, you worm!
You little handful of Israel!
Your saviour is the Holy One of Israel.

First song of the servant
42: 1–7
Here is my servant whom I uphold,
my chosen one in whom I delight.
I have sent my spirit upon him.
He will bring justice to the nations.
He does not cry out or raise his voice,
his voice is not heard in the street;
he does not break a reed that has been crushed
or snuff out a flickering wick.
Faithfully he brings justice. (. . .)
This is what the Lord God says,
who created the heavens and spread them out,
who hammered the earth into shape and what comes from it,
who gave breath to the people in it,
and spirit to those who walk on it: I, the Lord, have
called you in saving justice,
I have grasped you by the hand and shaped you;
I have given you as a covenant to the people and
a light to the nations,
to open the eyes of the blind,
to set the prisoners free,
and to bring out from the dungeon
those who live in darkness.

God's work was to be completed by "his Servant", who would not appear as a powerful warrior, but as a righteous man, called to complete the true covenant between the Lord and his people.

There will be a new Exodus

43: 16–21

This is what the Lord says,
who made a way through the sea, a path in the raging waters,
who led out chariot and horse
together with an army of picked troops:
they lay down never to rise again,
they were snuffed out, put out like a wick.
No need to remember past events,
no need to think about what was done before.
Look, I am doing something new,
now it emerges; can you not see it?
Yes, I am making a road in the desert (. . .)
and rivers on the wastelands for my people to drink. (. . .)

The prophet announced their approaching freedom by recalling the exodus from Egypt and taking up again the images of these historic events.

The prophet showed how, whoever he was, the Servant had been kept in reserve by the Lord to intervene at the right moment. He also indicated that the servant would appear to fail before he would see his righteousness triumph.

Cyrus, the instrument of God

45: 1, 2, 4

This is what the Lord says to his anointed one, to Cyrus whom,
he says, I have grasped by his right hand, to make the nations bow
before him and to disarm kings,
to open gateways before him
so that their gates be closed no more:

I myself shall go before you, I shall flatten the high ground, I
shall shatter the bronze gateways, I shall smash the iron bars. (. . .)

It is for the sake of my servant Jacob and of Israel my chosen
one that I have called you by your name.

I have given you a title though you do not know me.

The prophet did not hesitate to declare that a pagan prince was God's chosen instrument, his "anointed One" — his "Christ". He thus showed that the Lord was really in charge of everything that happened. Cyrus was his "servant". But soon the prophet saw that the warrior who brought freedom to his people was only a pale foreshadowing of the true servant of God, the only one able to bring a lasting salvation.

The end of the Exile

48: 20–1

Come out from Babylon! Flee from the Chaldaeans!
Declare this with cries of joy, proclaim it,
make it known in the remotest parts of the earth, say,
"The Lord has redeemed his servant Jacob!"
They never went thirsty
when he led them through dry land;
he made water flow for them from the rock,
he split the rock and out streamed the water.

The prophet seemed to think that the Servant who would re-create the world was the entire Israelite people. At the same time, though, he foresaw that the Servant would be the one who would re-unify the people and would therefore be an individual person.

Second song of the servant
49: 1–7

Coasts and islands, listen to me,
pay attention, distant peoples.
The Lord called me when I was in my mother's womb,
before my birth he had spoken my name.
He made my mouth like a sharp sword,
he hid me in the shadow of his hand.
He made me into a sharpened arrow
and kept me safe in his quiver.
He said to me, "Israel, you are my servant,
I will show my glory through you."
But I said, "I have wasted my time.
I have tired myself out for nothing, to no purpose."
Yet all the time my cause was in the Lord's hands
and my reward with my God.
And now the Lord has spoken,
who formed me in my mother's womb to be his servant,
to bring his people back to him
and to re-unite Israel to him (. . .):
"I shall make you a light to the nations
so that my salvation may reach the remotest parts of earth."
This is what the Lord says, the redeemer, the Holy One of Israel.

The joy of return
49: 13–23

Shout for joy, you heavens; let the earth rejoice!
For the Lord has consoled his people,
he is taking pity on those in deep distress.
    My people were saying, "The Lord has abandoned me, he has forgotten me."
Can a woman forget her tiny baby?
Does she feel no pity for the child she has
given birth to? But even if these women
were to forget, I shall not forget you.
Look! I have engraved your name,
on the palms of my hands.
I am always watching over the ramparts of your cities.
Those who will rebuild you are hurrying to help you,
while those who have destroyed and wrecked you will
soon go away.

Lift up your eyes and look around you:
everyone is gathering together, coming to you.
By my life, I give you my promise, declares the Lord,
you will put them all on like jewels,
like a bride, you will fasten them on.
For from now on, the parts of your country which lie devastated,
empty and in ruins, will be too cramped for your inhabitants (. . .).
Then you will think to yourself,
"Who bore these children for me?
I was all alone, without any children,
exiled, turned out of my home; who has brought these up?
I was left all alone, so where have these come from?"

This is what the Lord God says:
Look, I am beckoning to the nations
and making a signal to the peoples:
they will bring your sons in their arms
and your daughters will be carried on their shoulders.
Kings will be like foster-fathers to you
and their princesses, your foster-mothers.
They will bow down before you with their faces to the
ground, and they will lick the dust at your feet.
And you will know that I am the Lord.
Those who hope in me will
not be disappointed.

The prophet sang of the coming freedom. The people of God would be like a woman abandoned by everyone who suddenly found a huge family. Everyone would want her. It would be a great triumph.

The next prophecy about the Servant who will bring salvation emphasises how attentive the Servant would be to the divine Word he came to proclaim. He would have to face terrible opposition, but would persevere in spite of it.

Third song of the servant

50: 4–8

The Lord has given me a tongue that is able to pass on his word, for me to know how to give a word of comfort to those who are weary. Morning by morning he makes my ear alert to listen like a disciple.
The Lord has taught me to listen,
and I have not resisted, I have not turned away.
I have offered my back to those who hit me,
my cheeks to those who pulled my beard;
I have not turned my face away from those who
insulted me and spat at me.
The Lord comes to my help,
this is why I have not become discouraged;
this is why I have made my face as hard as flint.
I know that I shall not be made to feel ashamed.
The one who gives me justice is near!

Jerusalem is liberated

52: 1–9

A feast day! Jerusalem was freed. Everywhere, messengers carrying the good news were welcomed with joy. The Lord had acted at last.

Awake, awake! Put on your finest clothes, Jerusalem,
Holy City! (. . .)
Shake off your dust; get up, captive Jerusalem!
The chains have fallen from your neck! (. . .)
  How beautiful on the mountains, are the feet of the messenger who comes to announce peace,
bringing good news and the message of salvation
and says to Jerusalem, "Your God is king!" (. . .)
  Break out together into shouts of joy, you ruins of Jerusalem; for the Lord has consoled his people, he has redeemed Jerusalem.

Fourth song of the servant

52: 13—53: 11

Look, my servant will find success,
he will grow great and will rise to great heights.
Many people were stunned by his appearance–
so badly disfigured was he that he no longer looked like a man.
Many nations will be astonished and
kings will not dare to say a word in his presence, when they see what they had never been told, learn what they had not heard before. Who has believed what we have heard?

And who among us has seen the Lord's hand in what has happened?
He grew up before the Lord like the shoot of a young tree,
like a root in dry ground.
He had no beauty or charm to attract us to him,
his appearance did not win our hearts;
he was despised, the lowest of men,
a man of sorrows, familiar with suffering,
one from whom, as it were, we turned our eyes away.
He was despised, and we paid no attention to him.
Yet ours were the sufferings he was bearing,
ours the sorrows he was carrying.
We thought he was being punished
and struck down with affliction by God.
But he was being wounded for our crimes,
crushed because of our guilt.
The punishment which brought us peace fell on him,
and we have been healed by his bruises.
We had all gone astray like sheep,
each taking his own way.
The Lord made him carry all our sins.
Ill-treated, he never protested or said a word,
like a lamb led to the slaughter-house,
like a sheep dumb before its shearers
he never opened his mouth.
He was forcibly arrested and then sentenced.
Which of his contemporaries showed any concern,
at seeing him led to his death
and struck down for his own people's crimes?
He was given a grave among the wicked,
and a tomb among the rich,
although he had done no violence,
had never spoken a lie.
It was the Lord's wish to crush him with pain.
In giving his life as an offering for sin,
he will see his descendants and prolong the days
of his life.
Through him, the Lord's plan will be accomplished.
After the ordeal he has endured,
he will see the light and be content.

Probably the most striking text in the book of Isaiah. Who is this man, despised, rejected, persecuted? His sorrows made the people think he must be the guiltiest man who ever lived. In fact, like a scapegoat, he took upon himself the curse of the whole human race. Apparently cursed, he sacrificed himself for all of us. But, at the same time, he opened the door to conversion for all of us.

To Christians, this is an amazing description of the work of Jesus.

Jerusalem is restored

54: 1–10

Jerusalem and the chosen people were compared to a woman abandoned and childless, who suddenly finds herself the mother of a large and happy family. The tent has to be enlarged to make room for all the children. It is because her husband, who seemed to have abandoned her, was now beside her for ever. That husband is God.

Shout for joy, barren one who has never had any children! Break into shouts of joy, you who were never in labour! For the children of the woman who was abandoned are more in number than the children of the married wife, says the Lord.

Make your tent larger, extend the curtains of your home, lengthen your ropes, make your tent-pegs firm, for you will burst out to the right and to the left.

Your children will extend into neighbouring lands and deserted towns will be filled with people again. Do not be afraid, you will not be made to feel ashamed. Do not worry, you will not be disgraced again! For you will forget the shame of your youth and no longer remember the dishonour of your widowhood.

For your Creator is your husband. His name is the Lord of the universe. The Holy One of Israel is your redeemer, he is called God of the whole world. Yes, the Lord has called you back as if you were a wife who had been abandoned and left in deep distress, like the divorced wife of his youth.

Your God says to you, I did abandon you for a brief moment, but moved by great pity I shall take you back. In a flood of anger, I turned my face away from you for a moment. But in everlasting love I have taken pity on you, says the Lord, your redeemer. (. . .) So now I swear I will never be angry with you again and I will never rebuke you again. For the mountains may fall down and the hills be shaken, but my faithful love will never leave you, my covenant of peace will never be shaken, says the Lord who takes pity on you.

Final invitation

55: 1–11

Oh, come to the water all you who are thirsty; though you have no money, come, buy and eat; come, buy wine and milk without money, free!

Why spend money on what cannot nourish and your wages on what fails to satisfy?

Listen carefully to me and you will have good things to eat and rich food to enjoy.

Pay attention and come to me; listen, and you will live.

I shall make an everlasting covenant with you and I will fulfil the promises I made to David. (. . .)

Let the wicked man abandon his wrong ways and the evil one his thoughts. Let him turn back to the Lord who will take pity on him, to our God, for he is rich in forgiveness.

For my thoughts are not your thoughts and your ways are not my ways, declares the Lord. For as high as the heavens are above the earth so high are my ways above your ways, and my thoughts above your thoughts.

The rain and the snow come down from the sky and do not return there without having watered the earth, fertilising it and making it germinate to provide seed for the sower and food to eat. It is the same with the word that leaves my mouth; it will not return to me without having carried out what I wanted it to, without having achieved what it was sent to do.

> **Water for the thirsty and free food for the hungry: God's feast is about to begin, the wedding-feast between himself and his people. Let everyone hurry to the feast, the only feast that exists! Let everyone be converted to the Lord, acknowledging that he alone is God, that he is the Almighty whose Word is capable of changing the world.**

THE 'THIRD ISAIAH' (Isa. 56–66)

The Jews who had escaped from exile were soon disappointed despite their return. Where was the brilliant future they had expected? An anonymous prophet tried to stand up to the defeatists and give the people back their hopes. His writings were to be joined onto the works of his predecessors. He reminded them that the obstacle to permanent salvation was sin: they should take up the struggle against idolatry and injustice again! God would give them a new world order, for he was always ready to forgive, and faithful to the people whom he chose once and for all.

The new prophet also dealt with the question of what attitude the Jews should take towards foreigners. Of course, he continued to thunder against the pagan nations, who remained stubbornly in their evil ways, but he called on the Jewish nation to welcome into the Temple those pagans who had been converted to the true religion. God would even choose priests from among them one day. By speaking in this way, the prophet destroyed the narrow world-view of many of the Jews who believed that God wanted them to keep themselves separate from the other nations.

The exile had forced them to change their ideas about foreigners. They had discovered that some foreigners were good people, and some of them had been attracted by the religion of Israel. The old way of seeing things excluded from the religious practices all those who, for example, were considered to be inferior: eunuchs who were unable to produce children, and non-Israelites in general. But it was now clear that the main thing was a desire to serve the Lord and keep his laws. The old "exclusivity" was no longer valid. It was a revolution in the Jewish way of thinking but was far from complete.

Promises to foreigners
56: 1–7

This is what the Lord says: Be concerned about fair judgements, act with justice, for soon my salvation will come and my saving justice will be revealed.

Blessed is anyone who does this, anyone who keeps firmly to it, observing the Sabbath, not misusing it, and avoiding every evil deed.

No foreigner who joins himself to the Lord should say, "The Lord will utterly exclude me from his people." No eunuch should think to himself, "Look, I am only a dried-up tree."

For the Lord says this: To the eunuchs who observe my Sabbaths and choose to do what pleases me, keeping faithfully to my covenant, I shall make room for them in my house and within my walls; I shall give them an everlasting name that will never be forgotten: it will be better for them than for sons and daughters.

As for foreigners who join themselves to the Lord to serve him, to love his name and become his servants, all who observe the Sabbath, not misusing it, and keep faithfully to my covenant: I shall lead them to my holy mountain and fill them with joy in my house of prayer. Their offerings and sacrifices will be accepted on my altar, for my house will be called a house of prayer for all peoples.

The kind of fasting that pleases God
58: 1–8

Shout for all you are worth, do not hold back,
raise your voice like a trumpet,
tell my people what they have done wrong.

They seek for me day after day, they long to know my ways
(. . .).
They ask me for laws that are just,
they long to be near God.
They demand to know: "Why have we fasted, if you do not see, why have we denied ourselves if you never notice?"

Look, it is because, on the days when you fast, you please yourselves, and you exploit all your workers (. . .).

Making a bed of sackcloth and ashes, is that what you call fasting, a day acceptable to the Lord?

This is the sort of fast that pleases me:

To break unjust chains, to undo the yoke which crushes, to let those who are oppressed go free, and to break every yoke.

Those who had escaped from exile had taken up their religious practices again but were surprised that it had so little effect. Wasn't God paying any attention? But what were the correct religious practices? The prophet spoke out strongly against the illusions of those who thought they sought God while continuing to live in sin and injustice.

It is sharing your food with the hungry, and sheltering the home-less poor; if you see someone lacking clothes, to clothe him, and not turning away from a member of your own family. Then your light will blaze out like the dawn

and your wound will be healed quickly, you will follow justice and the glory of the Lord will follow you.

The splendour of Jerusalem

60: 1–6, 16–19

Arise, shine out, for your light has come,

and the glory of the Lord has risen on you.

Look! though night still covers the earth

and darkness the peoples, the Lord is rising over you like the sun, and his glory can be seen over you.

The nations will come to your light

and kings to the brightness of your dawn. Lift up your eyes and look around you: they are all gathering together; they are coming towards you.

Your sons are coming from far away and your daughters are being carried in people's arms.

When you see them, you will become radiant,

your heart will throb and swell with joy,

since the riches of the sea will flow towards you,

the wealth of the nations will come to you.

Herds of camels will fill your streets,

loaded with goods from Midian and Ephah.

Everyone will come from the land of Saba,

bringing gold and incense and proclaiming the

praises of the Lord. (. . .)

You will suck the milk of nations,

you will fill yourselves with the wealth of kings,

and you will know that it is I, the Lord, who

saves you (. . .).

Violence will no longer be heard of in your

country, nor devastation and ruin within your

borders. You will call your walls "Salvation"

and your gates "Praise".

You will no longer need the sun to give you

daylight, nor the moon to shine on you,

for the Lord will be your everlasting light,

your God will be your splendour.

Jerusalem would one day be the capital of the universe. It would be the centre of a humanity that was unified at last. The Evangelist Matthew saw the coming of the three Wise Men as the beginning of the fulfilment of this prophecy.

The last chapter of Revelation used images from this text in order to describe the 'new Jerusalem' as God's gift to humankind.

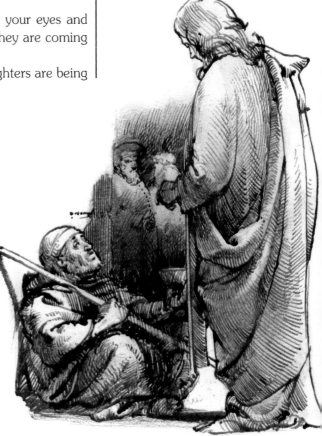

JEREMIAH

Who is able to stand back and see things during times of crisis and the collapse of societies to assess clearly the situation without sinking into despair? Anyone who dares to do so will be persecuted and rejected. That was what happened to Jeremiah.

The kingdom of Judah was going from bad to worse and the Chaldaean threat was increasing. This was in about BC 630. The society was corrupt morally and religiously, yet nobody saw clearly what was happening: everyone was optimistic about the future.

Jeremiah was born into a family of priests and God called him to be a prophet in 626. He began to proclaim that the kingdom of Judah was doomed although he was tormented by the uncertainty himself.

For a brief moment, he was hopeful as he watched the religious reforms carried out by Josiah. But his hopes were shattered when the king was killed in battle, and after that the prophet could only see sorrows ahead. He advised the people to surrender to the Chaldaeans, but was accused of accepting defeat too easily, and narrowly escaped being put to death. He cried out in despair and was angry with God for giving him a job to do which made him so alone (this is what the chapters we have called "Jeremiah's confession" are all about).

Surprisingly, it was at this, his darkest moment after the first fall of Jerusalem to the Chaldaeans, that Jeremiah began to proclaim his prophecies of happiness. He was certainly more downtrodden than ever but he looked forward to the time when God himself would come to create his messianic kingdom. The coming catastrophe was inevitable but would give the society a fresh start. Then the Lord could make a *new covenant* with his people.

Jeremiah was inspired by God but those he loved could not understand him. In spite of his difficulties, however, he had absolute faith in the Lord. One day, Christians would recognise him as the man who, by his words and way of life, showed most clearly what Jesus would be like.

The call of Jeremiah

1: 4–10

The word of the Lord came to me, saying: "Before I formed you in your mother's womb I knew you. Before you were born I consecrated you; I chose you to be a prophet to the nations." I then said, "Ah, Lord God, I really do not know how to speak: I am only a child!" But the Lord replied, "Do not say, 'I am only a child,' for you must go to all to whom I send you and say whatever I command you. Do not be afraid when you stand in front of them, for I am with you to rescue you, the Lord declares." Then the Lord stretched out his hand and touched my mouth. He said to me: "There! I have put my words into your mouth.
Look, today I have put you in charge over the nations and king-doms, to uproot and to knock down, to destroy and to overthrow, to build and to plant."

> From the outset, God's chosen prophet tried to turn down a mission whose difficulty he saw immediately. God's call was stronger than that: Jeremiah was to see the nation's final collapse, but he would also see the birth of a new reality.

Israel is reproached for being unfaithful

2: 1–7, 13

The word of the Lord came to me, saying, "Go and shout this in Jerusalem's ears: Say to them:

This is what the Lord says: I remember the love you used to show me, the affection of the days when we were first engaged. Then you followed me through the desert, through that land where nothing grew.

Israel was holy to the Lord, like the first-fruits of his harvest; I was angry with those who ate from this produce and I sent disaster on them. (. . .)

What wrong did your ancestors find in me, that they have gone so far as to follow worthless idols and become worthless them-selves? (. . .)

I brought you to a country of plenty, to enjoy its produce and good things; but when you entered my country, you ruined it, you made my heritage a place to be hated. (. . .)

They have abandoned me, the fountain of living water, and dug their own cracked water-tanks that hold no water. (. . .)"

> God is described here as a young man who remembers with nostalgia the time when his fiancée loved him. Now she had betrayed him for no reason and had gone in search of other lovers. Israel was in fact like a prostitute since politically and religiously it was a slave of powerful Egypt and Chaldaea.

2: 20–2
Israel, you said, "I will not serve!"
Yet on every high hill and under every green tree you have laid yourself down like a prostitute.
Yet I had planted you, a red vine taken from completely sound stock.
How is it you have turned into seedlings of a vine that is unknown to me?
Even though you scrub yourself with soda
and add plenty of soap,
the stain of your guilt would still remain visible to me, the Lord declares. (. . .)

2: 28, 32–5
Where are the gods you made for yourself?
Let them get up if they can save you
when trouble comes! (. . .)
Does a girl forget her jewels,
or a bride her sash?
And yet my people have forgotten me, for too many days to count.
How well you knew where to go to find love!
And so you have even made yourself familiar with the ways of crime.
The blood of the poor is found on your clothes. (. . .)
And in spite of all this, you say, "I am innocent,
I do not deserve God's anger."
But I am going to judge you.

Attack on the Temple

7: 1–15
The message that came to Jeremiah from the Lord, saying: "Stand at the gate of the Temple of the Lord and proclaim this message: Listen to the word of the Lord, all you men of Judah who come in through these gates to worship the Lord. The Lord of the universe, the God of Israel, says this: Change your behaviour and your actions and I will let you stay in this place. Do not believe the lies of those who say: 'This is the Temple of the Lord, the Temple of the Lord, the Temple of the Lord!' But if you really make changes to your behaviour and your actions, if you really treat one another fairly, if you stop exploiting foreigners, orphans and widows, if you do not shed the blood of innocent people in this

A little statuette used in the cult of Astarte.

The Judaeans were convinced of their superiority over the Israelites at the time when the kingdom was split: didn't they have the Temple of David? Jeremiah condemned this false security. God would destroy the Temple if it just gave them an excuse to indulge in all the sins available. God did not want them to go through the motions of pretending to be religious.

place and if you do not follow other gods, leading to your own downfall, then I shall let you live in this country which I gave long ago and for ever to your ancestors. But you put your trust in lies. What! You steal, murder, commit adultery, you do not keep your promises, you burn incense to idols and follow other gods you do not know, and then you come and stand before me in this Temple that bears my name, and say: 'Now we are safe!' and go on doing these awful things! In your eyes is this Temple that bears my name a den for bandits? I, at any rate, can see straight, declares the Lord. Go and see what I have done at Shiloh, the place which used to be set apart for me. At one time I gave my name a home there.

"Go and see what I have done to it to punish the wickedness of my people Israel! And now, since you have done all these things, the Lord declares, and since you refused to listen when I spoke to you so urgently, and so persistently, I shall treat this Temple that bears my name, and in which you put your trust, the place that I gave you and your ancestors, just as I treated Shiloh. I shall chase you out of my sight just as I did your brothers."

Jeremiah recalls the covenant

11: 1–12

The word that came to Jeremiah from the Lord, "Remind yourselves of the terms of our covenant!

"Tell the people of Judah and the citizens of Jerusalem: This is what the Lord, the God of Israel, says: Cursed be anyone who will not listen to the terms of this covenant which I made with your ancestors when I brought them out of Egypt, out of that iron-foundry. I told them: Listen to my voice, carry out all my orders; then you will be my people and I shall be your God. I will fulfil the promise I made to your ancestors, to give them a country flowing with milk and honey, the land where you find yourselves today."

I replied, "So be it, Lord!" Then the Lord said to me, "Proclaim this message in the towns of Judah and in the streets of Jerusalem, saying: Listen to the terms of this covenant and obey them. For when I brought your ancestors out of Egypt, I solemnly warned them, and have kept on warning them right up until today, saying: Listen to my voice. But they did not listen to me, they did not pay attention. Instead each person has stubbornly insisted on following his own evil desires. And so, I have put into action the words of

This text dates from the time when King Josiah was trying to bring about religious reform and reinstating the idea of the Ten Commandments which had just been rediscovered in the Temple (the text was from Deuteronomy and had been placed there by Jews escaping from the kingdom of Israel). Jeremiah was pleased about the reforms and wanted to believe in them, but he knew very well that it was too late: the rot had set in.

this covenant which I had ordered them to obey but which they have not put into practice."

The Lord said to me, "There is clearly a conspiracy among the people of Judah and the citizens of Jerusalem. They have fallen back into the sins of their ancestors by refusing to listen to my words. They too are intent on following other gods and serving them. The House of Israel and the House of Judah have broken my covenant which I made with their ancestors. And so, the Lord says this: I shall now bring a disaster on them which they will not be able to escape. They will call to me for help, but I shall not listen to them. The towns of Judah and the citizens of Jerusalem will then go and call for help to the gods to whom they burn incense, but these will be no help at all to them. (. . .)

"You, for your part, must not intercede for this people, you must neither plead nor pray on their behalf. For I will not listen when in their distress they call to me for help."

The waistcloth and the wine jugs

13: 1–14

The Lord said this to me, "Go and buy a linen waistcloth and put it round your waist. But do not dip it in water." And so, as the Lord had ordered, I bought a waistcloth and put it round my waist. Then the word of the Lord came to me a second time, "Take the waistcloth that you have bought and are wearing round your waist. Get up, go to the River Euphrates and hide it there in a hole in the rock." So I went and hid it by the Euphrates just as the Lord had ordered me. A long time later, the Lord said to me, "Get up, go to the Euphrates and fetch the waistcloth I ordered you to hide there." So I went to the Euphrates, searched for the waistcloth and took it from the place where I had hidden it. It was ruined, no use for anything. Then the Lord spoke to me in the following words, "The Lord says this: In the same way I shall ruin the pride of Judah, the great pride of Jerusalem. This evil people, these people who refuse to listen to my words, who insist on doing what pleases them and on running after other gods, serving and worshipping them — this people will become like this waistcloth, no good for anything. For just as a man ties a waistcloth around him, so I have tied the House of Israel and the House of Judah to me, the Lord declares, to be my people, my glory, my honour and my pride. But they have not listened.

Jeremiah performed little dramatic gestures in order to make the divine message more easy to understand. He acted out two parables. Through the first, he spoke out against the corruption of Israel following from the influence of Chaldaea (of which the main river was the Euphrates). In the second, he presented the Judaeans as jugs which needed to be broken. (A waistcloth was worn as underwear, like underpants today.)

"You will also say this to them: The Lord, God of Israel, says this: Any jug can be filled with wine. And if they answer you, 'We know that!' you are to say, the Lord says this: Look, I shall fill all the inhabitants of this country, the kings who rule on the throne of David, the priests, the false prophets and all the citizens of Jerusalem, so full with wine that they become drunk.
Then I shall set them one against the other,
parents and children all together,
the Lord declares. I shall destroy
them without pity, without
mercy and without relenting."

Jeremiah visits the potter

18: 1–12
The word of the Lord came to Jeremiah:
"Get up and make your way down to the
potter's house, and there I shall tell you
what I have to say."
So I went down to the potter's house;
and there he was,
working at the
wheel.

But the pot he was making turned out wrong, as sometimes happens with clay when a potter is at work. So he began again and shaped it into another pot, and this time it worked out well.

Then the Lord said to me: "House of Israel, can I not do to you what this potter does? the Lord demands. Yes, House of Israel, in

The prophet used symbolical gestures in order to express himself more strikingly. Israel was no more than a clay pot in the hand of God. A pot! The potter would break it if he considered it a failure: he could always make another. That was God's message to Jerusalem.

my hands you are like clay in the potter's hand. Sometimes I announce that I shall uproot, break down and destroy a certain nation or kingdom. But if the nation I have spoken against turns away from its wickedness, I then change my mind about the disaster which I have intended to bring upon it. In the cases of other nations or kingdoms I announce that my purpose is to build up and plant. But if that nation does what is evil in my eyes and refuses to listen to my voice, I then change my mind about the good which I was intending to send upon it. So now, say this to the people of Judah and the inhabitants of Jerusalem: The Lord says this:

I am preparing to send a disaster on you; I am working out a plan against you. So now, each one of you, turn away from the evil path you are following, take steps to improve your conduct and actions.''

The broken jug
19: 1–5, 10–11

The Lord said to Jeremiah, ''Go and buy a jug from the potter. Take some of the people's elders and some of the senior priests with you. Go out towards the Valley of Ben-Hinnom, just outside the Gate of the Potsherds. There you will speak the words I give you. You must say: Kings of Judah, people of Jerusalem! Listen to the word of the Lord of the universe, the God of Israel: I am about to bring a terrible disaster on this place. The ears of every one who hears of it will ring in shock. For they have abandoned me and have made this place unrecognisable. They have offered incense here to other gods which neither they nor their ancestors nor the kings of Judah ever knew before. They have shed the blood of innocent people in this place. For they have built altars to the god Baal and they have sacrificed their sons on them, a thing I never ordered, never mentioned, that had never entered my thoughts. (. . .) You must break this jug in front of the men who are with you, and say to them: This is what the Lord of the universe says: I am going to break this people and this city just as one breaks a potter's pot, so that it can never be mended again.''

20: 1–6

Now the priest Pashhur, who was the chief of police in the Temple of the Lord, heard Jeremiah making this prophecy. Pashhur hit the prophet Jeremiah and then put him in the stocks. (. . .)

Next day, Pashhur had Jeremiah taken out of the stocks. Then

Another story about pots: the prophet went to break the pot in the place where children were sacrificed to foreign gods as a symbol of punishment. But things went wrong for Jeremiah: he was arrested and put in chains. He spoke out angrily against those who thus dared to silence the word of God.

Jeremiah said to him, "The Lord no longer calls you Pashhur but Terror-on-every-Side. For this is what the Lord says: A time of terror lies ahead of you and all your friends; they will be killed by the sword of their enemies, your own eyes will see it. I shall also hand the whole nation of Judah over to the king of Babylon; he will carry them off as his captives to Babylon and will kill them with the sword. (. . .)

"As for you, Pashhur, you and your whole household will go into captivity. You will go to Babylon and you will die there, and be buried there, you and all your friends to whom you have prophesied lies."

Jeremiah's complaints

20: 7–18

You have seduced me, Lord, and I have let myself be seduced; you have overpowered me: you were stronger than me. People laugh at me all day long, they all make fun of me.
For whenever I speak, I have to cry out
and proclaim, "Violence and ruin!"
For me, the word of the Lord means being insulted and laughed at all day long.
I would say to myself, "I will not think about him,
I will not speak in his name any more."
But then there is like a fire burning in my heart,
imprisoned in my bones.
I wore myself out trying to hold it in, but I could not do it.
I heard so many insulting me with the words,

Jeremiah was broken by the constant struggle he sought to maintain in the name of God. He would have liked to abandon his mission, but he could not do so: he had to speak out. God was stronger than him.
The prophet came to curse the day of his birth: he was extremely unhappy.

"Terror on every side! Denounce him! Let us denounce him!"
Even those who were on good terms with me
watched for my downfall,
"Perhaps we can catch him out.
Then we shall get the better of him and take our revenge!"
But the Lord is at my side and he fights with me like a mighty
hero. My opponents will stumble, in defeat:
they will be confused by their failure and deeply disgraced.

Lord of the universe, you test the righteous,
you pay attention to their motives and thoughts.

I have put my cause in your hands.
I will see you take revenge on them. (. . .)

A curse on the day when I was born!
No one should have celebrated the day my mother gave birth to me
A curse on the man who brought my father the news,
"A son, a boy has been born to you!" filling him with joy. (. . .)
Why was I born?
To see heartache and pain and end my days in shame!

God can see our most secret thoughts.

The future king 23: 1–5

"Disaster is coming to the shepherds who lose and scatter the sheep of my pasture, declares the Lord. This, therefore, is what the Lord, God of Israel, says about the shepherds who are meant to look after my people: You have made my flock scatter, you have driven them away and have not taken care of them. Right, I shall take care of you for your misdeeds, the Lord declares! But I myself will come and gather what is left of my flock from all the countries where I have scattered them, and bring them back to their folds. They will be fruitful and increase in numbers. I shall raise up shepherds for them who will care for them and lead them to good pasture. They will no longer live in fear or terror; not one of them shall be lost, declares the Lord!

"Look, the days are coming when I will cause a righteous Branch to spring up from the line of David; he will reign as a wise king, doing what is just and righteous in the country."

Today, Israel had only weak kings. But tomorrow there would be a just king, the true heir of David, a real shepherd to his flock.

Jesus used this image of the shepherd to describe himself.

All this caused a violent reaction against the prophet. Jeremiah was arrested by the priests, official prophets and the people after he had announced that the Temple was going to be destroyed, like the one at Shiloh in the northern kingdom. They wanted to put him to death but Jeremiah stood by his prophecy. Some people then took his side and refused to take part in what they now saw as a crime. It was a big risk; other prophets had been lynched by angry mobs in the past.

THE BOOK OF CONSOLATION

Salvation is promised to Israel

30: 1–3

This is the word which came to Jeremiah from the Lord: (. . .)
"Look, the days are coming, when I shall bring back the captives
of my people Israel. I shall make them come back to the country
I gave to their ancestors and they will take possession of it. (. . .)
So do not be afraid, my servant Jacob!
Israel, do not be alarmed,
for I shall rescue you from distant countries,
I shall lead your descendants back from the country where they
have been held prisoner." (. . .)

Jeremiah's announcements were not all gloom and doom. They could also console the people and give them courage. But only when all seemed lost. Thus it was that this message of hope came immediately after the destruction of the northern kingdom of Israel. There was life beyond apparent death.

30: 17–21

For I shall bring you back to health and heal your wounds, declares
the Lord, you who used to be called "Outcast", "Zion for whom
no one cares".
The Lord says this: Look, I shall put the tents of Jacob back where
they once were,
I shall take pity on the places where his people live,
the town will be rebuilt on its hill,
the stronghold will stand again in its place.
Thanksgiving and shouts of joy will come from them.
I shall make them increase, they will not decrease.
I shall make them honoured, never again to be humbled.
Their sons will be as they once were,
their community will be secure before me,
and I shall punish all their oppressors.
Their prince will be one of their own people,
their ruler will come from among them.
I shall permit him to approach me freely.
Who, otherwise, would be bold enough to approach me?
asks the Lord.
You will be my people, and I shall be your God.

31: 8–9, 20
Watch, I shall bring them back from the land
of the north and gather them together from
the far ends of the earth. Among them there
will be the blind and the lame, pregnant
women and women giving birth.
There will be a great crowd returning here!
They will return in tears.
I shall lead them to streams of water,
along a smooth path
where they will not stumble.
For I am a father to Israel. (. . .)
My people are so dear to me that they are like
a favourite child. Whenever I mention him I remember
him with love.
That is why my heart longs for him.
I must take pity on him.

The new covenant

31: 31–4
The Lord declares, "Look, the days are coming, when I shall make
a new covenant with the House of Israel (and the House of Judah).
But it will not be like the covenant I made with their ancestors the
day I took them by the hand to bring them out of the land of
Egypt, that covenant which they broke, even though I was their
Master.

"But this is the covenant I shall make with the House of Israel
when those days come. I shall put my Law within them, writing it
on their hearts. Then I shall be their God and they will be my
people. No one will need to teach his neighbour
or his brother, saying, 'Learn to know the
Lord!' for they will all know me, from
the least to the greatest. I shall forgive
their guilt and forget their sin for ever,
declares the Lord."

The people would be transformed on the day when God came to redeem them. They would no longer obey the law out of fear, but out of love. There would be a new covenant between God and humanity.

Jesus was thinking of this passage when he announced the "New Covenant" (of the "New Testament") that he created himself by shedding his blood for us.

Jeremiah's actions symbolised the imminent catastrophe that nobody wanted to believe in. War broke out suddenly; Jerusalem was besieged and was about to fall. It was at that moment, when everybody was pessimistic, that the Lord told his prophet to return to his home village and buy a field. Jeremiah had difficulty understanding the instruction. To speculate about the future at such a time seemed incredible. But God is never wrong and, for once, Jeremiah's action was a sign of hope, beyond the coming defeat (ch. 32). The prophet continued to speak out strongly against the corrupt state of Judah's society.

34: 8, 10–12, 15–17

The message came to Jeremiah from the Lord after King Zedekiah had made a covenant with all the people in Jerusalem to issue a proclamation freeing their slaves. All the chief men and all the people who had entered into the covenant had agreed that everyone should free his slaves, men or women, and no longer keep them as slaves. Afterwards, however, they changed their minds, recovered the slaves, whom they had set free, and forced them to be slaves again. Then the word of the Lord came to Jeremiah as follows: (. . .) "Today you repented and did what pleases me by announcing freedom for your neighbour; you made a covenant before me in the Temple that bears my name. And then you changed your minds and, bringing dishonour to my name, each of you has taken back his slaves (. . .).

"So the Lord says this: You have disobeyed me, by not giving freedom to your brother and your neighbour. Very well, I shall give freedom to the sword, to famine and to plague to deal with you. All the kingdoms of the earth will be horrified at your suffering."

King Jehoiakim did not want to listen to Jeremiah's opinions. One day, Jeremiah sent his secretary, Baruch, to the Temple to present a message of warning to the country. The council of ministers was worried and alerted the king that the message was about to be read. The king's men cut up each column of scroll and threw it on the fire as soon as his secretary had read it. Jehoiakim hunted for the prophet and for Baruch to arrest them, but they managed to escape (ch. 36).

However, events were taking their course. The Chaldaeans took Jerusalem and a large part of the population was deported together with their king. Nebuchadnezzar appointed his uncle, Zedekiah, in the king's place although his powers were limited severely.

Zedekiah became involved in a revolt. The Chaldaeans returned to besiege Jerusalem. Jeremiah again announced catastrophe but the noblemen at court were united in fury against the prophet and accused him of accepting defeat too easily. When Jeremiah left the city during a brief pause in the siege, they took advantage of his absence to accuse him of treason and have him arrested. The king tried to avoid the worst but he had to give in to those who demanded the prisoner be put to death. It was to an Ethiopian, a court eunuch, that Jeremiah owed his life.

Jeremiah's mission was painful and we can understand how he could write one day like Job: "Curse the day that I was born!"
The persecution he faced makes him a prefiguration of Christ, as the Servant of Israel mentioned by Isaiah (ch. 53). The description in Isaiah may have been inspired by the life of Jeremiah.

38: 4–13

Then the chief men said to the king, "You must have this man put to death! There is no doubt he is discouraging the soldiers who are left in the city, and all the people too, by talking like this. This man is not seeking the welfare of the people but their ruin." King Zedekiah answered, "He is in your hands as you know, for the king is powerless to do anything to stop you." So they took Jeremiah and threw him into the well of the king's son Malchiah in the Court of the Guard; they let him down with ropes. There was no water in the well, only mud, and Jeremiah sank into the mud.

But Ebed-Melech the Cushite, a eunuch attached to the palace, heard that Jeremiah had been put into the well. As the king was sitting in the Benjamin Gate, Ebed-Melech came out from the palace and spoke to him: "My lord king, these men have done a wicked thing by treating the prophet Jeremiah like this: they have thrown him into the well. He will starve to death there, since there is no more food in the city." So the king gave Ebed-Melech the following order: "Take thirty men with you from here and pull the prophet Jeremiah out of the well before he dies." Ebed-Melech took the men with him and went into the palace to the Treasury wardrobe; out of it he took some torn, worn-out rags which he lowered on ropes to Jeremiah in the well.

Ebed-Melech then said to Jeremiah, "Put these torn, worn-out rags under your armpits to pad the ropes." Jeremiah did this. Then they dragged Jeremiah up with the ropes and pulled him out of the well. And Jeremiah stayed in the Court of the Guard.

When Jerusalem fell, in 586, the Chaldaeans spared Jeremiah, who remained in the ruined city. But the new governor appointed by the Chaldaeans was assassinated by terrorists. The people were terrified and feared Nebuchadnezzar would hit back. They dragged Jeremiah with them as they fled towards Egypt which was against his advice.

Jeremiah lived a sad life in Egypt. His fellow-countrymen still believed their defeat was because they had been unfaithful to Astarte, the queen of the skies! Until the end, the prophet remained alone and in the dark, with no hope of being present to see the birth of the wonderful world order he had foreseen. He was to die without ever being understood.

LAMENTATIONS

Jerusalem had fallen and the city had been destroyed. All religious faith seemed useless. But there were still some faithful people who believed that it all had a meaning: the Lord had punished his faithless people but would forgive them. Wasn't that what the prophets had said, especially Jeremiah, who was normally so severe about the Holy City?

An anonymous poet expressed these sentiments in five poems, composed in the style of contemporary funeral hymns. He presented Jerusalem as an abandoned queen, in slavery and mourning her lost happiness, begging fellow human beings and God for pity, but also talking of hope.

1: 1–2

How deserted the city is,
  that once thronged with people!
Once she was the greatest of nations,
  but now she is like a widow.
Once she was a princess ruling over states,
  now she is forced to work like a slave.
All night long she weeps,
  tears running down her cheeks.

The Church uses these texts during the liturgy on Good Friday, to express the sorrow of the Virgin Mary at the time of the Passion.

The "lovers" of Jerusalem are her former allies: Jeremiah and Ezekiel both spoke out against certain political alliances: they thought Jerusalem had been unfaithful to God, her true husband.

Not one of all her lovers
   is left to comfort her.
Her friends have all betrayed her,
   and become her enemies. (. . .)

1: 11–12
All her people are groaning,
   looking for something to eat;
they have given their treasures in exchange for food,
   to keep themselves alive.
Lord, look and see
   how despised I am!
All you who pass this way,
   look and see:
is any sorrow like the sorrow
   inflicted on me,
with which the Lord struck me
   on the day of his burning anger?

5: 1–5, 17–22
Lord, remember what has happened to us;
   look, and see how we have been humiliated.
Our inheritance has passed to strangers,
   our homes to foreigners.
We are orphans, we are fatherless;
   our mothers are like widows.
We have to buy our own water to drink,
   we have to pay for our own wood.
The yoke is on our necks; we are persecuted;
   we are exhausted, allowed no rest. (. . .)
This is why our hearts are sick;
   this is why our eyes have grown dim:
because Mount Zion is like a wasteland,
   jackals roam to and fro on it.
Yet you, Lord, rule for ever;
   your throne is secure and lasts from age to age.
Why have you forgotten us?
   Why have you abandoned us for so long?
Make us come back to you, Lord, and we will come back.
   Give us back the life we had before.
Unless you have totally rejected us,
   and your anger knows no limit.

BARUCH

We often need to get away from home and stand back from those things we take for granted, before we realise what we have lost, sometimes through our own fault. In the same way, the exile and scattering (or in Greek, the *diaspora*) of the Jews to foreign lands enabled them to see the real meaning of their ancestors' old traditions. This is what we discover in the book of Baruch.

The book was written by a group of the descendants of the deported Jews. This group had remained in Babylon after the destruction of Chaldaea by Cyrus in 539. Baruch was Jeremiah's secretary. We do not know his real name: this was the name he assumed when he became a priest. A letter thought to have been written by Jeremiah was added later to the book and is a vivid satire on the popular pagan cults.

Confession of sins and prayer for help
1: 15–19; 2: 11–15

Saving justice belongs to the Lord, while for us there is only shame; for the people of Judah, the inhabitants of Jerusalem, for our kings and princes, our priests, our prophets, and for our ancestors, because we have sinned against the Lord. We have disobeyed him, and we have not listened to the voice of the Lord our God telling us to follow the commandments he gave to us. From the day when the Lord brought our ancestors out of Egypt until today we have been disobedient to the Lord our God; we have been disloyal, and we have refused to listen to his voice. (. . .)

And now, Lord, God of Israel, who brought your people out of Egypt with great power, with signs and wonders, we recognise that we have sinned, we have been unfaithful and have broken your laws. Let your anger turn away from us since there are so few of us left among the nations where you have scattered us. Lord, listen to our prayers and our cries for help, save us for your own sake and help us win the favour of the people who have carried us to their lands, so that the whole world may know that you are the Lord our God, since Israel and his descendants are called by your name.

The faithful believers repented of the sins of their people while in captivity in Babylon. They felt involved in the sins of the past and humbly asked the Lord to forgive them, for they wanted to return to him.

EZEKIEL

BEYOND A COLLAPSING WORLD,
A NEW WORLD ORDER IS IN SIGHT

The kingdom of Judah had collapsed. Already, in 598, some of the inhabitants of Jerusalem had been taken prisoner to Chaldaea and, in 587, the ruin of the city was complete with more captives being sent to join the first. Everything caused despair. That was when a new prophet came to declare that the old system must collapse before a new one could grow up in its place.

Ezekiel was a priest who had been among the first to be captured. He quickly opposed those who hoped that Zedekiah's revolt against Nebuchadnezzar would result in speedy rescue for them: their cause was lost, and even the Temple was no longer a guarantee against disaster. Ezekiel stated that the future was in the hands of the prisoners. He advised each individual to think about his or her own personal responsibility for the disaster and to repent. This would make a new beginning possible.

The prophet became a messenger of hope after the final collapse of their illusions. He proclaimed that God would come to renew his people by the gift of his Spirit, and that Israel would be returned to life, although at present it was like a skeleton compared with its former self. He described how the pagan nations would be punished at the end of a great battle against the forces of evil.

Ezekiel spoke out against those who were responsible for the defeat, the leaders and the priests, bad shepherds of the flocks God had placed in their care. He announced that God would one day send a good shepherd who would give his life for the sheep. Sheep here is a symbol of the chosen people.

Ezekiel glimpsed the rebirth of Israel and tried to describe its new institutions: in particular the new temple around which the desert would flower.

Ezekiel's vision

1: 1–28

Then I found myself on the bank of the River Chebar, heaven opened and I saw visions from God. It was the fifth year of exile for King Jehoiachin.

I looked; a stormy wind blew from the north, a great cloud with flashing fire and brilliant light round it, and in the middle, in the heart of the fire, a brilliance like that of amber. In the middle I made out what seemed to be four living creatures which had human form. Each had four faces and four wings. (. . .) They touched one another with their wings. They did not turn as they moved; each one moved straight forward. This is what they looked like: all four had a human face to the front, a lion's face to the right, a bull's face to the left, and an eagle's face.

In the middle of these living creatures were what looked like blazing coals, like torches, darting backwards and forwards between them. The fire gave off a brilliant light, and lightning flashed from the fire. The living creatures kept disappearing and reappearing like flashes of lightning. (. . .)

I also heard the noise of their wings. When they moved, they sounded like flood-waters, like the voice of the Almighty, like the noise of a storm, like the noise of an army camp. When they stood still, they lowered their wings and even then there was still a noise.

Beyond the solid surface above their heads, there was something that looked like a throne made of sapphire. High above sitting on the throne was a figure with the appearance of a human being.

I saw a brilliance like amber, like fire, radiating from what appeared to be the waist upwards; and from what appeared to be the waist downwards, I saw what looked like fire, giving a brilliant light all round. The radiance of the encircling light was like a brilliant rainbow in the clouds on rainy days. The sight was like the glory of the Lord. I looked and fell to the ground. Then I heard the voice of someone speaking to me.

Ezekiel had his vision on the banks of a Chaldaean river. This was different from Isaiah whose visions had occurred in the Temple at Jerusalem: the change of venue was a sign that God was not confined to the Holy City, contrary to the beliefs of those who had thought Jerusalem was invincible. The images used by the prophet to describe what he saw are borrowed from Babylonian sculpture: but he emphasised that these were only very approximate images: it is impossible to describe God; he is far greater than his creation.

The first exiles in Babylon were hoping that the revolt against Nebuchadnezzar in Jerusalem would succeed. They did not realise the extent to which their world was doomed. Ezekiel then fell silent, causing his followers to become anxious. It was a sign: why bother to talk to people who did not want to hear? Ezekiel spoke only in mime until the final fall of the city. That was why he built a brick model of the besieged town in front of an amazed audience; and why he also ate forbidden foods similar to those that the prisoners would soon be forced to eat unless they were willing to die of hunger.

A strange, but meaningful gesture from the prophet: he left his house secretly through a hole in the wall and carried a poor bundle on his back. This was to be the fate of the inhabitants of Jerusalem.

The mime of the exile   12: 1–15

The Lord spoke to me in the following words, "Son of man, you are living among a band of rebels who have eyes but never see, they have ears but never hear. So, son of man, pack an exile's bundle and set off during the day while they watch. You will leave your home and go somewhere else while they watch. Then perhaps they will see that they are a band of rebels.

"You will pack your baggage by daylight, while they watch. You will then leave like an exile in the evening, while they watch. Make a hole in the wall, and go out through it. While they watch, you will put your pack on your shoulder and go out into the darkness. You will cover your face so that you cannot see where you are going. I have given you the job of warning the House of Israel what is about to happen."

I did as I had been told. By daylight I packed my baggage like an exile's bundle, and in the evening I made a hole through the wall with my hands. Then I went out into the darkness and put my pack on my shoulder while they watched.

Next morning the Lord spoke to me again, "Son of man, didn't the House of Israel, that band of rebels, ask you what you were doing? Say: The Lord says this: This prophecy concerns Jerusalem and the whole House of Israel who live there. Say: This is a warning to you of what is about to happen to Jerusalem and the whole country. They will be taken into exile. Their prince will himself have to put his pack on his shoulders in the darkness and go out through the wall (. . .). Then they will know that I am the Lord when I scatter them throughout the nations, in foreign countries."

"We are being punished for the sins of others, the sins of our ancestors! It's not fair!" cried the Israelites. There was actually no such thing as a sense of personal responsibility in ancient Israel. The nation was regarded as a single unit: if the king sinned then all the people would deserve punishment.

Individual responsibility   18: 1–32

The Lord spoke to me in the following words, "Why do you keep repeating this proverb in the land of Israel: 'The parents have eaten unripe grapes; and the children's teeth are set on edge?'

"I guarantee that you will have no further cause to repeat this proverb, says the Lord. Look, all life belongs to me; the father's life as well as the son's life. It is the one who has sinned who will have to die.

"But if a man is righteous, his actions law-abiding and just (. . .), if he keeps my laws and sincerely seeks to do what is right, living according to the truth, he will live, declares the Lord.

"But if he has a son who is violent and bloodthirsty, who commits all kinds of evil deeds even though his father never has (. . .), that son will not live (. . .). Having committed all these terrible crimes he will die and he will be responsible for his own death. (. . .)

"The one who has sinned is the one who must die. A son is not to bear his father's guilt, nor a father his son's guilt. The righteous man will be given credit for his righteousness, and the wicked man for his wickedness.

"If, however, the wicked man has a change of heart and is sorry for all the sins he has committed and if he decides instead to live according to my laws, doing what is right and just, he will most certainly live; he will not die. None of the crimes he committed will be remembered against him from then on. He will most certainly live because of his righteous actions. Am I pleased when wicked men die? Certainly not, says the Lord: I am pleased when the wicked man turns away from doing wrong and lives.

"But if the righteous man abandons his good way of life and does wrong by copying all the evil practices of the wicked, will he live? All his righteous actions will be forgotten from then on. He will most certainly die because he has been unfaithful and has sinned. Do not come to me and say, 'The Lord is acting in an unjust way.' Is it me who is acting in an unjust way? Is it not rather you? (. . .) So in future, House of Israel, I shall judge each of you by what that person does, declares the Lord. Repent and turn away from all your crimes, that there may be no more opportunities for guilt. Shake off all the crimes you have committed, and make yourselves a new heart and a new spirit! Why die, House of Israel? I do not take pleasure in the death of anyone — declares the Lord. So repent and live!''

This is the beginning of a meditation on a difficult problem: does God reward or punish people according to their merits? and, if so, why do good people suffer? This question is also asked in the book of Job and, above all, in the Gospels.
    That's not God's way, declares the prophet. Each of us is responsible for our own deeds and will be punished or rewarded accordingly, although it is always possible to come back to God after having sinned, just as it is possible to come to a bad end after having begun well.

An allegorical history of Jerusalem and Samaria
23: 1–35

The Lord spoke to me in the following words: "Son of man, there were once two women, two sisters. From their youth in Egypt, they lived their lives as prostitutes. Even as young girls they let men fondle their breasts. As regards their names, Oholah is Samaria, Oholibah is Jerusalem. Now Oholah was a prostitute, even though she belonged to me. She ran after her lovers, her neighbours the Assyrians, dressed in purple, governors and magistrates, all of them young and desirable, and skilful horsemen. She gave herself to all of them, the pick of Assyria, and in their homes she came into contact with all their idols and she became defiled (. . .). That

This was a terrible accusation to level at the two kingdoms of Israel and Judah: they are compared to two prostitutes who have betrayed their husbands and given themselves to anyone who wants them. Jerusalem was no better than Samaria, and could have benefited from the lesson the Samaritans were forced to learn.

is why I have handed her over to her lovers, to the Assyrians with whom she was in love. (. . .) "Her sister Oholibah saw all this, but she was even more depraved. The way she prostituted herself was even worse than her sister. She fell in love with her neighbours the Assyrians (. . .). But no sooner had she seen pictures carved into the wall of men from Chaldaea wearing clothes the colour of vermilion, with sashes round their waists and elaborate turbans on their heads, all looking so dignified, than she fell in love with them at first sight and sent messengers to them in Chaldaea. The Babylonians came to her, shared her love-bed and defiled her with their prostitutions. (. . .) I took my love away from her as I had done from her sister. (. . .) And so, Oholibah, this is what the Lord says: I shall set all your lovers against you. I shall bring them to attack you from all directions.

"From the north, they will come against you with chariots and wagons. A fully armed international army will attack you from all sides. I shall give them the task of passing sentence on you and they will pass sentence on you as they think fit. I shall direct my jealousy against you; they will treat you with great anger; they will cut off your nose and ears, and what is left of your family will be killed by the sword. They will capture your sons and daughters, and those who are left will be burnt. They will strip you of your clothes and rob you of your jewels. (. . .) This is what the Lord says: Since you have forgotten me, you will have to carry the full weight of your immoral behaviour and prostitutions."

The two cities were punished like women who had committed adultery.

Ezekiel suddenly found his tongue again in 587 after the fall of Jerusalem. He now wanted to give hope to his downtrodden fellow-countrymen.

Blame had to be allotted: the leaders of Israel had been bad shepherds and were responsible for the scattering of the flocks. God himself would one day

The shepherds of Israel   34: 1–6, 10–16

The Lord spoke to me in the following words, "Son of man, prophesy against the shepherds of Israel; prophesy.

"Say to them: Shepherds, this is what the Lord says.

"Disaster is in store for the shepherds of Israel who feed themselves! Are the shepherds not meant to feed the flock? Yet you have fed on milk, you have dressed yourselves in wool, you have sacrificed the fattest sheep, but you have not fed the flock. You have not made weak sheep strong, or cared for the sick ones, or bandaged up the injured ones.

"You have failed to bring back stray sheep or look for the lost. You have treated them cruelly and harshly. For lack of a shepherd they have been scattered, to become the prey of all the wild animals. My flock has gone astray on every mountain and on every high hill; my flock has been scattered all over the world; no one bothers about them and no one goes to look for them. (. . .)

"Very well, shepherds, hear the word of the Lord: because of all this I am against the shepherds.

"I shall take my flock out of their charge and from now on I will not allow them to feed my flock. And the shepherds will stop feeding themselves. I shall rescue my sheep from their mouths to stop them from being food for them.

"This is what the Lord says: Look, from now on I myself shall take care of my flock and look after it. I shall look after my sheep as a shepherd looks after his scattered flock. I shall rescue them from wherever they have been scattered on the day of darkness and catastrophe. I shall bring them back from the peoples where they are; I shall gather them back from the countries and bring them back to their own land. I shall pasture them on the mountains of Israel, in the valleys and in all the parts of the country where people live. I shall lead them to good pasture (. . .). I myself shall lead my sheep to good pasture and I myself shall give them rest, declares the Lord. I shall look for the sheep which are lost, bring back those which have strayed away, bandage up those which are injured and make those which are sick strong again. I shall watch over those which are fat and healthy. I shall be a true shepherd to them. (. . .)"

34: 23–4, 30–1

"I shall raise up one shepherd, my servant David, and put him in charge of them to lead them to good pasture; he will lead them to good pasture and be their shepherd. I, the Lord, shall be their God, and my servant David will be their ruler. (. . .)

"So they will know that I, their God, am with them and that they, the Israelites, are my people — declares the Lord. And you, my sheep, are the flock of my human pasture, and I am your God, declares the Lord."

become the shepherd of his sheep.

He would choose for himself a true shepherd, a new David. Peace and prosperity would reign everywhere on that day. Jesus took up this idea when he presented himself as the Good Shepherd (John 10: 11–18).

Foreign nations had seized the land and brought God's people under their control. The Lord would avenge his honour by restoring his heritage. He would save Israel, not because Israel deserved it, but to show them who he was. He would change the hearts of his people and give them a new spirit. On that day, Israel would be sincerely sorry for its sins and there would be forgiveness and rejoicing.

Promise of salvation
36: 22–36

"Say to the House of Israel: The Lord says this: 'I am not acting because you deserve it, House of Israel, but because of my holy name, which you have profaned among the nations where you have gone. (. . .) And the nations will know that I am the Lord when I display my holiness in you before their eyes, declares the Lord.

"For I shall take you from among the nations and gather you back from all the countries, and bring you home to your own country. I shall pour clean water over you and you will be made clean. I shall cleanse you of all your filth and of all your foul idols. I shall give you a new heart, and put a new spirit in you; I shall remove the heart of stone from your bodies and give you a heart of flesh instead. I shall put my spirit in you, and make you keep my laws, and do what I judge to be right. You will live in the country which I gave your ancestors. You will be my people and I shall be your God. (. . .) Then you will remember your evil conduct and actions. You will detest yourselves for your guilt and your terrible practices. I assure you that I am not doing this for your sake, declares the Lord. Be ashamed and blush for your conduct, House of Israel.

"This is what the Lord says: On the day I cleanse you from all your guilt, I shall fill your cities with people again and I shall cause the ruins to be rebuilt. The land, once devastated, will be farmed again. And the nations left round you will know that I, the Lord, have rebuilt what was demolished and replanted what was ruined. I, the Lord, have spoken and I shall do it."

The dry bones

37: 1–14

The hand of the Lord was on me. The spirit of the Lord carried me away and set me down in the middle of the valley, a valley full of bones. He made me walk up and down among them. There were bones everywhere and they were completely dry. He said to me, "Son of man, can these bones live?" I said to him, "Lord, only you know." He said to me, "Prophesy over these bones. Say: Dry bones, hear the word of the Lord.

"This is what the Lord says to these bones: I am now going to make breath enter you, and you will live. I shall put sinews on you, I shall make flesh grow on you, I shall cover you with skin and give you breath, and you will live; and you will know that I am the Lord."

I prophesied as I had been told to. At that moment, there was a noise, a clattering sound; it was the bones coming together. And as I looked, they were covered with sinews; flesh was growing on them and skin was covering them, but there was still no breath in them. He said to me, "Prophesy to the breath; prophesy, son of man. Say to the breath: The Lord says this: Come from the four winds, breath; breathe on these dead, so that they come to life!" I prophesied as he had told me to, and the breath entered them. They came to life and stood up on their feet: a great, an immense army.

Then the Lord said to me, "Son of man, these bones are the

All seemed lost. Israel was like a heap of dry bones in the desert, such as could be seen on the road to Babylon and exile, but God would breathe new life into those bones, inspiring them with his Spirit and would restore them to prosperity and power.

This is one of Ezekiel's most beautiful prophecies. The Christians saw it as a prediction of the coming of the Holy Spirit which brought the Church into being soon after the death of Jesus and the apparent failure of the Apostles.

EZEKIEL AND THE SPRING
IN THE TEMPLE

House of Israel. They keep saying, 'Our bones are dry, our hope has gone; we are done for.' So, prophesy. Say to them: The Lord says this: I am now going to open your graves, my people, and lead you back to the land of Israel. When I open your graves and bring you out from your graves, my people, you will know that I am the Lord. I shall put my spirit in you, and you shall live, I shall settle you back on your own soil, and you will know that I, the Lord, have spoken and done this, declares the Lord.''

Ezekiel was sure his people would be rescued and began to foretell the future. He dreamed in particular of a new temple, the symbol of the covenant that God would re-establish with his people. He was guided by an angel (in human form) and even described at length the details of this temple, giving all its measurements. He showed how the new building would be a source of blessing to the whole country.

The spring in the Temple
47: 1–12

The man brought me back to the entrance of the Temple.

A stream flowed eastwards from under the threshold of the Temple. He took me out by the north gate and led me right round as far as the east gate where the water flowed out on the right-hand side. The man went off to the east holding his measuring line and measured off a thousand cubits. He then made me wade across the stream; the water reached my ankles. He measured off another thousand and made me wade across the stream again; the water reached my knees. He measured off another thousand and made me wade across the stream again; the water reached my waist. He measured off another thousand; it was now a river which I could not cross, for the stream had swollen until it had become a river.

He then said, "Do you see, son of man?" He then took me and brought me back to the bank of the river. Now, when I reached it, I saw an enormous number of trees on each bank of the river. He said, "This water flows to the east, down to the Arabah, and to the sea. It flows into the sea and makes its waters clean. Wherever the river flows, all living creatures teeming in it will live. Fish will be very plentiful, for wherever the water goes it brings health, and life teems wherever the river flows. Along the river, on either bank, every kind of fruit tree will grow. The leaves of these trees will never wither, and they will never stop producing fruit; they will produce new fruit every month, because this water comes from the sanctuary. And their fruit will be good to eat and the leaves will bring healing.''

This description is the most interesting in the whole of Ezekiel's vision. The spring flowing from the Temple would revive the whole land, the desert and even the Dead Sea. Streams in that country normally get lost in the sand-dunes but this stream would grow larger as it flowed onwards: this is an image of divine grace spreading throughout the world. These images were often to be found in the symbolic pictures of the first Christians and also in the New Testament (especially when Jesus presented himself as the source of the water of life, in the book of John, and in the final chapter of Revelation). The spring in John's Gospel no longer comes from the Temple, however, but from the wound in the side of Jesus' body as it hung on the cross.

DANIEL

UNDER AN OPPRESSIVE DICTATOR: AN UNDERCOVER WRITER DECLARES THE ABSOLUTE SUPREMACY OF GOD

When a State becomes totalitarian and forces people to adhere to an official ideology people often band together to form a resistance. Authors are sometimes able to keep up the hopes of the resistance by writing books with a political message "in code". They are in danger, though, and may be facing torture and death for their resistance.

The Jews were under Greek occupation in BC 164 and King Antiochus Epiphanes wanted to force all his subjects to adopt the Greek way of life and its religion. A writer at that time put a work into circulation which he said had been written during the exile in Babylon a long time previously. Its author was Daniel who was said to have foretold all the events of the future and announced that the persecution would end soon. His message was thus received with joy: it was a source of hope.

The book seems rather strange to us and contains two very different types of stories.

Religious tales

The first story tells of the persecution that Daniel and his companions faced in Babylon. Not only did they resist faithfully and were saved miraculously from execution, but Daniel was able to interpret the dreams of Nebuchadnezzar and the vision of Belshazzar. He announced that God was master of the universe and would soon come and punish the persecutors.

Another story tells of a virtuous woman called Susanna (representing Israel) who was falsely accused by two old men who had not been able to make her sin. (These men represent the pagan nations which had not been able to make Israel forget its covenant with God.) The court was about to condemn the accused woman when the young Daniel proved that the accusers were acting out of spite, and the two men were punished.

An apocalypse

Apocalypses are writings which aim to give people hope by "putting all their cards on the table". Using descriptions full of symbolism, they show that events as we see them are only the visible and outward appearance of a deeper reality. Persecution is only a reflection of a gigantic battle between God and the forces of evil. But the Lord triumphs victoriously at the end of the fight and those who have been faithful to him are rewarded.

Daniel's visions, when decoded with the help of an angel, declare that God would soon triumph over the wicked when a mysterious character called "the Son of Man", who would come upon the clouds, intervened.

VISIONS AND ADVENTURES OF DANIEL IN BABYLON

Nebuchadnezzar's dream

Daniel and his companions were taken captive to Babylon. They were the talk of the town because nobody had ever seen such brilliant and dynamic young men. The explanation was their obedience to the Jewish Law which gave them more insight than any amount of learning could.

    King Nebuchadnezzar had just had a strange dream and none of his official magicians could interpret it. He concluded that they were all impostors and so he would have to get rid of them.

    Daniel on the other hand was able to tell the king all about his dream and to explain its meaning.

2: 31–45

The vision presented in a figurative way the great empires that had come and gone since the time of the exile. The latest to date was the empire of the persecutor Antiochus Epiphanes. This vision brought comfort to those who were suffering under his rule: God would intervene and crush him.

The Christians took up this idea of a stone which brought destruction (a stumbling block) which was to become the cornerstone of the Church founded by God.

"You have had a vision, Your Majesty; you saw a great statue standing before you. It was extremely bright and it was terrible to look at. The head of this statue was made of fine gold, its chest and arms were made of silver, its stomach and thighs of bronze, its legs of iron, and its feet were part iron, part clay. You were gazing at it. Suddenly without anyone touching it, a stone broke away and hit the statue, striking its feet of iron and clay and shattering them. Then, at the very same moment, iron and clay, bronze, silver and gold, all shattered into tiny pieces as fine as the chaff from corn when it is threshed in the summer. The wind blew them away, without leaving any trace behind. And the stone that had struck the statue grew into a great mountain, filling the whole world.

    "Now this is what your dream means: O king of kings, the God of heaven has given you a kingdom, power and honour. (. . .) You are the golden head. And, after you, another kingdom will rise, not as great as yours, and then a third, of bronze, which will rule over the whole world. A fourth kingdom will be as hard as iron which crushes and smashes everything into dust. The feet you saw, part clay, part iron, are a kingdom which will be split in two. (. . .) In the days of those kings, the God of heaven will set up a kingdom which will never be destroyed, and this kingdom will never be taken over by any other nation. It will shatter and absorb all the previous kingdoms, and last for ever: that is why you saw a stone break away from the mountain without anyone touching it and smash bronze, clay, silver and gold to dust. The Great God has shown the king what is going to take place."

King Nebuchadnezzar gave glory to Daniel's God and gave the prophet a high position at his court.

    But shortly afterwards the king had a golden statue made and tried to force his subjects to worship it. The young Jews refused to bow down to the idol. The king tried to force them and, when they resisted, commanded that they be thrown into a red-hot furnace. That was when an amazing thing happened.

The song in the furnace

3: 24–50

They walked in the heart of the flames, praising God and blessing the Lord. Azariah stood in the heart of the fire, praying aloud in these words:

May you be blessed and honoured, Lord, God of our ancestors, may your name be glorified for ever. For you are righteous, in all that you have done for us. All your deeds are true, all your ways right, all your judgements true. (. . .)

Yes, we have sinned, and done wrong by turning away from you, yes, we have sinned greatly,

and we have not listened to your commandments (. . .).

You have handed us over to our enemies,

to a lawless people, the worst of the godless,

to an unjust king, the worst in the whole world;

today we have no right to open our mouths (. . .).

Do not abandon us for ever, remember us for your name's sake and do not cancel your covenant with us.

Do not withdraw your favour from us, for the sake of Abraham, your friend, of Isaac, your servant, and of Israel, your holy one (. . .). Let confusion seize all those who harm your servants (. . .). Let them learn that you alone are God and Lord, glorious over the whole world.

And the angel of the Lord came down into the furnace beside Azariah and his companions. He beat the flames of the fire outwards and, in the centre of the furnace, he blew cool air to them like the breeze and dew, so that the fire did not touch them at all and caused them no pain or fear.

The song of Azariah was a "confessional" hymn. The faithful man acknowledged the sins of his people and repented in hope of divine mercy.

3: 51–90

The song of the three young men was a hymn of triumph to the God who saved them. Their blessings were inspired by the Jewish liturgy, and were followed by a song in which all God's creatures praise him, based on images in the book of Genesis.

The conclusion affirms that God drags us away from the "mouth of hell" and from death. The trial by fire thus appears as the introduction to a new life.

The text is part of what Protestants call "the Apocrypha" and has been preserved only in Greek and Syriac.

Then, all three young men in unison began to glorify and bless God in the furnace, singing:

May you be blessed, Lord, God of our ancestors,
may you be praised and exalted for ever. Blessed be your glorious and holy name, may it be praised and exalted for ever. (. . .)
Bless the Lord, angels of the Lord,
praise and glorify him for ever!
Bless the Lord, heavens,
praise and glorify him for ever!
Bless the Lord, all the waters above the heavens,
praise and glorify him for ever! (. . .)
Bless the Lord, sun and moon,
praise and glorify him for ever! (. . .)
Bless the Lord, all rain and dew,
praise and glorify him for ever! (. . .)
Bless the Lord, whales, and everything that moves in the waters,
praise and glorify him for ever!
Bless the Lord, every kind of bird,
praise and glorify him for ever!
Bless the Lord, all animals wild and tame,
praise and glorify him for ever! (. . .)
Bless the Lord, spirits and souls of the righteous,
praise and glorify him for ever!
Bless the Lord, you faithful people, with humble hearts,
praise and glorify him for ever!
Hananiah, Azariah and Mishael, bless the Lord,
praise and glorify him for ever!
For he has rescued us from the mouth of hell,
he has saved us from the hand of death,
he has snatched us, from the burning fiery furnace,
he has pulled us out from the heart of the flames!

Give thanks to the Lord, for he is good.
Bless the Lord, the God of gods, all you who fear him,
give praise and thanks to him, for his love lasts for ever!

Then King Nebuchadnezzar was overcome and had the young men released and forbade anyone to speak against their God. He gave them high posts in his administration.

Daniel interpreted another dream after Nebuchadnezzar's death, this time for the king's successor, Belshazzar. The new king had seen a mysterious hand writing on the wall while he was feasting one day. The young prophet explained that, through a play on words, the message foretold the imminent destruction of the kingdom which would be "counted", "weighed", and "shared out" between the Medes and the Persians. In fact, the king was killed that very night, during an enemy attack.

The trials continued under the next king, here called Darius the Mede. Daniel was ordered to worship the king as a god in spite of his high rank. The young man continued to pray only to his own God, without trying to hide the fact. His enemies had him arrested and thrown into a pit full of hungry lions, but the beasts did him no harm. The king, who had condemned his minister very half-heartedly, then had him released and worshipped the one true God, the God of Daniel, who had shown himself through this miracle.

That was when Daniel himself had a vision.

The vision of the Ancient of Days and the Son of man

7: 9–14

While I was watching thrones were set in place, and the Ancient of Days took his seat. His robe was white as snow, the hair of his head as pure as wool. His throne was a blaze of flames, its wheels were a burning fire. A stream of fire poured out from his presence. A thousand thousand were there to serve him, ten thousand times ten thousand stood before him. The court was in session and the books lay open. (. . .)

I was gazing into the visions of the night. Then I saw, coming on the clouds of heaven, as it were a Son of man. He approached the Ancient of Days and was led into his presence. He was given authority, honour and kingly power, and all the peoples of the earth from every nation and language became his servants. His rule will last for ever, and his kingship will never come to an end.

The "Ancient of Days" is God himself. The Son of man was interpreted by Jewish tradition as a superhuman figure, representing both the Jewish people as a whole and the long-awaited Messiah.

Two centuries after this was written, Jesus claimed to be the Son of Man. That claim was the reason given for condemning him to death.

HOSEA

Everything changes when love bursts into our lives and the whole world appears in a new light. Even our religious lives can be transformed by it: isn't God a God of love? The ordinary word love suddenly takes on a new and unexpected power.

Hosea loved his wife but sadly she continually betrayed his trust. He was furious and separated from her. Hosea finally forgave her: love triumphed over bitterness and she returned to him after a trial period.

That was when the domestic drama took on an extraordinary meaning, for Hosea saw how it reflected the relationship between God and his people. The Lord loved Israel as a husband loves his wife, but Israel kept betraying the One who had given it everything. Around BC 750, although the kingdom of Israel was at the height of its economic prosperity, it was sliding further and further away from God. God used Hosea and his troubles as an instrument to announce their inevitable punishment (which was to be the Assyrian invasion). God also declared that he would be eternally faithful: the wife of his youth would be taken back one day and he would purify her.

Israel would be converted and return to the Lord: love would have triumphed.

The Lord and his unfaithful wife

2: 4–22

Take your mother to court and bring an accusation against her! For she is no longer my wife and I am no longer her husband. She must stop her prostitution and put an end to all her adulterous ways. If she does not, I shall strip her and expose her naked as the day she was born.

I shall make her as bare as the desert,

I shall make her as dry as parched land,

and let her die of thirst.

And I shall feel no pity for her children since they are the children of her prostitution.

Yes, their mother has lived as a prostitute. She who brought them into the world has disgraced herself.

She has said, "I shall run after my lovers; they will provide me with what I need to live, my wool, my flax, my oil and my drinks."

This is why I shall block her way with thorn-bushes,

and put a wall around her to stop her in her tracks.

Then if she chases her lovers she will not catch them.

If she looks for them she will not find them.

Then she will say, "I shall go back to my first husband, I was better off then than I am now."

She never realised that I was the one who was giving her the grain, new wine and oil, giving her more and more silver and gold which they have spent on Baal!

This is why I shall take back my grain at harvest-time and my new wine, when the season for it comes. I shall remove my wool and my flax which were meant to cover her naked body. I will let her lovers see her disgrace and then no one will take her from me! (. . .) I mean to make her pay for the feast-days on which she burnt incense to the Baals, when she decked herself out in her earrings and necklaces to chase after her lovers, and forget me! declares the Lord.

But look, I am going to woo her back; I will lead her into the desert and speak to her heart. There I shall give her back her vineyards, and make the Vale of Achor a door of hope. There she will respond to me as she did when she was young, as she did on the day when she came out of Egypt.

When that day comes, declares the Lord, you will call me, "My husband", you will no longer call me, "My Baal". (. . .) When that day comes I shall make a treaty on their behalf with

God revealed through Hosea's drama that he intended to "divorce" the people with whom he had united himself. Israel thought prosperity came from the Baals, their fertility gods. God therefore had to reduce the country to poverty and make the people turn back to him to see that he had loved them "since the time in the wilderness".

the wild animals, with the birds of heaven and the reptiles of the earth. I shall break the bow and the sword, I will ban war from the country, and I will let my people sleep in safety. I shall make you my bride for ever. I shall make you my bride in righteousness and justice, and faithful love and tenderness.

Yes, I shall make you my bride in loyalty and you will know the Lord.

General corruption 4: 1–3

The prophet spoke out against Israel's religious and moral corruption.

Israelites, hear what the Lord says, for the Lord is bringing a case against the citizens of the country: in the country there is no loyalty, no faithful love, no knowledge of God, there is only swearing and lying, murder, theft, adultery, violence, and bloodshed after bloodshed.

This is why the country is in mourning and all its citizens are pining away (. . .).

5: 14—6: 6
For I shall be like a lion to Ephraim,
like a young lion to the House of Judah;
I myself shall do them harm, then go on my way, I shall carry them off as my prey, and no one will be able to rescue them. I shall go back to my place until they confess their guilt and seek me. In their distress they will seek eagerly for me again.
Come, let us return to the Lord.
He has wounded us but he will heal us; he has struck us but he will bind up our wounds.
After two days he will revive us, and on the third day he will raise us up and we shall live in his presence.
Let us get to know the Lord, let us do our very best to know him. That he will come is as certain as the dawn. He will come to us like a shower, like the rain in springtime as it waters the earth.
What am I to do with you, Ephraim? What am I to do with you, Judah?
For your love is like morning mist,
like the dew that disappears so quickly.
This is why I have hacked them to pieces by means of the prophets, why I have killed them with words from my mouth.
My judgement will appear suddenly like the dawn.
For faithful love is what pleases me, not sacrifice;
the knowledge of God, rather than offerings.

The people turned back to their God and begged for mercy when their punishment came – but their change of heart was only motivated by self-interest and would not last.

God's love forgives

11: 1–9

When Israel was a child I loved him, and I called my son out of Egypt. But the more I called, the further they went away from me; they offered sacrifice to Baal and burnt incense to idols.

I myself taught Ephraim to walk. I myself took them by the hand. They did not understand that I was the one caring for them. I was leading them with human ties, with cords of love. In my love for them, I was like someone lifting a young child to his cheek. I bent down towards him and gave him food to eat.

He will not have to go back to Egypt, but instead Assyria will be his king! Since he has refused to come back to me, his cities will be devastated by the sword, and their gates will be destroyed. Because of their plots their lives will be ruined.

My people insist on ignoring me. If they are called to come up, not one of them makes a move.

Ephraim, how could I part with you? Israel, how could I give you up? (. . .) My heart within me is overwhelmed, my inmost being trembles. I will not give way to my fierce anger. I will not destroy the house of Ephraim again, for I am God and not man. I am the Holy One in your midst. I shall not come to you in anger.

God was like an infinitely-loving father to his children. He had brought his people up out of Egypt and now he would punish them by letting them fall into the hands of the Assyrians. In the end his love was to be stronger than his anger, and he promised to pardon and reunite those of his children scattered throughout the world. Peace would be restored.

JOEL

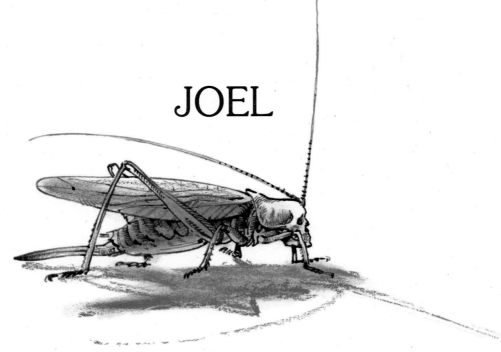

T here was a natural disaster around BC 400 when an invasion by locusts took place. Joel, a Judaean prophet, took this as a sign that the terrible "Day of the Lord" was near when God would come to devastate the earth. Joel called on the chosen people to repent so that God would restore the earth and save his people by the gift of his Spirit, even while everything around them collapsed.

The day of the Lord's anger was near. It would come in the form of a plague of locusts devouring everything in their path. Perhaps the Lord would spare them if the people repented?

A call to repentance
2: 1–2, 10–17

Blow the ram's-horn in Zion,
sound the alarm on my holy mountain!
Let everybody in the country tremble,
for the Day of the Lord is coming,
yes, it is near.
Day of darkness and gloom,
day of cloud and blackness.
Like the dawn, across the mountains,
spreads a vast and mighty people
such as has never been before,
such as will never be again (. . .).
As they approach, the earth quakes, the skies tremble.
The sun and moon grow dark,
the stars lose their brilliance.
The Lord's voice rings out at the head of his troops! (. . .)
The Day of the Lord is great and very terrible. Who can face it?
"But now, declares the Lord,
come back to me with all your heart,
with fasting, weeping and mourning."

Tear your hearts and not your clothes.
Come back to the Lord your God,
for he is gracious and compassionate,
slow to anger, rich in faithful love,
and he relents about sending disaster. (. . .)
Blow the ram's-horn in Zion! Order a fast, proclaim a solemn meeting, call the people together, summon the community, assemble the elders, gather the children, even babies at the breast! Call the bridegroom from his bedroom and the bride from her dressing-room! Let the priests, the ministers of the Lord, stand weeping between the portico and the altar. Let them cry, "Spare your people, O Lord!
Do not let your people be put to shame and mocked by the nations! Why give the nations cause to say, 'Where is their God?' "

The last days

3: 1–5

In those days I shall pour out my spirit on all humanity.
Your sons and daughters shall prophesy,
your old people shall dream dreams,
and your young people see visions.
In those days I shall even pour out my spirit
on the slaves, both men and women.
I shall show signs in the sky and on earth,
blood, fire and columns of smoke.
The sun will be turned into darkness, and the moon into blood,
before the Day comes, that great and terrible Day.
All who call on the name of the Lord will be saved,
for those who have escaped will be on Mount Zion,
and the survivors whom the Lord is
calling will live in Jerusalem.

Joel was referring to a famous text from Exodus (34:6), in which God revealed both his demanding nature and his mercy.

Signs in the sky would mark the hour of salvation for God's chosen ones. They would be lifted up by the Spirit and thus escape the general catastrophe.

Peter quoted this text in his first sermon on the day after Pentecost. The apostle saw Pentecost as the beginning of the fulfilment of Joel's predictions.

AMOS

We are mainly concerned with material success in our rich society and woe betide anyone who tries to remind us that poverty and oppression exist. We quickly dismiss such reminders in the name of power, of the common good or even of religion itself.

This is nothing new: we can already see it in the kingdom of Israel in BC 760. Israel was at the height of its prosperity although separated from the kingdom of Judah. Samaria was a magnificent city; religion was fashionable; Bethel was a rival centre of worship to Jerusalem and attracted crowds of people, and experienced an economic boom. It was then that a shepherd and farmer from Judah came on the scene. Amos was shocked at what he saw at Bethel. He spoke out passionately against the social inequalities and the way the poor were being exploited. He shouted at the people. They tried to throw him out so he only cried out all the more: "How can people who were once slaves themselves allow such injustice? This nation is rotten to the core! You are running to your own destruction." And the prophet foretold that Assyria would soon invade the land and cause its ruin.

The book of Amos did, however, end on a note of hope: the Lord would be faithful and would not destroy his people completely. He would save a remnant to be the seeds of the future. Life would go on after the catastrophe.

1: 1–2

Words of Amos one of the shepherds of Tekoa. These are the visions he had about Israel, in the time of Uzziah king of Judah and Jeroboam son of Joash, king of Israel (. . .). He says: The Lord roars from Zion, and he makes himself heard from Jerusalem.

Warnings to Israel

2: 6–7, 10, 13–16

This is what the Lord says:

For the three crimes, the four crimes of Israel, I have made my decision and I will not relent. Because they have sold innocent people for silver and the poor for a pair of sandals, because they have trampled the weak into the dust and pushed the rights of those who are oppressed to one side (. . .).

It was I who brought you up from Egypt, and for forty years led you through the desert in order to give you this country (. . .). I shall crush you where you stand like a cart overloaded with sheaves. There will be nowhere for the swift to run, the strong man will have no chance to exert his strength nor will the warrior be able to save his life (. . .). On that day, even the bravest of warriors will throw down his weapons and run away, declares the Lord.

3: 8, 10–12

The lion roars: who is not afraid?

The Lord has spoken: who will not prophesy? (. . .)

They cram their palaces full with violence and extortion.

The Lord says: This is why an enemy will soon invade the land, he will bring down your strength and your palaces will be looted.

The Lord says this: From the lion's mouth the shepherd rescues two legs or the tip of an ear. That is all that will be rescued of the children of Israel who now lounge about in Samaria, lying on their beds or on their couches.

4: 1–3

Listen to this saying, you cows of Bashan, you who live on the hills of Samaria, exploiting the weak and ill-treating the poor, saying to your husbands, "Bring us something to drink!"

The Lord God has sworn by his holiness:

Look, the days will soon come when you will be dragged away with hooks and fish-hooks, and each of you will run for your life, leaving through the holes in the wall and taking the path straight ahead of you.

What an unwelcome prophet! Amos came from an enemy country and spoke in the name of the God who reigned over the rival shrine; he was predicting troubles not only for their enemies in Damascus, Gaza, Tyre, Edom, Ammon and Moab but also for themselves.

God's anger turned against his chosen people, for they behaved as badly as the surrounding pagans.

The Lord had spoken. Amos could not remain silent so he spoke out against the corruption he saw among the upper classes.

Amos compared the rich women of Samaria to the cows kept for milk in the rich pastures of Bashan (Golan), to the east of Jordan.

5: 11–14, 18

You trample on the poor man and make him pay tax on his wheat. Although you have built houses in fine stone, you will not live in them. Although you have planted pleasant vineyards, you will not drink wine from them. For I know how many crimes you have committed and how serious your sins are, you who oppress the innocent, who hold people to ransom and stand in the way of the poor receiving justice. That is why anyone who has any sense keeps silent now, since the time is evil.

Seek good and not evil so that you may survive, and so that the Lord may be with you as you claim he is. Hate evil, love good, let justice reign (. . .).

Disaster will come to those of you who long for the Day of the Lord! What will the Day of the Lord mean for you? It will mean darkness, not light! (. . .)

Against outward show   5: 21–2
I hate, I scorn your festivals.
I take no pleasure in your solemn assemblies.
When you bring me your offerings,
I do not accept them.
I do not even look at the fat cattle you sacrifice to me.
Spare me the din of your chanting!
Don't make me listen to the strumming of your lyres.
But let justice flow like water,
and righteousness like a never-failing stream!

Conflict with the priest of Bethel   7: 10–17
Then Amaziah, the priest of Bethel, sent word to Jeroboam, king of Israel, "Amos is plotting against you in the heart of the land of Israel. The country cannot put up with his speeches any longer. For this is what Amos says, 'Jeroboam is going to die by the sword, and Israel will be taken into captivity far from its native land.' "
Then Amaziah said to Amos himself, "Go away, you prophet. Take yourself off to Judah. Earn your living there by being a prophet! But you must stop prophesying at Bethel, for this is a royal sanctuary, a national temple."

Amos replied to him, "I am not a prophet by profession. I am merely a herdsman and dresser of sycamore-figs. But the Lord took me as I followed the herd, and he said to me, 'Go and prophesy to my people Israel.'

Those who were carrying out this injustice claimed to be living in hope of the day of God's triumph. They would do better to fear it!

God could not stand religious feasts and outward show, if they only covered up injustice.

Who gave this foreigner the right to speak? His messages of doom were causing trouble at the royal shrine. The right came from God, replied Amos, and he predicted terrible punishment for the priest who tried to throw him out.

sycamore

The fruit of the sycamore can be prevented from becoming inedible as it ripens if the farmer prunes it back before it reaches maturity . . . The sycamore is a good symbol for the work of the prophet who must change hearts of stone into flesh and blood. Luke brought this prophetic activity to mind when he showed Zacchaeus perching in the branches of a sycamore tree, his hard heart about to be transformed by Jesus (Luke 19: 1–10).

"So now you who tell me not to prophesy against Israel, listen to what the Lord says (. . .): 'Your wife will become a prostitute in the streets, your sons and daughters will be killed by the sword, your land will be parcelled out by measuring line, and you yourself will die on polluted soil and Israel will be taken into captivity far from its own land!' "

Against cheats   8: 4–7, 10

Listen to this, you who crush the poor and would like to make those who are in need disappear from this country.

You say, "I can't wait for the festival to be over so that we can sell our corn and for the Sabbath to come to an end, so that we can market our wheat. Then, we can make the weights smaller and tamper with the scales. We can buy up the weak for silver and the poor for a pair of sandals; we can even sell the sweepings of the wheat."

The Lord makes a solemn vow: "Never will I forget anything they have done. I shall turn your festivals into times of mourning and all your singing into cries of distress."

Hope for the future   9: 11–15

On that Day, I shall rebuild the tottering hut of David. I will repair the gaps in it, restore its ruins and rebuild it as it was in days gone by. (. . .) The days are coming, declares the Lord, when the man who ploughs will follow closely behind the man who reaps, and the man who treads the grapes will follow closely behind the man who sows the seed. The mountains will run with new wine and the hills will all flow with it. I shall restore the fortunes of my people Israel (. . .). And I shall plant them on their own soil and they will never be uprooted again from the country which I have given them, declares the Lord your God.

God's last words were of hope. He would come to restore life to his people one day and the land would then see a time of lasting peace and prosperity.

OBADIAH

Would God never take revenge for his people who had been oppressed by evil men through all their lives?

Yes! replied the prophet Obadiah, who recalled how Israel's neighbours had taken advantage of the Chaldaean invasion in 587 to raid the land belonging to the people of God. He foretold the day when God would take revenge and when the chosen people would return to their own land.

Christians believe that God has indeed acted on his people's behalf, but in a different way to that predicted by the prophet.

The Edomites were thought to be descended from Esau, the rival brother of Jacob. Their capital was on the site now occupied by the Nabataean's capital city of Petra, which is also called "the rock" because it is built out of the rock. Some members of this Arab tribe were to become part of the first Christian community (Acts 2:11).

Sentence against Edom
1b-4

This is what the Lord God says:
Look, I have made you become the smallest of the nations,
you are now beneath contempt!
Your proud heart has misled you,
you who make your home in the crannies of the rock,
who make your home in the high places, who think to yourself,
"Who can bring me down to earth?"
Though you soar like an eagle,
though you make your nest among the stars,
I shall bring you down from there! declares the Lord.

Israel's revenge
17

But those who have escaped will find safety on Mount Zion.
It will be a holy place and the House of Jacob will recover what is rightfully theirs.

The Church, the new Israel, was to stretch its frontiers further still and would be used to show the true divine "vengeance of God".

20

The children of Israel will take possession of the land of the Canaanites as far as Zarephthah, and the exiles from Jerusalem now in Sepharad will have the cities of the Negeb.
Victorious, they will climb Mount Zion
to rule over Mount Esau,
and the Kingdom will be the Lord's!

JONAH

Sometimes we see certain religious groups claiming to have a monopoly on God's favour, seeing others as wicked instead of appreciating their own responsibility as God's people towards those who may not have had the opportunity to know the Lord.

This was the case with Judaism in about the fifth or fourth century BC. The people of God were called to become a light to the nations but were too inward-looking and had forgotten their mission.

So someone wrote a satire with a deep underlying meaning. He told how Jonah fled from the mission God had given to him, and how the Lord eventually forced him to carry it out. Until the end, however, Jonah remained small-minded and unable to understand God's mercy and generosity.

Jesus was to recall the "sign of Jonah". Some of the disciples thought he was referring to the story of Jonah lost in the depths before returning to life and thus to the death and resurrection of the Lord while others interpreted it in another way, realising that Jesus was the one who really responded to the divine call and brought salvation to all people everywhere.

God asked Jonah to go and preach repentance in Nineveh, which was a great pagan city and one of Judah's enemies. Jonah refused to fulfil his mission and ran away in the opposite direction. The boat in which he sailed was caught in a storm. Jonah recognised the storm as a sign that God was following him and asked the sailors to throw him into the sea to make the storm come to an end. He was then swallowed by an enormous fish and remained in its belly for three days and nights.

2: 2–8, 11

From the belly of the fish, Jonah prayed to the Lord, his God; he said: "In my distress I cried to the Lord and he answered me. From deep within the world of the dead I cried out, and you heard my voice!

"For you threw me into the deep waters; into the heart of the seas, and the floods closed round me. All your waves and breakers surged over me.

"Then I thought, 'He has sent me away for ever. How shall I ever see your holy Temple again?' (. . .) When my soul was growing ever weaker, Lord, I remembered you, and my prayer reached you in your holy Temple." (. . .)

Jonah was condemning himself to death by running away from his duty. God would not abandon the one he had called, though, and he brought Jonah back to life in order to fulfil his task.

Jonah at last agreed to go and preach in Nineveh although he hoped the city would not turn to God and would therefore be punished by the Lord. Nineveh did repent.

Nineveh is converted
3: 5–10

The pagans were converted when God called. Even the animals did penance. After all, everything is possible for God!

The people of Nineveh believed in God; they declared a fast and put on sackcloth, and everyone took part, from the oldest to the youngest. When the news reached the king of Nineveh, he got up from his throne, took off his robe, put on sackcloth and sat down in ashes. He then sent the following proclamation throughout Nineveh, by order of the king and his nobles: "No person or animal, herd or flock, may eat anything; they may not graze, they may not drink any water. All must put on sackcloth and call on God with all their strength; and let everyone turn away from his evil ways and violent behaviour. Who knows? Perhaps God will change his mind and turn away from his fierce anger, so that we shall not die."

God saw their efforts to turn away from their evil behaviour. And God relented about the disaster which he had threatened to bring on them, and he did not bring it.

Jonah was very indignant. He had climbed up onto the hill, expecting to see the city destroyed at God's hand. He was angrier still when the castor-oil plant giving him shelter from the sun was attacked by a worm and died. He complained bitterly to God.

God's answer
4: 8b-11

Jonah's pettiness burst out, but God had shown mercy towards all creatures, even the lowest. Luke's Gospel places particular emphasis on this idea.

He begged to die, saying, "I might as well be dead as go on living." God said to Jonah, "Are you right to be angry about the castor-oil plant?" He replied, "I have every right to be angry, so angry I could die!" The Lord replied, "You are concerned for the castor-oil plant which has not cost you any effort and which you did not grow, which came up in a night and has withered in a night. So why should I not be concerned for Nineveh, the great city, in which there are more than a hundred and twenty thousand people who cannot tell their right hand from their left, to say nothing of all the animals?"

MICAH

History is a record of the great and the good. It is rare for people to remember the cries of the poor and the oppressed although theirs is the greatest suffering during times of war and crisis. Their impressions are no less important than the accounts of their leaders' exploits.

One of these was Micah, a Judaean peasant who took refuge in Jerusalem at the time of the Assyrian invasion in the eighth century BC. He protested because he was sickened by the sight of the Holy City's inhabitants exploiting those who came there to find protection. He accused the official prophets and the priests of "bending the rules" in matters of right and wrong. He declared God's anger at what was happening and was also able to affirm his confidence in the future by recalling the events of the past: all the nations would one day be purified and their people united around the Holy City.

God decided to take action when faced with the sin of his people.

God comes to judge his people
1: 2–5
Listen, all you peoples!
Pay attention, earth and everyone on it!
The Lord is going to give evidence against you!
The Lord is going to leave his holy temple.
Look, the Lord is leaving his home:
down he comes, he treads on the high places of the earth.
The mountains melt beneath him and valleys are torn open,
like wax near a fire,
like water pouring down a slope.
All this is because of the crime of Jacob,
the sin of the House of Israel. (. . .)

Against the rulers who oppress the people
3: 1–2, 9–12
"Kindly listen, you leaders of the House of Jacob,
you princes of the House of Israel.
Surely you are the ones who ought to know what is right,
and yet you hate what is good and love what is evil! (. . .)
You hate justice, and try to divert it from its proper course,
you who build Zion on bloodshed and Jerusalem on crime!
Her leaders take bribes for their verdicts,
her priests take a fee for their rulings,

The prophet painted a very critical picture involving whole sections of Jerusalem's population.

her prophets take money for their words about the future.

Yet they pretend to rely on the Lord and say, 'Isn't the Lord among us? No disaster is going to come upon us.'

That is why, thanks to you, Zion will be ploughed like a field,

Jerusalem will become a heap of rubble

and the mountain where the Temple stands will become a wood.''

The future reign

4: 1–7

But in days to come the mountain where the Lord's Temple stands will tower above all the other mountains, and will be higher than all the hills.

Then the peoples will stream to it,

then many nations will come and say,

''Come, let us go up to the mountain of the Lord,

to the Temple of the God of Jacob, so that he may teach us his ways and we may walk in his paths.

For the Law comes from Zion and the word of the Lord from Jerusalem.''

He will judge between many peoples

and settle disputes between mighty nations.

They will hammer their swords into ploughs

and their spears into knives for pruning.

Nation will not lift sword against nation

or ever again be trained to make war.

But each man will sit under his vine and fig tree

with no one to trouble him. (. . .)

On that day, declares the Lord, I shall gather in the lame and bring together those who have strayed away and those whom I have treated harshly.

I shall make a new nation from those with sore feet,

and a mighty nation from the far-flung.

And the Lord will reign over them

on Mount Zion, from then on and for ever.

5: 1–3

But you (Bethlehem) Ephrathah, the smallest of the clans of Judah, from you will come for me a future ruler of Israel.

His origins go back to the distant past, to the days of old. (. . .) He will take his stand and he will be their shepherd with the power of the Lord, with the majesty of the name of his God.

He condemned the powerful who took advantage of people and led them to catastrophe, believing that God would stop any harm coming to them.

The nations of the earth would one day gather together around the Holy City; and peace would then reign as the Lord gathered his scattered flock.

It was not from the arrogant city of Jerusalem, but from the humble town of Bethlehem that the longed-for Messiah would come and bring peace to his people.

NAHUM

We cannot fail to be glad when a cruel regime topples.

In the olden days, the Assyrians were a particularly cruel people. Some of the prophets of Israel had explained that they were an instrument of God's anger but they still spoke out against the Assyrians' crimes. The inhabitants of Judah were delighted on hearing the news that Nineveh had fallen to the Chaldaeans, in 612. At last God had shown how he punished the wicked.

Nahum composed a hymn of triumph.

1: 2
The Lord is a jealous and avenging God!
The Lord takes revenge, he is full of anger!
The Lord takes revenge on his enemies (. . .).

3: 1–4
Disaster to the city of blood,
packed with lies, stuffed with booty,
where there is no end to looting!
The crack of the whip!
The rumble of wheels!
Galloping horses,
jolting chariots, charging cavalry,
flashing swords, gleaming spears,
a mass of wounded, the dead everywhere,
too many corpses to count!
They stumble over corpses.
All this is because of the countless acts of prostitution in
the city of prostitution
which, with its immoral behaviour, made
the nations its slaves. (. . .)

3: 19
There is no remedy for your wound!
Your injury is past healing.
All who hear the news of your downfall will clap their hands.
For who has not suffered again and again from your cruelty?

HABAKKUK

The prophet Habakkuk wondered what his people had done to deserve their punishment when Israel was oppressed by its enemies in the seventh century BC. Surely their enemies were even worse than they? How could God allow them to triumph?

"Be patient," replied the Lord. "The wicked will be punished." Faithfulness was all the Lord wanted at that moment from his righteous people. The prophet was sufficiently reassured that he was able to curse the oppressors and to hope that one day God would restore justice in the world.

1: 2–4

How long, O Lord, am I to cry for help while you will not listen;
to cry, "Violence!" in your ear while you will not save?
Why do you make me see wrong-doing everywhere I go,
why do you look on while your people are oppressed?
I see nothing but looting and violence,
disputes and arguments are the order of the day.
And so the law loses its grip and justice is forgotten.
The criminal outwits the righteous man
and so the course of justice is always perverted.

2: 1–4

I shall stand at my post,
I shall station myself on my watch-tower.
I will wait to see what he will say to me,
what answer he will make to my complaints.
Then the Lord answered me:
"Write the vision down, inscribe it on tablets
so that it can be read easily.
For it does not apply to the present moment,
but it will certainly be fulfilled in the end.
Although its fulfilment may take some time, wait for it,
for it will certainly come before too long.
You see, anyone whose heart is not righteous
will give in.
But the righteous will live because they are
faithful."

ZEPHANIAH

How can we avoid feeling that the world is heading for disaster when we see evil spreading everywhere? God's terrible anger will fall upon it all one day.

That was what Zephaniah had in mind in about BC 640: Judaea was going into decline while the threat from Assyria grew all the time. So the prophet made an accusation against Jerusalem, but also against the other nations. Soon the "Day of the Lord" would come, and it would be terrible. Only the poor of the earth would escape God's anger. They would form a tiny, pure remnant, and God would gather them in on his holy mountain.

The Day of the Lord
1: 14–18

God prepared to destroy a corrupted world as at the time of the Flood. The faithful should humble themselves and pray to be spared from the fury of the Lord.

The great Day of the Lord is near.
It is near, and it is coming with great speed.
What a bitter sound there will be on the Day of the Lord!
It will be like a warrior shouting out his war-cry.
That Day is a day of punishment,
a day of distress and trouble,
a day of ruin and devastation,
a day of darkness and gloom,
a day of cloud and thick fog,
a day of trumpet blast and battle cry
against fortified town and high tower.

The Church liturgy used this text for a long time in a hymn called the *Dies irae*, which was sung at burials. Like the oracle, the dramatic liturgy ended with a song of hope.

I shall bring such distress on the human race that they will grope
like the blind to find their way (. . .).
Neither their silver nor their gold will be able to save them.
On the Day of the Lord's anger,
the whole earth will be consumed by the fire of his jealousy.
For he will destroy. Yes, he will wipe out
everyone living on earth.

2: 3
Seek the Lord, all you humble people of the earth,
who obey his commands.
Seek justice, seek humility.
Then perhaps you may find shelter
on the Day of the Lord's anger.

The nations turn to God

3: 9, 12–18

Yes, I shall give the people pure lips so that they may all call on the name of the Lord (. . .).

But I shall allow only a modest and humble people to survive among you, and those who are left in Israel will take refuge in the name of the Lord.

They will do no wrong, they will tell no lies;
nor will a deceitful tongue be found in their mouths.

But they will be able to graze and rest with no one to make them afraid.

Shout for joy, daughter of Zion, Israel, shout aloud!

Rejoice, celebrate with all your heart, daughter of Jerusalem!

The Lord has taken your punishment away,
he has turned your enemy away.

The Lord is king among you, Israel,
you have nothing more to fear. (. . .)

The Lord your God is there with you,
the Saviour who fights for you.

He will rejoice over you with happy song,
he will renew you by his love,
he will dance with shouts of joy for you,
as on a day of festival.

Very soon, God would purify his sinful people. The remnant of Israel would be gathered in on the holy mountain.

3: 19–20

When that time comes I will rescue the lame,
and bring back the strays,
and I will win them praise and fame when I restore their fortunes.
At that time I shall be your guide,
at the time when I gather you back together.

HAGGAI

We are often struck by the contrast between our modest modern churches and the splendid cathedrals of the past. The difference shows the Church's loss of power in our modern society. Doesn't that lead us to doubt the power of God himself? This was already the state of the Jews' mind as they returned from captivity, when they compared the modest temple they were rebuilding with the splendour of Solomon's Temple.

Haggai brought them a message of hope. The glory of the new Temple would be even greater than that of the old. They should continue rebuilding with enthusiasm.

Perhaps King Herod had this text in mind when, several centuries later, he undertook the extension and refurbishment of the Temple and made the building more impressive. From a Christian point of view, however, the real fulfilment of the promise came from Jesus, the true dwelling-place of God in the world.

Zerubbabel was the governor of Judah in BC 520.

2: 4–9

Take courage now, Zerubbabel! the Lord declares.

Courage, Joshua, high priest!

Courage, all you people of the country! the Lord declares.

To work! I am with you, declares the Lord Almighty, and my Spirit is present among you.

Do not be afraid! For the Lord says this: A little while now, and I shall shake the heavens and the earth, the sea and the dry land. I shall shake all the nations.

Then the treasures of all the nations will flow in, and I shall fill this Temple with glory, says the Lord Almighty.

The silver and the gold are mine! declares the Lord Almighty. The glory of this new Temple will be greater than that of the old, says the Lord Almighty, and in this place I shall give peace.

ZECHARIAH

It sometimes happens that a person with vision can suddenly give back hope to his people. His message speaks of a brilliant future using apparently insignificant signs even when the way ahead seems blocked.

This was the case in Judah, in about BC 520. Hopes soon fell after their initial joy of returning from exile in Babylon. The Persians still occupied the land, and there was nothing to indicate when their shame would be over. For example, very little power was held by Zerubbabel, the high commissioner of Judah, and Joshua the high priest, because they had been appointed by the ruling power.

The prophet Zechariah had strange visions which revealed a glimpse of a totally different state of affairs which was both frightening and reassuring. He announced that the anger of God was going to fall upon the wicked and that Jerusalem would be freed. Zerubbabel and Joshua had God's support from that time but, later on, it was the Messiah (here called the "Branch"), who would bring a new world into being. God himself would then be present in his Temple.

Meanwhile, the prophet called the people to repentance, reminding them that true fasting was the practice of justice and righteousness, and penance could thus become a joy.

The people began to despair again a century after Zechariah's vision: when would the promise be fulfilled? Another prophet then added six more chapters to the book of Zechariah. He assured the people that God would not fail to come and deliver his people, but explained that rescue would not occur without difficult times and inner struggles. He also foretold the coming of a king who would be humble, just and good; he would not force his reign upon them, but would enter the city riding on a donkey. Oddly enough, the prophet also spoke of a man who would be pierced by his own people.

The early Christians recognised the figure of Jesus in all these apparently varying texts.

Peace for the future

8: 1–8

The word of the Lord Almighty came, saying:
This is what the Lord Almighty says:
I have been burning with jealousy for Zion,
I have been gripped with anger for her sake.
This is what the Lord says:
I am coming back to Zion
and shall live in the heart of Jerusalem.
Jerusalem will be called Faithful City
and the mountain of the Lord Almighty
will be known as the Holy Mountain.
This is what the Lord Almighty says:
Old men and women will sit once
again in the squares of
Jerusalem. They will each have a stick
to lean on because of
their great age.

> The prophet speaks about what will happen when God intervenes in world history, and then describes an idyllic vision of the Holy City where God himself would live among his people.

And the squares of the city will be full
of boys and girls playing there. (. . .)
This is what the Lord Almighty says:
Look, I shall rescue my people
from the countries of the east
and from the countries of the west.
I shall bring them back
to live in the heart of Jerusalem,
and they will be my people
and I shall be their faithful and just God.

8: 14–17
For the Lord Almighty says this, "When your ancestors made me
angry, I decided to punish you and I did not waver from my
decision. But now I have changed my mind and intend to treat
Jerusalem and the House of Judah well. Do not be afraid!

"These are the things that you must do. Speak the truth to one
another; in your public places, give fair judgements which lead to
peace; do not secretly plot evil against one another; do not tell lies
under oath. For these are the things I hate, declares the Lord."

Jerusalem the centre of the world

8: 20–3

The Lord Almighty says this: "In the future, peoples and citizens of many cities will come. They will go to one another and say: We must certainly go to plead for the Lord's favour and seek out the Lord Almighty. As for me, I am going. Yes, many peoples and great nations will seek out the Lord Almighty in Jerusalem to plead for his favour."

The Lord Almighty says this, "In those days, ten men from nations of every language will take a Jew by the sleeve and say: We want to go with you, since we have learnt that God is with you."

All the nations would realise that God was really with his people on the day he intervened. Many would then be converted to the true faith.

The coming of the Messiah

9: 9–10

Sing with all your heart, daughter of Zion!
Shout for joy, daughter of Jerusalem!
Look, your king is coming to you,
he is just and victorious,
humble and riding on a donkey,
on a colt, the foal of a donkey.
He will make the chariots of war disappear from Ephraim
and horses from Jerusalem.
The weapons of war will be banished from the land.
He will proclaim peace to the nations.
His empire will stretch from sea to sea,
from the River to the ends of the earth.

After showing God moving forward like a devastating high tide, Zechariah's successor described the king of the new world: a humble character who would bring peace.

12: 10–11

On that day I shall pour out a spirit of grace and prayer on the House of David and the inhabitants of Jerusalem and they will look to me. They will mourn for the one whom they have pierced as though for an only child. They will weep for him as people weep for a first-born child. When that day comes, there will be great mourning in Jerusalem (. . .).

The death of the Pierced One reminded people of the Servant mentioned by Isaiah. John the Evangelist was to see in this text a prophecy of the death of Jesus (cf. John 19: 37) and compare it with the image of a fountain purifying Jerusalem with the gift of the Holy Spirit (cf. John 7: 37–9).

13: 1

When that day comes, a fountain will be opened for the House of David and the inhabitants of Jerusalem, to wash sin and uncleanness away.

MALACHI

"**R**eligion is old-fashioned." People who think they are "with it" have been saying this for centuries. A prophet writing around BC 460 was already reacting against such attitudes. This author was anonymous, and was given the name Malachi some time later; the name means "my messenger" which is a word repeated in 3:1. He protested against the Jews of his time who were abandoning the traditions of their people. He accused the priests of neglecting the religious practices, and the worshippers of offering only the leftovers of their belongings. He spoke out against the break-up of marriages, especially divorce. He predicted the day of the long-awaited Messiah who would offer God the true sacrifice that he required. The messenger of God would judge those who oppressed their fellow human beings.

Accusation against the priests

1: 10–11

The prophet spoke out against the decline of the religious practices. God wants sincere sacrifice and not empty rituals.

I am not pleased with you, says the Lord Almighty. I do not accept the offerings you bring me. But from the farthest east to the farthest west my name is great among the nations, and everywhere incense and a pure gift are offered to my name. For my name is great among the nations.

Divorce is condemned

2: 14–16

The prophet condemned divorce and demanded faithfulness between husbands and wives, while recalling the message of Genesis which stated that man and woman formed a single being.

The Lord stands as witness between you and the wife of your youth, whom you have betrayed, even though she was your partner and your wife by covenant. Did he not make one single being, having flesh and the breath of life, from the two of you? And what does this single being seek? Children given by God! Have respect for your own life then, and do not break your promise to the wife of your youth. For I hate divorce, says the Lord, God of Israel.

God's messenger will come

3: 1–4

Soon the messenger of God would purify the Levites whose duty it was to encourage people to worship God. On that day, the Lord would be given the sacrifice he wanted. That would be true worship.

Look, I shall send my messenger to prepare a way before me. And suddenly the Lord whom you seek will come to his Temple; yes, the angel of the covenant, for whom you long, is on his way, says the Lord Almighty. Who will be able to endure the day of his coming? Who will remain standing when he appears? For he will be like a refiner's fire, like soap from the laundry. He will take his seat as refiner and purifier. He will purify the sons of Levi and refine them like gold and silver, so that they can make their offerings to the Lord with righteousness. The offering of Judah and Jerusalem will then be acceptable to the Lord as it was in former days.

THE NEW TESTAMENT

A group of young people who were extremely dynamic and united in their purpose were asked one day to explain what motivated them. They all said it was an older person, the organiser of their movement, to whom they were particularly attached. He had disappeared one day in tragic circumstances and the group was so devastated it had almost fallen apart. Then they had seen a letter from their former leader to a friend of his saying how sad it made him to see his young friends lacking in initiative and continually falling out. "I realised that the group was only united because of me," he said. "Perhaps I need to go away in order to make them take charge."

That was the spark they needed and their days of waiting and dreaming were ended. They held a group meeting which became an extraordinary celebration — and everything changed from that moment. They stopped living in the past and feeling sorry for themselves: the leader's strength became the strength of the entire group.

A simple story, but one that may help us to understand the

NEW TESTAMENT.

On the road to Emmaus

Two people were walking along a road in Judaea, almost two thousand years ago. They were deeply troubled and explained their confusion to a passing stranger. In a time of crisis, they had put their faith in Jesus of Nazareth, an amazing man who had just been arrested and crucified. Their hopes that a new life was just beginning had now fallen apart.

Then the stranger spoke. He discussed with his two companions the meaning of the hope of the Messiah. His was a new way of seeing things and he explained how Jesus' apparent failure could in fact be the starting-point for a new way of living. They should not expect a mighty saviour coming to save the world to be like a magician with a magic wand. They must become servants just as the crucified Jesus had been a servant, and that way a new life could begin.

The two people were amazed to discover that the speaker was Jesus himself. Through his death, which

he had accepted out of love, he was alive. They had to go and tell the Good News (or in Greek, the *gospel*) to the whole world.

Life changes completely for all who discover the Good News although the world itself stays just the same, with its dramas, struggles and sorrows. But we can face all our difficulties with courage once we have discovered true life, just as Jesus faced troubles.

The real secret of strength is that we recognise Jesus as the Son of God himself and it shows us just how much God loves us. How can we not face the future with confidence?

God made a New Covenant with those who found him, and also between the believers themselves. This covenant renewed the one God made with his chosen people and it brought a new and wonderful dimension to the old agreement.

The Church was born from the experience of Jesus' death and resurrection; it gave a name to the New Covenant:

NEW TESTAMENT.

The writings which proclaim the Good News

The disciples at Emmaus and the Apostles of Jesus went into the world to announce the Good News, that is, the New Testament — the renewal of the covenant between God and people through Jesus Christ. They talked a great deal but both they and their immediate disciples also wrote. Their first writings were usually simple letters which we call the Epistles. Perhaps some of them have been lost, but the most important ones remaining are the letters of Paul of Tarsus, a convert who became an apostle.

There were soon collections of memories also. First, accounts of Jesus' Passion and then collections of the teachings of Jesus, stories of the miracles, and lists of his parables to help preachers remember them.

One day, several decades after the events themselves had taken place, some writers noticed how these memories linked together and used them as a basis for the GOSPELS. Their aim was not to give a journalistic account of events, but to show the Christian community how Jesus' message affected them. They did not hesitate then to organise their account in such a way as to emphasise whatever aspect of the Good News seemed most important to those to whom they were speaking.

Later on, the Evangelist Luke was concerned to show also how the Gospel was spread throughout the world by the power of the Holy Spirit: that is what he aimed to show in the ACTS OF THE APOSTLES.

To all these pieces of writing was added a strange text which used symbols and images, and was aimed at giving confidence to Christians under persecution. This text was intended to show that God was the conqueror in the great battle which continues to be fought in the world between the forces of evil and those of Jesus: this text is the book of REVELATION.

All these works are grouped together under the name of what, in one way or another, they are all about: THE NEW TESTAMENT.

To summarise the comparison we started with, the NEW TESTAMENT consists of a collection of accounts by the people within the group which gathered around the person of Jesus. His message is now spread by his Spirit.

Understanding the Gospels

We need to know something about the situation in Palestine at the time of Jesus in order to understand the Gospels.

Politically, the Jews had lost their freedom a long time previously. The king employed by the Romans at the time of Jesus' birth was a bloodthirsty tyrant called Herod the Great. Only Galilee in the North of the country had any kind of independence after Herod's death, under the rule of his son, Herod Antipas. The Jews did not trust this cruel and immoral foreigner.

Samaria, in the centre, and Judaea, in the South, were under the direct authority of a Roman magistrate, Pontius Pilate, who normally lived in Caesarea, on the coast. However, the day-to-day business of Judaism was governed by a council, or Sanhedrin, presided over by the high priest.

Racially, the inhabitants of the land were divided. The Judaeans were a pure race and looked down on the Samaritans, a mixed race since the time of the Assyrian occupation. The Samaritans had closed in on themselves and built their own temple on Mount Gerazim.

The Judaeans also despised the Galileans, who had mixed a great deal with the Gentiles. They thought of them as simple people with naïve religious ideas.

Religiously, the divisions ran deep. The Sadducees were the clerical elite. They controlled Temple life and earned their money from it. They were traditionalists who liked order and hated new ideas, which was why they did not believe in the resurrection of the dead.

The Pharisees, who were generally quite ordinary people, were very much attached to the Law and prided themselves on following it in detail. Some of them followed Jesus, who in many ways, was quite close to their own spiritual beliefs, but other Pharisees were shocked by the way he mixed with sinners. The Sadducees hated the Pharisees and the feeling was mutual. However, they got on well with the Scribes, who were specialists in the interpretation of the Holy Scriptures. The early Church came into conflict with the Pharisees and tended to show them in a bad light in their writings.

The Essenes were a sort of community of monks established on the shores of the Dead Sea. They were full of spiritual fervour and were led by a "master of justice", but they had cut themselves off from the Temple at Jerusalem and from other religious groups.

The Zealots were the hardliners. Refusing to call anyone lord or master, they were violently opposed to Roman control, and they never stopped spreading unrest. Some of them put their hopes in Jesus for a short time, but were quickly disappointed.

Socially: the Sadducees were the upper class. The ordinary people and craftsmen were more likely to be Pharisees.

There was also a mass of poor and marginalised people, beggars who were often disabled or ill, and the prostitutes. These people were despised and considered irrelevant.

Publicans and tax-collectors were also shunned. They were often rich but were scorned because they collaborated with the hated authorities and were often dishonest.

It is evident that we are looking at a deeply divided society. Some people still held on to the great hopes of the past and looked forward to the coming of the promised Messiah. Unfortunately, everyone seemed to have a different idea of what the Messiah would be like, with people using ideas taken from their own individual ways of seeing things. Many felt as though none of that was at all relevant to them and tried simply to get by as best they could.

It was into this troubled world that the son of a carpenter from Nazareth called Jesus began his ministry one day. The Gospels are all about him.

THE GOSPEL ACCORDING TO MATTHEW

The first three Gospels are known as the "synoptic" or parallel Gospels, because they are all constructed in the same way and are similar to one another (even though each one is marked by the personality of its author). John's Gospel, however, is rather different.

We have chosen to print only Mark's Gospel (traditionally the second of the four), in full (see p. 24). Of the others, we have reproduced only those extracts which best show the originality of each Evangelist and complete the picture of Jesus given by Mark.

Some scholars think that Matthew's Gospel was written in Antioch, Syria. We know that in about AD 80 the Christians in that area were facing major difficulties. They were Jewish in origin and believed that in following Jesus they were being faithful to their religion. The Jews who were hostile to Christianity accused these early Christians of betraying their homeland, which had just suffered a crushing defeat by the Romans, and of being unfaithful to the true traditions proclaimed by Moses.

It was then that a writer took up a number of traditions and documents about Jesus and used them to show how he was in fact continuing what was seen in the Old Testament. It was the Jews who had misunderstood what God wanted from them. The true people of God were those of the Church. So we can see why the Evangelist frequently quotes passages from the Old Testament.

He is also careful to present the events and words he reports to enable his readers to see the parallels between Christ and Moses. Moses was the true founder of the Old Covenant. Jesus took up the work of his distant predecessor and revealed its full meaning by creating the people of the New Covenant.

Jesus is the way to the true Promised Land: the Kingdom he talks about. Just as Moses gave people the Law which is God's rule for freeing humanity, so Jesus showed them how to live now that they were saved.

He really was the long-awaited Messiah but was not a triumphant king. He was the humble and suffering servant predicted by the prophet Isaiah.

He was the Son of David, whom the prophets had seen from afar, but his Kingdom was the Kingdom of Love and not the rule of the mighty.

He was the Son of God who showed people the love of God the Father.

The Kingdom announced by Jesus became a reality in the Church. No doubt it was imperfect and still is far from perfect, but anyone who looks at it with faith will find the presence of the Lord in it.

The Church is called to spread itself throughout the world and is open to everyone.

Christians need no longer fear their enemies if they understand this. They can face the truth and therefore can go on into the future.

Matthew began with the family tree of Jesus: he showed how Jesus fitted into the troubled history of the human race. Although Jesus was born of a virgin, Matthew then showed how Jesus was related to David through Joseph, who agreed through faith to be the legal father of the child.

Matthew was careful to remind the Jews that Jesus was indeed the one they had been waiting for.

Joseph adopts Jesus as his son
1: 18–25

This is how Jesus Christ came to be born. His mother Mary was promised in marriage to Joseph. However, before they began to live together, she discovered she was going to have a baby through the Holy Spirit. Her husband Joseph was a righteous man and did not want her to be disgraced publicly, so he decided to divorce her quietly. He had made up his mind to do this when suddenly the angel of the Lord appeared to him in a dream and said, "Joseph, son of David, do not be afraid to take Mary home as your wife, because the child she has conceived comes from the Holy Spirit. She will give birth to a son and you must name him Jesus, because he is the one who will save his people from their sins." Now all this took place to fulfil what the Lord had spoken through the prophet: *Look! the virgin is with child and will give birth to a son, and they will call him Immanuel*, a name which means "God-is-with-us". When Joseph woke up he did what the angel of the Lord had told him to do: he took his wife to his home. He had not had sexual intercourse with her when she gave birth to a son. He named him Jesus.

The visit of the Magi

2: 1–12

Jesus was born at Bethlehem in Judaea during the reign of King Herod. Now some wise men came to Jerusalem from the east asking, "Where is the king of the Jews who has recently been born? We saw his star as it rose and have come to worship him." When King Herod heard this he was worried, and so was the whole of Jerusalem. He called together all the chief priests and the scribes of the people, and made enquiries about where the Christ was to be born. They told him, "At Bethlehem in Judaea, for this is what the prophet wrote:

And you, Bethlehem, in the land of Judah,
you are by no means the least among the tribes of Judah,
for a leader will come from you
who will be the shepherd of my people Israel."

Then Herod had the wise men called to see him privately. He asked them the exact date on which the star had appeared and sent them on to Bethlehem, saying to them, "Go and find out all about the child, and when you have found him, let me know, so that I too may go and worship him." Having listened to what the king had to say, they set out. And suddenly the star they had seen in the east went ahead of them and stopped over the place where the child was. The sight of the star filled them with joy, and going into the house they saw the child with his mother Mary. Falling to their knees they worshipped him. Then, opening their treasures, they gave him gifts of gold, frankincense and myrrh. But they were given a warning in a dream not to go back to Herod, and returned to their own country by a different way.

Matthew emphasised that, beside Herod, Jesus was the true king of Israel. Already his light was shining in the world and the wise men from the east saw it. This fulfilled the prophecies of Micah as quoted by Matthew. Isaiah had also announced that the kings of the earth would bring their treasures to Jerusalem to worship the true God (Isa. 49: 60). It is clear that the struggle between the representative of the kingdom of the earth and the representative of God's Kingdom had begun.

Flight into Egypt and massacre of innocent children   2: 13–18

After they had left, suddenly the angel of the Lord appeared to Joseph in a dream and said, "Get up, take the child and his mother with you, and escape into Egypt. Stay there until I tell you, because Herod intends to search for the child and have him killed." So Joseph got up and, taking the child and his mother with him, left that night for Egypt. He stayed there until Herod was dead. This was to fulfil what the Lord had spoken through the prophet: *I called my son out of Egypt.*

Herod was furious when he realised that he had been tricked by the wise men. In Bethlehem and its surrounding district he had all the male children killed who were two years old or less, reckoning by the date he had been careful to ask the wise men. Then the words spoken through the prophet Jeremiah were fulfilled:

A voice is heard in Ramah,
the sound of great mourning and bitter tears.
It is Rachel weeping for her children,
refusing to be comforted because they are no more.

Return from Egypt
3: 19–23

After Herod's death, suddenly the angel of the Lord appeared in a dream to Joseph in Egypt and said, "Get up, take the child and his mother with you and go back to the land of Israel. For all those who wanted to kill the child are dead." So Joseph got up and, taking the child and his mother with him, went back to the land of Israel. But when he learnt that Archelaus was now the ruler of Judaea in his father Herod's place he was afraid to go there. Having been warned in a dream he went down to the region of Galilee. There he settled in a town called Nazareth. In this way the words spoken through the prophets were fulfilled:

He will be called a Nazarene.

Like Mark, Matthew followed the baptism of Jesus by John the Baptist with a detailed description of the temptation in the desert.

Testing in the desert
4: 1–11

Then Jesus was led by the Spirit out into the desert to be put to the test by the devil. He fasted for forty days and forty nights. After that he was hungry. The tempter came and said to him, "If you are Son of God, tell these stones to turn into loaves." But Jesus replied, "Scripture says:

Human beings do not live on bread alone
but on every word that comes from the mouth of God."

The devil then led him to the holy city, to the parapet of the Temple, and said to him, "If you are Son of God, throw yourself down; for scripture says:

He has given his angels orders about you,
and they will carry you in their arms
in case you trip over a stone."

Jesus said to him, "Scripture also says:

Do not put the Lord your God to the test.

Next, taking him to a very high mountain, the devil showed him all the kingdoms of the world and their splendour. And he said to him, "I will give you all these, if you fall at my feet and worship me." Then Jesus replied, "Away with you, Satan! For scripture says:

The Lord your God is the one
you must worship,
you must serve only him."

Then the devil left him, and suddenly angels appeared and looked after him.

In a brief account, this text sums up all the problems Jesus faced during his public life. Unlike the Hebrews during the Exodus, and the people who wanted only power, status and immediate success, Jesus chose an attitude which was to lead him to apparent failure, but which actually made him the only human being truly capable of escaping the traps of sin. The Kingdom would be brought into being not through money, nor a popular hero to win the crowds, nor by compromising with the prince of this world, but by being totally obedient to God's Word.

The texts of the Bible quoted by the Devil are taken from the book of Deuteronomy and from Psalm 91.

Jesus then began his ministry in Galilee. He called the first apostles and some disciples to follow him, just as Moses had called his people to follow him into the wilderness long before. Matthew used the form of a long opening speech to summarise the basic teaching of Jesus on the subject of the new humanity which he called into being when announcing the Kingdom of God.

The Beatitudes

5: 1–12

Seeing the crowds, Jesus went up on to the mountain. When he had sat down his disciples came to him. Then he began to speak. This is what he taught them:

How blessed are the poor in spirit,
the kingdom of Heaven is theirs.
Blessed are the gentle,
they shall inherit the earth.
Blessed are those who mourn,
they shall be comforted.
Blessed are those who are hungry and thirsty,
they shall have their fill.
Blessed are the merciful,
they shall have mercy shown them.
Blessed are the pure in heart,
they shall see God.
Blessed are the peacemakers,
they shall be called children of God.
Blessed are those who are persecuted in the cause of righteousness,
the kingdom of Heaven is theirs.
　"Blessed are you when people insult you
and persecute you and speak all kinds of lies
against you falsely because of me.
Rejoice and be glad,
for your reward will be great in heaven.
This is also how they persecuted
the prophets before you."

Salt for the earth and light for the world

5: 13–16

"You are the salt for the earth. But if salt loses its taste, what can make it salty again? It is good for nothing, and can only be thrown out to be trampled under people's feet."

"You are light for the world. It is impossible to hide a city which is built on a hill-top. No one lights a lamp to put it under a bucket; they put it on the lamp-stand where it shines for everyone in the house. In the same way your light must shine where people can see it, so that they see your good works, and may give praise to your Father in heaven."

The fulfilment of the Law

5: 17–19

"Do not imagine that I have come to abolish the Law or the Prophets. I have not come to abolish but to complete them. In truth I tell you, till heaven and earth disappear, not one dot, not one little stroke, is to disappear from the Law until all its purpose is achieved. Therefore, anyone who disobeys even one of the least important of these commandments and teaches others to do the same will be considered the least in the kingdom of Heaven. On the other hand, the person who keeps them and teaches them will be considered great in the kingdom of Heaven."

Jesus showed that he intended to remain faithful in full to the religious traditions of his people by referring to the Law of Sinai. At the same time, however, he showed how God's Kingdom was much more demanding than that of Moses.

Jesus not only condemned wrong outward actions but also wrong inner intentions leading to them.

5: 20–4

"For I tell you, unless you are more righteous than the scribes and Pharisees, you will never get into the kingdom of Heaven.

"You have heard how it was said to our ancestors, *You shall not kill*; and if anyone does kill he must answer for it before the court. But I say this to you, anyone who is angry with a brother will have to answer for it before the court; anyone who calls a brother 'Fool' will have to answer for it before the council; and anyone who calls him 'Traitor' will have to answer for it in hell fire. So then, if you are bringing your offering to the altar and you remember that your brother has something against you, leave your offering there in front of the altar, go and be reconciled with your brother first. Then come back and present your offering."

5: 38–47

"You have heard how it was said: *Eye for eye and tooth for tooth*. But I say this to you: do not try to resist an evil person. On the contrary, if anyone hits you on the right cheek, offer him the other cheek as well; if someone wishes to take you to court to get your shirt, let him have your coat as well. And if anyone asks you to go with him for one mile, go with him for two. Give to anyone who asks you; do not turn your back on anyone who wants to borrow from you.

"You have heard how it was said, *You will love your neighbour and hate your enemy*. But I say this to you, love your enemies and pray for those who persecute you, so that you may be children of your Father in heaven; for he causes his sun to rise on the bad as well as the good, and sends down rain to fall on both the righteous and the wicked.

The Mosaic Law had limited the right to take revenge and had thus brought about progress in the system of justice. Jesus went a great deal further: he called on people always to work for reconciliation in relationships. This alone could cause love to grow and break the vicious circle of hatred. This was the true fulfilment of the text in Leviticus: "Be holy, for I, the Lord your God, am holy" (Lev. 19:2).

"For if you love those who love you, what reward will you get? Even the tax collectors do that much, don't they? And if you only greet your brothers, are you doing anything out of the ordinary? Even the gentiles do that much, don't they? You must therefore be perfect, just as your heavenly Father is perfect."

6: 1–6

Jesus followed the example of the prophets and severely criticised the superficial religion which is practised only for show. True religion meant building a relationship with God, not trying to impress other human beings.

"Be careful not to carry out your good deeds in public to attract attention; otherwise you will lose all your reward from your Father in heaven. So when you give gifts to the poor, do not draw people's attention to it by sounding a trumpet; this is what the hypocrites do in the synagogues and in the streets to make everyone admire them. In truth I tell you, they have already had their reward. But when you give gifts to the poor, your left hand must not know what your right is doing; your giving must be secret, and your Father who sees all that is done in secret will reward you.

"And when you pray, do not do what the hypocrites do: they love to say their prayers standing right in the middle of the synagogues and on street corners for people to see them. In truth I tell you, they have had their reward. But when you pray, go to your room, shut the door, and pray to your Father who is in that secret place; and your Father, who sees all that is done in secret, will reward you."

The choice between God and money
6: 19–21

This text seems to go against common sense in a world more conscious of economic problems than ever before. It was also addressed to wandering disciples whose practical needs were met by their more settled friends by setting up a brotherly and welcoming community. But it reminds us that some worries about the future are in conflict with the spirit of the Kingdom. Sometimes the desire for "total security" can stop us being able to act. Even today we must learn to live by faith and trust.

"Do not store up treasures for yourselves on earth, where moth and woodworm destroy them and thieves can break in and steal. But store up treasures for yourselves in heaven, where neither moth nor woodworm destroys them and thieves cannot break in and steal. For wherever your treasure is, there will your heart be too."

6: 24–34

"No one can be the slave of two masters. He will either hate the first and love the second, or be attached to the first and despise the second. You cannot be the slave both of God and of money.

"That is why I am telling you not to worry about what you are to eat in order to live, nor about what you are to wear. Surely there is more to life than food, and more to the body than clothing! Look at the birds in the sky. They do not sow or reap or gather

into barns; yet your heavenly Father feeds them. Are you not worth much more than they are? Who among you can add one single day to your life by worrying? And why worry about clothing? Think of the flowers growing in the fields; they never have to work or spin. Yet I assure you that not even Solomon in all his royal robes was ever as finely dressed as one of these. Now if that is how God clothes the wild flowers growing in the field which are there today and thrown into the fire tomorrow, will he not do much more for you, you who have so little faith? So do not worry; do not say, 'What are we to eat? What are we to drink? What are we to wear?' These are the things the gentiles set their hearts on. Your heavenly Father knows you need them all. Set your hearts on God's kingdom first, and on his justice, and all these other things will be given to you as well. So do not worry about tomorrow: tomorrow will take care of itself. Each day has enough trouble of its own.''

The wild flowers mentioned here were similar to anemones, with a deep crimson colour, which is why they reminded Jesus of the royal wealth of Solomon.

Attitude towards others

The true disciples of Jesus do not put themselves at the centre of everything: they are open to their brothers and sisters and think of them with love.

7: 1–5, 12

"Do not judge, and you will not be judged. For you will be judged in the way that you judge other people, and the standard you use will be the standard others use for you. Why do you look at the splinter in your brother's eye and never notice the great log in your own? And how dare you say to your brother, 'Let me take that splinter out of your eye,' when, look, there is a great log in your own? Hypocrite! Take the log out of your own eye first, and then you will see clearly enough to take the splinter out of your brother's eye. (. . .)

"So always treat others as you would like them to treat you; that is the Law and the Prophets."

False and true disciples

Jesus strongly criticised false religion and its desire to impress. He spoke out against false prophets, who were always ready to attract people, but unable to lead them to the truth. True disciples could be recognised by their actions rather than by their clever words.

7: 13–14

"Enter by the narrow gate. The road that leads to destruction is wide and spacious, and many take it. But the gate to life is narrow and a hard road leads to it, and only a few find it."

7: 24–9

"Therefore, anyone who listens to my words and puts them into practice will be like a wise man who built his house on rock. Rain came down, floods rose, gales blew and pounded against the house, and it did not fall down. It was built on rock. But anyone who listens to my words and does not put them into practice will be like a foolish man who built his house on sand. Rain came down, floods rose, gales blew and beat against that house, and it fell. It was totally ruined."

When Jesus had finished what he wanted to say, the people were amazed by his teaching: for he taught them with authority, not like their own scribes.

Matthew shows in the second part of his Gospel how Jesus formed a new world through his miracles (cf. Mark). He called his apostles to spread the Good News of his Kingdom, without fear of the opposition which was bound to come.

The third part of the Gospel tried to show what that Kingdom would be like. It was a reality that only the humble could grasp and the rich and powerful found difficult to understand.

A series of parables describes different aspects of this mystery.

13: 24–30, 36–43

He told them another parable. "The kingdom of Heaven is like a man who sowed good seed in his field. While everybody was asleep his enemy came and sowed weeds all among the wheat. When the new wheat sprouted and ripened, then the weeds began to appear as well. The labourers went to the owner and said, 'Sir, was it not good seed that you sowed in your field? If so, where have the weeds come from?' He said to them, 'One of my enemies has done this.' And the labourers said, 'Do you want us to go and weed it out?' But he said, 'No, because when you take out the weeds, you risk pulling up the wheat as well. Let them both grow till the harvest. At harvest time I shall say to the reapers: First collect the weeds and tie them in bundles to be burnt. Then gather the wheat into my barn.'" (...)

Leaving the crowds, he went back to the house. His disciples came to him and said, "Explain to us the parable about the weeds in the field." He replied, "The one who sows the good seed is the Son of man. The field is the world; the good seed is the subjects of the kingdom; the weeds, the subjects of the Evil One; the enemy who sowed it, is the devil; the harvest is the end of the world; the reapers are the angels. Well then, just as the weeds are gathered up and burnt in the fire, this is what will happen at the end of time. The Son of man will send his angels and they will gather out of his kingdom everything which causes evil and all those who do evil, and they will throw them into the blazing fire, where there will be weeping and grinding of teeth. Then the righteous will shine like the sun in the kingdom of their Father. Anyone who has ears should listen!"

Matthew added other parables to those told already by Mark. The parable of the weeds growing amongst the corn shows how the Kingdom of God is a mixture of good and bad elements while it is growing. It would be a mistake to try to create a totally "pure" community immediately. We must be patient with ourselves as well as with others.

Parables of the treasure and of the pearl
13: 44–6

Anyone who understands the value of the Kingdom of God will give up everything else in order to obtain it.

"The kingdom of Heaven is like treasure hidden in a field which someone has found. He hides it again and goes off full of joy. He sells everything he owns and buys the field.

"Again, the kingdom of Heaven is like a merchant looking for fine pearls. When he finds one of great value he goes and sells everything he owns and buys it."

Parable of the dragnet
13: 47–51

The first priority is to fish and not to be choosy about what we want to fish for; the selection process will come later. The parable of the weeds amongst the corn has already said as much in a different way.

"Again, the kingdom of Heaven is like a dragnet that is thrown in the sea and brings in a catch of all kinds of fish. When it is full, the fishermen bring it ashore; then, sitting down, they collect the good fish in baskets and throw away those that are no use. This is how it will be at the end of time. The angels will appear and separate the wicked from the righteous, to throw them into the blazing furnace, where there will be weeping and grinding of teeth.

Those who understood these parables were good interpreters of Jewish tradition. They discovered things that they had never suspected were there. That was what Matthew himself was doing when he quoted the Old Testament with reference to Jesus.

"Have you understood all this?" They said, "Yes." And he said to them, "Well then, every scribe who becomes a disciple of the kingdom of Heaven is like a householder who brings out from his storeroom new things as well as old."

Matthew used episodes already recounted by Mark to show how the community started by Jesus grew gradually as the first seed of the Church. Some of the Master's ideas showed how the members of the Kingdom should live. The Kingdom is about humility, working for the common good, the desire to help others and being able to forgive.

Forgiveness of sins and the parable of the unforgiving servant
18: 21–35

Then Peter went up to him and said, "Lord, how often must I forgive my brother if he sins against me? As often as seven times?" Jesus answered, "Not seven, I tell you, but seventy-seven times.

"And so the kingdom of Heaven may be compared to a king who decided to settle his accounts with his servants. He had just begun when they brought him a man who owed him ten thousand talents. Since he had no way of paying him back, his master gave orders that he should be sold, together with his wife, his children and all his possessions, to pay off the debt. At this, the servant threw himself down at his master's feet and begged him, 'Be patient with me and I will pay the whole sum.' And the servant's master felt so sorry for him that he let him go and released him from the debt. Now as this servant went out, he happened to meet a fellow-servant who owed him one hundred denarii; and he grabbed him by the throat and began to try and choke him, saying, 'Pay me what you owe me.' His fellow-servant fell at his feet and pleaded with him, saying, 'Be patient with me and I will pay you back.' But the other man would not agree. On the contrary, he had him thrown into prison till he could pay off the debt. His fellow-servants were deeply distressed when they saw what had happened, and they went to their master and reported the whole story to him. Then the master sent for the man and said to him, 'You wicked servant, I made you a present of the enormous sum of money you owed me when you pleaded with me. Should you not, then, have had pity on your fellow-servant just as I had pity on you?' And in his anger the master handed him over to the torturers until he was able to pay off all his debt. And that is how my heavenly Father will deal with you unless you each forgive your brother from your heart.''

Forgiveness has no limits in Jesus' Kingdom. Anyone who doubts such forgiveness should think of their own debts towards God and should refuse to be like the unforgiving servant who remembered his brother's tiny debt when God had forgiven him his huge one.

Parable of the labourers in the vineyard   20: 1–16

"Now the kingdom of Heaven is like a landowner going out early in the morning to hire workers for his vineyard. He made an agreement with the workers to pay them one denarius a day and sent them to his vineyard. He went out again at nine o'clock and saw others standing about in the market place with no work to go to. He said to them, 'You go to my vineyard too and I will give you a fair wage.' So they went.

The landowner went out again at midday and at three o'clock in the afternoon, and did the same. Then at five o'clock in the evening he went out and found more men standing around, and he said to them, 'Why have you been standing around here all day with nothing to do?' 'Because no one has hired us,' they answered. He said to them, 'You go into my vineyard too.' In the evening, the owner of the vineyard said to his foreman, 'Call the workers and pay them their wages, starting with those who were the last to arrive and ending with the first.' So those who were hired at about five o'clock came forward and were paid one denarius each. When the turn of the workers who had been hired first came, they expected to get more, but they too were paid one denarius each. They took it, but grumbled at the landowner saying, 'The men who came last have done only one hour's work, and you have

This parable challenges do-gooders who pride themselves on their obedience to the commandments, but have no sense of gratitude for God's grace. God is not an accountant; he welcomes all who come when he calls. This is unacceptable to those who think that "good works" give them a right to God's grace. It would be foolish to read this parable as a charter of workers' rights: that is exactly what Jesus was rejecting. He was not talking about the law.

treated them the same as us, though we have done a hard day's work in all the heat.' He answered one of them and said, 'My friend, I am not being unfair to you; did we not agree on one denarius? Take your earnings and go. I want to pay the workers who came late as much as I pay you. Have I not got the right to do what I like with my own money? Why should you be envious because I am generous?' This is how the last will be first, and the first, last.''

Parable of the wedding feast
22: 1–14

Jesus began to speak to them in parables once again, ''The kingdom of Heaven is like a king who gave a feast for his son's wedding. He sent his servants to call those who had been invited, but they would not come. Next he sent some more servants with the words, 'Tell those who have been invited: Look, my banquet is all prepared. My oxen and cattle have been slaughtered. Everything is ready. Come to the wedding.' But they were not interested: one went off to his farm, another to his business. The rest seized his servants, tortured them and killed them. The king was furious. He sent in his troops who destroyed those murderers and burnt down their town. Then he said to his servants, 'The wedding is ready; but those who were invited showed they were not worthy. So, go down to the main crossroads and invite everyone you can find to come to the wedding.' So these servants went out onto the roads and collected together everyone they could find, bad and good alike; and the wedding hall was filled with guests.

''When the king came in to look at the guests he noticed one man who was not wearing wedding clothes, and said to him, 'How

Matthew used this parable to emphasise the difference between Christians and followers of the Jewish faith at the time he was writing. The Jews were indeed the first to have been invited to the feast of the Kingdom, but they had been unable to see beyond the traditional ways which had become more and more rigid, and which Jesus came to bring to an end. The Good News about the Kingdom was addressed to the gentiles from that time. But they still had to be converted and purify themselves.

did you get in here, my friend, without wedding clothes?' And the man was silent. Then the king said to the servants, 'Tie up his hands and feet and throw him into the darkness outside, where there will be weeping and grinding of teeth.' For many are invited but not all are chosen.''

Chapter 24 is the beginning of the "eschatological speech", which means the speech about the end of the world. Matthew included extra parables after describing the difficulties of the last times.

Parable of the good and bad servant
24: 45–51

"Who, then, is the wise and faithful servant whom the master put in charge of his household to give them their food at the proper time? Blessed is that servant if, when his master arrives back, he finds him doing exactly that. In truth I tell you, he will put him in charge of everything he owns. But if the servant is dishonest and says to himself, 'My master is taking his time,' and begins beating his fellow-servants and eating and drinking with drunkards, his master will come at a time when he is not expecting him. The master will throw him out and make him share the same fate as the hypocrites, where there will be weeping and grinding of teeth.''

The true servant may not know when his master is going to return from his journey, but he is always ready to welcome him home. Believers should be the same: they will always rejoice to see the Lord return at the end of the world.

Parable of the ten young girls
25: 1–13

"The kingdom of Heaven is like ten young girls who took their lamps and went to meet the bridegroom. Five of them were foolish and five were sensible. The foolish girls, though they took their lamps, took no oil with them, whereas the sensible ones took flasks of oil as well as their lamps. The bridegroom was late, and they all grew drowsy and fell asleep. But at midnight there was a cry, 'Look! The bridegroom is arriving! Go out and meet him.' Then all the girls woke up and trimmed their lamps. The foolish girls said to the sensible ones, 'Give us some of your oil: our lamps are going out.' But they replied, 'There may not be enough for us and for you; you had better go and buy some for yourselves.' They had gone off to buy it when the bridegroom arrived. Those who were ready went in with him to the wedding hall and the door was closed. The other girls arrived later and said, 'Lord, Lord, open the door for us.' But he replied, 'In truth I tell you, I do not know you.' So stay awake, because you do not know either the day or the hour.''

The young girls invited to the traditional wedding procession did not know the exact time of the groom's arrival. But the wise ones among them had seen to it that they were ready. Only they were able to take part in the festivities. It will be the same for Christians; they should be ready to greet Christ whenever he returns.

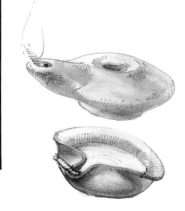

God has given gifts to all of us. He will call us all to account for them and demand to see how each of us has used our talents (in those days a talent was a large sum of money). Woe betide those who waste their lives without bothering to think about what the Lord expects of them!

The final form of the parable is deliberately challenging. It shows how we are drawn into a spiral of either good or evil through our own choices.

Parable of the talents   25: 14–30

"It is like a man about to go abroad who called his servants and gave his property to them to look after. To one he gave five talents, to another two, to a third one, each in proportion to his ability. Then he set out on his journey. The man who had received the five talents quickly went and traded with them and made five more. The man who had received two made two more in the same way. But the man who had received one went off and dug a hole in the ground and hid his master's money.

"Now a long time afterwards, the master of those servants came back and went through his accounts with them. The man who had received the five talents came forward bringing five more. 'Sir,' he said, 'you gave me five talents to look after; here are five more that I have made.' His master said to him, 'Well done, good and faithful servant. You have been faithful in small things; I will trust you with greater; come and join in your master's happiness.' Next the man with the two talents came forward. 'Sir,' he said, 'you gave me two talents to look after; here are two more that I have made.' His master said to him, 'Well done, good and faithful servant; you have shown you are faithful in small things; I will trust you with greater; come and join in your master's happiness.' Then the man who had the single talent came forward. 'Sir,' said he, 'I had heard you were a hard man: you reap where you have not sown and gather a harvest even in places where you have not scattered seed. So I was afraid, and I went off and hid your talent in the ground. Here it is; it was yours, you have it back.' But his master answered him, 'You wicked and lazy servant! So you knew that I reap where I have not sown and gather in places where I have not scattered? Well then, you should have deposited my money with the bankers, and on my return I would have got my money back with interest. So now, take the talent from him and give it to the man who has the ten talents. For to everyone who has will be given more, and he will have more than enough; but anyone who has nothing, even the little he has will be taken away. As for this good-for-nothing servant, throw him into the darkness outside, where there will be weeping and grinding of teeth.''

The Last Judgement

25: 31–45

"When the Son of man comes in his glory, with all the angels by his side, then he will take his seat on his throne of glory. All nations will be gathered before him and he will separate people one from another as the shepherd separates sheep from goats. He will place the sheep on his right hand and the goats on his left. Then the King will say to those on his right hand, 'Come, you whom my Father has blessed, inherit the kingdom prepared for you since the beginning of the world. For I was hungry and you gave me food, I was thirsty and you gave me drink, I was a stranger and you made me welcome, I was naked and you gave me clothes to wear, sick and you visited me, in prison and you came to see me.' Then the righteous will say to him in reply, 'Lord, when did we see you hungry and feed you, or thirsty and give you drink? When did we see you a stranger and make you welcome, naked and give you clothes to wear? When did we find you sick or in prison and go to see you?' And the King will answer, 'In truth I tell you, in so far as you did this to one of the least of these brothers of mine, you did it to me.' Then he will say to those on his left hand, 'Get away from me, you who are under God's curse, to the eternal fire prepared for the devil and his angels. For I was hungry and you never gave me food, I was thirsty and you never gave me anything to drink, I was a stranger and you never made me welcome, naked and you never gave me clothes to wear, sick and in prison and you never visited me.' Then it will be their turn to ask, 'Lord, when did we see you hungry or thirsty, a stranger or naked, sick or in prison, and did not come to your help?' Then he will answer, 'In truth I tell you, in so far as you did not do this to one of the least of these, you did not do it to me.' And they will go away to eternal punishment, and the righteous to eternal life."

The last of Jesus' speeches reported by Matthew shows what God will take into consideration when he judges human beings: the attitude of love towards those who are suffering. Jesus declared that any service done to the poor and humble has been done to himself.

Matthew's account of the Passion is very similar to Mark's. It is worth noting, however, that he puts the first verse of Psalm 22 into the mouth of the dying Jesus: "My God, my God, why have you forsaken me?" In the psalm, however, the cry of despair used to express the very depths of Jesus' agony ends in a song of hope.

The Evangelist told us in his account of the resurrection how some Jews tried to make people believe that the empty tomb was a trick by the apostles.

The last appearance of Jesus to his friends ended with the call to a world-wide mission: "Go, therefore, make disciples of all the nations; baptise them in the name of the Father and of the Son and of the Holy Spirit and teach them to observe all the commands I gave you. And know that I am with you always; yes, to the end of time."

Mark's Gospel is the earliest of the four Gospels. It was either written for the Romans or at least for a Christian community strongly influenced by the Roman culture. The new believers Mark was addressing were in difficulties. They often wondered whether their faith were not just a meaningless dream: where was the evidence of the triumph of Christ, the Son of God?

So Mark tried to show them that the glory of Christ was not at all what people had been expecting. It was revealed on the cross: the splendour of God shown in Jesus the servant of his brothers and sisters. True faith did not mean focusing on the most visible aspects of Jesus' great deeds, but the discovery of how his real power appeared behind them. He continually gave new life to all he met through love, and he himself lived on for ever.

The believers should stop looking for him where he was not. They should come to true faith, the faith that could save them. Their problems would no longer get them down but would challenge them.

Mark emphasised how much Jesus had shaken people up in order to show this. He overturned ideas about the Messiah God would send. Certainly, his actions raised enthusiasm, and Mark was good at presenting the work of Jesus as a real "show stopper". But the crowd's enthusiasm was based on a misunderstanding, which explained why even his apostles abandoned him on the day he was condemned to death. God showed how great he is by dying on the cross, as recognised by the gentile soldier who said: "This was the Son of God."

Right until the last moment, Jesus forbade people to talk about what seemed to be the most extraordinary thing about him (we call this the "messianic secret"). He knew that the people were dreaming of a glorious Messiah, one sent by God to free them from Roman occupation, and restore a political kingdom. It was not until that false hope was smashed by his death on the cross, and it seemed as if he had failed, that it became possible to proclaim the truth about who he really was.

Mark emphasised the difficulties experienced by the apostles when coming to real faith. Jesus had to shake them up again and again. The Evangelist tries to make his readers realise that faith is not easy; he says that faith demands that we pass through trials and death, but life springs from these.

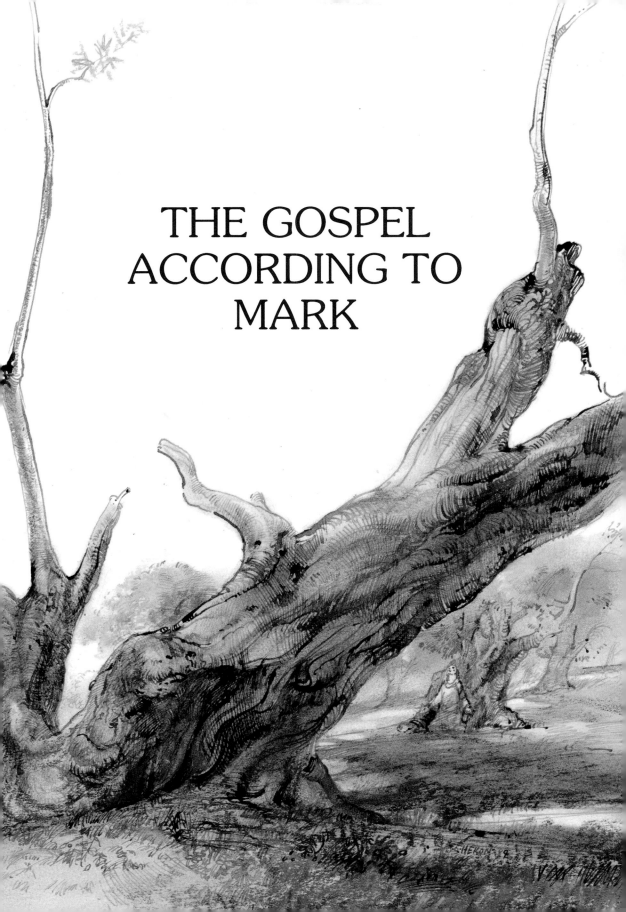

THE GOSPEL
ACCORDING TO
MARK

PREPARATION FOR THE PUBLIC MINISTRY OF JESUS

A prophet was making people sit up. He was announcing the arrival soon of someone far greater than himself: the one who would baptise people "with the Holy Spirit".

1: 1–8

The beginning of the gospel about Jesus Christ, the Son of God. It is written in the prophet Isaiah:

"Look, I am going to send my messenger in front of you
to prepare your way before you.
A voice of one that cries out in the desert:
Prepare a way for the Lord,
make his paths straight."

John the Baptist was in the desert, proclaiming a baptism of repentance for the forgiveness of sins. All the people of Judaea and all the citizens of Jerusalem made their way to him, and as they were baptised by him in the river Jordan they confessed their sins.

John wore a garment made of camel-skin. He lived on locusts and wild honey. In the course of his preaching he said, "The one who is coming after me is more powerful than me. I am not worthy to kneel down and undo the strap of his sandals. I have baptised you with water, but he will baptise you with the Holy Spirit."

Jesus is baptised
1: 9–11

It was at this time that Jesus came from Nazareth in Galilee and was baptised in the Jordan by John. And as he was coming up out of the water, he saw the heavens torn apart and the Spirit, like a dove, descending on him. And a voice came from heaven, "You are my beloved Son; my favour rests on you."

Jesus did come. God showed that Jesus was truly the "beloved son" when he was baptised by John and marked by the Spirit of God.

Testing in the desert
1: 12–13

And at once the Spirit made him go into the desert and he stayed there for forty days, and was put to the test by Satan. He was with the wild animals, and the angels looked after him.

It was in the wilderness that the great men chosen by God had learned their call. It was there too that Jesus meditated about his mission and made some basic decisions.

JESUS' MINISTRY IN GALILEE

Jesus begins to preach   1: 14–20

The Jews were expecting God to come in triumph to establish his reign on earth. Jesus talked of the Kingdom that was coming but for him it was the end of a long wait. He did not say any more about it, but his announcement was enough to provoke a wave of hope.

After John had been arrested, Jesus went into Galilee. There he proclaimed the gospel from God. He said: "The time is fulfilled, and the kingdom of God is close at hand. Repent, and believe the gospel."

As he was walking along by the Lake of Galilee he saw Simon and his brother Andrew casting a net in the lake — for they were fishermen. And Jesus said to them, "Follow me and I will make you into fishers of people." And at once they left their nets and followed him.

A little further on, he saw James, the son of Zebedee and his brother John. They too were in their boat, mending the nets. At once he called them. Leaving their father Zebedee in the boat with the men he employed, they began to follow him.

Jesus causes a stir in Capernaum   1: 21–8

Jesus began his fight against evil there and then. His words hit home. A man possessed by a demon (probably mentally ill) reacted in a violent way. Jesus did not want to be seen as some kind of magician so he first made the demon be quiet before making it leave the man.

They went as far as Capernaum, and at once on the Sabbath Jesus went into the synagogue and began to teach. Everyone was impressed by what he taught them because, unlike the scribes, he spoke with authority.

But there was a man who was possessed by a demon, and he shouted, "What are you doing here, Jesus of Nazareth? Have you come to destroy us? I know who you are: the Holy One of God." But Jesus rebuked it saying, "Be quiet! Come out of him!" And the unclean spirit shook the man violently and came out of him with a loud cry. The people were so astonished that they started asking one another what it all meant, saying, "What this man says is new! He speaks as if he knows what he is talking about. He gives orders to demons and they obey him." And at once his reputation spread everywhere, through the whole of Galilee.

Jesus heals   1: 29–31

Life seemed to spring up around Jesus. Evil collapsed. It really was a new world being born at the very heart of normal life.

On leaving the synagogue, he went straight to the house of Simon and Andrew, accompanied by James and John. Now Simon's mother-in-law was in bed with a fever. At once they told him about her. He went in to her, took her by the hand and helped her up. The fever left her and she began to serve them.

Many are healed   1: 32–4

That evening, after sunset, they brought to him all who were sick and those who were possessed by demons. The whole town was there, crowding round the door. He healed many who were sick with diseases of one kind or another; he also drove out many demons. But he would not allow them to speak, because they knew who he was.

Jesus' success was immediate. Everyone came to him. But did they really understand what he was trying to do? Jesus was afraid they would see him as a faith healer without understanding that his actions were signs of the Kingdom coming on earth.

Jesus leaves Capernaum   1: 35–9

In the morning, long before dawn, Jesus got up and went off to a lonely place. He prayed there. Simon and his friends went to look for him. When they found him they said, "Everybody is looking for you." He answered, "Let us go elsewhere, to the neighbouring country towns. I must preach the message there too, because that is why I came." And he went all over Galilee, preaching in their synagogues and driving out demons.

Jesus went to God for guidance as at every important moment in his life. He refused to listen to those who wanted to hold him back: he had to go on.

A leper is healed   1: 40–5

A leper came to him and pleaded on his knees saying, "If you are willing, you can heal me." Feeling sorry for him, Jesus stretched out his hand, touched him and said to him, "I am willing. Be healed." And at once the leprosy left him and he was healed. Jesus sent him away and said to him firmly, "Do not tell anyone what has happened. Go straight to the priest and let him examine you, and make an offering, as Moses instructed. This will be a witness to them."

But once the man had left, he began to speak freely about it and told the story everywhere, so that Jesus could no longer go openly into any town: he stayed outside in deserted places. Even so, people from all around kept coming to him.

Jesus took an interest in outcasts rejected by others. Having healed a leper, he sent him to the priests to have his healing confirmed, as instructed by the Law so that he could be accepted back into his village; the old Law kept lepers out of all social and religious life. Jesus' reputation grew but again he ordered silence. He did not want to be taken for a hoax miracle worker.

A paralysed man is healed   2: 1–12

Jesus returned to Capernaum. Some time later word went round that he was in the house. So many people gathered there that there was no room left, even in front of the door. He was preaching the word to them when some people came bringing him a paralysed man carried by four men. As they could not get the man to him through the crowd, they stripped the roof over the place where Jesus was; they made a hole and lowered the stretcher with the paralysed man. Seeing their faith, Jesus said to the paralysed man, "My child, your sins are forgiven." Now some scribes were sitting

Jesus showed clearly what he had come to do by forgiving the paralysed man's sins: he had come to reconcile the human race to God and to himself, which meant to heal everything that prevented people from going forward. He really shocked the scribes, though, who did not think he had any right to forgive sins. Jesus justified his power to forgive sins by healing the paralysed man.

Jesus was treading on more and more people's toes although the crowd was enthusiastic.

there, and they thought to themselves, "How can this man talk like that? This is blasphemy! Who but God can forgive sins?" And at once, Jesus, aware that this is what they were thinking, said to them, "Why do you have these thoughts in your hearts? Is it easier for me to say to the paralysed man, 'Your sins are forgiven' or, 'Get up, pick up your stretcher and walk'? But to prove to you that the Son of man has authority to forgive sins on earth" — he said to the paralysed man — "I order you: get up, pick up your stretcher, and go off home." And the man got up, and at once picked up his stretcher and walked out in front of everyone. They were all astonished and praised God saying, "We have never seen anything like this."

The call of Levi   2: 13–14

Jesus dared to call a tax-collector, a member of a shameful social group, to join him. This really provoked the "do-gooders".

He went out again to the shore of the lake. All the people came to him, and he taught them. As he was walking along he saw Levi, the son of Alphaeus, sitting at the tax office, and he said to him, "Follow me." Levi got up and followed him.

Eating with sinners   2: 15–17

Jesus shocked them even more by eating with people known for their immoral way of life. He reminded them of his mission: to save those who were lost.

One day Jesus was at dinner in his house. A number of tax collectors and sinners were with Jesus and his disciples; for there were many of them among his followers. When the scribes of the Pharisee party saw him eating with sinners and tax collectors, they said to his disciples, "Why does he eat with tax collectors and sinners?" Jesus heard this. He said to them, "It is not healthy people who need the doctor, but the sick. I came to call sinners, not righteous people."

A discussion on fasting   2: 18–22

Jesus came to create a universe of joy. The world he created replaced a religious universe which had lost all its original enthusiasm and sincerity. But the Pharisees were shocked. They could not understand Jesus' freedom which was so different to the so-called "traditional" rules.

John's disciples and the Pharisees were fasting. Some people came to him and said, "Why is it that John's disciples and the disciples of the Pharisees fast, but your disciples do not?" Jesus replied, "Surely the bridegroom's friends do not fast while he is still with them? That is not the time for fasting. But when the time comes for the bridegroom to be taken away from them, then they will fast. No one sews a new piece of material on an old cloak; otherwise, the new patch pulls away from the old cloth, and the tear gets worse. And nobody puts new wine into old wineskins; otherwise, the wine will burst the skins, and the wine is lost and the skins too. No! Put new wine into fresh skins!"

Picking corn on the Sabbath
2: 23–7

In the religious world of the Pharisees described by the Gospel in a controversial context, the Law had become rigid and had lost its sense of being a way to freedom. In Jesus' view, the Law was there to serve life and the Sabbath was there for freedom (cf. Exod. 20: 9), a freedom that King David had been able to use.

One Sabbath day Jesus was taking a walk through the cornfields. His disciples were picking ears of corn. And the Pharisees said to him, "Look, why are they doing something on the Sabbath day that is forbidden?" And he replied, "Have you never read what David did one day when he and his followers were hungry? At the time when Abiathar was high priest, he went into the house of God and ate the loaves given for the offering. He also gave some to the men with him. Really, only the priests are allowed to eat them."

And he added, "The Sabbath was made for man, not man for the Sabbath; that is why the Son of man is master even of the Sabbath."

Healing of a man with a withered hand
3: 1–6

Jesus challenged the prejudices of those people who had twisted the meaning of the Law, by healing someone on the Sabbath and in the heart of the synagogue. Hatred for Jesus brought together former enemies in a league against him.

Jesus went back to the synagogue. There was a man there who had a withered hand. They were watching him to see if he would heal him on the Sabbath day, for they wanted to accuse him of doing something wrong. He said to the man with the withered hand, "Get up and stand in the middle!" Then he said to them, "On the Sabbath day are we allowed to do good, or to do evil; to save life, or to kill?" But they said nothing. Then looking angrily at the crowd, he said to the man, "Stretch out your hand." He stretched it out and his hand was healed. The Pharisees went out and met at once with supporters of King Herod to discuss how they could kill him.

The crowds follow Jesus
3: 7–12

The crowds enthused about Jesus. But how many people understood the meaning of the title "Son of God" as it was shouted out by sinful people who had recognised that Jesus was a real enemy to them? In fact, people were attracted by the most obvious aspects of the Master's work and misunderstandings began to grow.

Jesus went back with his disciples to the Lake of Galilee. A great crowd followed him. People came from Judaea, from Jerusalem, from Idumaea and Transjordan and the region of Tyre and Sidon. They had heard of all he was doing and came to him. He asked his disciples to have a boat ready for him, to stop him being crushed by the crowd. For he had healed so many that all who were ill were crowding forward for him to touch them. Whenever they saw him, the unclean spirits would fall down before him and shout, "You are the Son of God!" But he forbade them to tell anyone who he was.

Jesus chooses the twelve apostles
3: 13–19

He now went up on to the mountain and called those he had chosen. He appointed twelve of them to be his companions, who would preach the message and would have the power to drive out demons. To Simon he gave the name Peter. He also chose James, the son of Zebedee, and John the brother of James: he called them Boanerges or "Sons of Thunder"; then Andrew, Philip, Bartholomew, Matthew, Thomas, James the son of Alphaeus, Thaddaeus, Simon the Zealot and Judas Iscariot, the man who was to betray him.

A reference to the twelve tribes of Jacob, which means the whole of the people of Israel Jesus had come to reunite. Jesus chose the twelve companions who were to continue his work. But would the apostles understand their mission? Mark is already indicating that one of them was to betray him.

His family are concerned about Jesus
3: 20–1

He went home again. There was such a crowd that neither he nor his disciples could even have a meal. When members of his family heard of this, they came to take charge of him. They said, "He is out of his mind."

Jesus' nearest and dearest did not understand him. They saw him merely as a great man. Gradually, Jesus found himself shut out from all the traditional institutions including his own family.

Jesus defends himself against the scribes' allegations
3: 22–30

The scribes who had come down from Jerusalem were saying, "Beelzebul is in him," and, "It is the prince of demons who gives him the power to drive demons out." So Jesus called them to him and spoke to them in parables, "How can Satan drive out Satan? If a kingdom is divided against itself, that kingdom cannot last. And if a family is divided, it can never last. Now if Satan has rebelled against himself and is divided, he loses his strength, he is lost. But no one can make his way into a strong man's house and rob his property unless he has first tied up the strong man. Only then can he rob his house.

"In truth I tell you, all human sins will be forgiven, and all the words of blasphemy they have ever spoken; but anyone who blasphemes against the Holy Spirit will never be forgiven, but is guilty of an eternal sin." Jesus said this because they were saying, "He is possessed by a demon."

The opposition grew. They slandered Jesus in the name of religion but were in fact filled with deep hatred. The conflict grew between the Galilean prophet and those representing the religious bodies in Jerusalem.

Jesus' outlook was very different. To him, his real family was not the one he was born into, but the one consisting of his disciples.

The true family of Jesus
3: 31–5

His mother and his brothers arrived. Standing outside, they sent in a message asking for him. A crowd was sitting round him at the time the message was passed to him, "Look, your mother, brothers and sisters are outside asking for you." He replied, "Who are my mother and my brothers?" He looked at those sitting in a circle round him and said, "Here are my mother and my brothers. Anyone who does the will of God, that person is my brother, my sister and mother."

Through this parable, Jesus was describing his own actions: he was sowing the word everywhere. But he knew very well that it would not grow everywhere. Only those who took it to their hearts would see it bear fruit.

Parable of the sower
4: 1–9

He began to teach them again by Lake Galilee. Such a huge crowd gathered round him that he got into a boat on the water and sat there. The whole crowd stood along the shore at the edge of the lake. He taught them many things using parables.

In the course of his teaching he said to them, "Listen! One day a sower went out to sow. Now, as he sowed, some of the seed fell on the edge of the path. The birds came and ate it up. Some seed fell on rocky ground where there was not much soil. It put up shoots at once because there was no depth of earth. When the sun came up it scorched the shoots and they withered away because they did not have any roots. Some seed fell into thorns; the thorns grew up and choked it, and it did not produce a crop. And some seed fell into rich soil. It grew tall and strong, and produced a good crop; the yield was thirty, sixty, even a hundred-fold." And he said, "Anyone who has ears should listen!"

Why Jesus spoke in parables
4: 10–12

The apostles wanted Jesus to speak in a clearer and more convincing way, but the Master reminded them that the Word of God could not be forced on people since it required personal effort. There were people who would always reject what, to others,

When he was alone, the Twelve, together with the others who travelled with him, asked what the parables meant. He told them, "You have received the secret of the kingdom of God. But the others only hear things in parables, so that *they may look and look, but never see and understand. For if they did, they might change their ways and be healed.*"

The parable of the sower explained
4: 13–20

He said to them, "Do you not understand this parable? Then how will you understand any of the parables? What the sower is sowing is the word. Those on the edge of the path where the word is sown are people who have no sooner heard it than Satan comes. He snatches away the word that was sown in them. Other people are like the seed sown on rocky ground. At first they welcome the word with joy. But they do not let it take root and so it does not last: as soon as some trial comes, or some persecution on account of the word, they fall away. Those who have received the word in thorns are those who have heard the word, but the worries of the world, the temptation of riches and other evil desires come in to choke the word, and so it produces nothing. Lastly, there are those who have received the word in rich soil; they hear the word, accept it and yield a harvest, some thirty times as much, some sixty and some a hundred."

seemed perfectly clear. Isaiah had already said the same thing, and Jesus quoted him here.

It is human desires which stop us accepting the Word of God. The only people who can really understand it are those who have freed themselves from all obstacles.

Parable of the lamp
4: 21–5

He said to them, "Does anyone bring in a lamp to put it under a tub or under the bed? Surely they put it on the lamp-stand? For everything that is hidden will be revealed, everything that is kept secret will be brought to light. Anyone who has ears should listen!"

He also said to them, "Pay attention to what you are hearing. Whatever standard you use for other people will be used for you — and you will receive more besides. Anyone who has, will be given more; anyone who has nothing, even the little he has will be taken away from him."

People are tempted to stop the light shining out, but it will always find a way, so the apostles should hold it up even if sometimes they fail.

Parable of the seed growing by itself
4: 26–9

He also said, "The kingdom of God is like a man who scatters seed on the land. Night or day, whether he sleeps or stays awake, the seed is sprouting and growing; how, he does not know. Of its own accord the land produces first the shoot, then the ear, then the full grain of corn. And when the crop is ready, he starts to reap at once because the harvest has come."

Have faith! When the Word has really begun to grow, when someone has begun to realise the full richness of the preaching about the Kingdom, it is unstoppable.

Parable of the mustard seed
4: 30–2

The Kingdom of God seems to be nothing at first but, little by little, it takes over everything and becomes the meeting point for all creation.

He also said, "What can we say that the kingdom is like? What parable can we find for it? It is like a mustard seed. At the time of its sowing, it is the smallest of all the seeds on earth. Yet once it is sown it grows into the biggest shrub of them all and puts out big branches so that the birds of the air can shelter in its shade."

The use of parables
4: 33–4

So each person receives the Word according to his or her own openness to the truth! Jesus tries to go further still with his disciples.

He spoke the word to them, using many parables like these, so far as they were capable of understanding it. He would only speak to them in parables, but he explained everything to his disciples when they were by themselves.

The calming of the storm
4: 35–41

Had the disciples really understood Jesus? The authority with which he calmed the storm made them feel very confused. They realised that he was quite different to themselves.

The evening of that same day, he said to them, "Let us cross over to the other side." Leaving the crowd behind they took him in the boat, just as he was. There were other boats with him. Then a strong gale blew up and the waves were breaking into the boat so that it was almost swamped. But he was in the stern, his head on the cushion, asleep. They woke him and said to him, "Master, don't you care? We are going to die!" And he woke up and rebuked the wind and said to the sea,

"Quiet now! Be calm!" The wind dropped, and there followed a great calm. Then he said to them, "Why are you so frightened? Have you still no faith?" They were seized by a great fear and said to one another, "Who is this man? Even the wind and the sea obey him."

Jesus heals a man with demons 5: 1–20

They reached the other side of the lake, in the territory of the Gerasenes. No sooner had Jesus climbed out of the boat than a man with an unclean spirit came out from the tombs towards him. The man lived in the tombs and no one could secure him any more, even with a chain: he had often been secured with ropes and chains but he had broken free from them, and no one had the strength to control him. All night and all day, he would remain among the tombs and in the mountains, crying out and gashing himself with stones. Catching sight of Jesus from a distance, he ran up and fell at his feet and shouted at the top of his voice, "What do you want with me, Jesus, son of the Most High God? In God's name, I beg you, do not torture me!" For Jesus had been saying to him, "Come out of the man, unclean spirit." Then he asked, "What is your name?" He answered, "My name is Legion, for there are many of us." And he begged him earnestly not to send them out of the district. Now on the mountainside there was a large herd of pigs feeding, and the unclean spirits begged him, "Send us to the pigs, let us go into them." So he gave them permission. With that, the unclean spirits came out of the man and went into the pigs, and the herd of about two thousand pigs charged down the cliff into the lake, and there they were drowned. The men looking after them ran off and told their story in the city and in the country round about. The people came to see what had really happened. They came to Jesus and saw the man who had been possessed sitting there, properly dressed and in his right mind, and they were afraid. And those who had witnessed it told them what had happened to the man with the demons and the pigs. Then they began to plead with Jesus to leave their neighbourhood.

As he was getting into the boat, the man who had been possessed begged to be allowed to stay with him. Jesus would not let him but said to him, "Go home to your people and tell them all that the Lord in his mercy has done for you." So the man went off and began to tell people in the Decapolis all that Jesus had done for him. And everyone was amazed.

Who was he? Mark says that this was the first time they had asked themselves such a question: it was to become more and more urgent.

This strange story is difficult for our logical minds to understand. Jesus healed a madman right in the middle of a pagan country, sending the powers of evil back to the depths of the abyss from which they came. The unusual healing upset the people of the country who had become used to the madman and who were rather fond of their pigs (which were considered unclean animals by the Jews anyway). This episode gives us a glimpse of the future mission of the apostles in gentile lands and also shows the difficulties they were to experience when trying to convince a world that wanted to reject salvation.

A sick woman is healed and Jairus' daughter is raised to life
5: 21–43

Faith has to keep growing. Jairus had to believe that Jesus had the power to raise the dead, when everything encouraged him to despair. The sick woman who tried to "steal" a cure out of self-interest had to accept a personal relationship with Jesus in order to be saved. It was a good question for the disciples as well as for the readers of Mark's Gospel: how strong was their faith? How far did it go?

Jesus crossed back to the other side of the lake in the boat. A large crowd gathered round him while he was still by the lake. Then the president of the synagogue, a man called Jairus, came up, and, as soon as he saw him, fell at his feet and begged him, "My little daughter is desperately sick. Please come and lay your hands on her that she may be saved and may live." Jesus went with him and a large crowd followed him; they were pressing all round him.

Now there was a woman who had suffered from a loss of blood for twelve years; after long and painful treatment under various doctors, she had spent all her money without being any the better for it; in fact, she was getting worse. She had heard about Jesus. Slipping up through the crowd behind him she touched his cloak, thinking, "If I can just touch his clothes, I shall be healed." And at once the loss of blood dried up, and she felt in herself that she was healed. Jesus became aware at once that power had gone out of him and, turning round to the crowd, asked, "Who touched my clothes?" His disciples said to him, "You see how the crowd is pressing round you; how can you ask, 'Who touched me?'" But he continued to look all round to see who had done it. Then the woman, frightened and trembling because she knew what had happened to her, threw herself at his feet and told him the whole truth. He said to her, "My daughter, your faith has made you well; go in peace and be healed of your illness."

He was still speaking when some people arrived from the house of the president of the synagogue to say, "Your daughter is dead. Why put the Master to any further trouble?" But Jesus overheard what they said and he said to the president of the synagogue, "Do not be afraid; only have faith." And he allowed no one to go with him except Peter, James and John, the brother of James. So they came to the house of the president of the synagogue, and Jesus noticed all the commotion, with people weeping and wailing loudly. He went in and said to them, "Why all this commotion and crying? The child is not dead, but asleep." But they laughed at him. So he turned them all out and, taking with him the child's father and mother and his own companions, he went into the place where the child was lying. And taking the child by the hand he said to her, "*Talitha kum!*" which means, "Little girl, I tell you to get up." The little girl got up at once and began to walk about, for she was twelve years old. Everyone was astonished. He gave them strict orders not to tell anyone, and told them to give her something to eat.

A visit to Nazareth   6: 1–6

Leaving there, he went back to his home town; his disciples followed him. On the Sabbath he began teaching in the synagogue; many people were astonished when they heard him. They said, "Where did the man get all this? What is this wisdom that has been given to him? How does he do these miracles? Isn't this the carpenter, the son of Mary, the brother of James and Joset and Jude and Simon? Aren't his sisters here with us?" And they would not accept him. And Jesus said to them, "A prophet is only despised in his own country, among his own relations and in his own house." He could do no miracles there, except that he healed a few sick people by laying his hands on them. He was amazed at their lack of faith.

The mission of the Twelve   6: 6–13

He made a tour round the villages, teaching. Then he called the Twelve to him and sent them out in pairs, giving them power over unclean spirits. And he instructed them to take nothing for the journey except a stick: no bread, no haversack, no money in their purses. They were to wear sandals but, he added, "Don't take any spare clothes." And he said to them, "If you enter a house anywhere, stay there until you leave the district. And if you are not welcomed in any place, and the people refuse to listen to you, as you walk away shake off the dust under your feet as a warning to them." So they set off and preached that people should repent; and they cast out many demons, and anointed many sick people with oil and healed them.

Herod and Jesus   6: 14–16

King Herod had heard about him, since by now he had become well-known. Some were saying, "John the Baptist has risen from the dead. That is why he has the power to work miracles. Others said, "He is Elijah," still others, "He is a prophet, like the prophets we used to have." But when Herod heard this he said, "It is John whom I beheaded; he has risen from the dead."

The words *Talitha Kum* are in Aramaic which is the language Jesus spoke.

Jesus came up against the unbelief of his nearest and dearest in contrast with the faith of the characters before. They could not understand that the power of God was showing itself in a man they all thought they knew well. In Nazareth, therefore, Jesus was unable to perform any miracles, because a miracle is no more than a bit of "magic" if performed without faith and is no longer a sign of the Kingdom.

It was the turn of the Twelve to act now. They had to go forward by letting go of anything that might hold them back. They should not think their mission was going to be easy! But they should give out signs of the Kingdom.

Jesus' fame was spreading: who was this man? There were many rumours and ideas. Herod had his own theory. He had a bad conscience.

The king could not forget the crime he had just committed. He had the prophet put to death at the request of Salome, who was encouraged by her mother's hatred for John the Baptist's rebukes.

John the Baptist beheaded
6: 17–29

Now it was this same Herod who had had John arrested and chained up in prison because of Herodias, his brother Philip's wife whom he had married. For John had told Herod, "It is against the law for you to take your brother's wife." Herodias was furious with him and wanted his death, but there was nothing she could do because Herod was afraid of John: knowing him to be a good and righteous man, he protected him. When he had heard him speak he was very puzzled, and yet he liked to listen to him.

An opportunity came on Herod's birthday when he gave a banquet for the nobles of his court, for his army officers and for the leading figures in Galilee. Herodias' daughter came in and danced, and she delighted Herod and his guests. So the king said to the girl, "Ask me anything you like and I will give it you." And he swore to her, "I will give you anything you ask, even half my kingdom." She went out and said to her mother, "What shall I ask for?" She replied, "The head of John the Baptist." The girl at once rushed back to the king and made her request, "I want you to give me John the Baptist's head, immediately, on a dish." The king was deeply distressed but he did not want to break his word to her because of his oath in front of his guests. At once the king sent one of the bodyguard with orders to bring John's head. The man went off and beheaded him in the prison. Then he brought the head on a dish and gave it to the girl, who gave it to her mother. When John's disciples heard about this, they came and took his body and buried it.

First miracle of the loaves   6: 30–44

Returning to Jesus, the apostles told him all they had done and taught. And he said to them, "Come away to a lonely place all by yourselves and rest for a while. For there were so many people coming and going that there was no time for them even to eat. So they went off in the boat to a lonely place where they could be by themselves. But people saw them going, and many recognised them; and from every town they all hurried to the place on foot and reached it before them. So as he stepped ashore he saw a large crowd; and he was filled with pity for them because they were like sheep without a shepherd, and he began to teach them many things. By now it was getting very late, and his disciples came up to him and said, "This is a lonely place and it is getting very late; so send them away, so that they can go to the farms and villages round about, to buy themselves something to eat." He replied, "Give them something to eat yourselves." They answered, "Are we to go and spend two hundred denarii on bread for them to eat?" He asked, "How many loaves do you have? Go and see." When they had found out they came back to him and said, "Five, and two fish." Then he ordered them to get all the people to sit down in groups on the green grass. Everyone sat down on the ground in squares of hundreds and fifties. Then he took the five loaves and the two fish, raised his eyes to heaven and said the blessing; then he broke the loaves and began handing them to his disciples to distribute among the people. He also shared out the two fish among them all. They all ate as much as they wanted. They collected twelve basketfuls of leftovers of bread and pieces of fish. There were five thousand men among the crowd who had eaten the loaves.

Jesus walks on the water   6: 45–52

And at once he made his disciples get into the boat and go on ahead to the other side near Bethsaida, while he sent the crowd away. After saying goodbye to the people he went off into the hills to pray. When evening came, the boat was right out in the middle of the lake, and he was alone on the land. He could see that the rowing was making them exhausted, for the wind was against them; late in the night he came towards them, walking on the sea. He was going to pass them by, but when they saw him walking on the sea they thought it was a ghost and cried out; for they had all seen him and were terrified. But at once he spoke to them and

The apostles gave an account of their mission. Jesus invited them to rest a little. Jesus had to deal with the crowds who were hungry to hear him speak. He took pity on the crowds who had no one to guide them, as a good shepherd would have done. He fed them with his teaching to make them his people. He also gave them food for their bodies, asking that they share the little they had. There was enough for everybody and they even gathered up plenty of leftovers.

This sign from Jesus is the only one reported in all four Gospels and is truly symbolic of the new world order Jesus created. It announced the day when God would gather all his people at the table of his feast.

The apostles were still ignorant at that time, as shown figuratively by the story of their return in the boat. Jesus, on the other hand, "walked on the water" because his mission kept him strong. He carried them along with him when they found that things were beyond them.

The crowds continued to flock to him: Jesus brought them life and salvation.

said, "Courage! It's me! Don't be afraid." Then he got into the boat with them and the wind dropped. They were utterly and completely amazed, because they had not seen what the miracle of the loaves meant; their minds were closed.

People are healed at Gennesaret 6: 53–6

Having made the crossing, they reached Gennesaret and moored there. They had hardly got out of the boat when people recognised him, and started hurrying all through the countryside, bringing the sick on stretchers to wherever they heard he was. And wherever he went, villages or towns or farms, they brought the sick to the open spaces and begged him to let them touch even the fringe of his cloak. And all those who touched him were saved.

Discussion on the traditions of the Pharisees 7: 1–13

The Pharisees and some of the scribes from Jerusalem gathered round him. They noticed that some of his disciples were eating with unclean hands, that is, without washing them. For the Pharisees, and all the Jews, keep the tradition of the elders and never eat without washing their arms as far as the elbow; and on returning from the market place they never eat without sprinkling themselves with water first. There are also many other practices which have been handed down to them to keep, concerning the washing of cups, pots and bronze dishes. So the Pharisees and scribes asked him, "Why do your disciples not respect the tradition of the elders but eat their food with unclean hands?" He answered, "How right Isaiah was when he spoke these words of prophecy about you hypocrites: *This people only honours me with their lips, while their hearts are far away from me. Their worship of me is worthless; the lessons they teach are nothing but human commandments.*

"You put aside the commandment of God to observe human traditions." And he said to them, "How cleverly you get round the commandment of God in order to keep your own tradition! For Moses said: *Honour your father and your mother*, and, *Anyone who curses father or mother must be put to death*. But you say, 'If a man says to his father or mother: Anything I have that I might have used to help you is Korban (that is, dedicated to God),' then he is forbidden from that moment to do anything for his father or mother. In this way you cancel out God's word for the sake of your tradition which you have handed down. And you do many other things like this."

The Pharisees were similar to Jesus in many ways although there were people among them who were set in their beliefs and traditions. The opposition grew between Jesus and these "do-gooders". Jesus rebuked them for being too rigid about their human rules; they were no longer thinking straight about important moral issues, and their religion was just outward show.

Teaching on what makes a person unclean   7: 14–23

He called the people to him again and said, "Listen to me, all of you, and understand. Nothing that goes into someone from outside can make that person unclean; it is the things that come out of someone that make that person unclean. Anyone who has ears should listen!"

When he had gone into the house, away from the crowd, his disciples questioned him about the meaning of the parable. He said to them, "Even you — don't you understand? Can't you see that nothing that goes into someone from outside can make that person unclean, because it goes not into the heart but into the stomach and then passes out of the body?" (By saying this he declared all foods fit to be eaten.) And he went on, "It is what comes out of someone that makes that person unclean. For it is from within, from the heart, that evil intentions come: fornication, theft, murder, adultery, greed, hatred, deceit, indecency, envy, slander, pride, foolishness. All these evil things come from within and make a person unclean."

A foreigner's daughter is healed   7: 24–30

Jesus left there and set out for the territory of Tyre. He went into a house and did not want anyone to know he was there; but he could not stay hidden. At once a woman whose little daughter had an unclean spirit heard about him and came and fell at his feet. Now this woman was a gentile, by birth a Syro-Phoenician. She begged him to drive the demon out of her daughter. And he said to her, "The children should be fed first, because it is not fair to take the children's food and throw it to little dogs." But she replied, "Ah yes, sir, but little dogs under the table eat the scraps from the children." And he said to her, "For saying this you may go home happy. The demon has gone out of your daughter." So she went

Jesus reminded people that true purity was that of the heart, which was the idea behind the Law of Moses.

Jesus seems originally to have thought that the salvation of the gentile world would take place when Israel was reunited, which would show everyone the splendour of God's work. But he had to rethink his original idea in view of the Canaanite's faith. God's plans surpassed the limits Jesus set on his plan of action.

People drag themselves along without understanding the truth and being unable to sing the glory of God. The healing of the deaf man with a speech impediment revealed his salvation, as shown also by the way the gentile crowds suddenly began to sing praises to Jesus.

off home and found the child lying on the bed. The demon had gone.

Healing of the deaf man   7: 31–7

Returning from the territory of Tyre, he made his way past Sidon towards the Lake of Galilee, right through the Decapolis territory. And they brought him a deaf man who also found it difficult to speak, and they asked him to lay his hand on him. He took him away from the crowd, to be by themselves, put his fingers into the man's ears and touched his tongue with saliva. Then looking up to heaven he sighed, and said to him, "*Ephphatha*," that is, "Be

opened." And his ears were opened, and at once the impediment of his tongue was removed and he spoke clearly. And Jesus ordered them not to tell anyone about it, but the more he insisted, the more widely they spoke of it. They were completely amazed and said, "Everything he does is good, he makes the deaf hear and the dumb speak."

Note Jesus' gesture, which is like the symbolic actions of the ancient prophets.

Second miracle of the loaves   8: 1–10

Once again a great crowd gathered, and they had nothing to eat. So he called his disciples to him and said to them, "I feel sorry for all these people; they have been with me for three days now and have nothing to eat. If I send them off home hungry they will collapse on the way; some have come a great distance." His disciples replied, "Where could anyone get these people enough bread to eat in a deserted place?" He asked them, "How many loaves do you have?" And they said to him, "Seven." He instructed

By telling the story of a second multiplication of the loaves, Mark showed that Jesus could perform the same miracle for gentiles as he did for the Jews. The disciples would see that they had all they needed to feed the crowds if they only believed in the Master's power. But they were not yet ready for their mission.

the crowd to sit down on the ground. Then he took the seven loaves, and after giving thanks he broke them and began handing them to his disciples to distribute. They shared them out among the crowd. They had a few small fishes as well. After he had blessed them, he ordered them to be distributed too. They ate as much as they wanted, and they collected seven basketfuls of leftovers. Now there had been about four thousand people. He sent them away. Then, getting into the boat with his disciples, he went to the region of Dalmanutha.

The Pharisees ask for a sign from heaven
8: 11–13

The Pharisees came up and started a discussion with him. They wanted to put him to the test and so they demanded a sign from heaven. And with a deep sigh he said, "Why does this generation demand a miracle? In truth I tell you, no miracle shall be given to this generation." And, leaving them again, he got back into the boat and went away to the other side.

The yeast of the Pharisees and of Herod
8: 14–21

The disciples had forgotten to take any bread and they only had one loaf with them in the boat. Then he gave them this warning, "Keep your eyes open; look out for the yeast of the Pharisees and the yeast of Herod." But they said to one another, "It is because we have no bread." Realising this, he said to them, "Why are you talking about having no bread? Do you still not understand, still not realise? Are your minds closed? Have you *eyes and do not see, ears and do not hear*? Or do you not remember? When I divided the five loaves among the five thousand, how many baskets full of leftovers did you collect?" They answered, "Twelve." "And when I divided the seven loaves among the four thousand, how many baskets full of leftovers did you collect?" And they answered, "Seven." Then he said to them, "Do you still not realise?"

Healing of a blind man at Bethsaida
8: 22–6

They arrived in Bethsaida, and some people brought to him a blind man whom they begged him to touch. He took the blind man by the hand and led him outside the village. Then, putting saliva on his eyes and laying his hands on him, he asked, "Can you see anything?'' The man, who was beginning to see, replied, "I can see people; they look like trees as they walk around." Then he laid his hands on the man's eyes again and he saw clearly; he was healed, and he could see everything plainly and distinctly. And Jesus sent him home, saying, "Do not even go into the village."

Peter's profession of faith
8: 27–30

Jesus and his disciples left for the villages round Caesarea Philippi. On the way he asked his disciples this question, "Who do people say I am?" And they told him, "Some say John the Baptist, others say Elijah, others again, one of the prophets." "But you," he asked them, "who do you say I am?" Peter spoke up and said to him, "You are the Christ." And he gave them strict orders not to tell anyone about him.

First prophecy of the Passion
8: 31–3

Then he began to teach them that the Son of man would have to face much suffering, and be rejected by the elders, the chief priests and the scribes, and be put to death, and after three days rise again; and he said all this quite openly. Then, taking him aside, Peter tried to rebuke him. But, turning and seeing his disciples, he rebuked Peter and said to him, "Get behind me, Satan! You are thinking not as God thinks, but as human beings do."

Conditions of following Christ
8: 34—9: 1

He called the people and his disciples to him and said, "If anyone wants to be a follower of mine, let him deny himself and take up his cross and follow me. Anyone who wants to save his life will lose it; but anyone who loses his life for my sake, and for the sake of the gospel, will save it. What gain, then, is it for anyone to win the whole world and lose his life? And indeed what can anyone offer in exchange for his life? For if anyone in this sinful and adulterous generation is ashamed of me and of my words, the Son of man will also be ashamed of him when he comes in the glory of his Father with the holy angels."

And he said to them, "In truth I tell you, there are some standing here who will not taste death before they see the Kingdom of God come with power."

---

his sight gradually, bit by bit. Mark was referring to Christian baptism which opens the door to divine light.

The eyes of the apostles seem at last to have been opened. Peter was the first to confess his faith in Jesus as the Christ, the anointed one of God. It was an important step in Mark's Gospel: the Word had taken root.

But this faith remained very limited. Peter refused to see things Jesus' way: he could believe that Jesus was Christ but he could not believe in the passion. So Peter was really taking the role of the tempter, the one who tried to dissuade his master from taking a path he himself could not accept.

The disciples had to leave their wrong dreams behind: the path of life went through death, which means laying down the human being's most basic desire. Such is the central and paradoxical message of the Gospel. Mark was probably thinking also of the persecution of Christians at the time of his writing: soon Jesus would call the persecutors to account (Mark thought the triumphal return of Christ was near at hand, which was a view held by many believers at that time).

The Transfiguration
9: 2–8

Jesus' glory was already very real. It was shown one day to some of the apostles: the witnesses to the resurrection of Jairus' daughter and the ones who would be with him at Gethsemane. Jesus really was the beloved Son of the Father accomplishing what the great men of history had only dreamed of. But they still had to work in the darkness since the time to live in that glory was yet to come.

Six days later, Jesus took with him Peter, James and John and led them up a high mountain on their own by themselves. There in their presence his appearance changed: his clothes became brilliantly white, whiter than any bleach on earth could make them. Then Elijah and Moses came to talk to Jesus. Peter said to Jesus, "Rabbi, it is wonderful for us to be here; so let us make three shelters, one for you, one for Moses and one for Elijah." He did not know what to say for they were so frightened. And a cloud came, covering them in shadow; and they heard a voice say from the cloud, "This is my beloved Son. Listen to him." Then suddenly, when they looked around, they saw no one with them any more but only Jesus.

The question about Elijah
9: 9–13

Elijah had been carried up to heaven in a fiery chariot according to the Bible. Some Jews expected that Elijah would return and put the world in order ready for the glorious coming of the Messiah. According to Jesus, Elijah had already come in the person of John the Baptist, but had not been welcomed. It would be the same for the Messiah himself.

As they were coming down from the mountain he forbade them to tell anyone what they had seen, until after the Son of man had risen from the dead. They observed the warning faithfully, though among themselves they discussed what "rising from the dead" could mean. And they asked him this question, "Why do the scribes say that Elijah must come first?" He said to them, "Elijah must indeed come first to set everything in order again. (. . .) But I tell you that in reality Elijah has already come and they treated him just as they pleased, as the scriptures said they would."

The epileptic boy
9: 14–29

As they were rejoining the disciples they saw a large crowd round them and some scribes arguing with them. When the crowd saw him, they were amazed and ran to greet him. He asked them, "What are you arguing about with them?" A man answered him from the crowd, "Master, I have brought my son to you; there is a spirit of dumbness in him. When it takes hold of him it throws him to the ground, and he foams at the mouth, grinds his teeth and goes stiff. I asked your disciples to drive it out but they were unable to." He replied, "You faithless people. How much longer must I stay with you? How much longer must I put up with you? Bring him to me."

They brought the boy to him. As soon as it saw Jesus, the spirit shook the boy violently, and he fell to the ground and lay there writhing and foaming at the mouth. Jesus asked the father, "How long has this been happening to him?" "From childhood," he said, "and it has often thrown him into fire and into water, in order to destroy him. But if you can do anything, have pity on us and help us." "If you can?" said Jesus. "Everything is possible for one who has faith." At once the father of the boy cried out, "I have faith. Help my lack of faith!" And when Jesus saw that a crowd was gathering, he rebuked the unclean spirit. "Deaf and dumb spirit," he said, "I command you: come out of him and never enter him again." Then it shook the boy violently and came out shouting, and the boy lay there as if he were dead, so that most of them said, "He is dead." But Jesus took him by the hand and helped him up, and he was able to stand. When he had gone indoors, his disciples asked him when they were by themselves, "Why were we unable to drive it out?" He answered, "This is the kind that can only be driven out by prayer."

Mark showed again how the power of God is revealed as soon as people believe. But the apostles did not yet have true faith. When were they going to start believing in the power of prayer? They would be able to free the world from the evil powers that held it prisoner when they did.

Second prophecy of the Passion
9: 30–2

After leaving that place they made their way through Galilee. He did not want anyone to know where he was, because he was instructing his disciples. He was telling them, "The Son of man will be handed over into the power of men and they will put him to death. Three days after he has been put to death he will rise again." But they did not understand what he said and were afraid to ask him.

Jesus' disciples preferred not to understand when he spoke of the suffering he was soon to face.

Who is the greatest?
9: 33–7

They came to Capernaum. When he got into the house he asked them, "What were you arguing about on the road?" They said nothing, because on the road they had been arguing about which of them was the greatest. So he sat down, called the Twelve to him and said, "If anyone wants to be first, he must make himself last of all and servant of all." He then took a little child and put him in the middle of them. He put his arms around the child and said to them, "Anyone who welcomes a little child such as this in my name, welcomes me. Anyone who welcomes me, does not welcome me but the one who sent me."

The disciples' biggest concern was which of them was the greatest. It was proof that they had not understood. The greatest? It was the servant, the simple little child. Jesus upset our normal way of thinking by identifying himself with such people.

On using the name of Jesus   9: 38–40

John said to him, "Master, we saw someone driving out demons in your name, and we tried to stop him because he was not one of us." But Jesus said, "You must not stop him. For no one can do a miracle in my name and then speak evil of me. Anyone who is not against us is for us.

The apostles wanted to hold onto their power and be the only ones to work with Jesus. Jesus rejected the idea of keeping people out. He said that anyone could claim to act in his name if they worked in the same way as he did.

Generosity towards the disciples   9: 41

"If anyone gives you a cup of water to drink because you belong to Christ, then in truth I tell you, he will most certainly not lose his reward.

On leading others astray   9: 42–9

"But if anyone causes the downfall of one of these little ones who have faith, it would be better for him to be thrown into the sea with a great millstone round his neck. And if your hand causes you to sin, cut it off; it is better for you to enter into life crippled, than to have two hands and go to hell, into the fire that can never be put out. And if your foot causes you to sin, cut it off; it is better for you to enter into life lame, than to have two feet and be thrown into hell. And if your eye causes you to sin, pull it out; it is better for you to enter into the kingdom of God with one eye, than to have two eyes and be thrown into hell where *their worm will never die nor their fire be put out.* For everyone will be salted with fire. Salt is a good thing, but if salt loses its flavour, how can you make it salty again? Have salt in yourselves and be at peace with one another."

The opposite attitude to that of the servant consists of shocking people and leading them into sin. Anything that got in the way of true life had to be stamped out mercilessly. The disciples should be sure to keep what made them special after purification: the sense of real service.

The question about divorce   10: 1–12

After leaving there, he came into the territory of Judaea and Transjordan. Again crowds gathered round him, and he taught them, as he usually did. Some Pharisees approached him and asked, "Is it lawful for a man to divorce his wife?" They were putting him to the test. He answered them, "What did Moses tell you to do?" They replied, "Moses allowed us to draw up a certificate of divorce and then send her away." Then Jesus said to them, "Moses allowed you to do this because he was taking into account the hardness of your hearts. But from the beginning of creation God *made them male and female. This is why a man leaves his father and mother, and the two become one.* They are no longer two, therefore, but one. So then, what God has joined together,

The men of tradition wanted to place Jesus in a difficult situation by asking him a delicate question: that of divorce. Jesus replied that from the point of view of the old covenant, in which the heart was not transformed, divorce had had to be tolerated. But marriage took on its true dimension of love when viewed from the Kingdom.

human beings must not divide." Back in the house the disciples questioned him again about this, and he said to them, "Whoever divorces his wife and marries another is guilty of adultery against her. And if a woman divorces her husband and marries another she is guilty of adultery too."

Jesus and the children
10: 13–16

People were bringing little children to him, for him to touch them. The disciples scolded them, but when Jesus saw this he was angry and said to them, "Let the little children come to me; do not stop them; for it is to such as these that the kingdom of God belongs. In truth I tell you, anyone who does not welcome the kingdom of God like a little child will never enter it." Then he put his arms around them, laid his hands on them and gave them his blessing.

The disciples would do well to learn from little children how to greet people instead of turning them away. The Kingdom of God is a gift and we must learn how to receive it with simple hearts rather than believing that we can claim it by right, as adults often do.

The rich young man   10: 17–22

He was setting out on a journey when a man ran up, knelt before him and asked him this question, "Good master, what must I do to inherit eternal life?" Jesus said to him, "Why do you call me good? No one is good but God alone. You know the commandments: *You shall not kill; You shall not commit adultery; You shall not steal; You shall not give false witness;* You shall not cheat; *Honour your father and mother.*" And he said to him, "Master, I have kept all these since I was young." Jesus looked steadily at him and he was filled with love for him. He said, "You need to do one thing more. Go and sell what you own and give the money to the poor, and you will have treasure in heaven; then come, follow me." But his face fell at these words and he went away sad, for he was a very rich man.

A rich man was filled with the desire to be perfect. Jesus looked at him, loved him and called him to follow him. There was one condition to following Jesus: he had to sell all his possessions. This was an obstacle the man could not overcome. Wealth shuts us in on ourselves and makes us forget our need for God.

The danger of riches

10: 23–7

Jesus looked round and said to his disciples, "How hard it is for those who have riches to enter the kingdom of God!" The disciples were amazed by these words. But Jesus said to them again, "My children, how hard it is to enter the kingdom of God! It is easier for a camel to pass through the eye of a needle than for someone rich to enter the kingdom of God." They were more astonished than ever and they said to one another, "In that case, who can be saved?" Jesus gazed at them and said, "For men it is impossible, but not for God. Everything is possible for God."

The disciples were amazed at Jesus' statement. Was it possible to give up so much? Surely Jesus was asking too much? "Definitely not," replied Jesus: all God's power is necessary if people's hearts are to be changed.

The reward of following Jesus

10: 28–31

Peter took this up. He said, "Look, we have left everything and followed you." Jesus said, "In truth I tell you, there is no one who has left house, brothers, sisters, mother, father, children or land for my sake and for the sake of the gospel who will not receive a hundred times as much in this life of houses, brothers, sisters, mothers, children and land — and persecutions too — and, in the world to come, eternal life. Many who are first will be last, and the last will be first."

Peter proudly said, "We have left everything behind" and Jesus replied, "Don't worry: you will receive a hundred times what you have given up now, and persecutions with it!" Thus he emphasised in a humorous way that the Christian life is a paradox: the greatest of joys in the midst of the greatest difficulties.

Third prophecy of the Passion

10: 32–4

They were on the road, going up to Jerusalem; Jesus was walking on ahead of them. They were in a daze, and those who followed were afraid. Taking the Twelve to one side once again, he began to tell them what was going to happen to him, "Now we are going up to Jerusalem, and the Son of man is about to be handed over to the chief priests and the scribes. They will sentence him to death and will hand him over to the gentiles: they will mock him, spit at him, whip him and put him to death. After three days he will rise again."

The disciples began to be afraid on the road to Jerusalem, the city from which the greatest opposition to Jesus had always come. The Master once again revealed the Passion to them and that he was walking right up to it.

The sons of Zebedee make their request
10: 35–40

James and John, the sons of Zebedee, came up to him and asked,

"Master, we want you to do us a favour." He said to them, "What do you want me to do for you?" They said to him, "Allow us to sit one at your right hand and the other at your left in your glory." But Jesus said to them, "You do not know what you are asking. Can you drink the cup that I shall drink, or be baptised with the baptism with which I shall be baptised?" They replied, "We can." Jesus said to them, "You shall indeed drink the cup that I shall drink, and be baptised with the baptism with which I shall be baptised. But it is not for me to decide who will sit on my right or on my left; for those seats belong to those who are destined to sit there."

The disciples remained totally blind. Two of them were fighting over the first place in the Kingdom! Jesus refused to give them an answer because the decision was not his to make. Jesus said that many trials had to be undergone (as symbolised by two images: that of the cup which is "hard to swallow", and the image of baptism which means a passage through the abyss) but the disciples were convinced that the trials did not present any problems.

Leaders must serve

10: 41–5

When the other ten heard this they began to feel angry with James and John. So Jesus called them to him and said to them, "You know that the rulers of the gentiles lord it over them, and their great men make their authority felt. This is not to happen among you. No; anyone who wants to become great among you must be your servant, and anyone who wants to be first among you must be slave to all. For the Son of man himself did not come to be served but to serve, and to give his life to save many other lives."

Jesus himself knew only one thing: he had come to serve. The apostles should also learn how to be servants, and then they would be the true masters.

The blind man of Jericho

10: 46–52

They reached Jericho. Just as he was leaving the town, surrounded by his disciples and a great crowd, the son of Timaeus (Bartimaeus), a blind beggar, was sitting at the side of the road. When he heard that it was Jesus of Nazareth who was passing by, he began to shout and cry out, "Son of David, Jesus, have pity on me." And many of them scolded him and told him to keep quiet, but he only shouted all the louder, "Son of David, have pity on me." Jesus stopped and said, "Call him here." So they called the blind man over, saying, "Courage, get up; he is calling you." So throwing off his cloak, he jumped up and went to Jesus. Then Jesus asked him, "What do you want me to do for you?" The blind man said to him, "Rabbuni, let me see again." Jesus said to him, "Go; your faith has saved you." And at once he was able to see again and he followed him along the road.

The blind man knew what he wanted and was so desperate to get it that he abandoned all politeness. Unlike many others, he was struck by Christ's words. He followed Jesus as soon as he could see, and went toward Jerusalem where the Passion was soon to take place.

JESUS' MINISTRY IN JERUSALEM

The Messiah enters Jerusalem
11: 1–11

Jesus chose the symbols which were to mark his entry into the Holy City. The crowds proclaimed him as the Messiah. He rode on a donkey as he entered (fulfilling the words of the prophet Zechariah) which showed clearly what kind of Messiah he claimed to be and the nature of the peace he was bringing. It had nothing to do with worldly power. The "Lord" was humble and poor.

On approaching Jerusalem, at Bethphage and Bethany, close by the Mount of Olives, Jesus sent two of his disciples and said to them, "Go to the village straight ahead of you. As you enter it you will find a colt tied up that no one has ever ridden. Untie it and bring it here. If anyone says to you, 'What are you doing?' say, 'The Master needs it and will send it back here at once.'" They went off and found a colt tied up near a door in the open street. They untied it. Some men standing there said, "What are you doing, untying that colt?" They replied as Jesus had told them to, and the men let them go. Then they took the colt to Jesus, threw their cloaks over its back, and he climbed on. Many people

spread their cloaks on the road, and others branches which they had cut in the fields. And those who walked in front and those who followed behind were all shouting, "*Hosanna! Blessed is he who comes in the name of the Lord!* Blessed is the coming kingdom of David our father! *Hosanna* in the highest heavens!"

He entered Jerusalem and went into the Temple. When he had looked all around, he went out with the Twelve to go to Bethany, for it was already late.

The barren fig tree

11: 12–14

Next day as they were leaving Bethany, he felt hungry. Seeing a fig tree in leaf some distance away, he went to see if he could find any fruit on it. But when he came up to it he found only leaves;

Jesus' strange reaction was puzzling and caught the attention of those present. The meaning of the episode is explained later on.

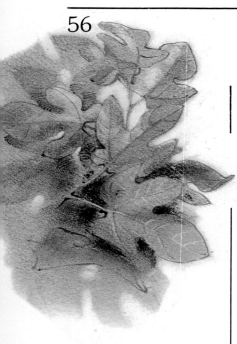

for it was not the season for figs. And he spoke to the fig tree, "May no one ever eat fruit from you again." His disciples heard him say this.

The dealers are thrown out from the Temple
11: 15–19

They reached Jerusalem. Jesus went into the Temple and began driving out those who were selling and buying there; he overturned the tables of the money changers and the seats of the dove sellers, and he would not allow anyone to carry anything through the Temple. Then he taught them and said, "Does scripture not say: *My house will be called a house of prayer for all peoples?* But you have turned it into *a den of thieves.*" This came to the ears of the chief priests and the scribes, and they tried to find some way of killing him; they were afraid of him because the people were carried away by his teaching. When evening came he went out of the city.

The fig tree withered. Faith and prayer
11: 20–6

Next morning, as they passed by, they saw the fig tree had completely withered. Peter remembered what had happened. He said to Jesus, "Look, Rabbi, the fig tree that you cursed has withered away." Jesus answered, "Have faith in God. In truth I tell you, if anyone says to this mountain, 'Be pulled up and thrown into the sea,' without any doubt in his heart, but believing that what he says will happen, it will be done for him. I tell you, therefore, everything you ask and pray for, believe that you have it already, and it will be yours. And when you stand in prayer, forgive anything you have against anybody, so that your Father in heaven may forgive your failings too."

The withered fig-tree (and the withered vine later on) symbolises Israel which was not bearing the expected fruit. Mark used this episode to report Jesus' teaching regarding the power of prayer when accompanied by faith.

Jesus' authority is questioned
11: 27–33

They came back to Jerusalem. As Jesus was walking in the Temple, the chief priests, the scribes and the elders came to him, and they said to him, "By what authority are you acting like this? Or who gave you authority to act like this?" Jesus said to them, "And I will ask you one question. Answer me and I will tell you my authority for acting like this. John's baptism, was it from heaven or from men? Answer me that." And they argued this way among

Jesus was asked what right he had to behave in this way. But he turned the tables on his questioners by talking to them about John the Baptist whose prophetic mission they had failed to recognise.

themselves, "If we say from heaven, he will say, 'Then why did you refuse to believe him?' But dare we say from men?" They feared the crowd for the people believed that John really was a prophet. So they made this reply to Jesus, "We do not know." And Jesus said to them, "Nor will I tell you my authority for acting like this."

Parable of the wicked tenants
12: 1–12

He began to speak to them in parables, "A man planted a vineyard; he put a fence round it, dug out a hole for the winepress and built a tower; then he let it out to tenants and went abroad. When the time came, he sent a servant to the tenants to collect from them his share of the produce of the vineyard. But they seized the man, beat him up and sent him away empty handed. Next he sent another servant to them; they beat him over the head and treated him in a disgraceful way. Then he sent another and they killed him; then he sent a number of others, and they beat some up and killed the rest. He still had someone left; his beloved son. He sent him to them last of all, thinking, 'They will respect my son.' But those tenants said to each other, 'This is the heir. Come on, let us kill him, and the vineyard will be ours.' So they seized him, killed him and threw him out of the vineyard. Now what will the owner of the vineyard do? He will come, put the tenants to death and give the vineyard to others. Have you not read this text of scripture:

"The stone which the builders rejected has become the corner-stone; this is the Lord's doing, and it is marvellous in our eyes?"

And they would have liked to arrest him, but they were afraid of the crowds. They realised that the parable was aimed at them. So they left him alone and went away.

Jesus attacked his enemies using a parable. He presented them as murderers who had stolen God's vineyard. But God would throw them out and give his vines to others (the gentile nations). At the same time Jesus presented the man who would throw out the murderous vinegrowers as the foundation stone of a new world order. The struggle between Jesus and his opponents had now passed the point of no return.

On paying tax to Caesar
12: 13–17

Next they sent to him some Pharisees and some members of Herod's party to catch him out in what he said. They came and said to him, "Master, we know that you are an honest man and that you are not afraid of anyone. You pay no attention to a person's rank, and you teach the way of God in all honesty. Are we permitted to pay taxes to Caesar or not? Should we pay or not?" Recognising their hypocrisy he said to them, "Why are you putting me to the test? Hand me a denarius and let me see it." They handed

Jesus had just been asked a trick question. The payment of taxes obviously had a political meaning because it meant recognising and accepting a hated foreign power. What should be done? Jesus put them in their place in a single phrase. We should not mix up human affairs with those of God.

Some of the Sadducees wanted to trap Jesus. These people were hostile to belief in the resurrection, so they asked him a question based on the law which said that the brother or brothers of a man who died without children had to marry his widow "to give him descendants". But Jesus rejected their twisted view of the life to come and proclaimed that God is the "God of the living".

The essence of religious life could be summarised in a few words from the Old Testament. A scribe who understood what he meant said he wished Jesus well. Jesus felt that they understood one another.

him one and he said to them, "Whose face is this? Whose title?" They said to him, "Caesar's." Jesus said to them, "Pay Caesar what belongs to Caesar — and God what belongs to God." And they were amazed at him.

The resurrection of the dead
12: 18–27

Then some Sadducees — who deny that there is a resurrection — came to him. They asked him this question, "Master, Moses gave us this law: if a man's brother dies leaving a wife but no child, he must marry the widow to provide children for his brother. Now there were seven brothers; the first married a wife and then died without having children. The second married the widow, and he too died without having children; with the third it was the same, and none of the seven left any children. Last of all the woman herself died. Now at the resurrection, when they rise again, whose wife will she be, since she had been married to all seven?"

Jesus said to them, "You are wrong, and the reason why is surely because you do not understand the scriptures or God's power. For when they rise from the dead, men and women do not marry; no, they are like the angels in heaven. Now about the dead rising again, have you never read in the Book of Moses, in the passage about the burning bush, how God spoke to him and said: *I am the God of Abraham, the God of Isaac and the God of Jacob?* He is not the God of the dead but God of the living. You are very much mistaken."

The most important commandment
12: 28–34

One of the scribes had heard them discussing. He saw that Jesus had given a good answer. He went up to him and said, "Which is the most important of all the commandments?" Jesus replied, "This is the most important: *Listen, Israel, the Lord our God is the one, only Lord, and you must love the Lord your God with all your heart, with all your soul, with all your mind and with all your strength.* The second most important commandment is this: *You must love your neighbour as yourself.* No other commandment is greater than these." The scribe said to him, "Well spoken, Master; what you have said is true, that there is only one God and there is no other. To love him with all your heart, with all your understanding and strength, and to love your neighbour as yourself, this is far more important than any offerings or sacrifices." Jesus, seeing how wisely he had spoken, said, "You are not far from the kingdom of God." And after that no one dared to question him any more.

Jesus not only son but also Lord of David

12: 35–40

While teaching in the Temple, Jesus said, "How can the scribes say that the Christ is the son of David? David himself, inspired by the Holy Spirit, said: *The Lord said to my Lord, take your seat at my right hand, till I have put your enemies under your feet.* David himself calls him Lord. How then can he be his son?" And the large crowd listened to him with delight.

To the Jewish way of thinking sonship meant being subject to the father. So Jesus answered his enemies' trick questions with another awkward question: he posed the problem of his own identity by quoting a biblical text.

In his teaching he said, "Be on your guard against the scribes who like to walk about in long robes, to be greeted respectfully in the market squares, to take the front seats in the synagogues and the places of honour at banquets. They get their hands on the property of widows and offer long prayers to show off. The punishment they receive will be severe."

Jesus severely criticised all those who crushed others in their quest for power and honour.

The widow's offering

12: 41–4

He sat down opposite the treasury and watched the people putting money into the box. Many of the rich people put in a great deal. A poor widow came and put in two small coins, the equivalent of a penny. Then he called his disciples and said to them, "In truth I tell you, this poor widow has put more in than all the others who have given to the treasury. For they have all put in money they could spare, but she in her poverty has put in everything she owned, all she had to live on."

The Temple had a box for offerings in common with all places of worship.

Jesus speaks about the end of the world

13: 1–4

As they were leaving the Temple one of his disciples said to him, "Master, look at the size of those stones! Look at the size of those buildings!" Jesus said to him, "You see these great buildings? Not one stone will be left on top of another; everything will be pulled down."

Many people thought the world was about to end at the time Mark wrote his Gospel. Accordingly, since the Temple was the centre of the universe to the Jews, Jesus referred to its destruction when he began what we call the "eschatological speech" which means a "speech about the end of time".

While they were sitting on the Mount of Olives, facing the Temple, Peter, James, John and Andrew questioned him when they were by themselves, "Tell us, when is this going to happen, and what will be the sign that the end of the world is coming?"

The beginning of sorrows

13: 5–13

Then Jesus began to tell them, "Take care that no one deceives you. Many will come using my name and saying, 'I am he,' and they will deceive many people. When you hear of wars and rumours of wars, do not be worried. This is something that must happen, but the end will not be yet. For nation will fight against nation, and kingdom against kingdom. There will be earthquakes in various places; there will be famines. This is the beginning of the sorrows.

The world was about to enter into such a crisis that the people would no longer know 'which saint to turn to'. It would be a time of persecution for the disciples but they were not to be afraid because the Spirit of God was with them. The gospel would be preached to all the nations.

"Be on your guard: you will be handed over to religious councils. You will be beaten in the synagogues; and you will be brought before governors and kings for my sake, to be my witnesses to them. The gospel must first be preached to all nations.

"And when they come to take you before the court, do not worry beforehand about what to say, but say whatever is given to you at that moment. It is not you who will be speaking, but the Holy Spirit. Brother will hand his own brother over to be put to death, and a father will betray his child. Children will come forward against their parents and have them put to death. Everyone will hate you on account of my name; but anyone who stands firm to the end will be saved.

Catastrophe in Jerusalem

13: 14–23

'The appalling abomination' is a quotation from the book of Daniel (9: 27) and describes the statue of Zeus taken into the Temple at Jerusalem at the time of the Maccabees.

"When you see the *appalling abomination* set up where it ought not to be (let the reader understand), then those who live in Judaea must escape to the mountains; if a man is on the housetop, he must not go inside to collect anything from his house; if a man is in the fields, he must not turn back to fetch his cloak. How terrible it will be for those who are pregnant or nursing babies when those days come! Pray that this may not happen in winter. For in those days there will be *great distress far worse than any since* God created the world, and there will never be anything like it again. And if the Lord had not decided to shorten that time, no human being would have survived. But for the sake of his chosen people he has shortened the time. "If anyone says to you then, 'Look, here is the Christ' or, 'Look, he is there,' do not believe it. For there will be false Christs and false prophets who will perform signs and miracles to try and deceive God's chosen people, if that were possible. You, therefore, must be on your guard. I have warned you of everything.

The Holy City had passed through many crises in the past. Jesus saw that an even greater crisis was ahead because the city was rotten to its core. Soon there would be total chaos in everyone's mind. God's chosen people should prepare themselves for the difficult times ahead.

The coming of the Son of man

13: 24–7

"But in those days, after that time of distress, the sun will be darkened, the moon will not give its light, the stars will come falling out of the sky and the powers in the heavens will be shaken. And then they will see the Son of man coming in the clouds with great power and glory. And then he will send the angels to gather his chosen ones from the four winds, from the ends of the world to the ends of the sky.

Jesus was using the vocabulary commonly found in the Old Testament prophets when they foretold the end of the world.

The time of this coming

13: 28–32

"Take the fig tree as a parable: as soon as its branches grow supple and its leaves come out, you know that summer is near. It is the same with you: when you see these things happening, you will know that he is near, right at the gates. In truth I tell you, all these things will happen before this generation has passed away. Sky and earth will pass away, but my words will not pass away.

"But as for that day or hour, nobody knows when it will happen, neither the angels in heaven, nor the Son; only the Father knows.

Soon the time of God's triumph through his chosen one, the 'Son of man', would come. It would be a time of gathering for the new world order.

Be on the alert

13: 33–7

"Be on the alert, stay awake, because you never know when the time will come. It is like a man travelling abroad: he has gone from his home, and left his servants in charge, each with his own work to do; and he has told the doorkeeper to stay awake. So stay awake, because you do not know when the master of the house is coming, evening, midnight, or in the morning. If he comes unexpectedly, he must not find you asleep. And what I am saying to you I say to all: Stay awake!"

"Be ready", insisted Jesus because "all these events are near at hand: learn to recognise the signs of their coming". But Mark reminded people that Jesus always refused to give a date for the end of the world.

The need to watch constantly corresponds to the urgent theme of Mark's Gospel, even from the beginning.

PASSION AND RESURRECTION

There was no stopping what would happen from then on. Jesus' enemies were only waiting for a chance to get rid of him "without fuss". Their fear of a scandal suggests that most of the people were on Jesus' side despite Mark's emphasis on the existence of the opposition.

The conspiracy against Jesus
14: 1–2

It was two days before the Passover and the feast of Unleavened Bread. The chief priests and the scribes were looking for a way to arrest Jesus using some sort of trick and have him put to death. For they said, "It must not be during the festivities, or there will be uproar among the people."

The anointing at Bethany
14: 3–9

Jesus was at Bethany at the house of Simon the leper. He was sitting eating when a woman came in with an alabaster jar of very expensive perfume. She broke the jar and poured the perfume on his head. Some of the people who were there were furious and said to one another, "Why was this perfume wasted? It could have been sold for over three hundred denarii and the money given to the poor''; and they were angry with her. But Jesus said, "Leave her alone. Why are you upsetting her? She has done a good work for me. You will always have the poor with you, and you can be kind to them whenever you wish, but you will not always have me. She has done what she could; she has anointed my body beforehand for its burial. In truth I tell you, wherever the gospel is preached throughout all the world, what she has done will be told as well, in memory of her."

> The woman's anointing of Jesus with perfume was both a sign of her respect and of her faith in the Messiah. It was to Jesus a symbol of his death and the embalming of his body; and his disciples were shocked by it. Three different ways of looking at the same incident corresponding to three different spiritual viewpoints.

Judas betrays Jesus
14: 10–11

Judas Iscariot, one of the Twelve, went to find the chief priests with an offer to hand Jesus over to them. They were delighted to hear it, and promised to give him money. He began to look for a good opportunity to betray him.

> Judas was one of the disciples from the beginning, yet he betrayed Jesus! What a lesson for Mark's readers who were being persecuted themselves!

Preparations for the Passover supper
14: 12–16

On the first day of Unleavened Bread, the day when the Passover lamb was sacrificed, his disciples asked him, "Where do you want us to go and prepare the Passover meal for you?" So he sent two of his disciples, with the instruction, "Go into the city and you will meet a man carrying a jar of water. Follow him. Say to the owner of the house which he enters, 'The Master says: Where is the room where I may eat the Passover with my disciples?' He will show you a large upper room furnished with couches, all prepared. Get everything ready for us there." The disciples set out for the city and found everything as he had told them. They prepared the Passover meal.

> Jesus made all the necessary arrangements for the meal. It is clear that he was in control of events even when he appeared to be at the mercy of those uniting against him. He accepted what was happening to him in a state of calm and full awareness.

The treachery of Judas foretold
14: 17–21

When evening came he arrived with the Twelve. And while they were at table eating, Jesus said, "In truth I tell you, one of you is about to betray me, one of you eating with me." The disciples were upset and said to him, one after another, "Not me, surely?" He said to them, "It is one of the Twelve, one who is dipping his bread into the same dish with me. Yes, the Son of man is going to die as the scriptures say he will, but how terrible it will be for that man by whom he is betrayed! It would be better for that man if he had never been born."

> Jesus had no illusions about the loyalty of his disciples. He had seen through Judas but did not turn against him or throw him out: he pitied him for having sunk so low.

The institution of the Eucharist
14: 22–5

Jesus took the normal Passover meal, already full of significance, and gave it a new meaning. It became a sign of his approaching death. His death was the sacrifice through which a new relationship between God and people was to be created. The last supper of Jesus also looked forward to the feast which would reunite all people in the Kingdom of God.

As they were eating Jesus took bread, and when he had said the blessing he broke it and gave it to them. He said, "Take it, this is my body." Then he took a cup, and when he had given thanks he handed it to them, and they all drank from it. He said to them, "This is my blood, the blood of the covenant, which is poured out for many. In truth I tell you, I shall not drink any more wine until the day I drink the new wine in the Kingdom of God."

Peter's denial foretold
14: 26–31

Jesus knew that none of the disciples, not even Peter, would be able to follow him at the time of the final test.

After the psalms had been sung they left for the Mount of Olives. And Jesus said to them, "You will all fall away. The scripture says: *I shall strike the shepherd and the sheep will be scattered.*

However, after my resurrection I shall go ahead of you into Gali-lee." Peter said, "Even if they all fall away, I will not." Jesus said to him, "In truth I tell you, this day, this very night, before the cock crows twice, you will have denied me three times." But he repeated even more strongly, "Even if I have to die with you, I will never deny you." And they all said the same.

The apostle was still fooling himself. He was not able to open his eyes and follow Jesus properly until forced to do so after the Passion when all his dreams seemed to have fallen apart.

Gethsemane
14: 32–42

The crucial 'Hour' had come at last. Jesus was suddenly afraid despite his calling to love until the end without weakening or running away from the trials ahead. But he showed that he really was the Son by abandoning himself in trust to God's call. The apostles were not aware of the drama taking place nearby and were fast asleep.

They came to a place called Gethsemane, and he said to his disciples, "Stay here while I pray." Then he took Peter, James and John with him. And he began to feel terror and anguish. And he said to them, "My soul is so full of sorrow, even to the point of death. Wait here, and stay awake." And going on a little further he threw himself on the ground and prayed that, if it were possible, this hour might pass him by. He said, "Abba, Father! For you everything is possible. Take this cup away from me. But let it be as you, not I, would have it." He came back and found them sleeping, and he said to Peter, "Simon, are you asleep? Did you not have the strength to stay awake one hour? Stay awake and pray not to be put to the test. The spirit is willing enough, but the body is weak." Again he went away and prayed. He came back again and found them sleeping, their eyes were so heavy; and they did not know how to answer him. He came back a third time and said to them, "You can sleep on now and have your rest. It is all over. The hour has come. Now the Son of man is to be betrayed into the hands of sinners. Get up! Let us go! The man who has betrayed me is not far away."

The arrest
14: 43–52

Jesus protested at his arrest. But he had known for a long time that it was inevitable and he had accepted all the consequences of what it would mean. From that time he faced his enemies alone.

He was still speaking when Judas, one of the Twelve, came up with a number of men armed with swords and clubs, sent by the chief priests, and the scribes and the elders. Now the traitor had agreed a signal with them, "The one I kiss is the man. Arrest him, and see he is well guarded when you take him away." So as soon as the traitor came, he went up to Jesus, said, "Master!" and kissed him. The others seized him and arrested him. Then one of the bystanders took out his sword, hit out at the high priest's servant and cut off his ear.

Then Jesus spoke, "Am I an outlaw that you had to set out to arrest me with swords and clubs? Day after day I was among you teaching in the Temple and you never tried to arrest me. But this is to fulfil the scriptures." The disciples all deserted him and ran away. A young man followed wearing nothing but a linen cloth. They caught hold of him, but leaving the cloth in their hand he ran away naked.

This detail is only given in Mark's Gospel. It has been suggested that the young man in question was the Evangelist himself.

Jesus before the Sanhedrin 14: 53–65

They led Jesus off to the high priest; and all the chief priests, the elders and the scribes were gathered there. Peter had followed him at a distance, right into the high priest's palace. Sitting with the servants he warmed himself at the fire.

The chief priests and the whole Sanhedrin were looking for evidence against Jesus in order to have him put to death. But they could not find any. Several witnesses told lies against him, but their stories did not agree. Some men stood up to make this false accusation against him, "We heard him say, 'I am going to destroy this Temple made by human hands, and in three days build another, not made by human hands.'" But their evidence did not even agree on this point.

The high priest then stood up before the whole assembly and asked Jesus this question, "Have you no answer to that? What is it these men are saying against you?" But he was silent and made no answer at all. The high priest asked him a second question, "Are you the Christ, the Son of the Blessed One?" "I am," said Jesus, "and you will see the *Son of man seated at the right hand of the Power and coming from heaven on the clouds.*" The high priest tore his clothes and said, "What further need do we have for witnesses? You heard his blasphemy. What is your decision?" They all agreed that he deserved to die.

Some of them started spitting at his face, hitting him and saying, "Be a prophet now!" And the servants hit him too.

Jesus was already condemned even though the trial was just beginning. His enemies had only to find a reason in law to justify the death sentence. In fact, the false witnesses contradicted each other and Jesus himself provided the grounds for the verdict by saying that he was indeed the Christ, the Son of God, and he quoted a psalm to them, together with a piece from the book of Daniel (7: 13–14). It was the first time he had ever claimed that title for himself: there was no longer any danger that people would get the wrong idea about what he had come for!

Peter denies Jesus 14: 66–72

Peter was down below in the courtyard. One of the high priest's servant-girls came up. Seeing Peter warming himself by the fire, she looked closely at him and said, "You too were with Jesus, the man from Nazareth." But he denied it. "I do not know, I do not understand what you are talking about," he said. Then he went out towards the entrance of the courtyard, and a cock crowed. The servant-girl saw him and again started telling the bystanders, "This man is one of them." But he denied it again. A little later the bystanders themselves said to Peter, "You must be one of them! Why, you come from Galilee too." But he started cursing and swearing, "I do not know the man you are talking about." And at once the cock crowed for the second time, and Peter remembered what Jesus had said to him, "Before the cock crows twice, you will have denied me three times." And he burst into tears.

Peter, too, was drawn into the hostile reactions to Jesus. He joined in with the others and denied his master.

Jesus before Pilate   15: 1–15

First thing in the morning, the chief priests, together with the elders, scribes and the rest of the Sanhedrin, had their plan ready. After having Jesus bound, they took him away and handed him over to Pilate.

Pilate asked him this question, "Are you the king of the Jews?" He replied, "It is you who say it." And the chief priests were accusing him of many things. Pilate questioned him again, "Aren't you going to answer? Listen to all the accusations they are making against you!" But, to Pilate's surprise, Jesus made no further reply.

At festival time Pilate used to release a prisoner for them, any one they asked for. Now at that time a man called Barabbas was in prison with the rebels who had committed murder during the uprising. The crowd gathered and began to ask Pilate for their usual favour. Pilate answered them, "Do you want me to release for you the king of the Jews?" For he realised that the chief priests had handed Jesus over out of jealousy. The chief priests, however, had stirred the crowd up to demand that he should release Barabbas for them instead. Then Pilate spoke again, "But in that case, what am I to do with the man you call king of the Jews?" They shouted back, "Crucify him!" Pilate asked them, "What harm has he done?" But they began to shout even louder, "Crucify him!" So Pilate, anxious to calm the crowd, released Barabbas for them and, after having Jesus whipped, he handed him over to be crucified.

Jesus crowned with thorns   15: 16–20

The soldiers led him away to the inside of the palace, that is, the Praetorium, and called the whole troop together. They dressed him up in purple, twisted some thorny branches together to make a crown and put it on him. They began saluting him, "Hail, king of the Jews!" They beat him over the head with a stick and spat at him; and they went down on their knees and bowed down to him. And when they had finished making fun of him, they dressed him in his own clothes.

The way of the cross   15: 21–2

They led him out to crucify him. They forced a passerby, Simon of Cyrene, father of Alexander and Rufus, who was on his way in from the country, to carry his cross. They brought Jesus to the place called Golgotha, which means the place of the skull.

The second trial was now concerned with the question: "Are you the king of the Jews?" Jesus did not actually claim that title for himself although he did not reject it either. The crowds present at the tribunal at that moment (perhaps only a small group) had turned against him and asked for Barabbas, a freedom fighter against Rome, to be released. Pilate himself does not seem to have been against Jesus but he gave in to cowardice and washed his hands of the whole affair.

It seemed ridiculous to think of Jesus as a king now. It would take real faith to see that this tortured man was the Messiah, the Son of God.

Simon of Cyrene was a passerby who had been roped in by chance. He was like all Jesus' disciples in that he was made to carry a cross without being asked whether he wanted to or not, as their Master had.

The crucifixion
15: 23–7

Mark's description echoes different passages of Scripture which had not previously been understood (cf. Ps. 22: 19, and Isa. 53:12). Jesus really was the one the prophets had foreseen yet he was not at all what they had expected the Messiah would be like.

They offered him wine mixed with myrrh to drink, but he did not take it. Then they crucified him, and shared out his clothing among them, casting lots to decide what each should get. It was nine o'clock in the morning when they crucified him. The inscription giving the charge against him read, "The King of the Jews". And they crucified two robbers with him, one on his right and one on his left.

Jesus on the cross
15: 29–32

The cross was a sign to those present that Jesus had been abandoned by God, but, to the believer, it shows the strength of a love which refuses to force itself on people, but quietly gives all of itself.

The passersby jeered at him. They shook their heads and said, "Aha! So you were going to destroy the Temple and rebuild it in three days! Then save yourself; come down from the cross!" The chief priests and the scribes mocked him among themselves, saying, "He saved others, but he cannot save himself. Let the Christ, the king of Israel, come down from the cross now, so that we can see and believe." Even those who were crucified with him taunted him.

The death of Jesus
15: 33–9

Jesus was abandoned by everybody and turned to his Father. He quoted a psalm expressing hope in spite of all the odds, while being in the depths of agony. He thus showed what it means to love God totally. The eyes of a Roman centurion at the very foot of the cross were opened: he was completely overwhelmed by it all.

At noon darkness fell over the whole land until three o'clock. At that moment Jesus cried out in a loud voice, "*Eloi, eloi, lama sabachthani?*" which means, "*My God, my God, why have you forsaken me?*" When some of those who were standing nearby heard this, they said, "Listen, he is calling on Elijah." Someone ran and soaked a sponge in vinegar and, putting it on the end of a stick, gave it to him to drink saying, "Wait! Let's see if Elijah will come to take him down." But Jesus gave a loud cry and died. And the curtain of the Sanctuary was torn in two from top to bottom. Seeing how he had died, the centurion, who was standing in front of him, said, "This man really was the Son of God."

The women at Calvary
15: 40–1

The disciples had fled. The only ones who stood by Jesus were some women who were mentioned here for the first time. They were to have the privilege of witnessing the events which followed.

There were some women watching from a distance. Mary of Magdala, Mary who was the mother of James the younger and Joset, and Salome were among them. They used to follow him and look after him when he was in Galilee. Many other women were also there who had come up to Jerusalem with him.

The burial
15: 42–7

Evening came. Since it was the time of preparation for the Sabbath, Joseph of Arimathaea, an important member of the Council, courageously went to Pilate and asked for the body of Jesus. Pilate was astonished that he should have died so soon. He called the centurion and asked if he had been dead for some time. Having heard his report, he allowed Joseph to take the body. He bought a linen sheet, took Jesus down from the cross, wrapped him in the sheet and laid him in a tomb which had been cut out of the rock. He then rolled a stone across the entrance to the tomb. Mary of Magdala and Mary the mother of Joset saw where the body had been placed.

The empty tomb   16: 1–8

After the Sabbath, Mary of Magdala, Mary the mother of James, and Salome, bought spices to go and anoint the body of Jesus. Very early in the morning on the first day of the week they went to the tomb.

They had been saying to one another, "Who will roll away the stone for us from the entrance to the tomb?" But when they looked up they saw that the stone — which was very big — had already been rolled back. On entering the tomb they saw a young man in a white robe sitting on the right-hand side. They were amazed. But he said to them, "Don't be afraid. You are looking for Jesus of Nazareth, who was crucified: he has risen, he is not here. See, here is the place where they laid him. But you must go and tell his disciples and Peter, 'He is going ahead of you to Galilee; that is where you will see him, just as he told you.' " The women came out and ran away from the tomb because they were frightened out of their wits. They did not say anything to anyone, for they were afraid.

Arriving at the tomb to embalm Jesus' body, the women were completely taken aback by the angel's message: it was so incredible. It seemed so impossible to believe that they did not even dare to pass the message on to the apostles.

Appearances of the risen Christ   16: 9–19

After he had risen in the morning on the first day of the week, he appeared first to Mary of Magdala from whom he had cast out seven demons. She then went to tell those who had been his companions, and who were mourning and in tears. But they did not believe her when she told them that he was alive and that she had seen him. After this, he showed himself in a different form to two of them as they were on their way into the country. They went back and told the others, who did not believe them either.

Last of all, he showed himself to the eleven disciples themselves as they were eating. He scolded them because of their lack of faith and because they were too stubborn to believe those who had seen him after he had risen.

And he said to them, "Go out to the whole world and preach the gospel. Whoever believes and is baptised will be saved; whoever does not believe will be condemned. These are the signs that will be associated with those who believe: in my name they will cast out demons; they will speak in new languages; they will pick up snakes in their hands. If they drink deadly poison it will not harm them. They will lay their hands on sick people and they will recover." After he had spoken to them, the Lord Jesus was taken up into heaven and took his place at the right hand of God. The disciples went out and preached everywhere. The Lord worked with them and showed that the word was true by the signs that accompanied it.

The angel had told them how the apostles would find Jesus again, alive in Galilee, a symbol of the world to which they now had to return. Mark's Gospel ended there, but some verses were added later to emphasise that Jesus' resurrection was real, difficult though it was to believe. Mark also outlined the mission of the Church which was to continue the Master's work. Nothing was finished: it was just beginning!

THE GOSPEL ACCORDING TO LUKE

W e are only too aware in our world, of poverty, of hunger, and of the suffering caused by all kinds of discrimination. Luke's Gospel shows us a side of Jesus which reveals the great love of God for the human race, including those who are poor and in difficult circumstances.

Luke was a doctor which might explain why he noticed all the details of the sufferings many people in that society had to cope with. This educated Greek had been a follower of the apostle Paul and had been struck by his teaching about God's mercy and grace.

He made detailed enquiries about Jesus' life and wrote his Gospel with the intention of showing Jesus' goodness. More than any other Evangelist, he showed that it was what people were like on the inside which determined whether or not they would be saved when they met Jesus.

On the one hand, there were people who held on tightly to their possessions: the rich (Luke had a lot to say about the question of money); there were also those who boasted about their reputation, or their goodness and who thought it gave them rights where God was concerned: the Pharisees and the doctors of the law; the scribes and the Sadducees — in fact all of them were blind to the Good News of God's mercy because all they thought about was themselves. Some of them were converted, however, for "everything is possible with God".

On the other hand, there were believers who were ready to open their hearts to the message of God's freely-offered love, because they did not put their trust in their possessions. They were often people living in difficult conditions: the poor and the sick; but also people who were considered to be of no importance, like women and children, and those who were openly rejected by society: the publicans (tax collectors, and others who collaborated with the Romans); prostitutes and Samaritans. Luke emphasised the special place of Mary among these 'poor' because she accepted the Word of God fully.

Jesus is obviously the central character in Luke's Gospel. Although Jesus shocked many people, others saw further than human appearances and realised that he was truly the Son of God. He made them "see" the deepest secret of God: the never-ending and merciful love offered to fallen humanity.

Nazareth was a little known village in Galilee. That was where Mary mysteriously heard God's call. She was to be the mother of the long-awaited Messiah. Jesus would be a gift from God and not a product of human desire. Mary was completely open to God and is thus the perfect representative of a person ready to respond to God's love when he comes looking for his lost creation.

The annunciation
1: 26–38

The angel Gabriel was sent by God to a town in Galilee called Nazareth, to a girl promised in marriage to a man named Joseph, a descendant of King David. The virgin's name was Mary. He went in and said to her, "Rejoice, you who enjoy God's favour! The Lord is with you." She was deeply troubled by these words and asked herself what this greeting could mean. But the angel said to her, "Mary, do not be afraid; you have found favour with God. Look! You will become pregnant and give birth to a son. You must name him Jesus. He will be great and will be called Son of the Most High. The Lord God will give him the throne of his ancestor David. He will rule over the House of Jacob for ever and his reign will never come to an end." Mary said to the angel, "But how can this come about, since I am a virgin?" The angel answered, "The Holy Spirit will come upon you, and the power of the Most High will cover you with its shadow. And so the child will be holy and will be called Son of God. And I tell you this too: your cousin Elizabeth has also become pregnant in her old age and will give birth to a son; people used to say she was sterile, but now she is in her sixth month, for nothing is impossible to God." Mary said, "I am the Lord's servant. Let it happen to me as you have said." And the angel left her.

The visitation 1: 39–56

Mary set out at that time and went as quickly as she could into the hill country to a town in Judah. She went into Zechariah's house and greeted Elizabeth. Now, as soon as Elizabeth heard Mary's greeting, the child leapt in her womb and Elizabeth was filled with the Holy Spirit. She gave a loud cry and said, "You are the most blessed of all women and blessed is the child you carry in your womb. Why should I be honoured with a visit from the mother of my Lord? Look, the moment I heard your greeting, the child in my womb leapt for joy. Yes, blessed is she who believed that the Lord's promise to her would be fulfilled."

Then Mary said:

Mary did not think about her own tiredness and rushed to see her cousin Elizabeth, who was to be the mother of John the Baptist. The first verses of Luke's Gospel showed that he too was a gift from God.

"My soul proclaims the greatness of the Lord and
my spirit *rejoices in God my Saviour; because he has looked
upon the humble circumstances of his servant.*

Yes, from now onwards, all generations will call me blessed, for
the Almighty has done great things for me.

Holy is his name,

*and his faithful love extends from generation to generation
of those who fear him.*

He has used the power of his arm, he has made those with
proud hearts run away.

He has pulled princes down from their thrones and lifted up
the humble.

He has filled the starving with good things, but sent the rich
away empty.

*He has come to the help of Israel his servant, and has remem-
bered his faithful love*

Mary sang a hymn of joy. God was
going to carry out his work through
her. He was going to respond to
the hopes of the poor who were
always ready to welcome him.

This song includes a number of
Old Testament texts.

as he promised our ancestors, to show mercy to Abraham and to his descendants for ever."

Mary stayed with Elizabeth for about three months and then went home.

The birth of Jesus and visit of the shepherds
2: 1–19

At this time Caesar Augustus issued a decree that a census should be made of the whole inhabited world. This census — the first — took place while Quirinius was governor of Syria. Everyone had to go to be registered, each to his own town. So Joseph set out from the town of Nazareth in Galilee for Judaea, to David's town called Bethlehem, since he was a descendant of David. He went to register with Mary who was promised to him in marriage. She was pregnant. Now while they were there, the time came for her to have her child. She gave birth to her first-born son. She wrapped him in swaddling clothes and laid him in a manger because there was no room for them in the living space.

In the countryside close by there were shepherds out in the fields keeping guard over their sheep during the night. An angel of the Lord stood in front of them and the glory of the Lord shone around them. They were terrified. But the angel said, "Do not be afraid. Look, I bring you news of great joy, a joy to be shared by the whole people. Today in the town of David a Saviour has been born to you; he is Christ the Lord. And here is a sign for you: you will find a baby wrapped in swaddling clothes and lying in a manger." All at once with the angel there was a great throng of the hosts of heaven, praising God with the words:

"Glory to God in the highest heaven, peace on earth to all men, whom he loves."

When the angels had gone back to heaven, the shepherds said to one another, "Let us go to Bethlehem and see this event which the Lord has made known to us." So they hurried away and found Mary and Joseph, and the baby lying in the manger. When they saw the child they repeated what they had been told about him. Mary treasured all these things and thought about them in her heart. And the shepherds went back glorifying and praising God for all they had heard and seen, which was just as they had been told. Eight days later, the child was circumcised, and they gave him the name Jesus, the name the angel had given him before he had been conceived.

All the details quoted by Luke will help us to understand the importance of the event. It was the decision of a gentile emperor which caused Jesus to be born in Bethlehem, as foretold by the prophet Micah. The presence of the angels was a way of showing the glory of the child, in contrast with the poverty of his birthplace. And the shepherds, who were looked down on by society, were the first to open their hearts with joy to the Good News while the rest of the world was still unaware of what was happening.

Luke emphasised the contrast between the humble life of Nazareth and the sudden glory which appeared with Jesus. Even at the age of twelve he was capable of impressing clever

Life in Nazareth and visit to Jerusalem   2: 39–52

When his parents had done everything the Law of the Lord required, they went back to Galilee, to their own town of Nazareth. The child grew, became strong and was filled with wisdom. God's favour was with him.

Every year his parents used to go to Jerusalem for the feast of the Passover. When he was twelve years old, they went up for the feast as usual. After the feast, when they set off home, the boy Jesus stayed behind in Jerusalem without his parents knowing it. They assumed he was among the group somewhere, and it was only after a day's journey that they went to look for him among their relations and acquaintances. When they could not find him they went back to Jerusalem looking for him everywhere.

Three days later, they finally found him in the Temple, sitting among the

teachers, listening to them, and asking them questions. All those who heard him were amazed at his intelligence and his replies. They were overcome with emotion when they saw him. His mother said to him, "My child, why have you done this to us? See how worried your father and I have been, looking for you." He replied, "Why were you looking for me? Did you not know that I must be in my Father's house?" But they did not understand what he meant.

He went back to Nazareth with them then and lived under their authority. His mother stored up all these things in her heart. And Jesus increased in wisdom, in stature, and in favour with God and with people.

men who specialised in the study of the Scriptures. Suddenly his parents could no longer understand him; a greater power seemed to be leading him. He declared that he had to do his Father's business: those words threw new light on his personality.

THE MINISTRY OF JESUS

As he reported Jesus' ministry, Luke included a number of events already mentioned by Mark and Matthew. But he also recalled others which particularly highlighted the Lord's goodness towards sinners and others rejected by society.

The woman who was a sinner

7: 36–50

One of the Pharisees invited him to a meal. He arrived at the Pharisee's house and took his place at table. Suddenly a woman came in, who had a bad name in the town. She had heard he was dining with the Pharisee and had brought with her an alabaster jar of perfume. She waited behind him at his feet, weeping, and her tears fell on his feet. She wiped them away with her hair, covered his feet with kisses and anointed them with the perfume.

When he saw this, the Pharisee who had invited him said to himself, "If this man were a prophet, he would know who this woman is who is touching him and what sort of a person she is: a sinner." Then Jesus spoke to him, "Simon, I have something to say to you." He replied, "Tell me, Master." "There were once two men who owed money to a money-lender: one owed him five hundred denarii, the other fifty. They were unable to pay, so he let them both off. Which of them will love him more?" Simon answered, "The one who was let off more, I suppose." Jesus said, "You are right."

Then he turned to the woman and said to Simon, "You see this woman? I came into your house, and you did not pour water over my feet, but she has poured out her tears over my feet and wiped them away with her hair. You did not give me a kiss, but she has been covering my feet with kisses ever since I came in. You did not anoint my head with oil, but she has anointed my feet with perfume. For this reason I tell you that her sins, many as they are, have been forgiven her, because she has shown such great love. It is someone who is forgiven little who shows little love." Then he said to her, "Your sins are forgiven." Those who were sitting at the table with him began to say to themselves, "Who is this man, that he even forgives sins?" But he said to the woman, "Your faith has saved you; go in peace."

The Pharisees and those in power either kept their distance from Jesus or were hostile, but the people who had been rejected by everyone else flocked to him. A woman known for her immoral life did something unheard of in polite society. Throughout her sinful life, she had been searching for true love and now she had found it, and the discovery changed and saved her.

The good Samaritan
10: 25–37

A lawyer stood up and asked him a question to test him, "Master, what must I do to have eternal life?" He said to him, "What does the Law say? What is your reading of it?"

He replied, "*You must love the Lord your God with all your heart, with all your soul, with all your strength, and with all your mind, and your neighbour as yourself.*" Jesus said to him, "You have answered right. Do this and life is yours."

But the man wanted to prove he lived a righteous life. He said to Jesus, "And who is my neighbour?" In answer Jesus said, "A man was once on his way down from Jerusalem to Jericho. He fell into the hands of robbers who stripped him, beat him and then made off, leaving him half dead. Now a priest happened to be travelling down the same road, but when he saw the man, he

The real value of life is found in love, as had already been made clear in Jewish Law (cf. Deut. 6: 5), so a lawyer decided to test Jesus about love. Jesus' parable reminds us that such love should have no limits. Using the excuse

passed by on the other side without stopping. In the same way a Levite who came to the place saw him, and passed by on the other side without stopping. But a Samaritan traveller who came along was moved with compassion when he saw him. He went up to him and bandaged his wounds, pouring oil and wine on them. He then lifted him onto his own animal and took him to an inn where he looked after him. Next day, he took out two denarii and handed them to the innkeeper and said, 'Look after him, and on my way home I will pay you back for any extra expense you have.' Which of these three, do you think, acted like a neighbour to the man who fell into the robbers' hands?'' He replied, ''The one who showed pity towards him.'' Jesus said to him, ''Go, and do the same yourself.''

of religious purity, and thus of obedience to the Law, the priest and the Levite avoided contact with the man wounded by thieves. The Samaritan showed the meaning of true love despite being a despised foreigner. He did not behave like a great man who condescended to love others but was the one who behaved in the image of God.

Martha and Mary

10: 38–42

On their journey Jesus came to a village, and a woman named Martha welcomed him into her house. She had a sister called Mary. She sat down at the Lord's feet to listen to what he was saying. Now Martha was taken up with all the work she had to do. She came to him and said, ''Lord, do you not care that my sister is leaving me to do the serving all by myself? Please tell her to help me.'' But the Lord answered, ''Martha, Martha,'' he said, ''you worry and fret about so many things. But only a few are needed, indeed only one. It is Mary who has made the right choice, and it is not to be taken away from her.''

Men living at the same time as Jesus and Luke took the view that conversations with women were a waste of time. From Jesus' point of view, however, the most important thing was the love between people's hearts that makes sense of the whole of life.

The Lord's prayer

11: 1–4

One day Jesus was praying. When he had finished, one of his disciples said, ''Lord, teach us to pray, as John taught his disciples.'' He said to them, ''When you pray, this is what to say: Father, may your name be held holy, your kingdom come; give us each day our daily bread, and forgive us our sins, for we ourselves forgive each one who is in debt to us. And do not put us to the test.''

The disciples were fascinated by Jesus' way of praying. The words of the prayer he taught them, addressed to God as Father, were all directed towards the coming of the Kingdom. They expressed the hope of the gift through which God gives life to men and women by allowing them to enter into a reality of grace and forgiveness.

The persistent friend

11: 5–8

Jesus also said to them, ''Suppose one of you has a friend and goes to him in the middle of the night to say, 'My friend, lend me three loaves, because a friend of mine who is on a journey has just arrived at my house and I have nothing to offer him.' The man answers from inside the house, 'Do not bother me. My door is locked and my children are with me in bed; I cannot get up to give it to you.' I tell you, if the man does not get up and give it to him because he is his friend, he will do it because he keeps on asking. He will give his friend all he wants.

Effective prayer
11: 9–13

The Psalms (6: 9–10, 22: 24; 28: 6, etc.) had already emphasised the fact that God listens to prayer.

"So I say to you: Ask, and it will be given to you; search and you will find; knock, and the door will be opened to you. For everyone who asks receives; everyone who searches finds; everyone who knocks will have the door opened. What father among you, if his son asked for a fish, would give him a snake? Or if he asked for an egg, would give him a scorpion? If you then, evil as you are, know how to give good things to your children, how much more will the heavenly Father give the Holy Spirit to those who ask him!"

Parables of God's mercy
15: 1–3

Jesus' attitude towards outcasts and sinners shocked those who thought they represented the purity demanded by the Jewish Law. Several parables show the nature of God's mercy as demonstrated by Jesus.

The tax collectors and sinners were all crowding round to listen to him. But the Pharisees and scribes were complaining, "This man welcomes sinners and eats with them." So he told them this parable:

The lost sheep
15: 4–7

"Which one of you, if he had a hundred sheep and lost one of them, would not leave the ninety-nine in the desert and go to look for the missing one till he found it? And when he found it, would he not joyfully put it on his shoulders and then, when he got home, call together his friends and neighbours, saying to them, 'Rejoice with me, I have found my sheep that was lost.' In the same way, I tell you, there will be more rejoicing in heaven over one sinner who repents than over the ninety-nine righteous people who have no need to repent."

The prodigal son

15: 11–32

Then he said, "There was a man who had two sons. The younger one said to his father, 'Father, let me have my share of the fortune that will come to me.' So the father divided the property between them. A few days later, the younger son got all his belongings together and left for a country far away. There he wasted all his money on immoral living.

"When he had spent it all, there was a severe famine in that country and he began to feel the pinch. So he hired himself out to one of the local people who put him to work on his farm to feed the pigs. He wished he could fill himself with the husks the pigs were eating but no one would let him have them. Then he came to his senses and said, 'My father's hired men have all the food they want and more, and here I am dying of hunger! I will leave this place and go to my father and say: Father, I have sinned against heaven and against you; I no longer deserve to be called your son; treat me as one of your hired men.' So he left there and went back to his father. While he was still a long way away, his father saw him and was filled with pity. He ran to the boy, put his arms around him and kissed him. Then his son said, 'Father, I have sinned against heaven and against you. I no longer deserve to be called your son.' But the father said to his servants, 'Quick! Bring out the best suit of clothes and put it on him; put a ring on his finger and sandals on his feet. Kill the calf we have been fattening, let's have a party, because this son of mine was dead and has come back to life; he was lost and is found.' And they began to celebrate.

"Now the elder son was out in the fields. As he got near to the house on his way back, he could hear music and dancing. He called one of the servants and asked what it was all about. The servant told him, 'Your brother has come back and your father has killed the calf we had been fattening because he has got him back safe and sound.' The son was angry then and refused to go in. His father came out and began to try to persuade him to come in. But he answered his father, 'All these years I have worked hard for you

It is the lost sheep which is the most important to the true shepherd (Jesus, the one whose coming had been announced by the prophets): there is great rejoicing when he finds it.

What a contrast between the
attitude of the father and the
brother! The father waited
hopefully for his son's return and
was ready to forgive him; the
brother was boxed in by his own
meanness and was therefore
unable to share his father's joy
because he felt deprived of the
rights he thought were owed to
him by his reluctant and
mechanical obedience.

Jesus did not say that the
dishonest steward was right, he
simply showed that he behaved
logically: he wanted money and
did all he could to get it. The
"sons of light", who are faithful
to God, should also be logical in
their efforts to get what is
important to them. Did the
dishonest steward make friends by
giving away things that did not
belong to him? Believers should
learn to make friends using their
belongings, even though they are
not completely pure. They should
be generous!

and never once
disobeyed any of your
orders, yet you never offered me so much
as a kid for me to have a party with my friends. But,
for this son of yours, when he comes back after wasting all your
money on women, you kill the calf we had been fattening.'

"The father said, 'My son, you are with me always and all I have
is yours. But it was only right we should celebrate and be glad,
because your brother here was dead and has come back to life; he
was lost and is found.' "

The dishonest steward   16: 1–9

He also said to his disciples, "There was a rich man whose steward
was accused of wasting his fortune. He called for the man and
said, 'What is this I hear about you? Give me a full set of accounts
because you are not to be my steward any longer.' Then the
steward said to himself, 'What am I to do now that my master is
taking my job away from me? Dig? I am not strong enough. Go
begging? I should be too ashamed. Ah, I know what I will do to
make sure that people still welcome me into their homes even
when I have lost my job.'

"Then he called the people who owed money to his master to
him one by one. To the first he said, 'How much do you owe my
master?' 'One hundred measures of oil,' he said. The steward said,
'Here, take your bill; sit down and quickly write fifty.' To another
he said, 'And you, sir, how much do you owe?' 'One hundred
measures of wheat,' he said. The steward said, 'Here, take your
bill and write eighty.'

"The master praised the dishonest steward for acting in such a
clever way. For the children of this world are much cleverer when it
comes to dealing with their own kind than the children of light are.

"And so I tell you this: even though it is corrupt, use money to win you friends. In this way you will make sure that when it runs out you will be welcomed into your eternal home."

The parable of the rich man and Lazarus   16: 19–30

"There was a rich man who always dressed in purple and fine linen clothes and ate wonderful meals every day. A poor man called Lazarus used to lie by his gate, covered with sores. He longed to fill himself up with the bits of food which fell from the rich man's table. Even dogs came and licked his sores. Now the poor man died and was carried away by the angels to Abraham's side. The rich man also died and was buried.

"In his torment in the world of the dead he looked up and saw Abraham a long way off with Lazarus at his side. So he cried out, 'Father Abraham have pity on me and send Lazarus to dip the tip of his finger in water and cool my tongue, for I am in agony in these flames.' Abraham said, 'My son, remember all the good things you had during your lifetime, and all the difficulties Lazarus had to face. Now he is being comforted here while you are in agony. But that is not all: between us and you a great gulf has been fixed, to prevent those who want to cross from our side to yours or from your side to ours.'

This text is extremely rich because it is filled with hidden references. Luke was particularly concerned to answer the questions of those who wanted "proof" from God. He seems to have told them to reread the Law (meaning Moses and the Prophets); but his version of the parable contains a controversial point against the Jews who did not believe in the resurrection of Jesus.

"So the rich man said, 'Father, I beg you then to send Lazarus to my father's house, since I have five brothers, to warn them so that they at least do not come to this place of torment too.' Abraham said, 'They have Moses and the prophets, let them listen to them.' The rich man replied, 'Ah no, father Abraham, but if someone comes to them from the dead, they will repent.' Then Abraham said to him, 'If they will not listen either to Moses or to the prophets, they will not be convinced even if someone should rise from the dead.' "

The ten lepers
17: 11–19

All of them were healed but the only one to be saved was the foreigner, which makes the account particularly moving.

One day Jesus was on his way to Jerusalem, and travelled along the border between Samaria and Galilee. As he entered one of the villages, ten lepers came to meet him. They stood some way off and called to him, "Jesus! Master! Take pity on us." When he saw them he said, "Go and show yourselves to the priests." Now as they were going away they were healed. When he saw that he had been healed, one of them turned back praising God at the top of his voice and threw himself at the feet of Jesus and thanked him. The man was a Samaritan. This led Jesus to say, "Weren't all ten healed? The other nine, where are they? Only this foreigner has come back to give praise to God." And he said to the man, "Stand up and go on your way. Your faith has saved you."

The Pharisee and the tax collector
18: 9–14

One of the men was really praying while the other was praising only himself.

He told the following parable to some people who were proud of the fact that they were righteous and looked down on everyone else, "Two men went up to the Temple to pray, one was a Pharisee, the other a tax collector. The Pharisee stood there and said this prayer to himself, 'I thank you, God, that I am not greedy, unjust, adulterous like everyone else, and particularly that I am not like this tax collector here. I fast twice a week; I give away a tenth of all I get.' The tax collector stood some distance away and did not even dare to lift his eyes up to heaven. But he beat his chest and said, 'God, be merciful to me, a sinner.' I tell you, this man, went home again forgiven; the other did not. For everyone who raises himself up will be humbled, but anyone who humbles himself will be raised up."

Zacchaeus
19: 1–10

Jesus was going through the town of Jericho. There was a man there whose name was Zacchaeus. He was one of the senior tax collectors and a rich man. He kept trying to see who Jesus was, but he was too short, and could not see him because of the crowd. So he ran on ahead and climbed a sycamore tree to catch a glimpse of him. When Jesus reached the spot he looked up and spoke to him, "Zacchaeus, come down. Hurry, because I am going to stay at your house today." Zacchaeus climbed down quickly and welcomed him joyfully. People complained when they saw what was happening. "He has gone to stay at a sinner's house," they said. But Zacchaeus said to the Lord, "Look, sir, I am going to give half my property to the poor, and if I have stolen from anybody I will pay him back four times the amount." And Jesus said to him, "Today salvation has come to this house, because this man too is a son of Abraham. For the Son of man has come to seek out and save what was lost."

Zacchaeus was a rich and hated tax collector. He was overwhelmed by the attention paid to him by Jesus when he invited himself to Zacchaeus' own house. It was a scandal for the 'good people' who prided themselves on being descended from Abraham.

The Law demanded that thieves should repay twice what was taken, so four times the amount was twice as much again.

Like the other Evangelists, Luke recounts Jesus' Passion but adds certain details which emphasised the way in which Jesus forgave even to the end.

The good thief 23: 39–43

One of the criminals hanging there shouted abuse at him: "Aren't you the Christ? Save yourself and us as well." But the other spoke up and rebuked him, "Have you no fear of God at all? You got the same sentence as he did, but in our case we deserved it: we are paying for what we did. But this man has done nothing wrong." Then he said, "Jesus, remember me when you come into your kingdom." Jesus answered him, "In truth I tell you, today you will be with me in paradise."

A dying thief next to Jesus at the moment of his death discovered the true nature of the Kingdom of Love and was saved!

In his record of the events surrounding the resurrection, Luke includes a detailed account of a story which Mark only mentions in passing.

Luke summarised the disciples' progress in this passage: they were attracted to the Master and followed him but did not yet understand in full what he had come to do. Their misunderstanding arose from a false picture of a God who could come and force himself on the world. That illusion had to collapse about them before they could open their hearts to the real message of the Lord. This was the truth that was revealed in the simple breaking of bread. Then they were totally overwhelmed: the meaning of the whole of their people's history, and the whole of their own past suddenly became clear! They rushed to take the Good News to others: Jesus was risen and alive, he was calling them to love: that was what life was all about!

The road to Emmaus
24: 13–35

Two disciples were on their way to a village called Emmaus, about seven miles from Jerusalem. They were talking together about everything that had happened. As they were talking together and discussing it, Jesus himself came up and walked by their side. But they did not recognise him. He said to them, "What are you talking about as you walk along?" They stopped, their faces very sad.

Then one of them, called Cleopas, answered him, "You must be the only person staying in Jerusalem who does not know what has happened over the last few days." He asked, "What things?" They answered, "All about Jesus of Nazareth. He showed that he was a prophet powerful in all he said and did before God and all the people. Our chief priests and our leaders handed him over to be sentenced to death, and had him crucified. We had hoped that he would be the one to set Israel free. And this is not all: two whole days have now gone by since it all happened; some women from our group have really amazed us! They went to the tomb in the early morning, and when they could not find the body, they came back to tell us they had seen a vision of angels who told them he was alive. Some of our friends went to the tomb and found everything exactly as the women had said. But they did not see him."

Then he said to them, "How foolish you are! So slow to believe all that the prophets have said! Was it not necessary for the Christ to suffer before entering into his glory?" Then, starting with Moses and going through all the prophets, he began to explain to them all the passages of scripture that talked about himself.

When they got near to the village to which they were going, Jesus made as if to go on. But they tried to persuade him to stay with them saying, "It is nearly evening, and the day is almost over." So he went in to stay with them. Now while he sat at the table with them, he took the bread and said the blessing; then he broke it and handed it to them. Their eyes were opened and they recognised him; but he had vanished from their sight. Then they said to each other, "Didn't our hearts burn within us as he talked to us on the road and explained the scriptures to us?"

They set out that instant and returned to Jerusalem. There they found the Eleven gathered together with their companions, who said to them, "The Lord has indeed risen and has appeared to Simon." Then they told their story of what had happened on the road and how they had recognised him when he broke the bread.

THE GOSPEL ACCORDING TO JOHN

Some things in life mean much more than their appearance alone would suggest. Think, for example, of the value of a present given by someone you love. Sometimes it takes years to realise fully what that person meant to say by the present and all the intentions that went into choosing the gift.

The Gospel of Saint John is an attempt to understand the full meaning of the great gift God gave us in Jesus. Through the words and actions of Jesus, John's Gospel shows how the Lord revealed his love to us.

John chose very carefully which of Jesus' words and actions to include. His choice is not the same as those of the other Evangelists, except for the miracle of the feeding of the five thousand, the Passion, the resurrection and a few other events. Those incidents he did include show us how God is still giving life to his Church through the great sacraments of the Eucharist and baptism.

John wanted to show us how faith allows us to understand the deep meaning of what is happening. That was why Jesus' enemies saw his important actions, and yet did not recognise them as "signs". (When John refers to the Jews as Jesus' enemies, he actually means more specifically Jewish religious leaders.) The Jewish leaders got no further than looking at the surface, just like when the message behind a present is ignored and only the object itself is seen. The Jews were not only incapable of recognising that this ordinary-looking man was the Son of God himself but that he was God's gift for the salvation of the whole human race also. This was because his enemies were part of "the world", by which John meant the universe of people who are selfish and concentrate only on themselves.

On the other hand, the mysteries of God were revealed to the poor and humble. The Gospel continually shows us people turning toward the light and finding life in all its fullness.

The Passion was the most important action in the life of Jesus. Certainly, it was forced upon him by his enemies, but he freely accepted the destiny to which his actions led him. He knew it was the moment at which men and women would finally discover the full impact of God's love, that is, the moment when Creator and his creation met: it was like the "wedding" of the Lord and his people. Jesus' whole life led up to this moment, so he referred to it as his "time".

God gave us "life" and "light" in Jesus and those who are filled with life and light live in a world of grace and joy.

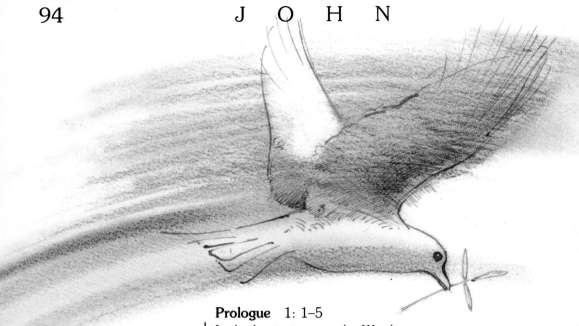

John touched on all the major themes of his Gospel in his prologue. God is reflected in his Word, the living reality that is also the Son, the second person of the Trinity. The Word is light and life and is present in all of creation.

Prologue 1: 1–5

In the beginning was the Word:
the Word was with God and the Word was God.
He was with God in the beginning.
Through him all things came into being,
not one thing came into being except through him.
What has come into being in him was life,
life that was the light of men;
and light shines in darkness,
and darkness could not overpower it.

1: 9–14

The Word was the real light
that gives light to everyone;
he was coming into the world.
He was in the world
that had come into being through him,
and the world did not recognise him.
He came to his own
and his own people did not accept him.
But to those who did accept him
he gave power to become children of God,
to those who believed in his name
who were born not from human stock
or human desire
or human will
but from God himself.
The Word became flesh,

The Word made itself known to men and women in Jesus. But those who are slaves to sin (the darkness) do not recognise him. In order to receive him, we need the Law which helps us to discover the one who is also known as the "meaning" of the world. Those who welcome him experience a second birth. They share in the life of God himself by entering into a state of grace. This truth is beyond human understanding.

he lived among us, and we saw his glory,
the glory that he has from the Father as only Son of the Father,
full of grace and truth.

1: 18
No one has ever seen God;
it is the only Son, who is close to the Father's heart,
who has made him known.

The first disciples of Jesus   1: 35–51

John was by the Jordan with two of his disciples. Seeing Jesus go by, he said, "Look, there is the lamb of God." And the two disciples heard what he said and followed Jesus. Seeing them following him, Jesus turned round and said, "What do you want?" They answered, "Rabbi" — which means Teacher — "where do you live?" He replied, "Come and see." So they went and saw where he lived, and stayed with him that day. It was about two o'clock.

One of these two who became followers of Jesus after hearing what John had said was Andrew, the brother of Simon Peter. The first thing Andrew did was to find his brother and say to him, "We have found the Messiah" — which means the Christ — and he took Simon to Jesus. Jesus looked at him and said, "You are Simon son of John; in future you will be called Cephas" (which means Rock).

The next day Jesus decided to leave for Galilee. He met Philip and said, "Follow me." Philip came from the same town, Bethsaida, as Andrew and Peter.

Philip found Nathanael and said to him, "We have found the one Moses wrote about in the Law and the prophets: it is Jesus son of Joseph, from Nazareth." Nathanael said to him, "Can anything good come from Nazareth?" Philip replied, "Come and see." When Jesus saw Nathanael coming he said of him, "There, truly, is an Israelite in whom there is no deceit." Nathanael asked, "How do you know me?" Jesus replied, "Before Philip came to call you, I saw you under the fig tree." Nathanael answered, "Rabbi, you are the Son of God, the king of Israel." Jesus replied, "You believe that just because I said: I saw you under the fig tree. You are going to see greater things than that." And then he added, "In all truth I tell you, you will see heaven open up and the angels of God ascending and descending over the Son of man."

The Evangelist (who may have been one of the first two disciples of Jesus) recalled the moment which changed his whole life. John the Baptist had just baptised Jesus. He was introduced by the Baptist with a strange title which made people think of the sacrifices offered to God by the Jews. Two of his disciples then left him to follow Jesus. The group grew quickly for Jesus had real charisma. Nathanael in particular was amazed when he referred to a deeply personal event in his own life, but Jesus claimed that they had not seen anything yet. Jesus referred to the story of Jacob's ladder (cf. Gen. 28: 12–18) and told them that through him the link between heaven and earth would be re-established one day.

The wedding at Cana　2: 1–12

Jesus reacted strongly when Mary drew his attention to the young couple's embarrassment because he realised there was a lot more in the service than his mother thought she was asking for. Changing the water into wine was a sign that the time for the wedding between God and humankind had come (when John wrote this, the union had just been completed by Jesus' death on the cross). Jesus was already thinking of his "time" when he helped his hosts; and his way of predicting it was through a sign. The disciples present later saw his action as a foretaste of the work Jesus had come to do.

On the third day there was a wedding at Cana in Galilee. The mother of Jesus was there, and Jesus and his disciples had also been invited. But they ran out of wine, since the wine provided for the feast had all been used. The mother of Jesus said to him, "They have no wine." Jesus said, "Woman, what do you want from me? My hour has not come yet." His mother said to the servants, *Do whatever he tells you.*

There were six stone water jars standing there, meant for the ceremonial washing that is customary among the Jews: each could hold twenty or thirty gallons. Jesus said to the servants, "Fill the jars with water," and they filled them to the brim. Then he said to them, "Pour some out now and take it to the president of the feast." They did this; the president tasted the water, and it had turned into wine. Having no idea where it came from — though the servants who had drawn the water knew — the president of the feast called the bridegroom and said, "Usually everyone serves good wine first and keeps the worse wine until the guests have had plenty to drink; but you have kept the best wine till now."

This was the first of Jesus' signs: it took place at Cana in Galilee. He let his glory be seen and his disciples believed in him. After this he went down to Capernaum with his mother, his brothers and his disciples. They only stayed there a few days.

Jesus meets a Samaritan woman   4: 5–34, 39

Jesus came to the Samaritan town called Sychar near the land that Jacob gave to his son Joseph. Jacob's well was there and Jesus, tired by the journey, sat down by the well. It was about the sixth hour.

A Samaritan woman came to draw water. Jesus said to her, "Give me something to drink." His disciples had gone into the town to buy food. The Samaritan woman said to him, "You are a Jew. How is it that you ask me, a Samaritan, for something to drink?" — Jews, of course, do not associate with Samaritans. Jesus replied to her: "If you only knew what God is offering and who it is that is saying to you, 'Give me something to drink,' you would have been the one to ask, and he would have given you living water."

"You have no bucket, sir," she answered, "and the well is deep: where do you get this living water from? Are you a greater man than our ancestor Jacob, who gave us this well and drank from it himself with his sons and his cattle?"

Jesus replied: "Anyone who drinks this water will be thirsty again; but no one who drinks the water that I shall give will ever be thirsty again. The water that I shall give will become a spring of water within, welling up for eternal life."

The woman said, "Sir, give me some of that water, so that I may never be thirsty again or have to come back to fetch water." Jesus said to her, "Go and call your husband, and come back here." The woman answered, "I have no husband." Jesus said to her, "You are right to say, 'I have no husband'; for although you have had five, the one you are living with now is not your husband. You spoke the truth there." The woman said, "I see you are a prophet, sir. Our fathers worshipped on this mountain, though you say that Jerusalem is the place where we ought to worship." Jesus said: "Believe me, woman, the time is coming when you will worship the Father, neither on this mountain nor in Jerusalem. You worship what you do not know; we worship what we do know; for salvation comes from the Jews. But the time is coming — indeed it is already here — when true worshippers will worship the Father in spirit and truth. That is the kind of worshipper the Father seeks. God is spirit, and those who worship must do so in spirit and truth."

The woman said to him, "I know that Messiah — that is, Christ — is coming. When he comes he will explain everything."

Jesus used the opportunity of asking a simple favour from a foreign woman to start an extraordinary conversation. He presented himself as "the spring" of eternal life. The Samaritan woman was both impressed and worried because Jesus seemed to know too much about her shocking life. She tried to avoid discussing her own affairs by mentioning a long-standing problem which had divided the Jews from the that the problem was no longer relevant. The woman was amazed and then converted along with her entire family. The Evangelist was thus able to show that Jesus, who had come to meet a spiritual thirst, called for old religious arguments to be laid to rest. He stated once and for all that the Jews were the ones who really knew God. At the same time he declared that the barriers between the two rival religions were about to fall: all that mattered was the religion of the heart, by which he meant people's deepest attitudes.

Jesus said, "That is who I am, I who am speaking to you."

At this point his disciples returned and were surprised to find him speaking to a woman. However, none of them asked, "What do you want from her?" or, "What are you talking to her about?" The woman put down her water jar and hurried back to the town to tell the people, "Come and see a man who has told me everything I have done; could this be the Christ?" This brought people out of the town and they made their way towards him.

Meanwhile, the disciples were urging him, "Rabbi, do have something to eat"; but he said, "I have food to eat that you do not know about." So the disciples said to one another, "Has someone brought him food?" But Jesus said: "My food is to do the will of the one who sent me, and to finish his work completely." (. . .)

Many Samaritans of that town believed in him because of what the woman had said, "He told me everything I have done."

He explained to his disciples that this was what the Father had sent him to reveal. The wish to respond to this mission was what he lived for and fed upon.

John followed Mark in telling the story of the multiplication of the loaves, but added an important discussion between Jesus and the people. The Lord reproached them for not having understood the "sign" which they had just been given: they only wanted material food, and did not understand that what makes people live is something quite different: faith in God. Then he began to talk about a mysterious bread which God had come to give. Jesus' ideas seemed strange at first and perhaps even shocking.

Discussion after the multiplication of the bread

6: 34, 41–4, 47–66

The people said to him, "Sir, give us that bread always." Jesus answered them: "I am the bread of life. No one who comes to me will ever be hungry, no one who believes in me will ever be thirsty." (. . .)

Meanwhile the Jews were complaining to each other because he had said, "I am the bread that has come down from heaven." They were saying, "Surely this is Jesus son of Joseph, whose father and mother we know. How can he now say, 'I have come down from heaven?'"

Jesus replied, "Stop complaining to each other. No one can come to me unless the Father who sent me draws him, and I will raise that person up on the last day. (. . .) In all truth I tell you, everyone who believes has eternal life. I am the bread of life. Your fathers ate manna in the desert and they are dead. This is the bread which comes down from heaven, so that a person may eat it and not die. I am the living bread which has come down from heaven. Anyone who eats this bread will live for ever. The bread that I shall give is my flesh, for the life of the world."

Then the Jews started arguing among themselves, "How can this man give us his flesh to eat?"

Jesus replied to them: "In all truth I tell you, if you do not eat the flesh of the Son of man and drink his blood, you have no life in you. Anyone who does eat my flesh and drink my blood has eternal life, and I shall raise that person up on the last day. For my flesh is real food and my blood is real drink. Whoever eats my flesh and drinks my blood lives in me and I live in that person. Just as the living Father sent me and I draw life from the Father, so whoever eats me will also live through me. This is the bread which has come down from heaven; it is not like the bread our ancestors ate: they are dead. Anyone who eats this bread will live for ever." (. . .)

After hearing it, many of his followers said, "This teaching is impossible. How could anyone accept it?" Jesus was aware that his followers were complaining about what he had just been saying and said, "Does this disturb you? What if you should see the Son of man go back up to where he was before?" (. . .) After this, many of his disciples went away and did not accompany him any more.

Then Jesus said to the Twelve, "What about you, do you want to go away too?" Simon Peter answered, "Lord, to whom shall

Jesus wanted to show people that what makes human beings live is their inner motivation. He gave them bread to eat because his greatest desire was to make them understand the full extent of his great love, which was leading him to give himself entirely to them. But the people saw only the external appearance because they had no spiritual insight (or faith).

Jesus then told them that he would literally give himself for the human race: he was referring to his Passion. He also taught them about the Eucharist, where he was to give them his own body and blood. The people were shocked at what he said. But Jesus was speaking of the true sacrament of his body and blood, a mystical eating of himself. He was not referring to a physical cannibalistic eating of his own dead body. Jesus then really put their faith to the test (you might say he asked them the "big question"). Jesus disappointed those who had hoped their material needs alone were to be provided; these people went away, so Jesus had just ruined his chances of popular success — yet the crowds had wanted to make him their king only the day before!

The apostles themselves were shocked because they saw that Jesus was ruining his chances. But they continued to trust him.

we go? You have the words of eternal life. We believe and we have come to know that you are the Holy One of God."

Jesus replied to them, "I am the one who chose the Twelve of you. Yet one of you is a devil." He meant Judas son of Simon Iscariot, since this was the man, one of the Twelve, who was to betray him.

The woman who had committed adultery   8: 2–11

At daybreak he went to the Temple again and all the people came to him. He sat down and began to teach them.

The scribes and Pharisees brought a woman along who had been caught committing adultery. They threw her into the middle of the circle and asked Jesus, "Master, this woman was caught in the very act of committing adultery. Now, in the Law, Moses has ordered us to stone women of this kind. What have you got to say?" In saying this, they wanted to put him to the test, so that they would have a reason to accuse him. But Jesus bent down and started writing on the ground with his finger. As they kept on with their question, he straightened up and said, "Let the one among you who is without sin be the first to throw a stone at her." Then he bent down and continued writing on the ground. When they heard this they went away one by one, beginning with the

There are two opposite attitudes in this account: that of the people who were always ready to condemn others, and that of Jesus who called people to be perfect from a loving heart; Jesus' heart was always ready to welcome sinners and give them another chance. Jesus escaped in an extraordinary way from the trap

eldest, until the last one had gone. Jesus was left alone with the woman, who was still in the middle of the circle. Jesus straightened up again and said, "Woman, where are they? Has no one condemned you?" "No one, sir," she replied. "Neither do I condemn you," said Jesus. "Go. From this moment do not sin any more."

The healing of the man born blind   9: 1, 6–41

As he went along, Jesus saw a man who had been blind from birth. (. . .) He spat on the ground, made a paste with the saliva and put this over the eyes of the blind man. He said to him, "Go and wash in the Pool of Siloam" (the name means "one who has been sent"). So the blind man went off, washed and came back able to see.

His neighbours and the people who were used to seeing him (for he was a beggar) said, "Isn't this the man who used to sit and beg?" Some said, "Yes, it is him." Others said, "No, it's someone who looks like him." The man himself said, "Yes, I am the one." So they asked him, "Then how is it that you can see again?" He answered, "The man called Jesus made a paste, put it on my eyes and said to me, 'Go off and wash at Siloam.' So that is what I did and now I can see again." They asked, "Where is he?" He answered, "I don't know."

They brought the man who had been blind to the Pharisees. It had been a Sabbath day when Jesus made the paste and gave the man back his sight. When the Pharisees asked him how he had regained his sight, he said, "He put a paste on my eyes, I washed, and I can see." Then some of the Pharisees said, "That man cannot be from God: he does not keep the Sabbath." Others said, "How can a sinner do signs like this?" And they differed among themselves. So they asked the blind man again, "What have you to say about him yourself, now that he has opened your eyes?" The man answered, "He is a prophet."

However, the Jews would not believe that the man had been blind without first sending for his parents. They asked them, "Is this man really your son who you say was born blind? If so, how is it that he is now able to see?" His parents answered, "We know he is our son and we know he was born blind. But we don't know how he can see and we don't know who opened his eyes. Ask him, he is old enough. Let him explain what happened." His parents spoke like this because they were afraid

set for him, because they would have accused him of rejecting the authority of the Law if he had declared it to be wrong. [PAGE 101]. He would have cut himself off from the very sinners he had come to save if he had condemned the woman.

By reporting this sign of Jesus, John was referring to baptism, which opens the door to the true light.

The man who was blind from birth was healed at the Pool of "the one who has been sent" (Jesus) by a word and a gesture from the Master. Opinions varied about the healed man: for example his relatives refused to commit themselves out of fear, but the Jewish authorities had the idea that anyone who healed on the Sabbath could not have come from God. They thought this way because to them religion was all about obeying rules.

of the Jews. They had already agreed to ban from the synagogue anyone who should acknowledge Jesus as the Christ. This was why his parents said, "He is old enough; ask him."

So the Jews sent for the man again and said to him, "Give glory to God! We know that this man is a sinner." The man answered, "I don't know whether he is a sinner; all I know is that I was blind and now I can see." They said to him, "What did he do to you? How did he open your eyes?" He replied, "I have told you once and you wouldn't listen. Why do you want to hear it all again? Do you want to become his disciples yourselves?" They began to throw insults at him, saying, "It is you who are his disciple, we are disciples of Moses. We know that God spoke to Moses, but as for this man, we don't know where he comes from." The man replied, "That is just what is so amazing! You don't know where he comes from and he has opened my eyes! We know that God doesn't listen to sinners, but God does listen to people who worship him, and do his will. Ever since the world began it has been unheard of for anyone to open the eyes of someone born blind. If this man did not come from God, he wouldn't have been able to do anything." They replied, "What! You have been a sinner from birth, and you're trying to teach us!" And they threw him out.

Jesus heard they had thrown him out. When he found him he

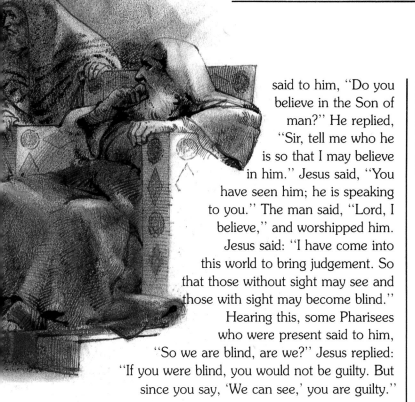

said to him, "Do you believe in the Son of man?" He replied, "Sir, tell me who he is so that I may believe in him." Jesus said, "You have seen him; he is speaking to you." The man said, "Lord, I believe," and worshipped him. Jesus said: "I have come into this world to bring judgement. So that those without sight may see and those with sight may become blind." Hearing this, some Pharisees who were present said to him, "So we are blind, are we?" Jesus replied: "If you were blind, you would not be guilty. But since you say, 'We can see,' you are guilty."

Finally, they threw the man out because they were embarrassed about his healing, but the former blind man had his eyes opened to the true light. The one who was blind now saw and those who thought they could see were still blind.

The good shepherd

10: 1–18

"In all truth I tell you, anyone who does not enter the sheepfold through the gate, but climbs in some other way, is a thief and a robber. The shepherd of the flock comes in through the gate. The gatekeeper lets him in and the sheep hear his voice. He calls his sheep one by one and leads them out. When he has brought out all those that are his, he goes ahead of them, and the sheep follow because they know his voice. They will never follow a stranger, but will run away from him because they do not recognise the voice of strangers."

Jesus told them this parable but they did not understand what he was saying to them.

So Jesus spoke to them again: "In all truth I tell you, I am the gate of the sheepfold. All those who have come before me are thieves and robbers, but the sheep took no notice of them. I am the gate. Anyone who enters through me will be safe. Such a one will go in and out and will find pasture. The thief comes only to steal, kill and destroy. I have come so that they may have life and have it to the full. I am the good shepherd. The good shepherd lays down his life for his sheep. The hired man, since he is not the shepherd and the sheep do not belong to him, abandons the sheep

Jesus presented himself as the "gate" of the sheepfold, or the opening that enabled people to enter the enclosure or to go out to pasture (the Kingdom of God).

Jesus also called himself the "shepherd": not one of those bad shepherds condemned by the prophets, especially Ezekiel (ch. 34), but the Good Shepherd promised by God. He would give his life for the human race and had come to gather them together. He responded generously to the call of the Father by his every action and gave himself totally. John particularly emphasised how freely Jesus' gift was given.

as soon as he sees a wolf coming, and runs away. Then the wolf attacks the sheep and they scatter. He runs away because he is only a hired man and does not care about the sheep. I am the good shepherd; I know my own and my own know me, just as the Father knows me and I know the Father; and I lay down my life for my sheep. And I have other sheep which are not of this fold. I must lead these too. They too will listen to my voice, and there will be only one flock, one shepherd. The Father loves me, because I lay down my life in order to take it up again. No one takes it from me; I lay it down of my own free will. I have power to lay it down, and power to take it up again. This is the command I have received from my Father.''

Martha and Mary from Bethany had just lost their brother, Lazarus. Jesus was not in Jerusalem. He heard the news but arrived too late.

The resurrection of Lazarus
11: 17–44

John saw in this seventh sign of Jesus the meaning of all his work: he came to give eternal life.

Jesus was risking his life by returning to Jerusalem because his enemies were determined to destroy him. Jesus was ready to give his life for his friend and, by raising him from the dead, he let them glimpse the coming resurrection for himself and for all who believed in him.

When Jesus arrived, Lazarus had already been in the tomb for four days. When Martha heard that Jesus was coming she went to meet him. Mary stayed sitting in the house. Martha said to Jesus, "Lord, if you had been here, my brother would not have died. But even now I know that God will give you whatever you ask of him.'' Jesus said to her, "Your brother will rise again." Martha said, "I know he will rise again at the resurrection on the last day." Jesus said:

"I am the resurrection. Anyone who believes in me, even though that person dies, will live. Whoever lives and believes in me will never die. Do you believe this?''

"Yes, Lord," she said, "I believe that you are the Christ, the Son of God, the one who was to come into this world.''

When she had said this, she went and called her sister Mary, saying in a low voice, "The Master is here and wants to see you." Hearing this, Mary got up quickly and went to him. Jesus had not yet come into the village; he was still at the place where Martha had met him. When the Jews who were in the house comforting Mary saw her get up so quickly and go out, they followed her, thinking that she was going to the tomb to weep there.

Mary went to Jesus, and as soon as she saw him she threw herself at his feet, saying, "Lord, if you had been here, my brother would not have died." At the sight of her tears, and those of the Jews who had come with her, Jesus was moved and troubled. He said, "Where have you put him?" They replied, "Lord, come and see." Jesus wept. The Jews said, "See how much he loved him!" But there were some who remarked, "He opened the eyes of the blind man. Could he not have prevented this man's death?" Deeply moved once again, Jesus reached the tomb: it was a cave with a stone across the opening. Jesus said, "Take the stone away." Martha, the dead man's sister, said to him, "Lord, by now he will smell; this is the fourth day since he died." Jesus replied, "Have I not told you that if you believe you will see the glory of God?" So they took the stone away. Then Jesus lifted up his eyes and said:

"Father, I thank you for hearing my prayer. I myself knew that you always hear me, but I speak for the sake of all these who are standing around me, so that they may believe it was you who sent me."

When he had said this, he shouted in a loud voice, "Lazarus, come out!" The dead man came out, his feet and hands wrapped with strips of material, and a cloth over his face. Jesus said to them, "Untie him, let him go free."

Jesus' enemies were annoyed at the resurrection of Lazarus: they had to get rid of him, at whatever cost. Jesus realised that the end (which he called his "hour") was near and that he would have a time of suffering, but he would also have completed his mission by showing fully the love of God for all people. From this point of view, he could say:

Jesus speaks of his glory through death
12: 23–6, 31–2
"Now the hour has come when the Son of man will be glorified. In all truth I tell you, unless a wheat grain falls into the earth and dies, it remains only a single grain. But if it dies it produces a rich harvest. Anyone who loves his life loses it; anyone who hates his life in this world will keep it for eternal life. Whoever serves me, must follow me, and my servant will be with me wherever I am. If anyone serves me, my Father will honour him. (. . .) Now is the time for this world to be judged. Now the prince of this world is to be driven out. And when I am lifted up from the earth, I shall draw all people to myself."

Jesus expressed in a few words the whole "paradox" of Christianity: death becomes life if accepted in love. Jesus' apparent failure was a turning point in the history of the human race: it showed clearly that evil could be defeated. The cross made people see their sin and come to true life by turning to God.

The washing of feet
13: 1–9, 12–15
Before the festival of the Passover, Jesus, knowing that his hour had come to pass from this world to the Father, having loved those who were his in the world, loved them to the end.

John is the only Gospel-writer who does not mention Jesus giving us the Eucharist. No doubt he felt he had already said enough, particularly with Jesus' speech following the miracle of the loaves. It is striking to see the way in which John showed Jesus indicating that his hour had now come: carrying out a service normally left to the most menial of the servants. Jesus called his apostles to recognise true greatness in being able to be a humble servant.

They were at supper, and the devil had already put it into the mind of Judas Iscariot son of Simon, to betray him. Jesus knew that the Father had put everything into his hands, and that he had come from God and was returning to God, and he got up from the table, removed his outer garments and, taking a towel, wrapped it round his waist. He then poured water into a basin and began to wash the disciples' feet and to wipe them with the towel he was wearing.

He came to Simon Peter, who said to him, "Lord, are you going to wash my feet?" Jesus answered, "At the moment you do not understand what I am doing, but later you will understand." Peter said, "You shall never wash my feet, never!" Jesus replied, "If I do not wash you, you can have no share with me." Simon Peter said, "Well then, Lord, not only my feet, but my hands and my head as well!" (. . .)

When he had washed their feet and put on his outer garments again he went back to the table and said, "Do you understand what I have done to you? You call me Master and Lord, and you are right, for so I am. If I, then, the Lord and Master, have washed your feet, you must wash each other's feet. I have given you an example so that you may copy what I have done for you."

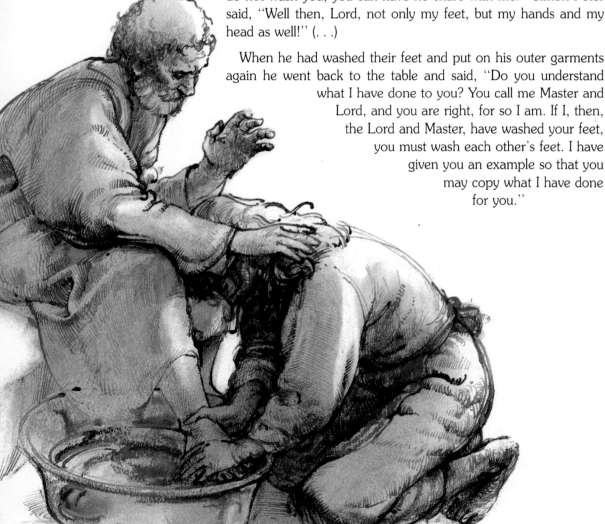

John repeated Jesus' ideas after this account: they are known as 'speeches after the Last Supper'. This was the moment when the Lord felt that his end was near and revealed all his deepest thoughts and gave a real 'spiritual testament'. The Evangelist recorded here some of Jesus' most beautiful words:

13: 34–5
"I give you a new commandment: love one another; you must love one another just as I have loved you. Everyone will know that you are my disciples if you have love one for another."

14: 6–7
"I am the Way, the Truth and the Life. No one can come to the Father except through me. If you know me, you will know my Father too."

14: 15–18
"If you love me you will keep my commandments. I shall ask the Father, and he will give you another helper: the Spirit, to be with you for ever, the Spirit of truth whom the world can never receive. (. . .) I shall not leave you orphans; I shall come to you."

14: 23
"Anyone who loves me will keep my word, and my Father will love him. We shall come to him and make a home in him."

14: 26–8
"Your helper, the Holy Spirit, whom the Father will send in my name, will teach you everything and remind you of all I have said to you. I leave you peace, I give you my own peace. It is a peace which the world cannot give, this is my gift to you. If you loved me you would be glad that I am going to the Father, for the Father is greater than I."

The true vine

15: 1–7, 10–16, 18
"I am the true vine, and my Father is the vinedresser. Every branch in me that does not bear fruit he cuts away. He prunes every branch that does bear fruit to make it bear even more. You are clean already, because of the word that I have spoken to you. Remain in me, as I in you. Just as a branch cannot bear fruit all

Jesus described the people of God using the image of the vine because this image had been used so often by the prophets. But the vine had always been ill-treated and neglected by dishonest workers. By contrast, the true vine bears fruit here. The main message of the parable is the need for unity between God and humankind. The sap is the source of life and represents the grace of love.

Anyone who wants to bear the fruit of love must allow themselves to be made holy by trials. They will then find joy.

The real disciple of Jesus, his friend, is the one who keeps the commandments, especially the one which summarises all the others: love one another.

Jesus reminded his disciples that they should expect the "world" (meaning those who were slaves to sin) to hate them, as it hated Jesus himself.

The disciples only understood Jesus properly after his death when they were filled with his Spirit and all had been revealed to them.

by itself, unless it remains attached to the vine, neither can you unless you remain attached to me. I am the vine, you are the branches. Whoever remains in me, with me in him, will bear much fruit. For cut off from me you can do nothing. Anyone who does not remain in me is thrown away like an old branch and withers. These branches are collected up, thrown on the fire and are burnt. If you remain in me and my words remain in you, you may ask for whatever you please and you will get it. (. . .) If you keep my commandments you will remain in my love, just as I have kept my Father's commandments and remain in his love. I have told you this so that my own joy may be in you and your joy may be perfect. This is my commandment: love one another, as I have loved you. No one can have greater love than to lay down his life for his friends.

"You are my friends, if you do what I command you. I shall no longer call you servants, because a servant does not know what his master is doing. I call you friends, because I have made known to you everything I have learnt from my Father.

"You did not choose me, no, I chose you; and I appointed you to go out and to bear fruit, fruit that will last. (. . .)

"If the world hates you, you must realise that it hated me before it hated you. If you belonged to the world, the world would love you as its own; but because you do not belong to the world, because I have taken you out of the world, that is why the world hates you."

The coming of the Holy Spirit

16: 6–7
"You are sad at heart. Still, I am telling you the truth: it is for your own good that I am going, because unless I go, your Helper will not come to you. But if I go, I will send him to you."

16: 12–13
"I still have many things to say to you but they would be too much for you to understand now. However, when the Spirit of truth comes he will lead you to the whole truth (. . .)."

16: 33
"I have told you all this so that you may find peace in me. In the world you will have to suffer. But be courageous! I have conquered the world."

The prayer of Jesus   17: 1–3, 9–26

"Father, the hour has come: give glory to your Son so that your Son may give glory to you (. . .). Give eternal life to all those you have given to him. And eternal life is this: to know you, the only true God, and Jesus Christ whom you have sent. (. . .) It is for those you have given me that I pray (. . .).

"I am no longer in the world. They are in the world, and I am coming to you. Holy Father, keep those you have given me true to your name, so that they may be one like us. (. . .) I am not asking you to take them out from the world, but to protect them from the Evil One. (. . .) Sanctify them in the truth (. . .). I pray not only for these but also for those who will come to believe in me through their teaching. May they all be one, just as, Father, you are in me and I am in you, so that they also may be in us, so that the world may believe it was you who sent me. (. . .) I have made your name known to them and will continue to make it known, so that the love with which you loved me may be in them, and so that I may be in them."

This prayer, which is often called the "sacerdotal prayer" (meaning the prayer of the priest or intercessor), expresses the deepest concerns and hopes of Christ. Even the believers were still far from obeying his call. Jesus was well aware of all the difficulties they would meet and which they would have to overcome one by one before they could reach perfect love and unity.

John's account of the Passion is generally similar to those of the other Evangelists but it does contain some passages which are particularly rich in meaning.

Jesus before Pilate   18: 28–40

The members of the Sanhedrin then led Jesus from the house of Caiaphas to the Praetorium. It was now morning. They did not go into the Praetorium themselves because they did not want to make themselves unclean and be unable to eat the Passover. So Pilate came out to meet them and said, "What charge do you bring against this man?" They replied, "If he were not a criminal, we should not have handed him over to you." Pilate said, "Take him yourselves, and try him by your own Law." The Jews answered, "We are not allowed to put anyone to death." This was to fulfil the words Jesus had spoken indicating the way he was going to die.

So Pilate went back into the Praetorium. He called Jesus to him and asked him, "Are you the king of the Jews?" Jesus replied, "Do you ask this of your own accord, or have others said it to you about me?" Pilate answered, "Am I a Jew? It is your own people and the chief priests who have handed you over to me: what have you done?" Jesus replied, "My kingdom is not of this world. If my kingdom were of this world, my men would have fought to stop me being handed over to the Jews. As it is, my kingdom does not belong here."

Pilate was aware that the political reason given by Jesus' accusers would not stand up in court. Jesus appeared to him to be no more than a harmless man with a vision who was not a threat to Rome. Pilate was a sceptic and did not understand a word Jesus said to him. But he was impressed by him and tried — though without taking any risks — to stop the accusers by making them look stupid.

Pilate said, "So, you are a king then?" Jesus answered, "It is you who say that I am a king. I was born and I came into this world to bear witness to the truth. All those who are on the side of truth listen to my voice."

Pilate said, "What is truth?" And with these words he went out again to the Jews and said, "I find no case against him. But you know I usually release one prisoner at the Passover; would you like me, then, to release for you the king of the Jews?" At this they shouted, "Not this man," they said, "but Barabbas." Barabbas was a robber.

John also reported the details of the last moments of Jesus' life.

Jesus and his mother
19: 25–7

Mary, in her grief, was told by her Son that, in sharing his own sorrows, she would become the spiritual mother of us all. That is what is meant by Jesus calling the disciple John her son.

Near the cross of Jesus stood his mother and his mother's sister, Mary the wife of Clopas, and Mary of Magdala. Seeing his mother and the disciple whom he loved standing near her, Jesus said to his mother, "Woman, this is your son." Then to the disciple he said, "This is your mother." And from that moment the disciple took her into his home.

The death of Jesus
19: 28–30

John emphasises the peaceful way in which Jesus died which contrasts with the accounts of the other Evangelists. He had completed his mission perfectly and gave himself up to the Father.

After this, Jesus knew that everything had now been completed and, so that the scripture should be fulfilled, he said: "*I am thirsty.*"

A jar full of cheap wine stood there; so, putting a sponge soaked in the wine on the end of a hyssop stick, they held it up to his mouth. After Jesus had taken the wine he said, "It is finished"; and bowing his head he gave up his spirit.

The pierced Christ
19: 31–7

The soldiers speeded up the death of the crucified men by making them suffocate. They did this by breaking their legs which meant that they could no longer lift themselves up in order to breathe. John noted the unique treatment of Jesus and thus showed that he was the sacrificial lamb whose bones were not allowed to be broken. His blood was a sign of a life offered up to God. The water which flowed from his side reminds us of the baptism by water and the Spirit.

It was the Day of Preparation for the Passover and to avoid the bodies' remaining on the cross during the Sabbath — since that Sabbath was an important day — the Jews asked Pilate to have the legs broken and the bodies taken away. So the soldiers came and broke the legs of the first man who had been crucified with him and then of the other. When they came to Jesus, they saw he was already dead, and so instead of breaking his legs one of the soldiers pierced his side with a spear; and immediately blood and water came out.

This is the evidence of one who saw it — true evidence, and he knows that what he says is true — and he gives it so that you may believe as well. Because all this happened to fulfil the words of scripture: "*Not one bone of his will be broken.*"

And in another place scripture says: "*They will look at the one they have pierced.*"

The Evangelist presented himself as a witness to the events he described and quoted texts from Exodus (12: 46) and Zechariah (12: 10).

Appearance to the apostles and to Thomas
20: 24–8

Thomas, called the Twin, who was one of the Twelve, was not with them when Jesus came. So the other disciples said to him, "We have seen the Lord!" But he answered, "Unless I can see the holes of the nails and can put my finger into the holes they made, and unless I can put my hands into his side, I refuse to believe." Eight days later the disciples were together in the house again and Thomas was with them. The doors were closed, but Jesus came in and stood among them. "Peace be with you," he said. Then he spoke to Thomas, "Put your finger here; look, here are my hands. Give me your hand; put it into my side. Do not be unbelieving any more but believe." Thomas replied, "My Lord and my God!" Jesus said to him: "You believe because you can see me. Blessed are those who have not seen and yet believe."

John added an important detail after mentioning the first time Jesus appeared to the apostles (in a similar way to Mark in 16: 14–18): the risen Jesus really was still the Jesus they all knew. It was not the fact of touching him that made them really believe in him, though, for his reality was much more than that of a revived corpse. Jesus was truly alive with God his Father for ever. Thomas realised this after meeting Jesus.

The appearance on the shore of Tiberias   21: 1–25

Jesus showed himself again to the disciples. It was by the Sea of Tiberias. It happened like this: Simon Peter, Thomas called the Twin, Nathanael from Cana in Galilee, the sons of Zebedee and two others were together. Simon Peter said, "I'm going fishing." They replied, "We'll come with you." They went out in the boat but did not catch anything that night.

Early in the morning Jesus stood on the shore. But the disciples did not realise that it was Jesus. Jesus called out, "Haven't you caught anything, friends?" When they answered, "No," he said, "Throw the net out on the right-hand side and you'll find something." So they threw the net out and did not have the strength to pull it back in because there were so many fish. The disciple whom Jesus loved said to Peter, "It is the Lord." At these words, "It is the Lord," Simon Peter put his clothes on (for he had nothing on) and jumped into the water. The other disciples came on in the boat, towing the net with the fish; they were only about a hundred yards from land.

Communion bread and fish.
Third century fresco. Calixtus
Cemetery, Rome.

The Evangelist was also referring
to the early days of the Church.
A miraculous catch of fish pointed
to the way in which the disciples
would have to gather together
those who were saved at the
Master's call. The sharing of the
meal reminds us of the
communion which links Jesus
with his people. A special
mission was given to Peter (Jesus
asked Peter the question three
times because the fisherman had
earlier denied his Master three
times; the apostle recognised that
Jesus was taking him back to his
own denial). Peter was now
capable of becoming a servant to
his brothers to the point of giving
up his life. The reference to the
"disciple whom Jesus loved"
was the object of much discussion
among the brothers (the first
Christians) but tradition has it that
John lived to a very old age.

As soon as they came ashore they saw a charcoal fire with some fish cooking on it and some bread. Jesus said, "Bring some of the fish you have just caught." Simon Peter went aboard and dragged the net ashore, full of big fish, one hundred and fifty-three of them; and in spite of the large number the net did not break. Jesus said to them, "Come and have breakfast." None of the disciples was brave enough to ask, "Who are you?" They knew quite well it was the Lord. Jesus then stepped forward, took the bread and gave it to them, and the same with the fish. This was the third time that Jesus showed himself to the disciples after his resurrection from the dead.

When they had eaten, Jesus said to Simon Peter, "Simon son of John, do you love me more than these others do?" He answered, "Yes, Lord, you know I love you." Jesus said to him, "Feed my lambs." A second time he said to him, "Simon son of John, do you love me?" He replied, "Yes, Lord, you know I love you." Jesus said to him, "Look after my sheep." Then he said to him a third time, "Simon son of John, do you love me?" Peter was hurt that he asked him a third time, "Do you love me?" and said, "Lord, you know everything; you know I love you." Jesus said to him, "Feed my sheep.

"In all truth I tell you, when you were young you put on your own belt and walked where you wanted to; but when you grow old you will stretch out your hands, and somebody else will put a belt round you and take you somewhere you would rather not go."

In these words he indicated the kind of death by which Peter would die and give glory to God. After this he said, "Follow me."

Peter turned round and saw behind him the disciple whom Jesus loved, the one who had leant back close to his chest at the supper and had said to him, "Lord, who is it that will betray you?" Seeing him, Peter said to Jesus, "What about him, Lord?" Jesus answered, "If I want him to stay behind till I come, what does it matter to you? You are to follow me." The rumour then went round among the brothers that this disciple would not die. Yet Jesus had not said to Peter, "He will not die," but, "If I want him to stay behind till I come."

This disciple is the one who is a witness to these things and has written them down, and we know that his account is true.

There were many other things that Jesus did. If they were written down in detail, I do not suppose the whole world would hold all the books that would be written.

THE
ACTS OF THE
APOSTLES

We tend to say "what a story!" when we hear an account of a string of unexpected events which keep postponing the rapid conclusion we expect.

"What a story" could also be said about the book of the Acts of the Apostles. How could a carpenter from a little known town in Galilee, crushed by the political and religious powers-that-be, transform the whole world despite the many things which opposed the spreading of his message?

Luke, the author of this book, replied that it was because the Spirit of God was in action. The Spirit gives new life, as had already been clearly seen in the resurrection of Jesus; this same Spirit acts against the forces of death (which erode at all groups of human beings until eventually they disappear completely).

The gospel was able to spread beyond the borders of a tiny corner of the Roman Empire and, in spite of all the obstacles, to reach the centre of the ancient civilised world: the Acts show how this unlikely series of events came about and how the mission to take the Good News to the ends of the earth was accomplished by Jesus trusting his friends to carry out his commission.

The distance covered by the gospel was accompanied by a change within the hearts of men and women. The early Christians were tempted to stay within their own Jewish communities despite the fact that their faith reached out to everyone. They had to accept the breaking down of the original boundaries and come to a new understanding of that faith, which would not be achieved without conflict.

Luke was not trying to write a "history of the early Church", but wanted perhaps to express his understanding of the action of the Spirit, so he concentrated on certain important events and a few typical personalities.

1. *Jerusalem*. The apostles were filled by the Spirit after the resurrection of Jesus. Their bold preaching of the gospel created communities where the Good News was put into practice. The Church hit opposition from the Jews and some were martyred even from the beginning. The power of the Spirit was able to shine through eventually, working through the disciples and especially Peter.

2. *The first missionary journey*. The Church was forced to open up to the outside world because of persecution, with Christians being scattered throughout the Greek world, but principally because of the inspiration of the Spirit itself. The Church welcomed foreigners (for example, Cornelius and his family) who were already adherents to Judaism.

3. *The mission of Paul and Barnabas*. Events began to speed up after Paul's conversion. The Church began to make progress among the gentiles. This caused an internal crisis in the Church which could no longer remain exclusive to the Jews but did not want to deny its own origins; some felt that these Jewish roots were stopping the progress of the gospel in the world. The Church was led by the Spirit to take the necessary step at the "Council of Jerusalem".

4. *Paul's missions*. Luke's account then concentrated on Paul, whose travelling companion he had become. He showed the rapid progress of the gospel in Asia Minor and from there to mainland Greece.

5. *The gospel at the heart of the Empire*. The Church showed that it was for everyone by reaching the heart of the ancient world. Luke ends his account at that point. Of course the story was far from finished because it is continued even now. The progress of the Spirit at the heart of human history will never end.

Luke used a short prologue to recall the instruction given by the risen Jesus to the apostles that they should remain in Jerusalem until the arrival of the Holy Spirit.

The ascension
1: 6–11

After the resurrection, the apostles were waiting for the triumphal arrival of the kingdom they still dreamt of. Jesus responded by talking about a mission which would lead them to the ends of the earth (in the Acts, this means Rome, the city opposed to Jerusalem). They were no longer to dream and watch the heavens but to turn towards the world so that one day, at the end of time, Jesus will be able to show himself fully there.

Now having met together, the apostles asked him, "Lord, has the time come for you to restore the kingdom to Israel?" He replied, "You do not have to know times or dates that the Father has decided by his own authority. But you will receive the power of the Holy Spirit which will come on you. Then you will be my witnesses not only in Jerusalem but throughout Judaea and Samaria, and indeed to the ends of the earth."

As he said this he was lifted up while they looked on, and a cloud took him from their sight. They were still staring into the sky watching him go, when suddenly two men in white were standing beside them. They said, "Why are you Galileans standing here looking into the sky? This Jesus who has been taken up from you into heaven will come back in the same way as you have seen him go."

1

THE CHURCH IN JERUSALEM

The central core of the Church consisted of the eleven apostles, Mary and a few other women. They were already making preparations to respond to the mission Jesus had given to them although the group seemed to be very poor. It was important that they should have twelve official witnesses to the resurrection of the Lord (twelve being the symbolic number for the perfect group, in memory of the twelve tribes of Israel). So they chose someone to replace the traitor, Judas.

Pentecost
2: 1–13

On the day of Pentecost they were all together, when suddenly there came from heaven a loud sound like a violent wind. It filled the whole house in which they were sitting. Then there appeared what looked like tongues of fire. These divided and came to rest on each of their heads. They were all filled with the Holy Spirit and began to speak different languages as the Spirit gave them power to express themselves.

Now at that time in Jerusalem Jews had gathered from every nation in the world. They all crowded together when they heard the noise and each one was bewildered to hear these men speaking his own language. They were amazed and astonished. They said, "Surely all these men speaking come from Galilee? How is it, then, that each of us hears them speaking in his own native language? Parthians, Medes and Elamites; people from Mesopotamia, Judaea and Cappadocia, Pontus and Asia, Phrygia and Pamphylia, Egypt and the parts of Libya round Cyrene; residents of Rome — Jews and proselytes alike — Cretans and Arabs, we hear them preaching in our own language about the wonderful things that God has done." Everyone was amazed and puzzled; they asked one another what it all meant. Some, however, laughed it off and said, "They have been drinking too much new wine."

The Jewish Pentecost was a reminder of the gift of the Law on Sinai, and thus of the real birth of the Jewish people. The Christian Pentecost marks the birth of the Church, formed by the Spirit of God. Luke tried to describe an indescribable experience by presenting it as the opposite of the episode of the Tower of Babel (Gen. 11: 1–9): people came back together and began to understand each other. Luke also used images from the Jewish accounts of the Pentecost at Sinai.

In a way, there was already a reunion of all humanity because the pilgrims were representatives of many different nations (they had come from all parts of the "diaspora" or dispersal). But the Jews who were converted were only the forerunners of the gentile world which was soon to enter the Church in its turn.

Peter, the same Peter who had denied Christ in fear and trembling, now boldly bore witness to the resurrection of Jesus. He called all those listening to enter the new world order; this order was offered to those willing to accept the amazing fact of God's call to men and women to be filled with the Spirit and live in close union with him through Jesus. He was lifting them above their purely human condition to share in his divine nature.

Peter's address to the crowd 2: 14ff

Then Peter stood up with the Eleven and spoke to them in a loud voice: "Men of Judaea, and all you who live in Jerusalem, listen to me. These men are not drunk, as you think; why, it is only nine o'clock in the morning. This is what the prophet was talking about when he said: 'In the last days — says the Lord — *I shall pour out my Spirit on the whole world.*

"*Your sons and daughters shall prophesy, your young people shall have visions, and your old people dreams. Even on slaves, men and women, I shall pour out my Spirit.*' (. . .)

"Men of Israel, listen to what I am going to say: Jesus the Nazarene (. . .) you took him and nailed him to the cross, having him killed by men outside the Law. But God raised him to life, freeing him from the power of death. God raised this man Jesus to life, and we are all witnesses of that. Now raised to God's right hand, he has received from the Father the Holy Spirit, who was

promised, and he has been poured out on us. (. . .) For this reason the whole House of Israel can be certain of this: God has made Jesus, whom you crucified, both Lord and Christ."

The first Christian community   2: 37-8, 41-7

Hearing this, they were deeply distressed and asked Peter and the other apostles, "What are we to do, brothers?" Peter answered, "You must repent, and every one of you must be baptised in the name of Jesus Christ for the forgiveness of your sins. Then you will receive the gift of the Holy Spirit." They accepted what he said and were baptised. That very day about three thousand were added to their number.

These remained faithful to the teaching of the apostles, to the brotherhood, to the breaking of bread and to prayer.

And everyone was filled with awe for the apostles worked many signs and miracles.

The believers shared everything in common. They sold their goods and possessions and shared the money out among themselves according to what each one needed.

Each day, with one heart, they regularly went to the Temple but met in their houses for the breaking of bread, sharing their food gladly and generously. They praised God and were looked up to by everyone. Day by day the Lord added to their community those who were being saved.

> A Christian is someone who turns away from sin to enter into the world of the Spirit through baptism in the name of Jesus.

> Luke presented an ideal picture of the first Christian community. The developing Church made an amazing impact. It remained linked to the Jewish world but showed its identity by its own rite: the "breaking of bread".

Jesus had shown the coming of the Kingdom by healing the sick. Luke reported that Peter had similarly healed a cripple by using the name of Christ. He explained the meaning of this miracle to the amazed crowd. He called Jews who might have misunderstood the true personality of the Christ to conversion: it was time for them to open their eyes following the resurrection. According to the promise made to Abraham, "All the families in the world will be blessed in your descendants". The moment was coming when the promise would be fulfilled in Jesus.

Like their Master, the believers experienced opposition from the Jewish authorities. Peter and John were dragged before the Sanhedrin (the religious court) where the leaders tried to forbid them to talk about Jesus. The two apostles replied proudly: "We cannot stop proclaiming what we have seen and heard." It was clear that the enemies of the growing faith could do nothing in the face of its strength, and this encouraged early Christians. They asked God with great urgency to give them the strength to continue to preach his word in all confidence.

However the Church came up against another danger but from within this time. Although the new members were very generous, there were also some imposters. Ananias and his wife Sapphira claimed to have sold all their belongings and given all the money to the community, when they had actually kept a large sum for themselves. Peter discovered their trick and reminded them that they had not been forced to share their belongings in this way, but that their hypocrisy was unacceptable. The two frauds fell dead at this rebuke. The Spirit cannot be fooled!

The new belief developed in an extraordinary way. It was becoming dangerous in the eyes of the Jewish religious authorities so the Sadducees had the apostles thrown into prison. But the apostles were miraculously freed in the middle of the night and were preaching in the Temple by early next morning.

A summons to appear before the Sanhedrin

5: 21–33

The opposition between the old Israel and the new was growing. But the first could not stop the second developing. The apostles spoke about their faith publicly before the same court which had condemned Jesus. They even rejoiced that they were being allowed to suffer for their Master as he had suffered for them.

The high priest arrived. He and his supporters convened the Sanhedrin — this was the full Senate of Israel — and sent for the apostles to be brought from the gaol. But when the officials arrived at the prison they did not find them there. So they went back and reported, "We found the gaol securely locked and the warders on duty at the gates, but when we unlocked the door we did not find anyone inside." When the captain of the Temple and the chief priests heard this news they wondered what could be happening. Then a man arrived with fresh news. He said, "Look! The men you imprisoned are in the Temple. They are preaching to the people." The captain went with his men and fetched them — though not by force, for they were afraid that the people might stone them.

They brought them in to face the Sanhedrin. The high priest demanded an explanation. "We gave you a strong warning not to preach in this name, and what have you done? You have filled Jerusalem with your teaching, and seem determined to fix the guilt for this man's death on us." In reply Peter and the apostles said, "We must obey God not men. The God of our ancestors raised up Jesus, whom you had killed by hanging him on a tree. By his own right hand God has now raised him up to be leader and Saviour, to give repentance and forgiveness of sins through him to Israel. We are witnesses to this, we and the Holy Spirit whom God has given to those who obey him." This made them so angry that they wanted to put them to death.

A universally-respected doctor of the Law came to their aid: "If this enterprise, this movement of theirs, is of human origin it will break up of its own accord; but if it does in fact come from God you will be unable to destroy them. Take care not to find yourselves fighting against God." His advice was accepted and they made do with having the apostles whipped and forbade them to continue their preaching of the message. But the apostles rejoiced that they had been allowed to suffer for the name of Jesus and only preached all the more.

2

THE FIRST MISSIONS

The Church now had to face new difficulties. Many of its members were Jews who came originally from the Greek world. There were divisions between these believers and those with a local Jewish background: it was not easy for them to live together. The apostles wanted to spend more time preaching so they appointed deacons in order to deal better with the problems caused by community life. The deacons were given the task of "serving at table".

Then members of several Jewish synagogues began to accuse the Church by picking on one of these deacons, Stephen. They said he had declared the Jewish Law and the Temple to be old-fashioned and useless.

Stephen was dragged before the Sanhedrin where he made a long plea. He went back to the origins of Israel and showed how the chosen people had always misunderstood the prophets sent by God. Furthermore, Judaism had tried to limit God by making him live in a house "that human hands have built". Stephen told his accusers, "you are resisting the Holy Spirit" and this made them very angry.

The stoning of Stephen. First persecution   7: 55—8: 3

But Stephen, filled with the Holy Spirit, gazed into heaven. He saw the glory of God, and Jesus standing at God's right hand. He said, "Look! I can see heaven thrown open, and the Son of man standing at the right hand of God." All the members of the council shouted out and put their hands over their ears. Then they all rushed at him at once, pushed him out of the city and stoned him. The witnesses put their clothes down at the feet of a young man called Saul. As they were stoning him, Stephen prayed, "Lord Jesus, receive my spirit." Then he fell on his knees and said with a loud cry, "Lord, do not hold this sin against them." And with those words he fell asleep in death.

Saul approved of his murder.

That day a bitter persecution started against the church in Jerusalem. Everyone except the apostles scattered to the country districts of Judaea and Samaria. (. . .) Saul then began doing great harm to the church; he went from house to house arresting both men and women and sending them to prison.

Stephen was speaking blasphemy in the eyes of those accusing him just as Jesus had done, since he dared to claim that Jesus was the triumphant "Son of man" spoken of by the prophet Daniel. Stephen had to die as his Master had and, like him, Stephen forgave his murderers.

In fact, persecution only speeded up the spreading of the gospel. That was how Philip came to be preaching the Good News in Samaria. The Jews had never wanted anything to do with that country, but it welcomed the word of God.

Another step forward: one day Philip met an important civil servant from the court of Ethiopia. This man was open to Judaism and told Philip he did not understand the passage in Isaiah about the lamb led to the slaughter (Isa. 53: 7–8). The apostle explained to him how this passage had been fulfilled in the person of Jesus. The Ethiopian was amazed and asked immediately to be baptised. So, the gospel began to spread in every direction.

The "Way" means "how to behave" or "way of living". In Acts, the word comes to mean Christians because they follow the "Way" of the Lord.

Saul's call   9: 1–9

Meanwhile Saul was still breathing threats of murder against the Lord's disciples. He went to the high priest and asked for letters addressed to the synagogues in Damascus, so that, if there were any followers of the Way there, men or women, he could arrest them and take them back to Jerusalem.

He was travelling to Damascus and approaching the city when suddenly a light from heaven shone all round him. He fell to the ground, and then he heard a voice saying, "Saul, Saul, why are you persecuting me?" "Who are you, Lord?" he asked, and the answer came, "I am Jesus, whom you are persecuting. Get up and go into the city, and you will be told what you are to do." The men travelling with Saul stood there speechless. Though they heard the voice they could see no one. Saul got up from the ground, but when he opened his eyes he could see nothing at all. They had to lead him into Damascus by the hand. For three days he could not see, and he neither ate nor drank.

There was a disciple named Ananias in Damascus. God told him in a vision to go to Saul and give him back his sight. The former persecutor was baptised with the name of Paul and became a passionate teacher of the gospel. He preached the gospel in the synagogues of the city to the amazement of everyone. The Jewish persecutors suddenly turned against him so that he needed help to flee from the city, eventually being lowered from the walls in a basket to escape from his enemies who were waiting at the gates. The new Christian then returned to Jerusalem where he managed, after some difficulty, to be accepted into the community which he had once persecuted. The Church then went through a short period of peace and continued to grow. Peter went from community to community. Like Jesus, he performed many signs which showed that a new world order had arrived.

There was a Roman centurion called Cornelius who was respected among the Jews and who had been converted to Judaism in Caesarea. One day this man had a vision in which he was ordered to send for Peter who was staying nearby. For his part, Peter had had a strange dream too: from the sky, a great sheet was lowered which was covered with foods the Jewish Law considered to be unclean. A voice had ordered him to eat some of them but Peter protested. The voice had repeated three times: "What God has made clean, you have no right to call unclean" and then the messengers from Cornelius arrived . . .

Conversion of a Roman centurion   10: 24–35, 44–8

Next day, he was ready to go off with them. Some of the brothers from Jaffa went with him. They reached Caesarea the following day, and Cornelius was waiting for them. He had asked his relations and close friends to be there. As Peter reached the house Cornelius

A startling new idea for a Church where people had thought the conversion of the gentiles could only take place after all Israel had been converted: God was now sending his message to all people everywhere. Already he was giving them his Spirit and was making room for them in his Church.

The barriers between Jews and gentiles were coming down. Jesus united all human beings in one single people from then on.

went out to meet him, and falling at his feet, honoured him. But Peter helped him up, saying, "Stand up, after all, I am only a man!" Talking together they went in and met all the other people gathered there. Peter said to them, "You know it is forbidden for Jews to mix with people of another race and visit them. But God has made it clear to me that I must not treat anyone as common or unclean. That is why I made no objection to coming when I was sent for. Tell me exactly why you sent for me." Cornelius replied, "At this time three days ago, at 3 o'clock in the afternoon, I was in my house praying, when I suddenly saw a man in front of me in shining clothes. He said, 'Cornelius, your prayer has been heard and your gifts to those in need have not been forgotten by God. Now send a messenger to Jaffa to fetch Simon known as Peter. He is lodging in the house of Simon the tanner, by the sea.' So I sent for you at once, and you have been kind enough to come. Here we all are, ready to hear all that God has told you to say." Then Peter began to speak, "I now really understand that God has no favourites, but that anybody of any nationality who fears him and does what is right is acceptable to him." (. . .)

While Peter was still speaking the Holy Spirit came down on all who were listening. The Jewish believers who had come down with Peter were all astonished that the gift of the Holy Spirit should be poured out on gentiles too; they could hear them speaking new languages and praising God for his greatness. Peter himself then said, "Could anyone stop these people being baptised with water, now they have received the Holy Spirit just as we have?" He then gave orders for them to be baptised in the name of Jesus Christ.

The news of Peter's visit to a gentile caused trouble in the community in Jerusalem. How could he be so unfaithful to the Jewish Law? Peter had to explain his action. It was like a ray of light for all of them. "God," they said, "has clearly granted the gentiles too the repentance that leads to life" and they gave glory to God.

The "Good News" was announced in Antioch a short time afterwards. The birth of Christianity in Antioch was a big step forward because it was the third largest city in the Roman Empire at that time. It was there that the first community of believers was formed which was made up entirely of Christians with a Greek background. It was also in that city that Jesus' disciples were called Christians for the first time. Links between the new local church and the Church in Jerusalem were formed immediately. Paul was introduced to the new community by Barnabas, the apostle sent by the mother Church.

Herod in Jerusalem had meanwhile ordered that Peter be arrested to please the Jews. The whole Church in the city began to pray for the prisoner.

Peter woke up suddenly one night as his cell was filled with light. The chains fell from him and a voice ordered him to leave the cell. All the doors were open. He first thought that he must be dreaming but then the apostle suddenly found himself free. The community had difficulty believing it really was him when he arrived on their doorstep. They helped him to flee to Caesarea. King Herod died shortly afterwards.

3

PAUL AND BARNABAS' MISSION:
THE COUNCIL OF JERUSALEM

The Church at Antioch decided to send out preachers to spread the Good News more widely. Paul and Barnabas were chosen under the inspiration of the Holy Spirit to carry out the plan. The two missionaries went to Seleucia and from there to Cyprus. The gospel was spreading beyond the areas of Syria and Palestine. But the messengers from Antioch always started their work by speaking first to the Jews in the synagogues of the country in which they were staying. Their preaching soon went further. Paul's preaching caused a strong reaction in Antioch in Pisidia which is now part of Turkey. The apostle was in fact showing how God's call to the ancestors of one particular race of people was now valid for everybody.

A person was no longer made right with God by obeying the Law but by a free gift from God who had resurrected Jesus Christ. The preacher was soon at the centre of conflict. Paul then declared: "We had to proclaim the word of God to you first, but since you have rejected it, since you do not think yourselves worthy of eternal life, here and now we turn to the gentiles." There was great rejoicing among the gentiles who welcomed Paul gladly; and there were many conversions.

But a group of "society ladies" began to stir up trouble. Paul and Barnabas had to flee in the face of persecution. They went to Iconium and the same thing happened there as in Antioch in Pisidia. So the two missionaries then went first to Lystra, and then to Derbe and its surroundings. They left living communities behind them everywhere, each one consisting of converted gentiles.

Paul healed a cripple at Derbe and the gentile crowds decided that Barnabas must be Zeus and Paul must be Hermes. They prepared to offer sacrifices to the two gods who had come down to earth. Paul protested in horror and made a speech to show how wrong it was to worship idols.

The Jewish opponents followed Paul and again stirred the people up to persecute the missionaries. Paul was stoned and left for dead but, still very much alive, he got up after his enemies had gone. Paul set up communities there with Barnabas and then went down to Pamphilia. He finally returned to his starting-point of Antioch in Syria. The new spread of the gospel in gentile countries was a source of joy and thanksgiving.

The growth of the Church among the gentiles raised a question which had already been discussed in the case of Cornelius: was it possible to welcome converts if they did not obey the Jewish Law, particularly as far as circumcision was concerned? Opinions varied so they eventually decided to consult the Church in Jerusalem. In fact, opinions were equally divided in Jerusalem. Some converted Pharisees were adamant that the Law must be followed: they demanded that all gentile converts should be circumcised and made to accept the commandments of Moses.

The Council of Jerusalem   15: 6–12

The apostles and elders met to look into the matter. After a long discussion, Peter stood up and spoke.

"My brothers, you know perfectly well that since the early days God chose me from among you so that the gentiles could learn the good news from me and so become believers. And God, who

Peter intervened in what has been called the "Council of Jerusalem". His words were decisive.

The apostle drew conclusions from the past by referring to his own experience with Cornelius. He showed how Paul's action was right. The Church became more and more open toward the gentile world from that time and began to detach itself from its Jewish roots. The new perspective was stated more clearly than ever: God is a God of freely-given mercy. The most important thing is faith and not the Law (the yoke).

knows everyone's heart, showed his approval of them by giving the Holy Spirit to them just as he had to us. God made no distinction between them and us, since he made their hearts pure by faith. Why do you put God to the test now by placing a burden on the disciples that neither our ancestors nor we were strong enough to carry? But we believe that we are saved in the same way as they are: through the grace of the Lord Jesus."

The whole meeting fell silent. They listened to Barnabas and Paul describing all the signs and wonders God had worked through them among the gentiles.

James was the leader of the Church in Jerusalem. He took Peter's side although he felt very strongly about Jewish tradition. He only asked that the whole of the Church should be in agreement about certain ground-rules. James' proposal was agreed on and a letter sent to Antioch rebuking those who had made trouble, and agreeing with the position of Paul and Barnabas who wanted gentile converts to be welcomed into the church. Peace seemed to have been re-established in a Church that was opening itself more and more toward the Greek world.

4

PAUL'S MISSIONS

Paul was free to go into the gentile world from that time on without any hesitation. He separated from Barnabas and was joined by Silas and then by Timothy who was the son of a converted Jewess. He crossed Syria, then Cilicia, and revisited the communities he had founded earlier at Derbe and Lystra. He next went across to Phrygia and the Galatian territory (which is part of modern-day Turkey) and returned to the coast at Troas, from where he set sail for a large city in Macedonia called Philippi.

The Christian preaching unsettled people. Paul healed a woman of a spirit which enabled her to tell people's fortunes. Her masters thus lost their source of income and roused the mob against the newcomers, who were whipped and thrown in prison.

Paul then went with Silas to Thessalonica. His speeches in the synagogue led to many conversions but at the same time caused opposition. They were forced to leave. The same thing happened at Berea. The apostle was pushed on by persecution till he came at last to Athens. When invited to explain his new teaching to them he said:

Paul's speech at the Areopagus   17: 22–34
"Men of Athens, I have seen for myself that you are very religious in all matters. As I strolled round your city looking at your sacred monuments, I even found an altar with the inscription: To An Unknown God. In fact, the unknown God you worship is the one I have come to tell you about.

"The God who made the world and everything in it, the Lord

of heaven and earth, does not make
his home in temples made by human
hands. Nor is he in need of anything, that he
should be served by human hands; on the contrary, it
is he who gives everything — including life and breath — to everyone. From one single origin he created the whole human race so

Saint Paul tried to make the Athenians listen to him by referring to Greek philosophy, but they could not accept the doctrine of the resurrection. His failure in Athens made Paul distrust the "prestige of wisdom" and of "vain philosophy".

that they could live all over the earth (. . .) and he did this so that they might seek the Lord and, by feeling their way towards him, succeed in finding him. Indeed he is not far from any of us. For it is in him that we live, and move, and exist. Indeed some of your own writers have said: 'We are all his children.'

"Since we are the children of God, we have no excuse for thinking that the divine being looks like anything in gold, silver or stone that has been carved and designed by a man.

"But now, wanting to forget the times of ignorance, God is telling everyone everywhere that they must repent, because he has fixed a day when the whole world will be judged with justice by a man he has appointed. And God has publicly proved this by raising him from the dead."

At this mention of rising from the dead, some of them burst out laughing; others said, "We would like to hear you talk about this another time." After that Paul left them. There were some, however, who joined him and became believers. Among them were Dionysius the Aeropagite and a woman called Damaris, and some others besides.

Paul was disappointed by his lack of welcome after speaking in an intellectual city. He went to Corinth which was a great and densely populated port that was famous for its corrupt society. He lived among simple people there and used his old job as a tent maker. A community gradually formed round him despite the opposition of the Jews in the synagogue.

His enemies tried once again to get rid of him by pulling him up in front of the local Roman court. But Gallio, the proconsul, refused to get involved in the affair.

Paul started his journey back to Antioch after some time in Corinth. He landed in Asia at Ephesus and left immediately for Caesarea, and at last reached his starting-point again.

Paul's third journey

The apostle left again almost immediately and went back through the territory of Galatia and Phrygia till he reached Ephesus. A serious incident took place there.

Ephesus was then the centre of a large pagan cult of the goddess Artemis, to whom they had built a impressive temple that attracted many pilgrims. A local goldsmith was worried by the progress of the Church because he made souvenirs of Artemis, and the Church might harm his trade. So he took the lead in a sort of anti-crusade for the defence of the mother goddess. The town was thrown into turmoil.

19: 23–8

It was during this time that a serious disturbance broke out in connection with the Way. A silversmith called Demetrius, who provided work for a large number of craftsmen making silver shrines of Diana, called a general meeting with others in the same trade. He said to them, "As you know, we depend on this industry for our prosperity. Now you must have seen and heard how, not just in Ephesus but nearly everywhere in Asia, this man Paul has converted a great number of people, persuading them that gods made with human hands are not gods at all. This threatens not only to discredit our trade, but also to make the sanctuary of the great goddess Diana become less and less important. It could end up by taking away the prestige of a goddess worshipped all over Asia, and indeed all over the world." This speech made them very angry, and they started to shout, "Great is Diana of the Ephesians!"

Paul left soon afterwards: he went from church to church but was now heading for Jerusalem.

5

THE JOURNEY TO JERUSALEM

20: 22–3, 28
"And now you see me on my way to Jerusalem as a prisoner of the Spirit; I have no idea what will happen to me there, except that the Holy Spirit, in town after town, has made it clear to me that imprisonment and persecution await me. (. . .)

"Be on your guard for yourselves and for all the flock which the Holy Spirit has placed in your care, to feed the Church of God which he bought with the blood of his own Son."

Statue of Artemis

Paul's friends were frightened by his plans to go to Jerusalem. Everyone knew he had terrible enemies in that city so they tried to dissuade him but, like Jesus, Paul knew that the Lord wanted him to go on without being distracted by the fear of death.

Some people in the city were getting worried: hadn't they heard that the apostle made Jewish converts to Christianity turn their backs on circumcision and the customs of their ancestors? Paul went to the Temple to explain himself and was accused — wrongly — of having brought Greeks into the sacred inner court: this caused a riot. Paul managed to calm the mob for a moment. He told them that he was both a Jew and a Pharisee and had been trained by the great Gamaliel himself "in the exact observance of the Law". He then explained how he had met Jesus. But the uproar became even more violent than before when he mentioned his mission to the gentiles. Paul was arrested but avoided being whipped by using his title as a Roman citizen. He was called before the Sanhedrin and cleverly took advantage of the disagreements between the Pharisees and Sadducees by presenting himself as a traditional Pharisee and then declared himself condemned because of his belief in the resurrection. The tribunal was divided immediately with the Pharisees defending Paul. The tribunal eventually decided to send him back to the fortress and then to have him sent to Caesarea, to appear before the Roman governor, Felix. Paul remained there as a prisoner for two years.

Festus, Felix' successor, had Paul brought before him again. Paul appealed to Caesar and was sent to Rome, but not without having previously appeared before King Agrippa and his sister, Bernice — the lady whose great love for Titus made her famous.

The journey to Rome

Paul set sail with several other prisoners. He lived under a fairly relaxed regime.

The ship went along the Asiatic coastline. In Lycia they changed to another ship and arrived eventually in Crete.

It was getting late in the season and the conditions were becoming dangerous. The centurion escorting the prisoners ignored Paul's advice and decided to set sail. A terrible storm broke out shortly afterwards and it was fourteen nights before they came within sight of land again. Everyone finally arrived safely on the island of Malta by either swimming or holding on to driftwood.

They were able to put to sea again at the end of three months. They landed at Syracuse, then at Rhegium and finally at Puteoli. Paul and his Christian companions met other believers there who welcomed them. Then the guards, the prisoners and their friends set out on foot for Rome.

Paul had quite a lot of freedom: he was allowed to stay in his own house with a soldier to guard him. He took advantage of the situation to continue his work: "He welcomed all who came to visit him, proclaiming the Kingdom of God and teaching the truth about the Lord Jesus Christ with complete freedom and without hindrance from anyone." The gospel was preached openly from that moment on. For Luke, the mission given by Christ to his Church was fulfilled. The Good News was preached in the heart of the gentile world. The writer had completed his task.

THE EPISTLES

LETTER TO THE ROMANS

Does religion really bring true life? Are all religions equally valid? The letter to the Romans sheds light on these important questions. Saint Paul wrote this letter in about AD 57 when he was thinking of going to Rome, so he addressed his message to the Christian community of that city.

His own past as a Pharisee gave him first-hand experience of the dead end reached by those who wanted to succeed through the Law alone. He had thought then that he was pleasing God by his exact obedience of a set of rules. In fact, this had only led him to be obsessed with sin, and to a persecuting attitude towards all those who did not think the same way as he himself did. At the time of his conversion, he had discovered with amazement the truth about God's freely-offered love. He was convinced from that instant that the only religion capable of freeing people and fulfilling all their needs was the faith brought about by recognising God's love. People could escape the obsessions and dreams they projected onto God by means of faith and then discover what it was to live in the Spirit.

This perspective helped Paul to look critically at both the gentiles and his fellow Jews. He reproached the gentiles for ignoring the voice of their conscience when creating gods in the image of their own desires. He explained to the Jews that the superiority of their Law, of which they were so proud, had led them to create an image of God as a terrifying and demanding character.

Everyone should recognise that the only truly valid religion was the one revealed in Jesus when he opened himself up with gratitude to the Father's gifts and responded with a love to match. Only this would enable the human race to be made right with God, that is, it would lead individuals to look at the world from God's point of view and by doing so to be renewed inwardly.

All believers without exception, even today, feel the occasional need to free themselves of narrow religious attitudes which suffocate them in order to open themselves up to the true God who brings life. That is why the letter to the Romans is relevant to us today although some of the ideas expressed in it are difficult.

SALVATION

Christian believers discover that the true way to relate to God is by means of faith. They know that God's love is free as shown in Jesus Christ. So they can live in peace and with a confident hope because they are now themselves filled with that divine love which the Holy Spirit stirs up in their hearts; they are gripped by the discovery of the gift Christ made of himself to people imprisoned in their own sin.

Release from sin, death and the law
We all find ourselves caught up in the same web of sin whether we act consciously or not. We must all stand before God because we are all related to Adam: this means we all end up at the same point of no return: death.

But all those who let themselves be caught up by the current of grace are saved because grace is released by Jesus Christ.

This is one of Paul's most important texts. We are tainted with an evil that infects us all like a contagious disease — modern history gives us plenty of examples. We can all be made holy by following Jesus in whom we rediscover our true identity.

5: 18–19

One man's sin brought condemnation on all humanity; and one man's good act has brought justification and life to all humanity. Just as by one man's disobedience many were made sinners, so by one man's obedience are many to be made righteous.

It is through baptism that Christians escape from the "old man", which means the way of life which separated them from God. We experience death and subsequent new life through the sacraments and so will experience going down into the pit and then rising to divine light: we take the road that Jesus took when he died and was resurrected.

6: 3–11

Jesus endured in love to the very end, and by his death, entered a new form of life which allows escape from the power of death.

You cannot have forgotten that all of us, when we were baptised into Christ Jesus, were baptised into his death. So by our baptism into his death we were buried with him, so that as Christ was raised from the dead by the Father's glorious power, we too should begin living a new life.

By identifying himself with Jesus the Christian enters into a movement he has never previously known in his life.

If, by dying a death like Christ's, we have been joined to him, so we shall be by a resurrection like his realising that our old self was crucified with him (. . .). But we believe that, if we died with Christ, then we shall live with him too. We know that Christ has been raised from the dead and will never die again. Death has no power over him any more. For by dying, he is dead to sin once and for all, and now the life that he lives is life with God. In the same way, you must see yourselves as being dead to sin but alive for God in Christ Jesus.

The Christian thus escapes from the grip of sin (which gave the illusion of being real life) because he is now fascinated by God and has finally discovered the truth of love. In fact, you could say that he is freed from his slavery to sin although on the other hand you could also say that he is now a slave to righteousness.

The world of sin is totally opposite to the world of God's justice: one leads to death while the other leads to life.

Those who are linked to Jesus can now "serve God in the new life of the Spirit". They are freed from the unbearable contradiction they felt inside that was caused by wanting to do good while being unable to achieve it.

The Christian life in the Spirit

The previous situation is reversed for the true believer, starting from the moment she is filled by the Spirit of Christ, because the direction of her desire is transformed. An attitude of rivalry is apparent prior to conversion and so God is seen as a jealous and judgemental God. This attitude disappears for it is God's Spirit who enters the believer: gone are the days when the Christian loved worldly goods which will not last. Paul calls these worldly goods "the flesh".

8: 14–18, 22–4, 28–39

All who are guided by the Spirit of God are sons of God. Understand that you did not receive a spirit of slavery to bring you back into fear. You received the Spirit of adoption, which makes us able to cry out, "*Abba*, Father!" The Spirit himself joins with our spirit to make us realise that we are children of God. And if we are children, then we are heirs, heirs of God and joint-heirs with Christ, provided that we share his suffering, so as to share his glory.

"Abba" is a child's word and full of tenderness. Jesus was the first person who dared to use it when referring to the Almighty God before whom all must bow.

For I consider that all we suffer in the present time is nothing compared with the glory which is going to be revealed for us. (. . .) We are well aware that the whole creation, until this time, has been groaning in the pain of childbirth. And not only that: we too, who have the first-fruits of the Spirit, even we are groaning inside ourselves, waiting with eagerness for our bodies to be set free. In hope, we already have salvation (. . .).

Paul emphasised the extent to which human beings are part of all creation. The creation is not just something for us to exploit: it has a meaning.

We are well aware that God turns everything to the good of those who love him and who have been called according to his purpose. He decided beforehand who were the ones destined to be moulded to the pattern of his Son, so that he should be the eldest of many brothers (. . .).

We can live in total confidence after we have understood the love God surrounds us with.

After saying this, what can we add? If God is for us, who can be against us? Since he did not spare his own Son, but gave him up for the sake of all of us, then will he not with him freely give us all his gifts? Who can bring any accusation against those that God has chosen? *It is God who justifies, who can condemn?* Are we not sure that Christ Jesus, who died — yes and more, who was raised from the dead and is at God's right hand — is praying for us?

Can anything cut us off from the love of Christ? Can hardships or distress, persecution, lack of food and clothing, or threats or violence? For as scripture says: "*For your sake we are being put to death all day long. We are treated like sheep that are going to be slaughtered.*" No; in all these things we are triumphantly victorious, by the power of him who loved us.

For I am certain of this: neither death nor life, nor angels, nor powers in the heavens, nothing already in existence and nothing still to come, nor the heights nor the depths, nor any created thing whatever, will be able to come between us and the love of God, known to us in Christ Jesus our Lord.

Exhortations

12: 1–6

Paul drew a practical conclusion from all this teaching by showing what a Christian life wholly led by the love of God should be like.

I urge you, then, brothers, remembering the mercies of God, to offer your bodies as a living sacrifice, holy and acceptable to God. That is the kind of worship that you must offer. Do not take the standards of the modern world as your example, but let God change your way of looking at things, so that you may understand for yourselves what is the will of God — what is good and acceptable and perfect. And through the grace that I have been given, I say this to every one of you: never think of yourself as being better than you really are, but have a wise view of yourself, recognising that God has given to each one his measure of faith. Each of us has one body with many parts, and the parts do not all have the same function. In the same way, though there are so many of us, we all make up one body in Christ, and we are all joined to one another, each having a different part to play. We have each received a different gift, according to the grace that was given to each of us (. . .).

12: 9–10

Let love be without any pretence. Avoid what is evil; stick to what is good. In brotherly love demonstrate your feelings of deep affection for one another and regard others as more important than yourself. (. . .)

12: 14–19

We form a single body in Christ and each of us must find our proper place in that body. The characteristics of the Christian community are humility and brotherly love.

Bless those who persecute you; never curse them, bless them. Rejoice with others when they rejoice, and be sad with those who are sad. Give the same consideration to all others alike. Pay no attention to social standing, but meet humble people on their own terms. (. . .) Never pay back evil with evil, but *bear in mind the ideals that all people consider to be good.* As much as possible, and as far as it depends on you, be at peace with everyone (. . .).

FIRST LETTER TO THE CORINTHIANS

How can we as Christians find the light to guide us in the new situations we meet every day?

The Scriptures rarely spell out the solutions to the moral issues of our own time. They do teach us however to consider them in the light of the choices Jesus made during his own lifetime. This was what Saint Paul did in his first letter to the Christians who lived in Corinth.

Paul probably sent this letter in the year AD 55 to a community he had founded some years earlier. Corinth was an important port famous for its many cults and its immoral living. The new Christians there had flocked enthusiastically to the faith but they still had their old way of thinking. Furthermore, their relationships with those around them created endless delicate situations.

The apostle therefore had to deal firmly with some wrong behaviour and react against certain sins. His letter is made up of a series of replies to questions that the Church elders had asked him previously. Paul was not satisfied with simply suggesting practical solutions to the problems raised, though: he always wanted to give reasons for his opinions based on years of study of the meaning of the Scriptures and the renewal of each individual made possible by Jesus.

No doubt some of the issues Paul discussed are no longer directly relevant to us today but the way he related Jesus' actions to the attitudes of the Church is certainly valid. Paul's letter can help us to shed light on problems we have today.

1. DIVISIONS AND SCANDAL

Divisions in the church at Corinth

1: 11–13

Indeed, brothers, I have been told that there are serious differences among you. I learn that each of you says, "I belong to Paul," or "I belong to Apollos," or "I belong to Cephas," or "I belong to Christ." Has Christ been split up? Was it Paul that was crucified for you? (. . .)

1: 17–25

After all, Christ sent me to preach the gospel; and not by means of clever words which would make the cross of Christ pointless. The message of the cross is foolish in the eyes of those who are on the way to ruin, but it is the power of God for those of us who are on the road to salvation. (. . .) Since the world, preferring to rely on human wisdom, was unable to recognise God's wisdom, it pleased God to use the foolishness of the gospel to save believers.

The eternal problem of divisions within the Church. Each one claimed to be under the authority of its own particular master (or "guru") and saw no further than the views of that individual. The apostle protested that he was not Jesus Christ but only the one Jesus spoke through. He was not even a great preacher with convincing arguments since clever words are often merely a smoke-screen. They are very inadequate when it comes to explaining the startling message of Jesus' death on the cross.

While the Jews demand miracles and the Greeks look for wisdom, we are preaching a crucified Christ: to the Jews an obstacle they cannot get over, to the gentiles foolishness (. . .). God's foolishness is wiser than human wisdom, and God's weakness is stronger than human strength.

The true role of the preacher 3: 5–17

For what is Apollos and what is Paul? The servants through whom you came to believe, each doing the work the Lord has given him to do. I did the planting, Apollos did the watering, but God made it grow. It does not matter who plants or who waters: only God matters, who makes it grow. (. . .)

By the grace of God which was given to me, I laid the foundations like a trained masterbuilder, and someone else is building on them. (. . .) For nobody can lay down any other foundation than the one which is there already, namely Jesus Christ. (. . .)

Do you not realise that you are a temple of God with the Spirit of God living in you? If anybody should destroy the temple of God, God will destroy that person. For God's temple is holy; and you are that temple.

Sexual immorality 6: 12–20

"Everything is permissible for me"; maybe, but not everything is good for me. True, everything is permissible for me, but I am not going to allow myself to be dominated by anything. (. . .) But the body is not intended for sexual immorality; it is for the Lord, and the Lord is for the body. God raised up the Lord and he will raise us up too by his power.

Do you not realise that your bodies are members of Christ's body? Do you think one can take parts of Christ's body and join them to the body of a prostitute? Out of the question! Or do you not realise that anyone who joins himself to a prostitute is one body with her? For as it is said, *the two become one body*. But anyone who joins himself to the Lord is one spirit with him.

Keep away from sexual immorality. All other sins that people may commit are done outside the body; but the sexually immoral person sins against his own body.

Do you not realise that your body is the temple of the Holy Spirit, who is in you and whom you received from God? You are not your own property, then; you have been bought at a price. So use your body for the glory of God.

The different groups within the Corinthian church were complaining about certain preachers. All these men working together helped to build the temple of the community in which the Holy Spirit lived.

Woe betide anyone who undermines the holy building of the Church.

Corinth was known for its depraved morals: there was much prostitution, for example. Paul's reaction was to remind people of the meaning of sexual intercourse. Our bodies are a temple of the Spirit and are thus involved in the process of salvation begun by Jesus. They therefore belong to God and should be used to give him glory.

2. SOLUTIONS TO VARIOUS PROBLEMS

Marriage and singleness

A Christian had asked Paul whether he should push his daughter into getting married. The apostle thought that the end of the world was near and so advised Christians that they should concentrate completely on the future and give up everything else including marriage.

The problem of food consecrated to idols

Could a Christian buy the meat of animals sacrificed to idols at the market? Paul replied that it did not matter at all because idols were nothing. But they should be careful! It was possible that eating such meat might shock other Christians who still saw such food as a sign of idol-worship. So Paul put the believers on their guard: "Only be careful that this freedom of yours does not in any way turn into an obstacle to trip the weak."

Then he reminded them how he himself could have used his freedom to insist on his rights (for example, the right to receive a salary to live on from the believers). He had always done whatever would be best for the spreading of the gospel even if that had led him to give up those rights. He had thus adapted himself to all possible situations:

9: 19–23

So though I was not a slave to any human being, I put myself in slavery to all people, to win as many as I could. To the Jews I made myself as a Jew, to win the Jews (. . .). To the weak, I made myself weak, to win the weak. I made myself all things to all men, so that by all possible means, I might bring some to salvation. All this I do for the sake of the gospel, that I may share its benefits with others.

Paul explained the meaning of Christian sacrifice. He himself had always practised it each time he had thought it would help him to communicate the message of the gospel more effectively. This sacrifice was clearly a difficult thing to do although it was necessary to establish priorities. Christian life is geared towards the final result and that result makes any sacrifice worthwhile.

Order in meetings

Paul tried to answer some questions which caused real controversy: they concerned the problems of how people should behave during meetings. He explained that he had opted in the end for the most generally accepted customs but he tackled a much more important question:

The early Christians celebrated the Eucharist after the end of a meal. It was the custom then to split into equal shares the food people had brought — in fact, the meaning of the Eucharist was being contradicted because there was no sharing out. Paul then reminded the church of how the Eucharist had come into being and, in so doing, wrote the earliest account we have of the Last Supper. The Last Supper must become a sign of brotherly love uniting all believers: it is not truly the "Lord's Supper" if it does not.

11: 18–34

In the first place, I hear that when you all meet together, there are divisions among you (. . .). So, when you meet together, it is not the Lord's Supper that you eat. For when the eating begins, each one of you has his own supper first, and one person goes hungry while another gets drunk. Surely you have homes for eating and drinking in? Or have you such disregard for God's church that you can put to shame those who have nothing? What am I to say to you? Congratulate you? On this I cannot congratulate you.

For I received from the Lord what I in my turn handed on to you. On the night he was betrayed, the Lord Jesus took some bread, and after he had given thanks, he broke it, and he said, "This is my body, which is for you; do this in remembrance of me." And in the same way, after supper, he took the cup and said, "This cup is the new covenant in my blood. Whenever you drink it, do this as a memorial of me." Whenever you eat this bread, then, and drink this cup, you are proclaiming the Lord's death until he comes. Therefore anyone who eats the bread or drinks the cup of the Lord in an unworthy way will have to answer for the body and blood of the Lord.

Everyone is to examine himself and only then eat of the bread or drink from the cup; because a person who eats and drinks

without recognising the body is eating and drinking judgement on himself. (. . .)

So then, my brothers, when you meet for the Meal, wait for each other. Anyone who is hungry should eat at home. Then your meeting will not bring judgement upon you.

Spiritual gifts 12: 1, 3

I want you to be quite certain about the gifts of the Spirit. (. . .) Nobody is able to say, "Jesus is Lord" except in the Holy Spirit.

12: 4–30

There are many different gifts, but it is always the same Spirit; there are many different ways of serving, but it is always the same Lord. There are many different forms of activity, but in everybody it is the same God who is at work in them all. The particular manifestation of the Spirit is given to each person for the general good. One person is given the gift of being able to speak words of wisdom from the Holy Spirit; to another the gift of being able to speak words of knowledge, in accordance with the same Spirit; to another, faith, from the same Spirit; and to another, the gifts of healing, through this one Spirit; to another, the working of miracles; to another, prophecy; to another, the power of distinguishing spirits; to one, the gift of different tongues and to another, the interpretation of tongues. But in all these the one and same Spirit is at work distributing his gifts to each individual as he pleases.

For just as the human body is a single unit although it has many parts — all the many parts of the body still making up one single body — so it is with Christ. We were baptised into one body in a single Spirit, Jews as well as Greeks, slaves as well as free men, and we were all given the same Spirit to drink. (. . .)

If one part is hurt, all the parts share its pain. And if one part is honoured, all the parts share its joy.

Now you are the body of Christ, each of you with a part to play in the whole. And in the Church those whom God has appointed are, first apostles, secondly prophets, thirdly teachers. Then there are those with miraculous powers, then gifts of healing, helpful acts, guidance, various kinds of tongues. Are all of them apostles? Or all prophets? Or all teachers? Or all miracle-workers? Do all have the gifts of healing? Do all of them speak in tongues and all interpret them?

Paul reacted against the ecstatic experiences of some Christians who, rightly or wrongly, claimed to have been inspired by the Holy Spirit. The presence of the Spirit can be seen through many different gifts. But, behind these gifts, it is always the same Spirit who cannot change the way he behaves.

The order of importance in gifts
Hymn to Love

12: 31

Set your mind on the higher gifts. And now I am going to put before you the best way of all.

13: 1–13

If I speak with both human and angelic languages but I do not have love, I am no more than a gong booming or a cymbal clashing. And if I have the power of prophecy, and understand all mysteries and knowledge, and if I have all the faith necessary to move mountains — if I am without love, I am nothing. If I should give away everything I have to the poor, and even give up my body to be burned — if I am without love, it will do me no good whatever.

Love is always patient and kind; love is never jealous; love is not boastful or conceited, it is never rude and never seeks its own advantage, it does not take offence or keep a record of wrongs. Love does not rejoice at wrongdoing, but finds its joy in the truth. It is always ready to make allowances, to trust, to hope and to endure whatever comes. (. . .) As it is, these remain: faith, hope and love. But the greatest of them is love.

In the end, love is the only essential quality for a Christian. The other gifts of the Spirit are only temporary while love lasts forever. It is love that will eventually enable us to know God as well as he now knows us.

3. THE RESURRECTION OF THE DEAD

15: 3–22

I want you to know what I myself received: that Christ died for our sins, according to the scriptures, and that he was buried; and that on the third day, he was raised to life, according to the scriptures; and that he appeared to Cephas; and later to the Twelve. Next he appeared to more than five hundred of the brothers at the same time, most of whom are still alive, though some have fallen asleep. Then he appeared to James, and then to all the apostles. Last of all he appeared to me too, as though I was a child who was born at the wrong time. (. . .)

Anyway, whether it was they or I, this is what we preach and what you believed.

Now if we preach that Christ has been raised from the dead, how can some of you be saying that there is no resurrection of the dead? If there is no resurrection of the dead, then Christ cannot have been raised either. But if Christ has not been raised, then our preaching is empty and so is your faith. (. . .) If our hope in Christ has been for this life only, we are to be pitied more than all other people.

In fact, however, Christ has been raised from the dead, as the first-fruits of all who have fallen asleep. For just as death came through one man, so the resurrection of the dead has also come through one man. Just as all die in Adam, so in Christ all will be brought to life.

15: 58

So, my dear brothers, keep firm and immovable, always full of energy for the Lord's work, being sure that nothing you do in the Lord's service is ever wasted.

> People have sometimes tried to limit the message of the gospel to speaking about our morals and the way we treat other people. The "Good News" is above all the message of the death and resurrection of Jesus. Christian life involves a relationship with the *living* Jesus.

Paul told the Corinthians about his travelling plans after having recommended that a collection be taken for the troubled church in Jerusalem. He also sent a few more personal messages. For example, he repeated his faith in Jesus' return and ended:

16: 23–4

The grace of the Lord Jesus Christ be with you.
My love is with you all in Christ Jesus.

SECOND LETTER TO THE CORINTHIANS

All Christians who serve the Church will sooner or later want to express their feelings: both their joy at seeing the fruits of their hard work but also their dismay at the hugeness of the task. They may also protest against lack of understanding and opposition, or state their care for those who have had such sacrifices made for them. But aren't these feelings too human? Isn't passion a form of pride? Shouldn't we accept failure as Jesus did and be strong in our belief that what seems to be death gives birth to life?

Those who are asking themselves these questions should read the second letter to the Corinthians. They will find their problems mirrored there and see how one of the apostles coped with them; Paul wrote about them with deep feeling.

Paul completed his third missionary voyage around AD 56. He was facing great difficulties at that time, but was also filled with joy when he saw the Church growing everywhere. Corinth was still a black spot though, and some people opposed his work by accusing him of weakness and self-interest. He had to send them a severe letter. Titus then went to visit the community on Paul's behalf and brought better news after rejoining him in Macedonia. The apostle was relieved and dictated another letter in which he could at last explain his position, tell them he forgave them and give encouragement to the repentant Corinthians. He took the opportunity to relaunch a collection for the Church in Jerusalem which was in financial difficulties. He had a heartfelt interest in this plan because it demonstrated the togetherness of the Church everywhere.

The second letter to the Corinthians probably draws together into a single text all — or most — of his letters. Its interest for us lies in the way it shows how action and thought were linked in Paul's life. He thought about what happened to him and saw continually the presence of the Father, the Son and the Holy Spirit in it. He reflected on his work in the light of Jesus' death and resurrection. It was through his weakness that God had pushed forward the work of salvation. This certainly made him feel humble and aware of the action of grace. It also gave him the courage he needed to complete the work he had already begun.

1. A LOOK BACK OVER INCIDENTS IN THE PAST

Paul had promised to visit Corinth and had been criticised for postponing the visit. Now he could explain why: a member of the community had attacked him very viciously. The incident had caused a scandal. Paul had thought it best not to come at such a tense time, and had written a severe letter instead. The guilty party had now repented and should be forgiven.

The apostle had travelled widely since leaving Ephesus. He was amazed by the ministry he was called to: he cried out with joy at being able to spread the "sweet aroma of Christ" everywhere and to help to spread the "new covenant" of the Spirit. Those who saw only the difficulties of his life pitied him: it was true that he seemed to have nothing at all. But in reality, how rich he was!

The apostle's mission

Here, again, Paul insisted on the huge contrast between the poverty of the messenger and the splendour of his mission.

4: 7–14

But we hold this treasure in clay pots so that it can clearly be seen that it is God's immense power and not our own. We face every kind of hardship, but we are never distressed; we see no way out but we never despair; we are persecuted but never abandoned; knocked down, but still have some life in us. We always carry with us in our body the death of Jesus so that the life of Jesus, too, may be seen in our body. Indeed, while we are still alive, we are continually being handed over to death, for the sake of Jesus, so that the life of Jesus, too, may be seen in our mortal bodies. In us, then, death is at work; in you, life.

But as scripture says: *I believed and therefore I spoke*, and we have the same spirit of faith; we, too, believe and therefore we, too, speak, realising that he who raised up the Lord Jesus will raise us up with Jesus in our turn, and bring us to himself — and you as well.

He had been given an extraordinary mission although he was no better than anyone else.

Paul wanted his readers to understand that his motivation was the love of God. That love was shown in the person of Jesus. The apostle saw those around him in a totally new way having been raised up by Jesus. He no longer looked at things from a human point of view, just as Jesus had not acted with human strength. What he saw in them was the new, spiritual, person created by the Lord.

2. THE ORGANISATION OF THE COLLECTION

Paul reminded the Corinthians that they themselves had started off the collection for the Church in Jerusalem, which was in financial difficulties. He told them about the generosity of the Macedonian Christians, who had responded to the Corinthian appeal. He then urged those he is writing to not to let the others outdo them in generosity.

8: 9, 13–14
You are well aware of the generosity which our Lord Jesus Christ had, that, although he was rich, he became poor for your sake, so that you should become rich through his poverty. (. . .)

It is not that you should leave yourselves in hardship in order to help those in need; but there should be a fair balance. What you have to spare at present can make up for what they are lacking, and another time they may be able to help you. (. . .)

The division of wealth: Paul founded a Church tradition when he recalled the way in which Christ had made himself poor in order to make us rich spiritually.

3. PAUL DEFENDS HIMSELF AGAINST HIS ACCUSERS

Some people accused Paul of being too scared to say what he thought in front of people. In fact, he was hoping not to have to be severe with them during his next visit. They also accused him of being ambitious although his only claim to glory was seeing the way God was working through him. Why did the community he had founded let itself be carried away by the "super-apostles" with their clever words?

Did Paul have to justify himself in this way?

11: 21—12: 1

This part of the letter is probably an extract from the warning letter with which Paul had reacted against his accusers. It was later added to the end of what we now call the second letter to the Corinthians. The apostle defended himself strongly and sometimes with biting sarcasm against those who thought themselves better than he was. He himself could have boasted quite easily about all sorts of things but realised how stupid all boasting really was: the true strength of God was most evident in the weakness of those he used as his instruments.

Whatever bold claims anyone makes — now I am talking like a fool — I can make them too. Are they Hebrews? So am I. Are they Israelites? So am I. Are they descendants of Abraham? So am I. Are they servants of Christ? I am talking nonsense — I am too, and more than they are: I have done more work, I have been in prison more, I have been whipped more severely, many times in danger of death. Five times I have been given the thirty-nine lashes by the Jews. Three times I have been beaten with sticks; once I was stoned, three times I have been shipwrecked. Once I have been in the open sea for a night and a day. Continually on the road, I have been in danger from rivers, in danger from robbers, in danger from my own people and in danger from the gentiles, in danger in the towns and in danger in the open country, in danger at sea and in danger from people pretending to be brothers; I have worked tirelessly for many nights without sleep; I have been hungry and thirsty, and often altogether without food or drink; I have been cold and had nothing to wear. And, besides all the other things, there is, day in day out, the pressure on me of my concern for all the churches. If anyone becomes weak, then I become weak as well; and when anyone is made to fall, I burn in agony myself. (. . .)

I am boasting because I have to. Not that it does any good, but I will move on to visions and revelations from the Lord. (. . .)

12: 7–10

That is why, to stop me becoming proud about these amazing revelations, I was given a thorn in the flesh, a messenger from Satan to batter me and prevent me from getting above myself. Three times I have pleaded with the Lord to take it away from me; but he has answered me, "My grace is enough for you: for my strength is shown in weakness." It is, then, about my weaknesses that I am happiest of all to boast, so that the power of Christ can be shown through me. (. . .) For it is when I am weak that I am strong.

Paul's main concern was not to defend himself personally: other peoples' opinion of him did not matter at all. What did matter was that the Corinthians should find the right path, and that is why Paul wanted to end the in-fighting which was harming the community.

13: 11–13

The Church uses the formula of Paul's greeting as a call to the Eucharist.

To end then, brothers, we wish you joy; try to grow perfect; encourage one another; be of one mind and live in peace, and the God of love and peace will be with you. (. . .) The grace of the Lord Jesus Christ, the love of God and the fellowship of the Holy Spirit be with you all.

LETTER TO THE GALATIANS

The Council of Jerusalem (described in Acts chapter 15) was a turning-point in the spread of the gospel. From that moment it became clear that it was possible to be a Christian without keeping all the Jewish practices, particularly that of circumcision: salvation depended on faith in the God who saved people freely rather than obeying a set of rules.

Paul was able to go out into the gentile world because he was so sure about this. He founded a very enthusiastic Christian community in Galatia in what is now northern Turkey.

There were some Christians who were attached to the old ways, who stirred up trouble by claiming that it was impossible to be a believer without obeying the rules. The Galatians were convinced.

Paul's reaction was strong because he saw this as a dangerous teaching. It was fine for the Jews themselves to live with their customs; it was not acceptable to claim that these were indispensable, because that would go against the message of the Gospels. Jesus did not come to trap people with rules and regulations — he came to bring them the freedom of the Spirit. Those who claimed otherwise were giving a false view of God by turning him into a kind of magistrate. In fact, God is above all a loving and merciful Father, who wants people to open themselves with thankfulness to the gift he has made to them of himself in the person of Jesus.

Paul defends his work

It was by relying on his personal experience of the risen Jesus that Paul wrote to the Galatians. He reminded them how he had been led to the doctrine he was now defending. He had initially been an enthusiastic supporter of the Jewish system of Law to the point of actively persecuting Christians. But Christ had opened his eyes and, since his conversion, he had become a living witness to the work of God which brings freedom.

Some Christians were critical of him. But the apostles had come round to his point of view by the time of the Council of Jerusalem. They did not defend him easily at first. Peter himself hesitated for a long time before taking the final step to break down the barriers created by the Jewish legal system (Acts 10); Paul even had to reproach him and Peter realised he was wrong.

Reflections on doctrine

The Galatians had experienced inner renewal by faith. Why did they want to return to a system of practices which would inhibit them? They should reread the Scriptures! Abraham was not saved by keeping an impossibly demanding set of rules but by believing in the divine promise. Those who believe are made right with God.

3: 26–9

For all of you are the children of God, through faith, in Christ Jesus. Every one of you that has been baptised has been clothed in Christ. There can be neither Jew nor Greek, there can be neither slave nor free man, there can be neither male nor female — for you are all one in Christ Jesus. And simply by being Christ's, you are children of Abraham, the heirs named in the promise.

Christians are equal in all things and are the true heirs of Abraham because they have the same Spirit.

4: 4–7
When the right time came, God sent his Son, born of a woman, born under the Law, to redeem the subjects of the Law, so that we could receive adoption as sons. As you are sons, God has sent into our hearts the Spirit of his Son crying, "*Abba*, Father". So you are no longer a slave, but a son; and if a son, then an heir, by God's own act.

Practical conclusions 5: 1
Christ set us free, so that we should remain free. Stand firm, then, and do not let yourselves be put under a yoke of slavery again.

5: 13–14
After all, brothers,
you were called to be free.
Do not use your freedom as an excuse
to be selfish. Be servants to one another
in love, since the whole of the Law can be summed up
in the one commandment: *You must love your
neighbour as yourself.*

5: 22–5
The fruit of the Spirit is love, joy, peace, patience, kindness, goodness, trustfulness, gentleness and self-control. There is no law against such things as these. All who belong to Christ Jesus have crucified self with all its passions and its desires. Since we are living by the Spirit, let our behaviour be guided by the Spirit.

LETTER TO THE EPHESIANS

orced inactivity often gives us the opportunity to think about things and sort them out; and the past appears in a new light. Such was Paul's experience.

Paul had just written to the Colossians between AD 61 and AD 63. He now took up his discussion of previous points but this time in greater depth. He considered the great design of God he was caught up in to be amazing: the Lord wanted to gather all people together in unity to follow Jesus. The Son of man was like the head of an immense body which was rich in its wide variety of believers. Christians should be aware of the beauty of their call and let themselves be filled with love.

These thoughts led Paul to give praise to God who had called him to take an active part in the work of salvation. This work showed him the splendour of the divine "mystery" in the world.

The mystery of salvation and of the Church

1: 3–5

Blessed be the God and Father of our Lord Jesus Christ, who has blessed us with all the spiritual blessings of heaven in Christ. Thus he chose us in Christ before the world was made to be holy and without fault before him in love, marking us out for himself beforehand, to be adopted sons, through Jesus Christ. (. . .)

> Paul gave glory to God as he thought about the divine plan to save the world through Jesus.

1: 22–3

He is above all things, the head of the Church, which is his Body, the fullness of him who fills all in all.

In Jesus, God restores unity to humankind

2: 13–22

Now in Christ Jesus, you that used to be so far off have been brought close, by the blood of Christ.

For he is the peace between us and has brought the two together to be one people, breaking down the barrier which used to keep them apart (. . .) to create in himself one New Man out of the two of them to restore peace and to reconcile them both to God in one Body through the cross. In his own person he killed the hostility. He came to bring the good news of *peace to you who were far away and peace to those who were near.* Through him, then, in the one Spirit we have free access to the Father.

So you are no longer strangers or foreign visitors. You are fellow-citizens with the holy people of God and part of God's household.

> There had been a wide gulf between Jews and gentiles but that was changed now. The Greeks had once been foreigners to the chosen people, but Paul was now able to say to them: you are members in your own right of the great family of God. Jesus had broken down the old barriers.

You are built upon the foundations of the apostles and prophets, and Christ Jesus himself is the cornerstone. (. . .) In him, you too are being built up into a dwelling-place of God in the Spirit.

Paul's prayer 3: 14–20

Paul prayed fervently that his readers might open their hearts to the message of the wonderful love of Christ.

This, then, is what I pray, kneeling before the Father, from whom every family takes its name in heaven or on earth. In the richness of his glory may he, through his Spirit, enable you to grow firm in power in your inner self; may Christ live in your hearts through faith, and may you be planted in love and built on love. Then, with all God's holy people, you will have the strength to grasp the breadth and the length, the height and the depth; so that, knowing the love of Christ, which is beyond knowledge, you may be filled with the utter fullness of God.

Glory be to him whose power, working in us, can do infinitely more than we can ask or imagine.

A call to a new life 4: 1–6, 13

Christians should live a life worthy of their call. Each should be filled with love right where they are, caught up in the great flow of people making their way to God led by Jesus. Christ and the Christians together would then form a single body, and Christ would make sure that together they all made progress.

I, the prisoner in the Lord, encourage you therefore to lead a life worthy of the call which you have received. With all humility and gentleness, and with patience, support each other in love. Take every care to keep the unity of the Spirit by the peace that binds you together. There is one Body, one Spirit, just as one hope is the goal of your calling by God. There is one Lord, one faith, one baptism, and one God and Father of all, over all, through all and within all. (. . .)

So we will all reach unity in faith and knowledge of the Son of God and form the perfect Man, fully mature with the fullness of Christ himself.

5: 1–2

As God's dear children, then, try to be like him, and follow Christ by loving as he loved you (. . .).

Paul made clear what the call could mean in different circumstances: for the young and for adults, and for slaves. He gives particular importance to the relationship between married couples:

Christian marriage 5: 25–33

Husbands should love their wives, just as Christ loved the Church. He gave himself for her to make her holy by washing her in water with a word. When he took the Church to himself he wanted her to be glorious, with no spot or wrinkle or anything like that, but holy and faultless. In the same way, husbands must love their wives as they love their own bodies. For a man to love his wife is for him to love himself. A man never hates his own body, but he feeds it and looks after it. That is exactly how Christ treats the Church, because we are parts of his Body. *This is why a man leaves his father and mother and becomes joined to his wife, and the two become one flesh.* This mystery has great significance, but I am applying it to Christ and the Church. To sum up: you also, each one of you, must love his wife as he loves himself; and every wife must respect her husband.

The relationship of a husband to his wife should be similar to that which links Christ to his Church: it should be based entirely on devotion and service. Jesus united himself with humanity as if to a wife whom he wished to make perfect. He purified her through baptism and watched over her with love.

This is the suggested model for love within marriage.

The spiritual battle

6: 11, 14–18
Put on the full armour of God so as to be able to resist the devil's tactics. (. . .)
So stand your ground, with *truth as a belt*

round your waist, and
righteousness as a breastplate,
wearing for shoes on your feet *the eagerness to spread the gospel of peace.* Always carry the shield of faith so that you can use it to put out the burning arrows of the Evil One. And then you must take *salvation as your helmet* and the sword of the Spirit, that is, the word of God. Live a life of prayer, asking God for his help. Keep praying in the Spirit on every possible occasion.

It is important to be armed against the forces of evil in this world. But our weapons must also be spiritual because it is a spiritual battle.

LETTER TO THE PHILIPPIANS

P aul had just been through a difficult time. He was a prisoner and had even been on the verge of being put to death. He now knew that he would soon be released and so he would be able to continue his work.

The Christians of Philippi had supported Paul during his imprisonment and had even sent someone to help him. The apostle had founded a community in the middle of a gentile land: the conversions had been sincere and the new Christians had shown great love towards their missionary. Paul wanted to thank them for their latest expressions of support and took the opportunity to talk freely about his deepest thoughts. He told them of the deep joy that carried him along and which gave him a feeling of amazing freedom. Christ had taken hold of him and only Christ mattered to him from that moment, even while Paul was in prison. He wrote for his friends one of the most magnificent hymns that we possess about Christ.

Keep humility in love

The true Christian attitude is being humble rather than competitive. Jesus himself set the example. Paul remembered this when he mentioned a text which may have been a early hymn used in worship. It is the oldest text expressing the Christian faith in the Son of God, as seen in the person of Jesus.

1: 8, 2: 1—11

For God will be my witness of how much I long for you all with the warm longing of Christ Jesus (. . .). So if in Christ there is anything that will move you, any comfort in love, any fellowship in the Spirit, any warmth or sympathy — I appeal to you, make my joy complete by being of a single mind, one in love, one in heart and one in mind. Do nothing out of jealousy or vanity; instead, in humility think of others as better than yourselves. Do not look after your own interests but those of others. Make your own the mind of Christ Jesus:

Who, being in the form of God, did not count equality with God something to be grasped.

But he emptied himself, taking the form of a slave, becoming as human beings are.

Being in every way like a human being, he was humbler yet, even to accepting death, death on a cross.

And for this God raised him high, and gave him the name, which is above all other names;

so that *all beings* in the heavens, on earth and in the underworld, *should bend the knee* at the name of Jesus

and that *every tongue should acknowledge* Jesus Christ as Lord, to the glory of God the Father.

The Philippians should shine out like lights in a corrupt world by living in Jesus' way as Paul himself did. They should live only for Christ's return.

3: 7–16

The advantages I once had I now consider as losses. Yes, I will go further: I count everything else as loss for the sake of knowing Christ Jesus my Lord. For him I have accepted the loss of all other things, and look on them all as rubbish if only I can gain Christ and be given a place in him, with the righteousness I have gained not from the Law, but through faith in Christ, a righteousness from God, based on faith. I want to know him and the power of his resurrection, and share in his sufferings by becoming like him in his death, striving towards the goal of resurrection from the dead. Not that I have yet reached my goal nor am yet perfect. I am still pressing on to take hold of the prize for which Christ Jesus took hold of me. (. . .) I am straining forward to what lies in front and I am racing towards the finishing line to win the prize of God's heavenly call in Christ Jesus. (. . .). Meanwhile, let us go forward from the point we have each reached.

> Paul said that there was nothing else worth being proud of when compared with the one really essential thing in life: the knowledge of Jesus.

Paul invites his readers to share in his joy after having written a few last recommendations:

4: 4–7

Always be joyful, then, in the Lord; I repeat, be joyful. (. . .) The Lord is near. Do not worry about anything. Tell God all your desires of every kind in prayer and petition, always being grateful, and the peace of God which is beyond our understanding will guard your hearts and your thoughts in Christ Jesus.

LETTER TO THE COLOSSIANS

C hristians are often tempted to let themselves be carried away by fashionable ideas and to forget the richness of their own faith. This was already true in Paul's day: previously, the apostle had founded a Christian community in Colossae. Some preachers were now spreading a doctrine which they claimed was only for a select few (gnosticism). It involved intellectual ideas about angels and had been taken from Jewish texts of that time, perhaps mingled with an Asiatic doctrine about the stars. Christ's part in all this was not clear.

Paul's reaction was to emphasise the central position of Christ in the universe. His view was that Christ reflected God: coming into the world and gradually revealing himself, more and more, until the moment when he showed himself fully in the person of Jesus. He had already been at work from the moment of the creation of the world. Whatever ideas people might have about angels, it should not lead them to forget what really mattered. The new practices suggested by fashionable theories had no meaning at all. What mattered was to be one with Christ. The believers should place the cross at the centre of their thinking: that was the true source of salvation. It brought the "new person" into being, who could then live in the recognition and action of the grace of God who loves us all.

1. The central place of Christ in God's work
Paul prayed for those he was writing to, to grow in faith:

1: 12–20

The power of Christ penetrates the whole of creation. He gives it life and meaning. Nothing is greater than he is. Raised from the dead, he is the head of the new creation, of the Church. It is through him that God fully realises his work of reconciliation and peace.

We give thanks with joy to the Father who has made you able to share the lot of God's holy people and with them to inherit the light.

Because that is what he has done. He has rescued us from the power of darkness and brought us into the kingdom of the Son that he loves, and in him we enjoy our freedom, the forgiveness of sin. He is the image of the unseen God, the first-born of all creation, for in him all things were created in heaven and on earth: everything visible and everything invisible, thrones, ruling forces, sovereignties, powers — all things were created through him and for him. He exists before all things and in him all things hold together, and he is the Head of the Body, that is, the Church. He is the Beginning, the first-born from the dead, so that he should be supreme in every way; because God wanted all fullness to be found in him and through him to reconcile all things to him, everything in heaven and everything on earth, by making peace through his death on the cross.

After having reminded the Colossians of his call to tell the gentile peoples about the wonderful message of Christ, Paul told them how much he cared about their faith:

2: 6–9

So then, as you received Jesus as Lord and Christ, now live your lives in him, be rooted in him and built up on him, held firm by the faith you have been taught, and overflowing with thanksgiving.

Make sure that no one takes you captive with an empty "philosophy" of the kind that human beings hand on, based on the principles of this world and not on Christ. In him, in bodily form, lives all the fullness of the divine nature.

Paul then asked them to leave behind the rituals they practised to get in touch with the invisible world. These drew believers' attention away from the only important point: their place in the "Body of Christ". Everything else was only religious in its outward appearance.

2. Principles of the Christian life

3: 9–15

You have stripped off your old behaviour with your old self, and you have put on a new self which is being transformed in the image of its Creator, in order to bring you to a full knowledge of him. There is no room for distinction between Greek and Jew, between the circumcised and uncircumcised, or between barbarian and Scythian, slave and free. There is only Christ: he is everything and he is in everything.

As the chosen of God, then, the holy people whom he loves, you are to be clothed in heartfelt compassion, in generosity and humility, gentleness and patience. Bear with one another; forgive each other if you have any reason to make a complaint against another. The Lord has forgiven you; now you must do the same. But above all, put on love, the perfect bond. And may the peace of Christ reign in your hearts, because it is for this that you were called together in one body. Always be thankful.

> Christians should reject behaviour linked to the "old person". Having taken on their "new person", they should live in the image of the God who created them. They are now united in Jesus who lives in them all. So they should be filled with love.

FIRST LETTER TO THE THESSALONIANS

For many people, the idea of the end of the world is frightening. The early Christians were different because they lived in joyful expectation of Christ's return which was to mark the end of time. Furthermore, they believed that he would come soon. That is the main point in Paul's letter to his readers in Thessalonica (now called Salonica).

The apostle only stayed in the city for a short time in AD 50 because the Jews soon threw him out. But he set up a stable little community with new believers from among the gentiles. Paul sent his disciple Timothy to get news of the small church as soon as he reached Athens. He was reassured and wrote to them.

4: 13–14

For the believer, faith in the resurrection changes the meaning of death. Even when experiencing pain it is possible to hope.

We want you to be quite certain, brothers, on the subject of death. You do not need to grieve, as others do who have no hope. We believe that Jesus died and rose again, and that in the same way God will bring with him those who have fallen asleep in Jesus.

Paul described that day using traditional Jewish imagery to represent the destruction of the earth, and the Lord coming down from the heavens. He concluded:

4: 17—5: 10

Paul himself, at the beginning of his ministry, seems to have thought that the return of Christ was near. But he wisely refused to predict a date and simply advised the Thessalonian Christians to be ready at all times. This is like the attentive servant waiting for his master who is mentioned in the Gospels.

Then we shall be with the Lord for ever. With such thoughts as these, then, you should encourage one another.

About times and dates, brothers, there is no need to write to you for you are well aware in any case that the Day of the Lord is going to come like a thief in the night. It is when people are saying, "How quiet and peaceful it is" that sudden destruction falls on them, as suddenly as labour pains come on a pregnant woman; and there is no escape.

But you, brothers, do not live in the dark, that the Day should surprise you like a thief. No, you are all children of light and children of the day: we do not belong to the night or to darkness, so we should not go on sleeping, as everyone else does, but stay wide awake and sober. (. . .) God destined us not for his anger, but to win salvation through our Lord Jesus Christ, who died for us so that, awake or asleep, we should still live united to him.

Paul then finished his letter with a few reminders about the demands of communal living and with a prayer for the grace of God.

SECOND LETTER TO THE THESSALONIANS

Paul's first letter to the Christians in Thessalonica seems to have been the cause of a somewhat Utopian enthusiasm. Why bother to work if the Lord was returning soon? This caused some trouble in the community and some of the Christians began to live on the efforts of others.

Paul called them back to order. Christians had first to go through times of trial whatever the date of the Lord's return. The young community probably knew plenty about suffering already because they lived in a time of persecution. They had worse to expect, however, with the coming of the "adversary" or "evil one" (which means the instrument of Satan). The return of Christ could only take place following that event (here Paul seems to be echoing certain Jewish writings which represented the triumph of God at the end of a terrible battle against the ultimate enemy).

The most important thing was for the community to put some order back into its life:

3: 6–16

In the name of the Lord Jesus Christ, we ask you, brothers, to keep away from any of the brothers who lives an undisciplined life and does not follow the teaching you received from us.

You know how you should take us as your model: we were not undisciplined when we were with you, nor did we ever ask anyone to give us the food we ate; no, we worked hard, night and day, so as not to be a burden on any of you. (. . .)

When we were with you, we gave you this rule: not to let anyone eat who refused to work. Now we hear that there are some of you who are living lives without any discipline, doing no work themselves but interfering with other people's. In the Lord Jesus Christ, we urge and call on people of this kind to go on quietly working and earning the food that they eat.

My brothers, never grow tired of doing what is right. (. . .)

May the Lord of peace himself give you peace at all times and in every way. The Lord be with you all.

Hillel, a famous rabbi who lived at the same time as Jesus, expressed the same idea when he said: "where there are no human beings, make every effort to be a human being".

A person with real faith would never be content to live off other people. On the contrary, believers express the strength of their faith by accepting their present responsibilities within the community.

THE PASTORAL EPISTLES

A group may form on the spur of the moment in a fit of enthusiasm. But eventually it will have to face the problems of organisation, or the initial enthusiasm will vanish amid general disorder.

The Pastoral Epistles are three letters giving advice about this organisation. They are addressed to pastors, which is the name given to the leaders of Christian communities.

The letters were signed by Paul but might not really be from him since the style is so different from the apostle's other letters. It is possible that he either asked one of his secretaries to write them, or that they were written by one of his followers, who was deliberately copying Paul's own work.

The letters were addressed to two community leaders (traditionally "bishops") who had been Paul's companions during his missionary voyages.

The interesting thing about them is that they show how, in the Church, even the most spiritual people cannot afford to ignore practical problems concerning the organisation of the group.

FIRST LETTER TO TIMOTHY

Paul reminded his disciple of the responsibility he had been given: he should take special care to fight against false teaching about salvation. There would always be people who were tempted to go back to the old system of the Jewish Law and Paul knew well that the Law was only a guide-line for those who were already on the slippery slope to sin. It could not save anyone. God's salvation was free as experienced first-hand by the apostle.

Paul returned constantly to the experience that had changed his life: the experience of the mercy of God, who came to seek him out when he was still a sinner. It was because of this that he believed in God's desire to save all people.

Paul on his own calling
1: 12–16
I thank Christ Jesus our Lord, who has given me strength. He considered me faithful enough to call me into his service, even though I used to be a blasphemer, a persecutor and an insolent man. He showed me mercy, however, because I acted in ignorance, a stranger to the faith. But the grace of our Lord filled me with faith and with the love that is in Christ Jesus. Here is a saying that you can rely on and nobody should doubt: that Christ Jesus came into the world to save sinners. I myself am the greatest of them. And if he was merciful to me, it is because Jesus Christ meant to show the full extent of his patience, making me an example for all the other people who were later to trust in him for eternal life.

Timothy himself should fight the good fight and never waver from the true faith. He should make sure that the believers continued to pray constantly and that the women kept their place in the meetings. He should be careful in his choice of bishops and deacons since the men chosen were to be worthy and competent. It was necessary to take into account the different living circumstances of the believers, and Paul gave advice to the teachers of the faith and the ''elders'' who led the life of the community concerning the treatment of widows, and slaves. The apostle ended the letter with a solemn call upon Timothy:

6: 12–16

Fight the good fight of faith and win the eternal life to which you were called and for which you made your noble profession of faith before many witnesses. Now, before God, who gives life to all things, and before Jesus Christ, who witnessed to his noble profession of faith before Pontius Pilate, I urge you to do all that you have been told, without any failures, until the appearing of our Lord Jesus Christ, who at the due time will be revealed by God, the blessed and only Ruler of all, the King of kings and the Lord of lords, who alone is immortal, whose home is in inaccessible light, whom no human being has seen or is able to see: to him be honour and everlasting power. Amen.

Paul was probably referring to the profession of faith which Timothy had made when he was baptised.

SECOND LETTER TO TIMOTHY

P aul was happy to make contact again with his dear friend. He reminded him of his responsibility.

2: 1–2

As for you, my dear son, be strong in the grace which is in Christ Jesus. Pass on to reliable people what you have heard from me through many witnesses so that they in turn will be able to teach others.

2: 8–13

Remember, ''Jesus Christ risen from the dead, a descendant of David'', according to my gospel. It is on account of this that I have to put up with suffering, even to being chained like a criminal. But God's message cannot be chained up. So I persevere for the sake of those who are chosen, so that they, too, may obtain the salvation that is in Christ Jesus with eternal glory.

    Here is a saying that you can rely on:

Paul was quoting a fragment of an early hymn which expressed the faith of the first Christians.

If we have died with him, then we shall live with him.
If we persevere, then we shall reign with him.
If we disown him, then he will disown us.
If we are faithless, he is faithful still, for he cannot disown his own self.

Paul sent his disciple a final appeal after warning him against those who taught false doctrines:

4: 1–5

Before God and before Christ Jesus who is to be judge of the living and the dead, I charge you, in the name of his appearing and of his kingdom: preach the message and, welcome or unwelcome, insist on it. Disprove false teaching, correct error, give encouragement — but do all with patience and with a desire to instruct. The time is sure to come when people will not accept sound teaching, but their ears will be itching for anything new and they will collect for themselves a whole series of teachers according to their own tastes; and then they will shut their ears to the truth and will turn to myths. But you must keep steady all the time; put up with suffering; do the work of preaching the gospel; fulfil the service asked of you.

This was a sort of testament from Paul to his disciple. He left him everything he had lived for: the word of God.

LETTER TO TITUS

Titus was continuing the work of spreading the gospel in Crete. Paul sent him several pieces of advice similar to those given to Timothy. Paul reminded him of the role of the bishops and elders and repeated the necessity of fighting against false doctrines. He underlined once more the idea of the new life the believers ought to lead: they must remember the day when God revealed all his goodness to them:

3: 4–7

Paul returned constantly to the basis of faith and the new life of all Christians: the salvation represented by Jesus Christ.

But when the kindness and love of God our Saviour for humanity were revealed, it was not because of any righteous actions we had done ourselves; it was for no reason except his own faithful love that he saved us, through cleansing water to give us new birth and through the Holy Spirit to give us new life. He has so generously poured this Spirit over us through Jesus Christ our Saviour; so that, justified by his grace, we should become heirs in hope of eternal life.

LETTER TO PHILEMON

There have always been arguments about whether we need to change society in order to make people good, or whether we first have to make people good so that society can change accordingly.

Nobody even thought about changing society in Paul's day. Some of the people on the edges of society occasionally rebelled against their allotted lives. Paul himself seems to have thought that the social order established by the Romans had at least brought peace in spite of its faults.

Paul then found himself in prison in Rome awaiting trial following his conflict with the Jews (Acts 21–22). It was while Paul was in Rome that he got to know Onesimus, a slave who had run away from his master, Philemon. Paul converted Onesimus to the faith and, by doing so, "gave him life".

Philemon had previously been converted to Christianity by Paul. The apostle sent his former slave back to him. Paul wrote to Philemon saying not only that he should forgive Onesimus but that he should welcome him as a brother. He even suggested that Philemon should free the slave.

By doing so, he showed that he was no revolutionary: slavery was considered perfectly normal in the society of his day. He was not suggesting new laws but showing that the fact of being a Christian completely changed relationships between people. Masters and slaves could become brothers, which was something that no decree of the abolition of slavery could ever enforce.

Among other things, he wrote:

9–20

I am speaking to you as Paul, an old man, and now also a prisoner of Christ Jesus. I am making a request on behalf of a child of mine, whose father I became while wearing these chains: I mean Onesimus. He was of no use to you before, but now he is useful both to you and to me. I am sending him back to you — that is to say, sending you my own heart. I should have liked to keep him with me; he could have been a substitute for you, to help me while I am in the chains that the gospel has brought me. However, I did not want to do anything without your consent (. . .). Perhaps you lost him for a time, so that you could have him back for ever, no longer as a slave, but something much better than a slave, a dear brother (. . .). Welcome him as you would me. If he has wronged you in any way or owes you anything, put it down to my account. I am writing this in my own hand. I, Paul, shall pay it back. But think of the debt, that you owe me: your very self. Well then, brother, I am counting on you, in the Lord.

Paul was a prisoner himself when he pleaded for the slave to be freed.

LETTER TO THE HEBREWS

Where are the magnificent ceremonies we used to have? We often hear old people talking nostalgically about the splendour of the Church in the past.

That was also the view of some Christian converts from Judaism, who missed the great ceremonies of the Temple in Jerusalem with their processions of priests and their solemn rites.

A Christian scholar answered their questions around the year AD 60. His thoughts were circulated in the form of a letter and later attributed to Paul. Perhaps the apostle did contribute to publicising the letter's contents. But it is possible that the real author was a famous preacher called Apollos who was highly thought of by Paul.

The scholar's answer, which shows an amazing grasp of biblical teaching, was as follows. Never look back on the past with regret because it is over and done with. Christ came to reveal the true reality to us: he accomplished the real sacrifice God wanted which was the sacrifice to end all sacrifices: he responded with love to the will of the Father and gave himself. In a sense he was the only true priest ever.

The author also explained that the past history of the chosen people was all a preparation for its own end in Jesus.

This letter is difficult for us because it deals methodically with all the elements of the Jewish liturgy in turn. The great interest of this letter is that it shows us the nature of the real sacrifice God wants from us: the gift of ourselves through love.

Prologue
1: 1–3

The introduction summarises in a few words the way in which throughout history God has revealed more and more of his purposes until it reached its climax in the gift of his Son. The full glory of the Father could be seen in him and he made possible humanity's journey back towards God. His title of "Son" puts him above all other creatures.

At many moments in the past and by many means, God spoke to our ancestors through the prophets; but in these days which are the last, he has spoken to us in the person of his Son, whom he appointed heir of all things and through whom he made the universe. He is the reflection of God's glory and bears the image of God's own being, sustaining the universe by his powerful command; and now that he has won the forgiveness of sins, he has taken his seat at the right hand of the divine Majesty on high.

Jesus did not offer sacrifices in the way the Levite priests did. He offered himself. He thus established the New Covenant announced by the prophet Jeremiah. This covenant was signed with Jesus' own blood. It was made once for all and based on the gift he made of his life:

The inadequacy of the ancient sacrifices
10: 5–7, 9–10

The author puts a quotation from Psalm 40: 7–9 into Jesus' mouth to summarise what motivated his whole life. It expresses the whole

On coming into the world, Christ said, *"You did not want sacrifices or cereal offerings, but you gave me a body. You did not want burnt offerings or sacrifices for sin. Then I said, 'Here I am, I am coming,' it is written of me in the scroll of the book, to do your will, God." (. . .)*

He is abolishing the old way of doing things to establish the new. And this *will* was for us to be made holy by the *offering* of the *body* of Jesus Christ made once and for all.

of his spiritual purpose: that of a Son responding totally to the love of his Father.

Christians should live by faith in the strong certainty that Jesus is the only high priest who can save them.

The faith of our ancestors

11: 1–2

Only faith can guarantee the blessings that we hope for, or prove the existence of realities that we do not see. It is for their faith that our ancestors are known.

11: 8–20, 32–3

(. . .) It was by faith that Abraham *set out* for a country that was the inheritance given to him and his descendants, and that *he set out* without knowing where he was going. By faith he *lived* in the Promised Land as though it were not his, living in tents with Isaac and Jacob, who were heirs with him of the same promise. He looked forward to the well-founded city, designed and built by God. It was by faith that Sarah too, in spite of being past the age, was made able to conceive a child, because she believed that he who had made the promise was faithful to it. Because of this, there came from one man, and one who already had the mark of death on him, descendants *as numerous as the stars of heaven and the grains of sand on the seashore which cannot be counted.*

All these died in faith, before receiving any of the things that had been promised, but they saw them in the far distance and welcomed them, recognising that they were only *strangers and nomads on earth.* People who use such terms about themselves make it quite plain that they are in search of a homeland. If they had meant the country they came from, they would have had the opportunity to return to it. But in fact they were longing for a better homeland, their heavenly homeland. That is why God is not ashamed to be called their God, since he has founded the city for them.

It was by faith that Abraham, *when put to the test, offered up Isaac.* He offered to sacrifice *his only son* even though he had yet to receive what had been promised, and he had been told: *Isaac is the one through whom your name will be carried on.* He was confident that God had the power even to raise the dead. So, he was given back Isaac from the dead and this was symbolic for us.

The author emphasised that faith means being certain in the midst of uncertainty. Faith makes us continue even when things are not entirely clear. It is a way of confidently entering into a future that God lets us see only dimly. Faith is demonstrated when people who have seen something of God at the heart of their existence leave their security to travel they know not where. Faith makes them capable of opening their hearts to God: faith then helps them to see clearly what they are relying on without even knowing it: Jesus. So, the whole of the past led to the coming of Jesus.

It was by faith that this same Isaac gave his blessing to Jacob and Esau for the still distant future. (. . .)

What more shall I say? There is not time for me to give an account of Gideon, Barak, Samson, Jephthah, or of David, Samuel and the prophets. These were men who through faith conquered kingdoms, did what was just, earned the promises and could keep a lion's mouth shut.

The example of Jesus Christ
12: 1–4

With so many witnesses in a great cloud all around us, we too, then, should throw off everything that weighs us down and the sin that clings so closely, and with perseverance keep running in the race which lies ahead of us. Let us keep our eyes fixed on Jesus, who leads us in our faith and brings it to perfection: for the sake of the joy which lay ahead of him, he endured the cross, paying no attention to the shame of it, and *has taken his seat at the right* of God's throne. Think of the way he persevered despite such opposition from sinners and then you will not lose heart and come to grief. In the fight against sin, you have not yet had to keep fighting to the point of bloodshed.

So Christians should not look back to the past. Such a lack of faith is sinful. They must continue as boldly as Jesus did and go into the future without fearing the difficulties.

LETTER FROM SAINT JAMES

All of us are going to be judged as Christians both by God and by other people. Such judgement will depend on our behaviour towards others rather than our clever words.

This is the essential gospel truth we are reminded of in the Epistle of Saint James.

This Saint James was not the apostle but the leader of the Church in Jerusalem. He was "the brother of the Lord" which may mean just a close relative.

Whoever the author really was, he was in touch with people of low social status from the Jewish culture. He was very sensitive to their worries regarding poverty and wealth.

But he also needed to respond to the situation in which some Christians, who tended to have "their heads in the clouds", were full of lovely ideas but did not put them into practice.

So his letter contains a series of practical moral considerations. They are based on the idea that all human beings are brothers and sisters in Jesus.

Material wealth is not true riches: it can even destroy those who possess it when wealth comes to them through the exploitation of the poor. All this follows directly from the teaching of the beatitudes.

James also gave valuable information on the way in which the early Christians prayed for the sick: the tradition of the "sacrament for the sick" in the Catholic Church is based on this text.

Here are some of James' thoughts:

Receive the Word and put it into practice

1: 22–7

But you must do what the Word tells you. Do not just listen to it and deceive yourselves. Anyone who listens to the Word and does not put it into practice is like someone who looks at himself in a mirror. Once he has seen what he looks like, he goes off and immediately forgets it. But anyone who looks steadily at the perfect law of freedom and keeps to it — not listening and forgetting, but putting it into practice — will be blessed in carrying it out.

> These words echo those of Jesus concerning the seed which fell on stony ground: the word that does not bear fruit is useless.

If anyone claims to be religious without keeping his tongue under control, he is deceiving his own heart; that person's religion is worthless. Pure, unspoilt religion, in the eyes of God our Father, is this: coming to the help of orphans and widows in their hardships, and keeping oneself free from the corruption of the world.

Respect for the poor

2: 1–9

My brothers, do not let class distinction enter into your faith in Jesus Christ, our glorified Lord. Now suppose a man comes into your meeting, well-dressed and with a gold ring on, and at the same time a poor man comes in, in shabby clothes. You take notice of the well-dressed man, and say, "Come this way to the best seats", then you tell the poor man, "Stand over there" or "You can sit on the floor at my feet." In making this distinction among yourselves have you not used a standard which is completely wrong?

> James' reminder builds on biblical tradition: we tend to notice only the external signs of wealth. In fact, the only wealth that matters is that of the heart, and this is usually possessed by the poor.

Listen, my dear brothers: God chose those who were poor in the world's eyes to be rich in faith and to be the heirs to the kingdom which he promised to those who love him. You, on the other hand, have looked down on the poor. Is it not the rich who lord it over you, who drag you into court, who insult the wonderful name which has been pronounced over you? If, however, you keep the royal Law of scripture: *you will love your neighbour as yourself*, you do well. But as soon as you make class distinctions, you are committing sin and the Law condemns you for your failure.

The letter of James shows how the New Testament is a continuation from the Old Testament: this text, like the whole of the epistle, is full of quotations (from Hosea, Isaiah and the Psalms).

5: 1–6

Well now, you rich! Weep and howl for the miseries that are coming to you. Your wealth is rotting, your clothes are all moth-eaten. All your gold and your silver are corroding away, and the same corrosion will be a witness against you and eat into your body. It is like a fire which you have stored up for the final days. Listen: the wages which you kept back from the labourers mowing your fields are crying out against you. The cries of the reapers have reached the ears of the Lord Almighty. On earth you have had a life of comfort and luxury. In the time of massacre you went on eating to your heart's content. It was you who condemned the righteous and killed them (. . .).

THE LETTERS OF SAINT PETER

1

The human race saved! Many revolutionaries have predicted this for the future. Christianity says redemption should come immediately, right in the middle of our sinful world. We do not have to wait for the world to change before we can set out to be holy. We only need to understand that we are called to holiness by the God of love, who makes us his children. This is what Peter's first letter is all about.

The author of this letter probably used the name of the apostle in order to give weight to his arguments. He was clearly in favour of a baptismal catechism and showed how baptism puts believers on the road to a real exodus. Believers can no longer lead corrupt lives as they have been delivered from captivity by Jesus, the Paschal Lamb. Believers thank God for his merciful love when they become brothers and sisters and this is the only sacrifice truly acceptable to God. The difficulties of the path are no longer important: despite slander and persecution, Christians are facing the future filled with joy.

2: 1–10

Rid yourselves, then, of all spite, deceit, hypocrisy, envy and criticism. Like new-born babies you should long for milk — the pure spiritual milk — which will help you to grow up to salvation, at any rate if *you have tasted that the Lord is good.*

Come to him, the living stone, rejected by human beings but chosen by God and precious to him. You, too, as living stones, are being built into a spiritual house as a holy priesthood to offer the spiritual sacrifices made acceptable to God through Jesus Christ. As scripture says: *Now I am laying a stone in Zion, a chosen,*

This quotation comes from Isaiah (28:16).

precious cornerstone and *no one who relies on this will ever be disappointed.*

To you believers it brings honour. But for unbelievers, it is rather a *stone which the builders rejected that became a cornerstone, a stumbling block, a rock to trip people up.* They stumble over it, because they do not believe in the Word. (. . .)

But you are *a chosen race, a kingdom of priests, a holy nation, a people to be a personal possession* to sing the praises of God who called you out of the darkness into his wonderful light. Once you were not *a people* and now you are the People of God; once you were *outside his pity*; now you *have received pity.*

> Peter is still quoting the Scriptures: Psalm 118: 22; Exodus 19: 5–6 and Hosea 1: 6–9.

2

Christ seems so far away to us. It must have been so much easier to believe in the early days of the Church. But how is it still possible for us to do so after so many years?

In fact, some Christians were already asking that very question at the beginning of the second century AD. The expectation of the Lord's early return had begun to fade. The Church was "just cruising along". Some of the believers had become lax; some of them had let themselves be attracted to new and fashionable ideas. Moral standards were also slipping.

The apostle Peter was one of the last remaining representatives of those who had actually been with Jesus. He took up his pen and wrote a letter in the form of a last will and testament intended to call to order those who were going astray: they should not say that God's judgement was taking too long to come because God worked in his own time. The end certainly would come. The writer also reminded them of the importance of the Scriptures and Paul's letters in particular.

False teachers   3: 3–4, 8–10

Do not forget that in the final days there will come scoffers whose life is ruled by their passions. They will say, "What has happened to the promise of his coming? Since our Fathers died everything has gone on just as it has since the beginning of creation!" (. . .) But there is one thing, my dear friends, that you must never forget: that with the Lord, a day is like a thousand years, and *a thousand years are like a day.* The Lord is not being slow in carrying out his promises, as some people think he is; rather he is being patient with you, not wanting anybody to be lost but everybody to be brought to repentance. The Day of the Lord will come like a thief (. . .).

> It is easy to poke fun at the teaching about the return of Christ but the author quotes Psalm 90 to remind us of God's patience.

3: 14

So then, my dear friends, while you are waiting, do your best to live blameless and pure lives so that he will find you at peace.

THE LETTERS OF JOHN

1

Can we still believe today? What is the truth we are to live for? some Christians ask, not wanting to waste time on what they consider old ideas which are no longer relevant.

Such Christians already existed at the end of the first century AD. In Asia Minor, there were certain mystics and intellectuals called gnostics who claimed that true knowledge and understanding were only accessible to a select few. They believed in Jesus, but "spiritualised" him in such a way that their image of him no longer bore much resemblance to the real Jesus, who was wholly human as well as wholly divine.

The first of Saint John's letters is an invitation to Christians to be aware of the richness and variety of their faith. They should not allow themselves to be deceived by false doctrines, but should remember that they are really the children of God. God is light. He is Love. He saves us. From these three certainties, we can see what a truly Christian life is all about. Through such an existence, a person enters into true fellowship with the Lord.

Introduction
1: 1–4

The author of this letter gave a very personal account of faith in the Word made flesh, which is the source of life.

Something which has existed since the beginning, which we have heard, which we have seen with our own eyes, which we have watched and touched with our own hands, the Word of life (. . .) we are declaring to you so that you too may share our life. Our life is shared with the Father and with his Son Jesus Christ. We are writing this to you so that our joy may be complete.

1. Walk in the light
1: 5–9

To live in the light of God is to see that we are sinners. But it is also to know that God forgives us. It is to obey the commandments. It is to love.

God is light. There is no darkness in him at all. If we say that we share in God's life while we are living in darkness, we are lying, because we are not living the truth. But if we live in light, as he is in light, we have a share in one another's life, and the blood of Jesus, his Son, cleanses us from all sin.

If we say, "We have no sin," we are deceiving ourselves, and truth has no place in us. If we acknowledge our sins, he is faithful and just, so that he will forgive our sins and will cleanse us from all evil.

2: 3–5

In this way we know that we have come to know him, if we keep his commandments. Whoever says, "I know him" without keeping his commandments, is a liar, and truth has no place in

him. But in anyone who does keep his word, God's love truly reaches its perfection.

2: 9–11

Whoever claims to be in light but hates his brother is still in darkness. Anyone who loves his brother remains in light and there is in him nothing to make him fall away. But whoever hates his brother is in darkness and is walking about in darkness. He does not know where he is going, because darkness has blinded him.

2. To live as God's children

3: 1–2

You must see what great love the Father has lavished on us by letting us be called God's children — which is what we are! The reason why the world does not acknowledge us is that it did not acknowledge him. My dear friends, we are already God's children. What we shall be in the future has not yet been revealed. We are well aware that when he appears we shall be like him, because we shall see him as he really is.

3. The source of love

4: 7–16

My dear friends, let us love one another, since love is from God and everyone who loves is a child of God and knows God. Whoever does not love does not know God, because God is love. This is how God showed his love for us. God sent his only Son into the world that we might have life through him. Love consists in this: it is not we who loved God, but God loved us and sent his Son to pay the penalty for our sins. My dear friends, if God loved us so much, we too should love one another. No one has ever seen God, but as long as we love one another God remains in us and his love

Christian tradition closely links the symbol of the eagle with Saint John — a symbol drawn from the vision of the prophet Ezekiel: four beings in human form, each with four wings and four faces, one like a man (Matthew), one like a lion (Mark), one like a bull (Luke) and one like an eagle (John). These representations of the Evangelists are often used in religious art.

comes to its perfection in us. This is the proof that we remain in him and he in us, that he has given us a share in his Spirit. (. . .) We have recognised for ourselves, and put our faith in, the love God has for us. God is love, and whoever remains in love remains in God and God in him.

4: 18

In love there is no room for fear, but perfect love drives out fear (. . .).

4: 20–1

Anyone who says "I love God" and hates his brother, is a liar. No one who fails to love the brother whom he can see can love God whom he has not seen. Indeed this is the commandment we have received from him, that whoever loves God, must also love his brother.

5: 1, 3–5

To believe is to be made new. It is to live a new life in the certain knowledge of conquering, in the face of a world that denies God.

Whoever believes that Jesus is the Christ is a child of God (. . .). This is what the love of God is: keeping his commandments. Nor are his commandments burdensome, because every child of God overcomes the world. And this is the victory that has overcome the world — our faith. Who can overcome the world but the one who believes that Jesus is the Son of God?

2

The second of John's letters, which was actually written before the first, is a short note addressed to a local church to fight against certain preachers who did not believe that the Son of God had come to earth as a man. The author reminds us that believers know the truth, and so they should love one another in accordance with the will of the Father. John rejoices to have met such believers.

4–6

John talks to the local church as though to the mother of the Christians.

It has given me great joy to find that children of yours have been living the life of truth as we were commanded by the Father. And now I am asking you, not as though I were writing you a new commandment, but only the one which we have had from the beginning: that we should love one another.

To love is to live according to his commandments: the first commandment is to live a life of love.

3

This letter is in fact the earliest of the three. It is a short warning note, written as a reaction against the sectarian attitude of Diotrephes, the leader of a local church. He had refused to welcome the missionaries John had sent to the gentiles in the area. On the other hand, John congratulated Gaius, to whom he was writing, who had shown himself to be a "child of God". He repeated his main advice:

5, 9–11

You have done loyal work in helping these brothers, even though they were strangers to you. (. . .) Diotrephes, who enjoys being in charge of it, refuses to accept us. So if I come, I shall tell everyone how he has behaved, and about the wicked accusations he has been circulating against us. Not content with that, he not only refuses to welcome our brothers, but prevents from doing so other people who would have liked to, and expels them from the church. My dear friend, never follow a bad example, but keep following the good one. Whoever does what is right is from God. No one who does what is wrong has ever seen God.

Strangers become friends in the church.

LETTER FROM SAINT JUDE

The epistle of Saint Jude is an odd text. Its author lived in a Jewish community strongly influenced by "apocalyptic" writings (writings about the end of the world), and which laid great importance on a whole mysterious universe of angels. This text shows Christian faith in a society strange to us today, as is often the case with small groups of people who live in a world of their own, cut off from others. However, it is interesting to us because it shows how seriously some Christians, marked by their own cultural and spiritual background, took their dedication to the true faith without letting themselves be distracted or corrupted.

20–1

But you, my dear friends, must build yourselves up on the foundation of your most holy faith, praying in the Holy Spirit; keep yourselves within the love of God and wait for the mercy of our Lord Jesus Christ to give you eternal life.

This epistle is a strange letter in many ways but shows that faith is the essential message of Christianity.

24–5

To him who can keep you from falling and bring you safe to his glorious presence, innocent and joyful, to the only God, our Saviour, through Jesus Christ our Lord, be glory, majesty, authority and power, before all ages, now and for ever. Amen.

REVELATION

History is moving on! It is a frightening concept to accept for those who are afraid of losing their power but a source of hope for those who are suffering in the present.

In writing the book of Revelation, the "man from Patmos" who saw a vision (who is normally identified as Saint John, but who could have been one of his disciples) wanted to encourage Christians who were going through persecution under the cruel regime of the Romans, during the reign of Domitian (AD 81–96). The believers were troubled: how were trials and tribulations possible if the resurrection of Jesus had really been the beginning of a new world order?

John's answer was to warn them against trusting appearances. They only saw how things looked on the surface: the truth was that the reign of God was coming. They should have faith.

A symbolical description of history

Revelation (or Apocalypse) means *unveiling*. The writer meant to unveil what was happening beneath the visible surface of events. Through images referring to the present, he showed how historical events were the outworking of a great battle between the forces of God and the power of Evil. But God's victory was already clear and a new universe was to be born.

The "present reality" John was referring to was that of the Church in troubled times. The book of Revelation begins with letters written to "the seven Churches" (which are symbols of the Church throughout the world) who were called to persevere in spite of difficulties.

Their struggles were only an episode in a universal drama. But Christ, "the sacrificial Lamb", had already won his victory in heaven (chapters 4–5).

The opening of the great book of History (with its seven seals) made it possible for the author to show how the fight had already been going on in Old Testament times. But the saints were saved and a great crowd had just joined them.

The action changed direction with the introduction of the "small scroll" (the New Testament): Judaism was dominated by gentile nations. But a remnant remained apart: that remnant was the Church (8:6 to 11).

A woman (Jerusalem, perhaps with a reference to the Virgin Mary) gave birth to a son (Jesus) who was chased by a Dragon (Satan). The son was carried up into heaven (the resurrection and the ascension). The remnant of the people of God continued to suffer persecution from Satan in the form of the two Beasts (Rome with its political power, and world views which gave no place to God). The remnant were fed by God while sheltered in the wilderness (the Eucharist). Judgement was now close at hand (12–16).

Babylon (Rome) eventually collapsed and the victory was won (17–19: 10).

But the battle was not finally over. It continued with the great final showdown which ended in God's victory (19: 11 to 20). The new Jerusalem (the Kingdom of Heaven) had been prepared since the beginning of time and then showed its glory which was the glory of God. It was the perfect city where humankind's hopes were finally fulfilled: God with us!

The wide use of symbols makes the book difficult to read. No other text in the New Testament has given rise to so many weird and wonderful interpretations. Sections have often been taken literally which never claimed to be any more than images. It is dangerous to try to find in them a precise description of events, as the book was only intended as a very general sketch of the meaning of history.

The Revelation brought the Bible to its climax: we find outlined in it the accounts of Genesis and Exodus and the great texts of the prophets. It shows the ending of humanity's long struggle toward God.

Prologue

1: 1

The Revelation was given in the name of the Father 'who is, and was and shall be', the name which reminds us of the word "Yahweh" (Exod. 3: 14) and of Jesus Christ. The Revelation was about the coming of God at the end of time. Christ was the beginning of history (the Alpha, which is the first letter of the Greek alphabet) and he is also its end (the Omega, the last letter of the Greek alphabet).

A revelation of Jesus Christ, which God gave him so that he could tell his servants *what is now to take place* very soon; he sent his angel to make it known to his servant John (. . .).

1. The letters to the churches of Asia

1: 4–8

John, to the seven churches of Asia: grace and peace to you from him who is, who was, and who is to come, from the seven spirits who are before his throne, and from Jesus Christ, *the faithful witness, the First-born* from the dead, *the highest of earthly kings.* He loves us and has washed away our sins with his blood (. . .). Look, he *is coming on the clouds*; everyone will see him, even *those who pierced him*, and *all the races of the earth will mourn over him.* Indeed this shall be so. Amen.

"I am the Alpha and the Omega," says the Lord God, who is, who was, and who is to come, the Almighty.

John recounted how he had a vision on the day of the resurrection (Sunday). He saw Jesus dressed in signs of power. He was alive once more after having been through death. He was present among the churches. He was about to reveal the meaning of history.

To each of the seven churches of Asia (Asia Minor), John proclaimed a message concerning the spiritual state of the community, calling on them to make the changes necessary. Thus he wrote as follows to the "angel" of the church in Laodicea:

3: 14–22

"Here is the message of the Amen, the faithful and true witness, the Principle of God's creation: I know about your activities: how you are neither cold nor hot. I wish you were one or the other, but since you are neither hot nor cold, but only lukewarm, I will spit you out of my mouth. You say to yourself: I am rich, I have made a fortune and have everything I want. You do not realise that you are wretched, pathetic, poor, blind and naked too. I warn you, buy from me the gold that has been tested in the fire to make you truly rich, and white robes to clothe you and hide your shameful nakedness, and ointment to put on your eyes to enable you to see. *I rebuke* and *train those whom I love*: so be serious and repent. Look, I am standing at the door, knocking. If one of you hears me calling and opens the door, I will come in and eat with him, and he with me. Anyone who is victorious I will allow to share my throne, just as I have myself overcome and have taken my seat with my Father on his throne. Let anyone who can hear, listen to what the Spirit is saying to the churches."

The city of Laodicea was proud of its textile industry, its banks, and its schools of optical medicine. But the church there was mediocre in spite of, or possibly because of, the situation of its members. The Christians should have thought carefully about the situation and really opened the door to the Lord, who was knocking to be let in. They would have been invited in their turn to God's table at the coming of his Kingdom if only they had welcomed him to their table.

The prophetic visions

The lead-up to the great day of the Lord.

The person seeing the vision was now introduced to the heavenly court with a throne occupied by a great "Somebody" (God, who is not named directly) at its centre. This Somebody was surrounded by Elders (representing the Old Testament) and the Living (the forces of nature) who worshipped him. God was holding the scroll on which all time past, present and future was written. Who was worthy to break the seals and read it? Nobody, except the "Lion of Judah" who was also the "Lamb" (the symbol of love offering itself up without trying to defend itself). Sacrificed (on the cross), the Lamb had triumphed. He deserved the same worship as God himself.

As he broke the first six seals, the Lamb revealed the meaning of the past (the Old Testament). In the words of the prophets, the coming of the "Day of the Lord" had already been discerned. The powers of evil were already defeated and the martyrs of the faith were carefully counted and each marked on the forehead with the sign of God (like Christians at baptism). The martyrs were gathered for the final judgement:

7: 9–17

After that I saw that there was a huge crowd, which no one could count, from every nation, race, tribe and language. They were standing in front of the throne and in front of the Lamb, dressed in white robes and holding palms in their hands. They shouted in a loud voice, "Salvation to our God, who sits on the throne, and

The faith of persecuted Christians was strengthened by this vision concerning the glory of past martyrs, and their faith was encouraged by that of people from all corners of the earth who had come to join them (salvation broke free from the boundaries of Israel). These chosen ones escaped the evil which was spreading throughout the world after being introduced to the court of heaven.

Many of the images used were taken from the great prophets.

to the Lamb!'' And all the angels who were standing in a circle round the throne, surrounding the elders and the four living creatures, bowed down before the throne, and touched the ground with their foreheads, worshipping God with these words:

"Amen. Praise and glory and wisdom, thanksgiving and honour and power and strength to our God for ever and ever. Amen."

One of the elders then spoke and asked me, "Who are these people, dressed in white robes, and where have they come from?" I answered him, "You can tell me, sir." Then he said, "These are the people who have been through the great trial; they have washed their robes white again in the blood of the Lamb. That is why they are standing in front of God's throne and serving him day and night in his sanctuary. And the One who sits on the throne will spread his tent over them. *They will never be hungry or thirsty* again; *sun and scorching wind will never harm them*, because the Lamb who is at the heart of the throne *will be their shepherd and will guide them to springs of living water*; and God *will wipe away all tears from their eyes.''*

The Lamb then broke the seventh seal on the scroll. It was a vital moment: the last times were beginning, the times in which believers lived. The universe was overturned. The powers of Hell were let loose but in spite of this people did not turn from their errors.

The seventh and last trumpet was blown, and John saw an angel holding a small book which described all events (the message of Christ). This represented the time the gospel arrived in the gentile world. John had to swallow the book symbolically, which at first tasted sweet in his mouth, but was bitter in his stomach afterwards (it was good news, but how could John not be dismayed at the thought of the persecution which the gospel would bring about). Finally, the seventh trumpet sounded, the Temple of God appeared in the heavens, amid lightning and hail, and as the earth shook . . .

The vision of the woman and the dragon

12: 1–11

The last battle began. The Woman (the people of God) gave birth to the Messiah. The Dragon (the powers of evil — Rome, which is a city with seven hills and seven emperors) tried to devour the Messiah but he was carried up to God (the resurrection) and the Dragon could do nothing to harm him.

Now a great sign appeared in heaven: a woman, clothed with the sun, standing on the moon, and on her head a crown of twelve stars. She was pregnant, and in labour, crying out in the pains of childbirth. Then a second sign appeared in the sky: there was a huge red dragon with seven heads and ten horns, and on each of the seven heads there was a crown. Its tail swept a third of *the stars from the sky and hurled them to the ground*, and the dragon stopped in front of the woman as she was at the point of giving birth, so that it could eat the child as soon as it was born. The woman *gave birth to a boy*, the son who was *to rule all the*

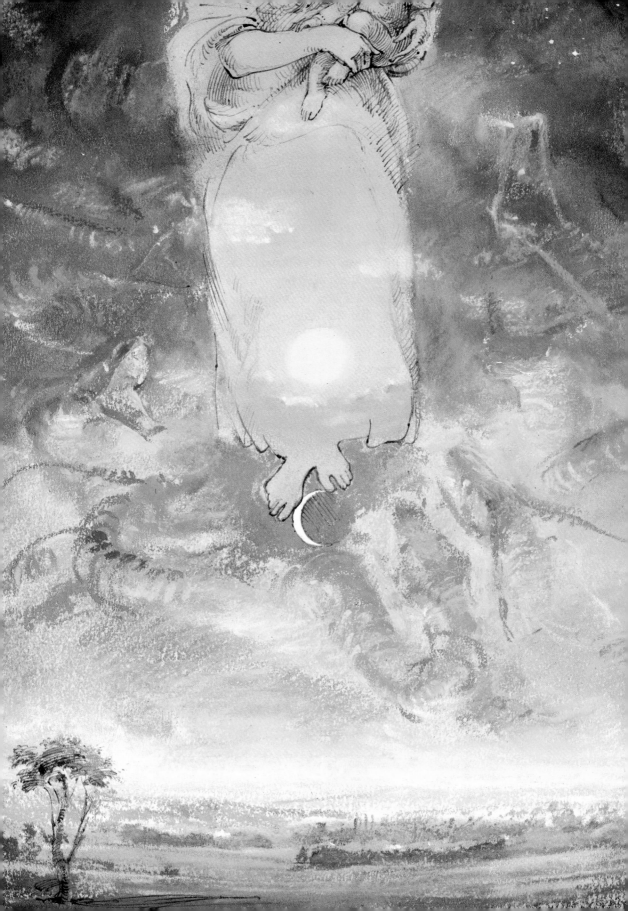

nations with an iron sceptre. The child was taken straight up to God and to his throne, while the woman escaped into the desert, where God had prepared a place for her to be looked after for twelve hundred and sixty days.

Then war broke out in heaven. *Michael* and his angels attacked the dragon. The dragon fought back with his angels, but they were defeated and driven out of heaven. The great dragon, the ancient serpent, known as the devil or Satan, who had led all the world astray, was thrown down to the earth with his angels. Then I heard a voice shout from heaven, "Salvation and power and the kingdom have been won for ever by our God, and all authority for his Christ, now that the accuser, who accused our brothers day and night before our God, has been brought down. They have triumphed over him by the blood of the Lamb and by the word to which they bore witness, because they did not cling to life even in the face of death."

12: 13–14, 17

The Dragon then bent toward the earth to pursue the Church and its children who had taken refuge. Their refuge was the wilderness where God protected and fed them as he fed his people Israel during the Exodus.

As soon as the dragon found himself hurled down to the earth, he began to pursue the woman, the mother of the male child, but she was given a pair of the great eagle's wings to fly away, far away from the serpent, into the desert to the place where she was to be looked after (. . .). Then the dragon was furious with the woman and went away to make war on the rest of her children, those who obey God's commandments and have in themselves the witness of Jesus.

The Beast seemed all-powerful: he was a worthy representative of Satan and was a symbol of the Roman Empire. It attracted all people by its power. Everyone had to be marked with the seal of God in order to escape from its fatal attraction.

Another Beast appeared. This one represented the ideologies of the time as used by the Roman Empire to maintain its power. This beast gave new strength to the persecution against the Christians. It was the real Antichrist.

There are still some who follow the Lamb who is pure when faced with persecution: they worship only God and have refused to prostitute themselves by following false cults.

The punishment of Babylon

The new Babylon was Rome, which never ceased leading people astray — just like a prostitute. Rome was a persecutor who lived on the blood of saints: she was the Beast with seven heads (the seven hills of the city) and seven kings (the seven emperors). The other ten kings were her accomplices. But the time of her final fall arrived: her fall (the fall of the city) was regretted by the servants of the Empire and those who profited by her power. The servants of God cried out a final "alleluia!" It was time for the wedding of the Lamb through whom God was wedded to his people.

The heavenly Jerusalem

21: 1–8

Then I saw *a new heaven and a new earth*, for the first heaven and the first earth had disappeared, and there was no longer any sea. I saw the holy city, the new Jerusalem, coming down out of heaven from God. It was beautiful, like a bride dressed for her husband. Then I heard a loud voice call from the throne, "Look, here God lives among human beings. He will make *his home among them; they will be his people*, and he will be their God, *God-with-them. He will wipe* away all *tears from their eyes.* There will be no more death, and no more mourning or sadness or pain. The world of the past has gone."

Then the One sitting on the throne spoke. "Look, I am making the whole of creation new. Write this, 'These words are faithful and true.' " Then he said to me, "It has already happened. I am the Alpha and the Omega, the Beginning and the End. I will give water from the well of life free to anybody who is thirsty. Anyone who is victorious will inherit these things; and *I will be his* God and *he will be my son.* But cowards, those who break their word, or worship obscenities, murderers, the sexually immoral, sorcerers, worshippers of false gods or any other sort of liars, their fate will be the burning lake of sulphur. It is the second death."

History thus had a happy ending. God had at last married his people through the gift of the Holy City which had been prepared since time began.

He created a new universe from which the sea (the threatening abyss) had disappeared.

The glory of God was visible in the Holy City. John explored it while accompanied by an angel. The city was made of precious stones and had twelve gates.

21: 22—22: 5

I could not see any temple in the city since the Lord God Almighty and the Lamb were themselves the temple. The city did not need the sun or the moon for light, since it was lit by the radiant glory of God, and the Lamb was its light. *The nations will come to its light* and the kings of the earth will bring it their treasures. Its *gates will never be closed during the day* — and there will be no night there — and *the nations will come, bringing their treasure* and their wealth. Nothing unclean may come into it: no one who does what is detestable or false, but only those who are listed in the Lamb's book of life.

Then the angel showed me the river of life, rising from the throne of God and of the Lamb and flowing crystal-clear. Down the middle of the city street, *on either bank of the river were the trees of life, which bear twelve crops of fruit in a year, one in each month; its leaves are for the healing of the nations.*

History was at an end and God was at last united with his people. A new paradise appeared to replace the paradise lost at the beginning of the Bible. A long journey for the human race was ended. This marvellous place was watered by the fountain of grace as a gift of the Spirit. This paradise contained the tree of Life which made human beings certain that they would live for ever. This was John's vision to comfort all Christians and to give them fresh hope in the fight in which they were involved.

The images used were taken from the prophets Isaiah and Ezekiel.

There will be no more curse. The throne of God and of the Lamb will be in the city; his servants will worship him. They will see him face to face, and his name will be written on their foreheads. And night will be abolished; they will not need a lamp or the sun to give them light, because the Lord God will be shining on them. They will reign for ever and ever.

Epilogue

22: 16–17

I, Jesus, have sent my angel to bear witness to these things to you for the sake of the churches. I am the shoot from the root of David and the bright star of the morning.

The Spirit and the Bride say, "Come!" Let everyone who listens answer, "Come!" Then *let all who are thirsty come and let them receive the water of life freely.*

22: 20–1

The one who bears witness to these things says: "I am indeed coming soon." Amen; come, Lord Jesus.

May the grace of the Lord Jesus be with you all. Amen.

All people should be filled with the immense hope placed at the heart of the Church by the Spirit! Their thirst will be satisfied because Jesus is coming. Christians are already living in the light of his grace.

TABLE OF CONTENTS

T A B L E   O F   C O N T E N T S

Impression CLERC S.A. - 18200 Saint-Amand-Montrond
Imprimé et relié dans la C.E.E.
Achevé d'imprimer en Juin 1999

Jerusalem in the time of David

Jerusalem from Solomon to Ezechias

Jerusalem after the Exile

SYRIA

Mount Hermon

Lake Huleh

Tyre

Chorazin

Bethsaida

Capernaum

Tabghka

Tiberias

Sea of Galilee
Lake Tiberias

Jord

Hills of Galilee

Mount of the Beatitudes

Acco/Ptolemais

Cana

Nazareth

Mount Tabor

Mount Gilboa

Beth-Shean

Zebulun Valley

Mount Carmel

Valley of Jezreel

Mountains of Samaria

Dor

Caesarea

Coastal plain

The Great Sea
(MEDITERRANEAN)